Palgrave Studies in the History of Finance

The study of the history of financial institutions, markets, instruments and concepts is vital if we are to understand the role played by finance today. At the same time, the methodologies developed by finance academics can provide a new perspective for historical studies. Palgrave Studies in the History of Finance is a multi-disciplinary effort to emphasise the role played by finance in the past, and what lessons historical experiences have for us. It presents original research, in both authored monographs and edited collections, from historians, finance academics and economists, as well as financial practitioners.

More information about this series at
http://www.springer.com/series/14583

Korinna Schönhärl
Editor

Decision Taking, Confidence and Risk Management in Banks from Early Modernity to the 20th Century

palgrave
macmillan

Editor
Korinna Schönhärl
University of Duisburg-Essen
Duisburg, Germany

Palgrave Studies in the History of Finance
ISBN 978-3-319-42075-2 ISBN 978-3-319-42076-9 (eBook)
DOI 10.1007/978-3-319-42076-9

Library of Congress Control Number: 2016958112

Printed on acid-free paper

This Palgrave Macmillan imprint is published by Springer Nature
The registered company is Springer International Publishing AG
The registered company address is: Gewerbestrasse 11, 6330 Cham, Switzerland

This volume provides a wealth of historical case studies of different techniques used over time by bankers to assess and mitigate their exposure to different sources of risk. By combining institutional, sociological and behavioral perspectives, it emphasizes the relevance of culture, social networks and institutional rules for bankers' perceptions of risk, lending decisions and investment strategies. An entertaining and instructive reading both for financial historians and banking practitioners

—Stefano Battilossi, Associate Professor, Universidad Carlos III Madrid, Spain, and Editor, Financial History Review

Acknowledgments

This book draws on papers presented during the workshop 'Decision Taking, Confidence and Risk Management in Banks: 19th and 20th Century' in February 2015. It took place at the KWI Essen (Kulturwissenschaftliches Institut, Institute for Advanced Study in the Humanities). The plan was to bring together an interdisciplinary and international group of researchers to discuss new methodological approaches to banking history, which sometimes seems to need fresh input. My interest in this topic emerged during my project 'Financers Desired Spaces. European Bankers and Greece in the 19th Century', which researches the motives of British, French, German and Swiss bankers to invest their money in that high-risk emerging market. All contributors to the workshop were invited to present one methodological approach or idea and to illustrate its use and function in an empirical case study taken from their current research. The workshop's discussions indeed offered plenty of helpful ideas and stimulation about how historians can deal with bankers' investment motives. Our chairs and commentators Dirk Baecker (Friedrichshafen), Johannes Bähr (Frankfurt a. M.), Boris Barth (Konstanz), Youssef Cassis (Florence), Christopher Kopper (Bielefeld) and Dieter Ziegler (Bochum) made major contributions to our results.

I extend my sincere thanks to Ute Schneider who, as Professor for Social, Cultural and Economic History at Duisburg-Essen University, provided me with the time and space to develop and execute this workshop independently. I also thank the KWI, where the workshop was held in a pleasant atmosphere. Furthermore I am very grateful to our partners for their generous funding of the workshop as well as the publication of the volume: Akku (Arbeitskreis für kritische Unternehmensgeschichte, Association for Critical Business History), DFG (Deutsche Forschungsgemeinschaft, German Research Foundation), Eugen-Gutmann-Gesellschaft e.V., EABH (European Association for Banking History), GUG (Gesellschaft für Unternehmensgeschichte, German Business History Association), Historische Gesellschaft der Deutsche Bank (Historical Association of Deutsche Bank), IfB (Institut für Bankengeschichte, Institute for Banking Historical Research), Sal. Oppenheim and Targo-Bank Foundation.

Finally yet importantly, I thank Katharine Thomas for language correction and Svenja Kiel for her essential help in organising the workshop and editing this volume.

This book is dedicated to my daughters Pauline and Ricarda, the source of my energy and happiness.

Korinna Schönhärl
Essen, in May 2016

Contents

Notes on Contributors

Bernardo Batiz-Lazo read economics (at ITAM, Mexico and Autónoma de Barcelona, Spain) and history (at Oxford) and received a doctorate in business administration from Manchester Business School. He has been studying financial markets and institutions since 1988. He joined Bangor as professor of business history and bank management after appointments at Leicester, the Open University and Queen's University of Belfast. He has combined full-time appointments with consulting and executive training in Europe, the Gulf States, Latin America and Asia. Bernardo has published over 40 refereed articles, three books and eight distance-learning books. He is a Fellow of the Royal Historical Society, research associate of Fundación Estudios Financieros (Fundef – ITAM), and edits a weekly report on new working papers in Payments and Financial Technology (see http://lists.repec.org/mailman/listinfo/nep-pay) and on Economic and Business History (http://lists.repec.org/mailman/listinfo/nep-his/). He is also the Executive Editor of www.nephis.org. Twitter: @BatizLazo

Andrew Dilley completed his Dr. Phil. at the University of Oxford in 2006. He is a Senior Lecturer in Imperial and Global History in the Department of History at the University of Aberdeen. His early publications, including his book *Finance, Politics, and Imperialism: The City of London, Australia, and Canada 1896–1914* (Palgrave, 2012), focused on the political impacts of London finance in the British dominions. He currently holds an AHRC Early Career Fellowship on *Commerce and the Commonwealth: Business Associations, Political Culture, and Governance, 1886–1975*, which aims to re-examine the economic and political history of the Commonwealth through the lens provided by business associations.

Matthew Hollow is an Associate Lecturer at the York Management School (UK). He holds a PhD (DPhil) in Modern History from Oxford University and has previously worked as a Research Associate on the Leverhulme Trust-funded 'Tipping Points' project at Durham University. Research-wise, his main interests include: the history of commercial crime, risk and risk management, business ethics, and shadow banking. His most recent book is entitled *Rogue Banking: A History of Financial Fraud in Interwar Britain* (2014).

Sebastian Knake studied history and social science at Universität Bielefeld and at Johns Hopkins University in Baltimore. In 2010 he wrote his master's thesis on the bicycle production cluster in the city of Bielefeld from 1880 to 1970. For this study he was granted the Gustav-Engel-Award of the 'Historischer Verein für die Grafschaft Ravensberg' in 2012. Since 2012 he has been working on his doctoral thesis on the expansion of business financing by the 'Braunschweigische Staatsbank' from 1919 to 1969 (funded by the 'Niedersächsisches Wirtschaftsarchiv' in Wolfenbüttel). Some parts of this research will be published as part of a study about the history of public banking in the former state of Brunswick in March 2016. In 2015 Sebastian took a position as research assistant in the project: 'Ersparte Krisen?' at Bayreuth University (funded by the Federal Ministry of Education and Research). The aim of the research is to examine changes and continuities in the saving behaviour of the (West-) German population between 1960 and 1980 on the basis of normative judgements concerning different forms of saving.

Nadia Matringe is an economic historian specialised in utilising business firm archives to analyse economic mechanisms at a macro level, such as market integration, network dynamics, and the evolution of banking systems. She completed her PhD at the European University Institute of Florence, for which she received the EBHA dissertation prize 2014. Currently an LSE Fellow in Accounting, and a researcher affiliated to IHMC (CNRS, Paris), she is focusing on the technical spread of financial techniques and expertise from the Mediterranean to North Western Europe in the Early Modern Age. The comparative history of accounting systems is at the core of this research project.

Anders L. Mikkelsen completed a PhD in financial history at King's College London in 2014 on the market practices and techniques of London issuing houses and their role in facilitating access of sovereign borrowers to the London capital market between 1870 and 1914. He currently works as a researcher at BH-DG Systematic Trading LLP and holds a Visiting Research Fellowship at the ICBH, King's College London.

Susie J. Pak is an Associate Professor in the Department of History at St. John's University (New York). A graduate of Dartmouth College and Cornell University, she serves on the editorial board of *Connections*, the journal of the International Network for Social Network Analysis (INSNA), and as co-chair of the Economic History Seminar at Columbia University. Her book, *Gentlemen Bankers: The World of J.P. Morgan*, was published by Harvard University Press in 2013.

Morten Reitmayer is Deputy Chair for Modern History at the University of Trier. He studied history, sociology and German literature at the University of Hannover. His dissertation thesis is: *Bankiers im Kaiserreich. Sozialprofil und Habitus der deutschen Hochfinanz* (1999); his habilitation thesis is: *Elite. Sozialgeschichte einer politisch-gesellschaftlichen Idee in der frühen Bundesrepublik* (2009). His fields of research comprise business history, intellectual history and the social history of modern European societies.

Victor Ricciardi is an Assistant Professor of Financial Management at Goucher College in Baltimore, Maryland, USA. He teaches courses in financial planning, investments, corporate finance, behavioural finance, and the psychology of money, and is a leading expert on academic literature and emerging research issues in behavioural finance. With Kent Baker, he co-edited the book *Investor Behavior: The Psychology of Financial Planning and Investing* (2014, as part of the Wiley Finance Series). This research endeavour is a contributor series book that incorporates 30 chapters written by 45 leading experts (academics and practitioners) on emerging research on investor psychology in personal finance, financial planning, and investment management. He received a BBA in accounting and management from Hofstra University, and an MBA in finance and Advanced Professional Certificate (APC) at graduate level in economics from St. John's University. He also holds a Graduate Certificate in personal family financial planning from Kansas State University. He can be found on Twitter @victorricciardi.

Friederike Sattler studied economic and social history, modern history and economics. She took her PhD from the Freie Universität Berlin in 2001. She has worked as a research fellow and lecturer in economic and social history at various institutions, among them the University Halle-Wittenberg, the Center for the Study of Contemporary History Potsdam and the Historical Commission at the Bavarian Academy of Sciences and Humanities in Munich. Today she is a lecturer in economic and social history at the Goethe-University Frankfurt. Her main fields of research include the economic and social history of the twentieth century, business history with a focus on banks and finance, European economic elites and the history of modern capitalism.

Korinna Schönhärl is assistant professor in the Department for Social and Economic History at the University Duisburg-Essen and fellow of the Historical College (Munich). Her thesis from Goethe-University Frankfurt is entitled *Knowledge and Visions. Theory and Politics of the Economists in the Stefan George Circle* (2009). Her research interest is the combination of cultural and economic history on an international level. Her second book project (just finished) is entitled *Financers desired spaces—European Banks and Greece in the 19th Century*. It examines the international relationships of French, British, Swiss and German banks with Greece from the time of her independence until World War I. Additional research foci are the history of migration (*Ruhr Area and Istanbul. The Economies of Urban Diversity, 2013*) and the history of tax morale.

Morten Reitmayer is Deputy Chair for Modern History at the University of Trier. He studied history, sociology and German literature at the University of Hannover. His dissertation thesis is: *Bankiers im Kaiserreich. Sozialprofil und Habitus der deutschen Hochfinanz* (1999); his habilitation thesis is: *Elite. Sozialgeschichte einer politisch-gesellschaftlichen Idee in der frühen Bundesrepublik* (2009). His fields of research comprise business history, intellectual history and the social history of modern European societies.

Daniel Velinov is a researcher at the *Centre National de la Recherche Scientifique* (CNRS) and is affiliated to the *Laboratoire de Recherche Historique Rhône-Alpes* (LARHRA) in Lyon. He holds a PhD from the *Freie Universität Berlin* and from the *Université de Paris 1*. In his thesis, he studied the working of exchange markets and of the international payment system based on the archive of the Antwerp banker de la Bistrate (1654–1674). He continues to work on early modern banking and exchange.

Daniel Wylegala is an economic and social historian specialised in utilising sociological theory in the field of German business history. Currently, he is finishing his doctoral thesis about the career of the former Deutsche Bank's co-CEO and President of the Bundesbank Karl Klasen at the Philipp University of Marburg and working as a scientific researcher at the Heinrich Heine University Düsseldorf, where he is examining the role of experiences and expectations for decision making in business using the example of innovations in the German iron and steel industry after 1945.

List of Figures

List of Tables

Introduction

Korinna Schönhärl

1 Bankers' Investment Decisions and Risk Management

During the recent years of crisis, public opinion has drawn a very negative picture of bankers and their investment decisions, which are considered to be predominantly motivated by profit maximisation, lacking all kinds of social responsibility (N.N. 2013). Certainly, profit has always been a driving force for bankers, as it necessarily is for all entrepreneurs who want to succeed. But when researching the worldwide history of investment, one soon realises that rational choice theory does not provide sufficient methodological approaches to understanding all variants of bankers' investment behaviour (Green and Pohle Fraser 2008). Sometimes banks have invested despite rather poor expectations of profits and insufficient risk

K. Schönhärl (✉)
Historical Institute, University Duisburg-Essen, Essen, Germany
e-mail: korinna.schoenhaerl@uni-due.de

K. Schönhärl (ed.), *Decision Taking, Confidence and Risk Management in Banks from Early Modernity to the 20th Century*,
DOI 10.1007/978-3-319-42076-9_1

premiums. Sometimes they let apparently good investment opportunities go to their competitors, although the risk seemed to be low. How can banking historians understand and explain their decision-making? Primarily it should be acknowledged that bankers are humans of flesh and blood with emotions and experiences and ethical norms, who cannot be squeezed into a narrow model of *homo economicus* (Berghoff 1999, 174). Bankers' investment decisions and the motives behind them should be looked at more closely. Why did bankers take their decisions in the way they did? What mechanisms of decision-taking were established in banking from early modern times until the twentieth century, and how did they change over time? What kinds of risk management techniques were used and to what extent did they succeed? How did bankers perceive risks and how did they try to limit them? Which factors contributed to the constitution of confidence and which factors damaged it? These questions can certainly only be answered with the help of elaborate methodological concepts. Thus this volume presents methodological approaches for banking historians to analyse questions pertaining to bankers' decision-making. The methodological tools are not only introduced in theory, but their practical application to empirical research based on archive material is also demonstrated in selected case studies.

2 Risk, Confidence and Decision-making: Some Definitions

In order to research risk management, it is necessary to define the term 'risk': the possibility that an action causes losses for or damage to the actor (Baecker 2008, III). Decisive for choices related to risk management is the interpretation of the situation by the actor as dangerous (i.e. influenced by external, non-controllable dangers) or as risky (dependent on one's own decisions and actions) (Hahn 1998, 49; Akerlof and Shiller 2009, 205). Risk, according to this definition, is always connected to one's own actions and one's own decisions. Different options for action have to exist, providing the actor with a choice. He or she could easily avoid the risk by taking an alternative course of action (e.g. not to invest), but in this case he or she would also lose the chance of winning something.

While uncontrollable dangers have to be avoided, consciously getting involved in risks can be profitable and desirable, as entrepreneurs can profit from the contingency of future developments by being repaid for the taking on of risks (risk premium). This is especially the case for bankers, who are responsible for the compensation of time differences in the economy. They deal with payment promises in a contingent future and have to secure the safety of payments through continued rescheduling and thus deal with various kinds of risk: risk of fraud, risk of insolvency, risk of illiquidity or risk of loan loss (Baecker 2008, VIf., 108–112).

So banks continuously have to take on risks and consequently develop risk strategies (Kahneman 2011, 340). Their business is unimaginable without risks. The most important aim for bankers was (and is) not to be taken in by an illusion of security because this would damage the chances of identifying and allocating risks. This is even more important because bankers often have to represent themselves to politics and the public as being risk averse (Pohle Fraser 1999, 2, 48). However, they have to clearly identify risks and use risk management to put themselves in a position that is as advantageous as possible in terms of risk-taking. In this process, banks must reduce the complexity of 'noise' in their environment (Pohle Fraser 1995, 28) and thereby differentiate between important and insignificant information in order to make investment decisions possible. Risk management works on three levels: firstly, the observation of markets to identify profitable business opportunities; secondly, risk management within the organisation to organise the conditions of risk-taking; and thirdly, the design of financial instruments to split risks (Baecker 2008, 126). The allocation of partial risks between reliable partners was (and is) one of the most important techniques of risk management. All three levels of risk management can be reconstructed using banks' archive materials.

However, even with elaborate risk management complete knowledge of one's counterpart, including the prognosis of his/her actions is not possible in business relationships, as indeed is the case in any other social interaction. The actions of the counterpart are always contingent (Simmel 2013, 268, 274). Increasing control over a business partner always involves rising transaction costs due to the provision of information. A reduction of these transaction costs is only possible by confidence (Berghoff 2004, 59). Confidence can be defined as a mechanism to stabilise insecure expectations and to reduce the complexity of human action (Ripperger 2005, 9). It reflects contingence, whereas hope eliminates it (Luhmann 2009, 29). Political science, sociology, anthropology and economics have developed various approaches to the term 'confidence' (or trust) in recent decades, without arriving at a consensus (Fukuyama 2001). The operationalisation of the term also remains difficult in historical research (Frevert 2013). Perhaps the most usable approach is that of new institutional economics, elaborated on by Tanja Ripperger. She defines confidence not as an end in itself or a moral aim, but as a competitive factor in business life due to the possibility of saving transaction costs (Ripperger 2005, 262). Francis Fukuyama similarly argues that it is the level of confidence inherent in a society which makes it successful in economic terms (1995, 150). Especially within the principal-agent relationship, confidence is a *sine qua non* of economic interaction. The principal has to intentionally bypass his/her lack of information concerning the intentions of the agent, for example by generalising his/her experiences with other members of the same group. But in the end confidence is always a voluntary act. All the reasons that may be mentioned as underlying it are only ways of legitimising a decision which cannot be based on pure rationality (ibid.). The decision to bestow confidence, after all, seems to possess many of the characteristics of a black box in historical research, as is the case for many other banking decisions.

In this unsatisfactory situation, behavioural psychology can provide new options for historians interested in the motives of decision-making. Choice theory intensively researches factors relevant to decision-taking and 'has uncovered substantial and systematic regularities in how people make decisions' (LeBoeuf and Shafir 2012, 243; Allingham, 2002). The rational choice model has been shown to be insufficient because it cannot explain many aspects of human decision-making. The assumption that individuals always choose the most profitable alternative has lost ground *vis-à-vis* more differentiated models. Behavioural finance transfers these approaches to the field of financial markets with the aim of explaining the decisions taken by individuals. It is especially concerned with questions of risk perception, the process 'by which an individual is in search of preeminent clarification of sensory information so that he or she can make a final judgement based on their level of expertise and past experience' (Ricciardi, 2008, 86). The main finding of behavioural finance is that risks are perceived very differently by different individuals and that 'objective' mathematical quantification is unhelpful in making sense of the decision taken in a certain situation by a certain actor on a certain financial market (ibid.). These results are gained mostly by empirical test series carried out in laboratories with selected probands. Here is the point where historians can enter with their qualitative methods and enrich the discussion with the results of their historical source-based research. How did bankers in the past perceive risk and how did they try to manage it? The analysis of archive material can produce valuable case studies and can therefore augment the behavioural finance perspective on investment behaviour. It is important to carefully investigate the question of whether the decision-making processes of actors today are comparable to those of actors in the past and the nature and significance of possible differences. Even if the differences indeed prove to be predominant, a new perspective on archive material can be gained. The explicit aim is to overcome a perspective in which the bankers are described either as responsible investors or as foolhardy speculators, depending on the outcome of their business decisions (Priemel, 2013). Instead, analysis of their state of knowledge and information at the moment of the decision is required.

The framework of this volume is defined by the three terms 'decision-making', 'risk management' and 'confidence'. The aim is to present carefully designed case studies that use different methodological tools to illuminate the black box of bankers' decision-making.

3 First Part: Recruitment of Personnel and Partners

Maybe the most delicate decisions that have to be taken in banks concern the recruitment of the next generation or adequate business partners. They are dealt with in the first part of this volume. Decisions made in this field involve high risks for the entire enterprise. This is true whatever the governance structure of the bank in question, be it a family bank or a joint-stock company. Susie J. **Pak** analyses the risks associated with the recruitment of non-family members to the House of Morgan from

1895 to 1940, when the family was no longer able to fill all the positions itself. She discusses how and according to which characteristics possible candidates were recruited, how they were judged, and how they were incorporated into in-house and broader social networks to make them more reliable. The resulting structures were still comparable with the preceding ones when belonging to the family was the essential characteristic. Pak includes all the non-family members of the House of Morgan in that period in her research, based on detailed tabular material which offers an analytic overview.

Daniel **Wylegala** also deals with the question of how an organisation's higher hierarchical levels can be filled and how the associated risks can be managed. Using Niklas Luhmann's system theory he views top careers as a process of selection and socialisation, in which a candidate has to prove his eligibility and ability to manage risks time and again. In a case study on Karl Klasen, President of the German Bundesbank, Wylegala demonstrates how a system theoretical perspective can be used to develop a consistent narrative of a top manager's biography.

Not only is the recruitment of in-house personnel a risky business for banks. The selection of cooperation partners also takes place under conditions of uncertainty and is connected with high risks. Friederike **Sattler**, after careful consideration of the methodological challenges, designs a model of experience-based expectation formation to explain the post-1960 decisions of German universal banks to enter the US-American market via club banking rather than alone. Sattler demonstrates a special interest in the banks' perceptions of the chances and risks of this kind of multilateral cooperative governance.

4 Second Part: Risk Management Techniques

Of course the recruitment of staff and partners is only one field of bankers' decisions. Another one concerns the question of investments. Close cooperation here can help to manage risk too, for example when issuing state loans. Anders L. **Mikkelsen** opens the second part of the volume by analysing the way in which British issuing houses dealt with underwriting and reputational risk from the 1880s onward when the gatekeeper positions of the banks weakened for certain countries. Their reaction was to cooperate by issuing syndicates and forming underwriting groups in which the underwriting risk could be spread over several strong shoulders and the position towards the creditor strengthened.

Such risk management always took place in a certain cultural and economic setting, in this case the British one. Is the national environment of any importance? Andrew **Dilley** instead proposes the financial centre as a unit of analysis. He understands it as a field in the sense of Bourdieu's praxeology, his 'theory of practice', causing a certain 'habitus' of risk perception. Habitus is understood here to refer to the structure of mind and emotions of the individual, socialised through education and social environment. Using, in addition, the new institutional economics perspective, Dilley argues that this habitus was influenced by economic and business structures, the role of states, social networks and cultural factors. He thus opens up a wide field for international banking historians to look beyond their own noses and examine cultural differences in banking more closely.

This was well demonstrated in Monika Pohle Fraser's analysis of the risk management techniques of German and French banks in the nineteenth century. Her focus was on the question of how bankers' justifications of investment decisions in these two different countries developed in this period. Sebastian **Knake** summarises the results of her unpublished dissertation and compares it with Thévenot and Boltanski's convention theory. He puts his results to the test in a case study on the risk management of the Braunschweigische Staatsbank in the 1950s and shows that it is very likely that some elements of risk management survived in banking practice until the first half of the twentieth century.

Matthew **Hollow** also deals with twentieth-century risk management. He researches how Barclays Bank dealt with the risks inherent in lending to small and local businesses. His results are in many points comparable with those of Knake and of Pohle Fraser of the nineteenth century: despite all the technical innovations, interpersonal relationships and networks remained very meaningful for the lending decisions.

Does this situation change with the emergence of computer technology in financial institutions? Bernardo **Batiz-Lazo** asks about the expectations of decision makers and shareholders in applying these new methods to retail deposit-accepting financial institutions and their outcome for the decision-making process. He is also interested in the impacts of these changes on the social composition of the bank's staff and the education of bankers.

5 Third Part: Methodological Tools for Historians: Network Theory, Principal-Agent Relationships, Behavioural Finance and Social Capital

In addition to the approaches already mentioned, the third part of the volume deals with further methodological tools with which historians can research risk perception and decision-making processes in banks. Nadia **Matringe** emphasises the role of networks in the decision-taking of early modern bankers. Networking was so important to the bankers (her case study is the banking house Salviati) that profit maximisation could actually be of subordinated importance. The integration into social networks could prevent the bankers from acting opportunistically.

Opportunistic behaviour of business correspondents is but one of the multiple risks early modern bankers had to deal with. Based on the archive of the Antwerp banker de la Bistrate, Daniel **Velinov** examines risk mitigation in the context of payments via bills of exchange in 17th century Europe. The close analysis of exchange transactions shows that it is the complex relationship between principals and agents that is the source of the important variety of risks that both principals and agents faced. Therefore, risk mitigation relies on procedures that regulate the principal-agent relationship or – to put it differently – that are inherent to the system of commission trading. Also the notions of credit and reputation relate intrinsically to the principal-agent relationship. This finding challenges the commonly attributed importance of familial, city-based, regional, national, ethnic or religious affiliations to generating trust, credit and risk mitigation.

The variety of motives that can contribute to investment decisions is the subject of the following chapter by Victor **Ricciardi**. As a researcher in financial management, he presents the basics of behavioural finance for banking historians, covering overconfidence, representativeness, anchoring, worry, herd behaviour, group polarisation and groupthink. In an interdisciplinary approach, Ricciardi considers the chances and challenges of behavioural finance for the research of bankers' investment decisions in the past, discussing the new and interesting perspectives that it opens up for work with archive material, despite the methodological snares that have to be negotiated.

This idea is put to the test by Korinna **Schönhärl** in the following chapter. She uses the behavioural finance approach to analyse the decision by the French bank Comptoir d'escompte to get involved in the construction of a maritime canal at Corinth in Greece (1882–1893). She shows that it is probable that 'belief in experts' and 'overconfidence', caused by imperial overestimation of French technical and financial capabilities, were meaningful for this investment decision. The behavioural finance approach opens up a new perspective on the archive material and helps to construct a narrative from the research.

But can attempts like this make banking history more attractive for 'general' historians? Morten **Reitmayer** is sceptical. Even if he judges the concept of social capital, which he explains in detail, to be a promising methodological approach, he does not believe it will bring banking history very much closer to the historical mainstream. Reitmayer instead proposes a range of subjects and themes where the expertise of banking and more general business historians are required where they could fruitfully contribute to historical and social discussion in general. He thus opens up the field for consideration of the future of banking history and the challenges with which it will be confronted.

6 Main Results of the Book

Addressing the questions of how bankers took their decisions and what their risk management looked like, the volume provides a couple of interesting results. On the one hand, it becomes clear that from the seventeenth to the twentieth-century new risk management techniques were continuously developed, employed and advanced. For early modern times the procedures of commission trading or the construction and care of networks of personal confidence are worthy of mention. In comparison to the observance of the rules of the game of commission trading or to the elaborate maintenance of networks, profit maximisation was often less important for early modern bankers. Later on, with the evolution of the banking business, risk management techniques also became more sophisticated. In the nineteenth century, the era of 'the banking revolution' (Cassis, 2009, 43; Chapman, 1984; Kynaston, 1994), banks made accessible new sources of capital by becoming joint-stock enterprises. With their new, completely revised governance structures they started the financialisation of a globalising industry. The challenges connected with this forced not only joint-stock but also more traditional family banks to adopt new methods of risk calculation and management. At this time several new mechanisms were proven as responses to new challenges: the construction of issuing groups as a method of risk sharing, the development of scientific expert systems, and, in the twentieth century, the employment of computer technology. But alongside these innovations other key elements of risk management like personal reputation, connecting elements like memberships in certain universities or clubs, shared contacts and confidence continued to be of importance throughout the centuries. Even if the bankers claimed to practise modern and technically up-to-date risk management, they *de facto* still relied on the second-order observation of colleagues, business partners and even scientific experts, checking their reputations and middle-class virtues as the basis of confidence. Even in-house careers in banks can be interpreted as the long-lasting probation of candidates, their gradual involvement in decision situations and the establishment of their reliability. The risk management techniques used by bankers alongside these traditional approaches often served more to legitimise decisions afterwards, as far as it is possible to distinguish between these two purposes at all.

It becomes clear that risk perception is a deeply culturally conditioned process, one that can be analysed only when embedded in the context of its social, political and cultural background, something that is indeed a challenge for banking historians. Culture, language and local habits do matter when considering bankers' investment decisions. Alongside this group level, some of the chapters of this book also prove the importance of the individual level, because they show that the decision-making of bankers is a highly individual process that can be understood only by considering the value background, the expectations and the past experiences of the actors involved. Another person might have made a different decision in an identical situation—an observation that has to be taken seriously.

So the research of bankers' risk management and investment decisions is not possible without an elaborate methodological approach that focuses on the evaluation of sources in the decision-making process. This volume offers a variety of proposals about how this focusing can be put into effect, taking one's own blind spots as a historical researcher seriously and trying to shed light on them. The broad field of methodological approaches from modern cultural history (Arcangeli, 2012; Burke, 2004; Daniel, 2001) thus becomes indispensable for writing the history of banks.

References

Akerlof, G. A., & Shiller, R. J. (2009). *Animal Spirits. How human psychology drives the economy, and why it matters for global capitalism.* Princeton: Princeton University Press.

Allingham, M. (2002). *Choice Theory. A very Short introduction.* Oxford: Oxford University Press.

Arcangeli, A. (2012). *Cultural history. A concise introduction.* London/New York: Routledge.

Baecker, D. (2008, 1st ed. 1991). *Womit handeln Banken? Eine Untersuchung zur Risikoverarbeitung in der Wirtschaft* Reprint. Frankfurt: Suhrkamp.

Berghoff, H. (1999). Transaktionskosten: Generalschlüssel zum Verständnis langfristiger Unternehmensentwicklung? Zum Verhältnis von neuer Institutionenökonomie und moderner Unternehmensgeschichte. *Jahrbuch für Wirtschaftsgeschichte/Economic History Yearbook, 2*, 159–176.

Berghoff, H. (2004). Vertrauen als ökonomische Schlüsselvariable. Zur Theorie des Vertrauens und der Geschichte seiner privatwirtschaftlichen Produktion. In: K.-P. Ellerbrock (Ed.), *Die Wirtschaftsgeschichte vor der Herausforderung durch die New Institutional Economics* (pp. 58–71). Münster: Ardey-Verlag.

Burke, P. (2004). *What is cultural history?* Cambridge: Polity-Press.

Cassis, Y. (2009). Private banks and the onset of the corporate economy. In: Y. Cassis & P. Cottrell (Eds.), *The world of private banking* (pp. 43–59). Aldershot: Ashgate.

Chapman, S. D. (1984). *The rise of merchant banking*. Boston: Allen Unwin.
Daniel, U. (2001). *Kompendium Kulturgeschichte. Theorien, Praxis, Schlüsselwörter*. Suhrkamp: Frankfurt.
Frevert, U. (2013). *Vertrauensfragen. Eine Obsession der Moderne*. München: Beck.
Fukuyama, F. (1995). *Trust. The social virtues and the creation of prosperity*. New York: Penguin.
Fukuyama, F. (2001). Differing disciplinary perspectives on the origins of trust. *Boston University Law Review, 81* (3), 479–494.
Green, E., & Pohle Fraser, M. (Eds.) (2008). *The human factor in banking history. Entrepreneurship, organization, management and personnel*. Athens: Alpha Bank, Historical Archives.
Hahn, A. (1998). Risiko und Gefahr. In: G. Graevenitz, O. von Marquard, & M. Christen (Eds.), *Kontingenz* (pp. 49–54). München: Wilhelm Fink.
Kahneman, D. (2011). *Thinking, fast and slow*. New York: Farrar Straus and Giroux.
Kynaston, D. (1994). *The city of London. Bd. 1: A world of its own, 1815-90; Bd. 2: Golden years, 1890-1914*. London: Chatto & Windus.
LeBoeuf, R. A., & Shafir, E. (2012, 1st ed. 2005). Decision making. In: K. J. Holyoak & R. G. Morrison (Eds.), *The Cambridge handbook of thinking and reasoning* (pp. 301–321). Cambridge: Cambridge University Press.
Luhmann, N. (2009). *Vertrauen. Ein Mechanismus der Reduktion sozialer Komplexität*. Stuttgart: UTB.
N.N. (2013). Crash course. The origins of the financial crisis. In: *The Economist*, 07.09.2013. http://www.economist.com/news/schoolsbrief/21584534-effects-financial-crisis-are-still-being-felt-five-years-article. [Accessed 05 Feb 2016].
Pohle Fraser, M. (1995). Risk, information and noise: Risk perception and risk management of French and German banks during the nineteenth century. *Financial History Review, 2* (1), 25–39.
Pohle Fraser, M. (1999). *Noisy optimists: Risk management in French and German banks in the 19th and early 20th centuries*. Unpublished thesis, Florence.
Priemel, K. (2013). Spekulation als Gegenstand historischer Forschung. *Jahrbuch für Wirtschaftsgeschichte/ Economic History Yearbook 2*, 9–26.
Ricciardi, V. (2008). The psychology of risk: The behavioral finance perspective. In: F. J. Fabozzi (Ed.), *Handbook of finance, Investment management and financial management* (Vol. 2, pp. 85–111). Hoboken: Wiley.
Ripperger, T. (2005, 2nd ed.). *Ökonomik des Vertrauens. Analyse eines Organisationsprinzips*. Tübingen: Mohr Siebeck.
Simmel, G. (2013, 7th ed., 1st ed. 1908). *Soziologie. Untersuchungen über die Formen der Vergesellschaftung*. Berlin: Duncker & Humblot.

Part I

First Part: Recruitment of Personnel and Partners

The House of Morgan: Private Family Bank in Transition

Susie J. Pak

1 The Transition from a Family Bank to a Managerial Corporation

In August 1926, three years after losing his daughter, Hope, in a stag hunt riding accident, H. Herman Harjes fell off his horse during a polo match and died in Deauville, France.[1] At the time of his death, Herman was the senior partner of Morgan, Harjes & Co., the French branch of the House of Morgan, and his untimely demise left the firm without a clear successor. Herman's brother, John H. Harjes, Jr., had been a partner but left after only a short period of time.[2] It was said that Herman's surviving male children were too young to take his place, but none of his three sons went on to join the firm (Rottenberg 2006, 40).[3] It was not unusual for family members to lose interest in the family business,

S.J. Pak (✉)
Department of History, St. John's University, Jamaica, NY, USA

K. Schönhärl (ed.), *Decision Taking, Confidence and Risk Management in Banks from Early Modernity to the 20th Century*,
DOI 10.1007/978-3-319-42076-9_2

particularly by the third generation, but French law dictated that the firm could not continue to use the Harjes name without an heir.[4]

The situation facing the Morgan bank epitomised one of the key challenges that all family firms face during their lifetime—how to establish continuity in the face of generational change. In fact, when Morgan, Harjes & Co. became Morgan et Cie (Morgan & Company) in 1926, it was not the first time that the Paris firm had changed its name due to a lack of family interest. Originally, the bank had been called Drexel, Harjes & Co. (f. 1868) after its founders, John H. Harjes, Herman's father, and Anthony J. Drexel, whose father, Francis Drexel, was the founder of the Philadelphia house of Drexel & Co. (f. 1847). When Anthony died in 1893, his three sons indicated they did not want to assume 'the cares and responsibilities' of the bank (Rottenberg 2006, 141, 172–175).[5] The Drexel name did not completely disappear, however, because Anthony Drexel had fortuitously combined his family's interests with that of London banker Junius Morgan in 1871. In 1895, the Morgan, Drexel, and Harjes firms were reorganised under the leadership of Junius's son, J. Pierpont Morgan.

The House of Morgan was made up of four firms: J.P. Morgan & Co. (New York), Drexel & Co. (Philadelphia), J.S. Morgan & Co./Morgan, Grenfell & Co. (London), and Morgan Harjes & Co./Morgan et Cie (Paris) (Burk 1989, 62).[6] Over the course of the twentieth century, each bank confronted challenges related to family succession. During the same period, they also began a related but distinct shift away from the partnership structure. This paper researches the social origins of partnership changes by looking at the makeup of the partnerships during the banks' transition to a managerial corporate structure. It studies how the type of institutions that went into selecting and recruiting partners changed over time. It asks: What can the history of the Morgan partnership contribute to the understanding of how the mechanisms of confidence and risk management work in tandem? How did the Morgans manage the risk of incorporating non-family members into the bank? How were traditions of decision-taking continued over time? How did they maintain confidence, continuity, and a sense of coherent identity during the transition period? How did the identity of the Morgan bank as a family firm persist despite the breaks in continuity in the family line, the overall decrease of kinship ties between the partners, and the loss of the partnership model?

The paper argues a key component of that continuity was the way in which the partners created common associations to other institutions in the society at large. This 'external architecture' of the bank's business, to use a phrase by Geoffrey Jones, included non-financial firms, such as governmental, educational and social organisations (Jones 2000, 227). The partners' ties to those interests created their own challenges, but they integrated the firm in an institutional network whose longevity was not limited by the life span of individual partners or specific kinship lines. The partners pursued these associations willingly and in ways that were meaningful to them as individuals such that they offer a view into the culture of the firm. Because the ties also required constant renewal by every subsequent generation, whether the partners had kinship claims or not, the resultant network is an important reminder that the family was but just one institution within modern society. In other words, they demonstrate the ways in which the family firm, like the family, was 'a historical institution, not a natural one' (Maynes and Waltner 2012, IX).

2 The Limits of Inheritance

When Pierpont Morgan died in 1913, his son, Jack, became the senior partner of the House of Morgan. Jack Morgan was raised in the tradition of merchant banking, and he had a strong sense of duty to the family firm. Despite the fact that he was not as forceful a personality as his father, he had the ability to command the respect of the head of his house.[7] The Morgans were fortunate in this regard because, as noted, family banks could not guarantee the availability of able and willing descendants even though family succession offered clear advantages for banking partnerships. Families had a natural way to monitor their members, and they operated under the assumption of shared interest and trust. When family members continued to play an active role in their firms, their economic capital was kept within the firm and outsider anxieties about the change in leadership were mollified by the appearance of continuity represented by the persistence of the family name.

At the same time, given that a partnership's most important asset was its human capital and because partners took a great personal risk by having unlimited liability, a private bank could not and did not simply award a partnership as a matter of inheritance. Family background did not guarantee quality nor did it imply the absence of conflict. For example, Herman's death in 1926 was untimely and tragic, but, as Martin Horn has described in great detail, his tenure at the firm was not uncomplicated, particularly during the Great War (Horn 2000, 85–112; 2002, 73–74). Seven years earlier, when the New York partners felt that Herman was not devoting enough attention to the bank or protecting the New York house's interests, the Morgans invited American banker Nelson Dean Jay, who had no family ties to the bank, to become a partner in the Paris house.[8]

Private banks may have been closely identified with kinship ties, but they were not exclusively so. Throughout the early twentieth century, the Morgans found enough talent outside the family network so that they developed a reputation for being more 'meritocratic' than their peers (Carosso 1987, 307). Whether or not that was the case, and even as the Morgans continued to include family members of the subsequent generation (either by marriage or birth), the partnerships became less and less populated by family members over the course of the early twentieth century. After Jack Morgan's death in 1943, the New York house ceased to be led by a family heir even though his oldest son, Junius, remained a member. By that time, the bank also began to move away from being family run for reasons that had nothing to do with a partner's natural life cycle.

3 The Great War and the Growth of State Power

In 1935, Jack Morgan's youngest son, Henry, formally left the partnership to create Morgan Stanley & Co., a new investment bank. His departure and those of Morgan partners Harold Stanley and William Ewing were the direct result of new regulations that separated commercial and investment banking under the Glass-Steagall Act. In 1934 these changes in American law led Morgan, Grenfell & Co. to become a limited liability company so that the American partners could remain affiliated with the bank (Burk 1989, 83).[9] The pressures created by the growth of state power accelerated the New York house's transition away from the partnership structure. In 1940, J.P. Morgan & Co. made the historic decision to become a limited liability corporation. Morgan et Cie followed in 1945.[10]

The loss of the unlimited liability structure was significant because as Kathleen Burk has written, 'Traditionally, merchant…[bankers'] liability was unlimited—otherwise they were not trusted...' (Burk 1989, 102). The Morgans would not have become a limited liability company if they had thought it would fundamentally change the identity of the bank, so the fact that they were willing to do so indicates they believed the essence of the bank would continue, even in an organisationally different form. Part of this confidence had to do with the fact that the Morgan bank had been expanding its network and adapting to a changing regulatory environment for several decades. It also reflected an appreciation for the rise of state power that developed organically within the firm and was not entirely imposed from without.

The Great War was an important turning point. At that time, the Morgans' attendance to state power became even more pronounced as their interests aligned with the Allied cause as a firm and as individuals. Led by Jack Morgan, their role as the buying agent for Britain and France set them apart, but like many others, the Morgans integrated state interests into their emotional and individual lives, meaning a nationalist spirit became a part of their collective identity as a result of the war. When the United States entered the war in 1917, many of the sons of the American partners and former partners went off to fight: Robert Bacon's son, Elliot C. Bacon, was a captain in the 304th Field Artillery of the 77th Division; Charles H. Coster's son, Charles H. Coster, Jr., served in the infantry; Jack Morgan's sons, Junius Spencer Morgan and Henry Sturgis Morgan, both served in the navy as did Henry P. Davison's sons, Henry P. Davison, Jr. and F. Trubee Davison, who was wounded; Thomas W. Lamont's son, Thomas Stillwell Lamont, was a private in field artillery; Edward R. Stettinius's son, William C. Stettinius, was a lieutenant with the Eleventh Infantry, Fifth Division, and wounded in France; and William Henry Porter's son, James Jackson Porter, was killed fighting in France in 1918.

Many of the sons who survived entered the firm after the war, and they were joined over the next two decades by partners across all four firms, who had also served in the war, including Randal Hugh Vivian Smith (17th Lancers—wounded); Francis James Rennell Rodd (Royal Field Artillery); Michael George Herbert (Lieutenant, UK); Thomas Sivewright Catto (British Ministry of Food, USA); Nelson Dean Jay (Lieutenant Colonel, A.E.F), Bernard S. Carter (Second Lieutenant, 103rd Infantry Regiment—wounded), Thomas Newhall (Lieutenant Commander, Navy), Charles D. Dickey (Lieutenant, Navy); Benjamin Joy (Major, Infantry), and Alan Vasey Arragon (Artillery regiment, France).[11]

From the Great War onward, the New York house began to incorporate partners whose background included government experience, such as John Ridgely Carter, who was a diplomat with the State Department for more than a decade before joining the Paris firm in 1914; Russell C. Leffingwell, a former Assistant Secretary of Treasury and partner at Cravath, Henderson, Leffingwell & de Gersdorff, who joined the New York house in 1923; S. Parker Gilbert, who was Leffingwell's colleague at the Department of Treasury and the Cravath firm, joined the firm in 1931. While links to the Cravath law firm dated back to the late nineteenth century, and recruiting partners from Cravath began with the introduction of partner Charles Steele in 1900 (when it was called Seward, Guthrie & Steele), the connections to the Department of Treasury and State Department were relatively new (see Tables 1 and 2).

There is much more to this story, but suffice it to say that the Great War was a transformative experience for the House of Morgan. In other words, it changed the firms' relationship to the American state, their role in international finance, and the makeup of the House.[12] The partnership changes that followed indicate that the Morgans adapted to shifts in the business and political environment by strengthening the network of institutions to which the firms were tied. These were not simply calculated additions. They were deeply personal and institutional, meaning they reflected the many individual choices by the partners and future partners, but they were made possible in part because the network from which the

Table 1 Partners who did not have family ties to another partner before joining the firm, J.P. Morgan & Co. and Drexel & Co., 1895–1920

Name	Date became partner	Place of birth	Education	Firm before went to JPM	Occupation of father if known	Wife's maiden name[a]	Occupation of wife's father if known
Robert Bacon	1895	Jamaica Plain, MA	Hopkinson's School; Harvard	E. Rollins Morse & Bros.	Merchant & shipper	Martha Waldron Cowdin	Importer
Charles H. Coster	1895	Newport, RI	Private schools	Fabbri & Chauncey	Merchant	Emily Pell	Auctioneer
Arthur E. Newbold	1895	Somerset County, PA	University of PA	W.A. Newbold, Son & Co.	Banker	Harriet Dixon	Farmer
Edward T. Stotesbury	1895	Philadelphia	Public schools; Friends' Central School	Harris & Stotesbury	Sugar refiner	Fannie Butcher/ Lucretia Eva Roberts Cromwell	N/A/lawyer
George C. Thomas	1895	Philadelphia	Episcopal Academy	Thomas & Shoemaker	Merchant	Ada Elizabeth Moorhead	Ironmaster
Charles Steele	1900	Baltimore	Private schools; University of Virginia; Columbia Law	Seward, Guthrie & Steele (law)	Lawyer & diplomat	Nannie Gordon French	Banker & broker

(continued)

Table 1 (continued)

Name	Date became partner	Place of birth	Education	Firm before went to JPM	Occupation of father if known	Wife's maiden name[a]	Occupation of wife's father if known
Edward F. Whitney	1900	Boston	E.S. Dixwell's Latin School; Harvard	Jacob C. Rogers agency	Shipmaster & merchant	Not married	Not married
George W. Perkins	1901	Chicago	Public grammar school	New York Life	Insurance agent	Evelina Ball	Lawyer & insurance agent
Henry P. Davison	1909	Troy, PA	Public school; Greylock Institute	First National Bank of New York	Farming implements salesman & inventor	Kate Trubee	Wholesale grocer
Thomas W. Lamont	1911	Claverack, NY	Phillips Exeter; Harvard	First National Bank of New York	Minister	Florence Haskell Corliss	Men's collar and shirt manufacturer
William H. Porter	1911	Middlebury, VT	Middlebury Academy; Saratoga High School	Chemical National Bank; Guaranty Trust	Farmer	Esther Jackson	Clerk
Horatio G. Lloyd	1912	Middletown, DE	Private schools; University of PA Law	Commercial Trust Co.	Farmer	Mary Helen Wingate	Military general & lawyer

Dwight Whitney Morrow	1914	Huntington, West VA	Public schools; Amherst College; Columbia Law	Reed, Simpson, Thacher & Bartlett (law)	President of college & professor	Elizabeth Reeve Cutter	Railroad executive
Edward R. Stettinius	1916	Chicago	St. Louis University; Mt. St. Mary's College	Diamond Match Company	Wholesale grocer	Judith Carrington	Tobacconist
Thomas Cochran	1917	St. Paul, MN	Phillips Exeter; Yale	Liberty National Bank	Lawyer & dealer in real estate	Martha A. Griffin	Farmer

[a] Slash indicates more than one marriage

Table 2 Partners who did not have family ties to another partner before joining the firm, J.P. Morgan & Co. and Drexel & Co., 1921–1940

Name	Date became partner	Place of birth	Education	Firm before went to JPM	Occupation of father if known	Wife's maiden name[a]	Occupation of wife's father if known
Thomas S. Gates	1921	Fairfield, CT	Germantown Academy; University of PA; University of PA Law	Philadelphia Trust Co.	President, Germantown mutual insurance co.	Marie Rogers/ Mary Emma Gibson/Emma Barton Brewster Gibson	N/A/ wholesale liquors/ lawyer
Russell C. Leffingwell	1923	New York	Yale; Columbia Law	Cravath, Henderson, Leffingwell & de Gersdorff	Businessman (iron)	Lucy Hewitt	Businessman (iron)
Arthur M. Anderson	1927	East Orange, NJ	Public Schools	Libbey & Struthers; L. von Hoffman & Co.	Bookkeeper & clerk in bank	Alice Mary Sloane	Educator
Francis D. Bartow	1927	Annapolis, MD	Rectory School, New Milford, CT	First National Bank of New York	Insurance agent	Sabina Redmond Martin	Businessman (insurance)
William Ewing	1927	St. Louis, MO	Yale	N.W. Harris & Co., Chicago	Businessman (dairy)	Maria Taylor	N/A

Harold Stanley	1928	Great Barrington, MA	Hotchkiss; Yale	Guaranty Trust Co.	Electrical engineer; inventor	Edith Thurston/ Louise Ross Todd Gilbert	N/A/ businessman
Edward Hopkinson Jr.	1929	Philadelphia	William Penn Charter School; University of PA; University of PA Law	Dickson, Beltler & McCouch (law)	Lawyer	May Theresa Sullivan/Edith Sullivan	Railroad executive & stockbroker
Thomas Newhall	1929	Philadelphia	Haverford School	Philadelphia & Western Railway	Sugar merchant & purchasing agent, Penn RR	Honora Guest Blackwell	Broker & lawyer
S. Parker Gilbert	1931	Bloomfield, NJ	Public schools; Rutgers College; Harvard Law	Cravath, Henderson & de Gersdorff (law)	Coal merchant & politician	Louis Ross Todd	Businessman

(*continued*)

Table 2 (continued)

Name	Date became partner	Place of birth	Education	Firm before went to JPM	Occupation of father if known	Wife's maiden name[a]	Occupation of wife's father if known
Charles D. Dickey	1932	New York City	St. Paul's; Yale	Brown, Brothers & Co.	Banker	Catherine Dunscomb Colt	Exporter
Henry C. Alexander	1939	Murfreesboro, TN	Public schools; Vanderbilt University; Yale Law	Davis, Polk, Wardwell, Gardiner, Reed (law)	Feed store operator; farm supplies merchant	Janet Hutchinson	Engineer & industrial executive
I.C. Raymond Atkin	1939	Springfield, Ontario, Canada	Public schools	Royal Bank of Canada	Farmer	Alice Winnifred Flanagan	Minister
William Arthur Mitchell	1939	Hamilton, Ontario	Public schools	Royal Bank of Canada	N/A	Georgie Lynn Brown	Secretary (auto co.)

[a] Slash indicates more than one marriage; N/A indicates information not available

Morgans could gain resources and experience expanded through their wartime experience.

It should be noted here that the shift in relation to state power may not have been as dramatic a change for Morgan, Grenfell & Co. Unlike the American firms or the French house, which was also primarily made up of men of American nationality, all of Morgan, Grenfell's partners were British except Harry Ashton Watkins, who was American. Many of their families had the experience of direct participation in government as members of the Foreign Service or had ties to Parliament (see Tables 3, 4, 5 and 6). As Youssef Cassis has written, the status of Member of Parliament had a 'social prestige' that was extremely meaningful to British bankers of their generation and represented but a fraction of their historic ties to politics or interests in state power (Cassis 1994, 267, 262–310).[13]

In relative terms, a closer association with the state was quite foreign to the Morgan bank's American branches under the tenure of Pierpont Morgan, who abhorred the world of politics. So it was a more dramatic shift for the American house to incorporate the idea of the banker as a public servant into the firm's identity by the 1930s (Pak 2013, 192–218). It is not that the state replaced the family model or that the firm had uncomplicated relations with state power from that point forward—far from it. But by that time, partners spoke of public service with a familiarity that was akin to other traditional characteristics like family background or work experience. Thus, when Thomas Lamont wrote a memorandum about the achievements of the partners, he noted:

> *The repute gained by the Morgans, senior and junior, as magnificent patrons of the arts, letters, charities, etc. The service of Robert Bacon as Assistant Secretary and for a brief period as Secretary of State. The public service of R.C.L. [Leffingwell] in the Treasury and of S.P.G. [S. Parker Gilbert] in the Treasury and in Germany—even though these services preceded their entry into the firm. H.P.D.'s [Henry P. Davison] work in the American Red Cross during the war. J.P.M.'s [Jack Morgan] service on the Bankers' Committee re. Reparations in 1922. His service on the Young Committee in 1929. T.W.L.'s [Thomas W. Lamont] ditto and in other lesser capacities. Activity of many firm members on educational boards and charitable foundations.* (Pak 2013, 214)[14]

Table 3 Partners who had family ties to another partner before joining the firm, J.S. Morgan & Co./Morgan, Grenfell & Co., 1895–1940[a]

Name	Date became partner	Place of birth	Education	Firm before joining House of Morgan	Father's profession	Wife's maiden name[b]	Wife's father's profession if known
Walter H. Burns	1890	New York City	Harvard University	Morton, Bliss & Co.; United States Mortgage Co.	Merchant	Mary Lyman Morgan	Banker
Walter Spencer Morgan Burns	1898	London	Eton; Trinity College, Cambridge	N/A	Banker	Ruth Evelyn Cavendish-Bentinck	Justice of the Peace; Member of Parliament
Vivian Hugh Smith	1905	London	Eton; Cambridge University	Hay's Wharf	Partner, Hay's Wharf; former Governor of Bank of England	Sybil Mary McDonnell	Earl of Antrim
Randal Hugh Vivian Smith	1930	London	Eton; Sandhurst	Andrew Yule & Co.; J.P. Morgan & Co.	Banker	Dorothea Gwenllian James	Justice of the Peace; 3rd Baron Northbourne
Francis James Rennell Rodd	1933	London	Eton; Balliol College, Oxford	J.P. Morgan & Co.; Bank of International Settlements	Diplomat & British ambassador to Italy	Mary Constance Vivian Smith	Banker

William Edward, 2nd Viscount Harcourt	1939	London	Eton; Oxford University	J.P. Morgan & Co.; Morgan Stanley & Co.	Secretary of state for the colonies (1st Viscount Harcourt)	Maud Elizabeth Grosvenor/ Elizabeth Sonia Snagge	Banker; 4th Baron Ebury/ banker

[a] Morgan, Grenfell & Co., Ltd. is included to reflect the continued association by the partners even though the firms were technically legally separated

[b] Slash indicates more than one marriage; N/A indicates information not available

Table 4 Partners who did not have family ties to another partner before joining the firm, J.S. Morgan & Co./Morgan, Grenfell & Co., 1895–1940[a]

Name	Date became partner	Place of birth	Education	Firm before joining House of Morgan	Father's profession	Wife's maiden name[b]	Wife's father's profession if known
Robert Gordon	1885	Dumfries, Scotland	Dumfries Academy	Maitland, Phelps & Co. (NY)	Lawyer	Frances Burton	N/A
Frederick William Lawrence	1885	N/A	N/A	N/A	N/A	N/A	N/A
Clinton E. Dawkins	1900	London	Cheltenham; Oxford, Balliol College	British Diplomatic Service, India	British foreign office	Louise Johnston	Brazil merchant
Edward Charles Grenfell	1904	London	Harrow; Trinity College, Cambridge	Brown, Shipley & Co.; Smith, Ellison	MP and director of Bank of England	Florence Henderson	Merchant importer
Charles Frederick Whigham	1912/1918[c]	Ayrshire, Scotland	Ayr Academy	N/A	Wine merchant	N/A	N/A
Michael George Herbert	1924	London	Eton; Oxford Balliol College	N/A	British ambassador to Washington	N/A	N/A

Thomas Sivewright Catto	1928	Tyneside, Scotland	Peterhead Academy (Scotland); Heaton School, Newcastle-upon-Tyne	Andrew Yule & Co.	Shipwright	Gladys Forbes Gordon	Partner, MacAndrews & Forbes (manufacturer & merchants)
Harry Ashton Watkins	1934	South Orange, NJ	Williams College	J.P. Morgan & Co.	Broker	Barbara Cheney/ Marion Moore Adams	Silk manufacturer/ N/A
Wilfred William Hill Hill-Wood	1939	London	Eton, Trinity College, Cambridge	None	Gentleman; MP	Diana Marian Wyld	N/A

[a] Morgan, Grenfell & Co., Ltd. is included to reflect the continued association by the partners even though the firms were technically legally separated

[b] Slash indicates more than one marriage; N/A indicates information not available

[c] Whigham became a salaried partner in 1912 and a general partner in 1918 (Burk 1989, 65)

Table 5 Partners who had family ties to another partner before joining the firm, Morgan, Harjes & Co./Morgan et Cie, 1895–1940

Name	Date became partner	Place of birth	Education	Firm before joining House of Morgan	Father's profession	Wife's name	Wife's father's profession if known
John Henry Harjes	1893	Bremen, Germany	N/A	Drexel, Harjes & Co.	N/A	Amelia Hessenbruch	Hardware merchant
John Henry Harjes, Jr.	1893	New York	N/A	Drexel, Harjes & Co.	Banker	N/A	N/A
Henry Herman Harjes	1898	New York	Private tutors	J.P. Morgan & Co.	Banker	Frederica Virginia Berwind	Berwind, White & Co. (Coal merchant)
Bernard Shirley Carter	1924	Biarritz, France	Groton; Harvard University; Harvard Law	J.P. Morgan & Co.; Morgan, Grenfell & Co.	Banker & diplomat	Louise Hope Thacher	Wool merchant

Table 6 Partners who did not have family ties to another partner before joining the firm, Morgan, Harjes & Co./Morgan et Cie, 1895–1940

Name	Date became partner	Place of birth	Education	Firm before joining House of Morgan	Father's profession	Wife's name	Wife's father's profession if known
Oscar Othon Siegel	1893	N/A	N/A	N/A	N/A	N/A	N/A
Hermann Peter Herold	1893	N/A	N/A	N/A	N/A	N/A	N/A
John Ridgely Carter	1914	Baltimore, MD	Trinity College (CT); Maryland University Law	Department of State	Lawyer	Alice Morgan	N/A
Nelson Dean Jay	1920	Elmwood, Illinois	Knox College	Guaranty Trust Co.	Merchant; insurance agent	Anne Augustine	Dry goods merchant
Benjamin Joy	1928	Boston	Groton; Harvard	Dillon, Read & Co.	Dry goods commission merchant	Not married	Not married
Maurice Charles Alphonse Paul Pesson-Didion	1931	N/A	N/A	N/A	N/A	N/A	N/A
Alan Vasey Arragon	1933	Chicago	Northwestern University	First National Bank of Chicago	Manager, Pianos; real estate dealer	Paulette Arragon	N/A

Given the changes the firms' partners experienced as a result of the War and political pressure, it is remarkable that the Morgans' identity was not perceived as more of a mishmash, as it could have been, rather than the seamless legacy that they believed it to be.[15] This is particularly true given that the idea of a continuous history was not based simply on a cult of their founder, who certainly would not have been familiar with a world in which the public service of bankers had become the expected norm. If generations of Morgan partners believed there was truth to this image of cohesion, it was because it had a tangibility made real by historical, institutional ties in which they were personally invested and that they pursued in a natural and organic way without a calculated purpose specifically for the benefit of the firm's image. In other words, changes in the Morgans' identity after the War were indicative of the firm's ability to adapt to unforeseen historical circumstances, but the ease with which it did so relied upon the presence of a network of relations, which pre-dated the War and continued well into the post-War period. The partners did not dwell on analysing the institutional network which existed outside the firm and made these ties possible, but they understood that their unity in the face of generational change was not just based on memories or wishful thinking.

4 Institutions and Confidence

To get a sense of the institutions that undergirded the partners' relations and their sense of cohesion, one need only to look at a letter from Thomas Lamont to John Ridgely Carter written eight months after Herman Harjes's death. At the time, the partners had not yet found another partner for the Paris house, and Lamont's letter to Carter, who became the senior partner in Paris, offers a window into the considerations that were involved. It is worth quoting at length. He wrote:

> *Dear Jack: We have all been terribly interested in this matter of a new partner for Paris. The situation with yourself, Dean [Nelson Dean Jay] and Bunny [Bernard S. Carter, Jack's son] has been constantly on the minds of us all since dear Herman's death. The Paris house is constantly growing in importance and usefulness. You are all overburdened; you must have competent assistance. When it comes to your choos-*

ing a partner, it is just as difficult and just as important as choosing a wife. We all feel that. Jack Morgan has, of course, been particularly active minded in the matter. Having spent so much time abroad, I think he sees and feels the intimate problems of Paris and London perhaps even more keenly than the rest of us. At any rate, not a week has gone by since last summer that he has not recurred to the question; and Dean had hardly arrived before he pounced on him and said that we must take up some suggestion to submit to you.

Lamont went on to tell Carter that the 'leading possibility' for the partnership 'in the minds of Jack and of all of us' was Harold Stanley. He wrote:

Even before Herman's death we had been talking of Harold among ourselves here and had wondered whether he might by any chance be available for Paris; so, he was the first man that we suggested to Dean, and we thought that we would exhaust that possibility before we cast about in any other direction.

Why did Lamont and the other partners feel that Stanley was such an ideal candidate? He wrote:

The way George Whitney and I, and in fact all of us, feel about Harold is that with the exception of his lack of French (which can be remedied) he is almost perfectly equipped to fit in with you all. He has high character, an excellent education (of course, he is only a Yale man, and Jack [Morgan], George and I feel that is against him, but we must admit that there are some good Yale men, including Tom Cochran, Russell Leffingwell and Buck [William] Ewing,) a charming personality, an analytical mind, excellent negotiating ability, including quite extraordinary straightforwardness, and long experience in banking. To be sure, his experience at the Guaranty has lain more along the security than the purely banking end, but he has had a wide variety of experience over there and knows all the problems of the banking end. My only misgiving is lest he should not be able to come. If he should, I am certain that you and Bunny would find him a wonderful and congenial partner, a fine playmate and a staunch friend. His qualities of loyalty are unexcelled.[16]

Lamont's letter is a remarkable document because it expresses the way in which partnership considerations were intensely personal. From their perspective, so much of being a good partner depended on whether a candidate would 'fit in'. Language, even for the French house, and specialised banking experience were not obstacles. Character, education, personality, loyalty, congeniality and experience were the key considerations. Lamont's informal way of referring to Carter as Jack, and his son Bernard, as Bunny (as he was known to his friends) reinforced the idea that an ideal partner was not just about being a competent colleague but also a 'playmate' and a 'friend' (Steel 1999, 463, 528).[17]

How did Stanley come to the attention of the Morgans? How did they get to know him as a person and under what circumstances? Lamont states that they had known him for years, but he was not related to anyone in the bank. How could they judge his character and personality and experience? How did they know they could confide in him and trust him? Stanley did not work at any of the Morgan firms before becoming a partner. His father, William Stanley, had served as the chief engineer of the Westinghouse Electric Company and was well known in the field of engineering as the inventor of the electrical transformer, but he was not a banker. How did they know he 'was perfectly equipped to fit in'? What made him a potential Morgan partner? It is important to look at what Lamont did not explain about Stanley, presumably because it was already understood—the Morgans knew Stanley because they were part of a wider community, meaning they had relationships with institutions to which Stanley was also affiliated.

To begin with, Stanley was a member of Guaranty Trust Co., a firm that historically had a close relationship with the Morgans. Guaranty Trust was founded in 1903, but in 1910 it was put under a voting trust made up of three men: Morgan partner Henry P. Davison, William H. Porter, who was at Guaranty and became a Morgan partner in 1911, and George F. Baker, Sr., president of First National Bank of New York, who was also a close friend and associate of Pierpont Morgan. Since that time, Guaranty had been identified closely with the Morgans, and the firms retained close institutional ties for decades, so much so that J.P. Morgan & Co. and Guaranty eventually merged in 1959 to become Morgan, Guaranty (Allen 2014; 1935, 121).[18]

No matter how competent a banker, the Morgans would only consider recruiting from firms they believed would either match or enhance their status and reputation. Recruiting Stanley from Guaranty

Trust thus reflected the relationship between the two firms as much as it did his relationship to the Morgans. Stanley joined Guaranty Trust in 1915 and became vice-president of the bond department in 1916. In 1921, he was made president of the Guaranty Company, a securities company that was a subsidiary of Guaranty Trust. As president, Stanley 'underwrote and sold bonds amounting to millions of dollars for governmental and private organisations. He worked with the house of Morgan in floating some of the largest bond issues'.[19] Guaranty Trust and Guaranty Co. were major participants in the Morgans' syndicates; both ranked with the top ten participants in the Morgans' syndicates (out of over 2400) between 1894 and 1934, even though Guaranty Co. was only founded after the war.[20]

Stanley's entrée into the firm was typical of partners who did not have family ties, in that they came from firms within the Morgan orbit. Nelson Dean Jay, who had been brought into the Paris firm in 1920, had also been recruited from Guaranty, and he and Stanley were good friends. William H. Porter, one of the members of the voting trust, preceded them in 1911. Lamont was recruited by the Morgan firm from First National Bank of New York, which had even stronger, closer ties to the Morgans (Pak 2013, 23–25). He was not the only partner recruited from First National. His mentor, Henry P. Davison, joined the firm in 1909, and Francis D. Bartow joined the firm in 1927 (see Tables 1 and 2). In other words, firms could and did act as substitutes for traditional kinship recommendations, reflecting the extent to which the external architecture of the bank business was changing. But because the firms were not families, they also created certain issues related to the foundations of trust and confidence.

5 Institutions and Identity

Though the Morgans tended to recruit from a select group of firms, one consequence of acquiring partners from outside existing kinship networks is that the firm's makeup became demographically more diverse, which created potential challenges for firm cohesion, particularly after 1910. In general, Morgan partners were native born, white, male, and Protestant (with the vast majority being Episcopalian), but partners that came from outside the family were more likely to be born outside the major cities, and more likely to have fathers without a background in banking. Stanley grew up in Great Barrington, Massachusetts, and his father was an inventor and engineer. Jay was from Elmwood, Illinois and the son of a general merchandise merchant. Porter was from Vermont, and his father was a farmer. Lamont's father was a Methodist minister, and he grew up in upstate New York. Davison was born in rural Pennsylvania and was the son of a farming implements salesman. Bartow was the son of an insurance agent and from Annapolis, Maryland (Tables 1 and 2).

Even the London firm, which was generally more cohesive than the American houses, demonstrated differences between the partners with or without family ties. With the exception of American Walter H. Burns, Junius S. Morgan, Sr.'s son-in-law and Pierpont Morgan's brother-in-law, all family partners were born in London. None were Scottish, in contrast to partners without family ties, three of whom were born in Scotland (Robert Gordon, Charles Frederick Whigham and Thomas Sivewright Catto) (see Table 4). None, except Harry A. Watkins, appears to have apprenticed with the Morgan bank. Like the American partners, they came to the British house from firms known to the Morgans (Table 3).

Theoretically, these types of differences could create the potential for friction because there was no denying that partners who were sons or relatives of former partners, had certain entitlements associated with kinship. Morgan partners with family ties either apprenticed at firms associated with their fathers or they did not have to have work experience at all before they joined the firm. They did not, in other words, need an outside introduction. Though there were exceptions, they were more homogeneous in terms of upbringing. They were more likely to be born in New York City, Philadelphia or Boston. They were more likely to have attended elite Episcopalian private schools in New England like Groton (f. 1884, MA) or St. Paul's (f. 1856, NH) rather than go to local public schools (see Table 7).[21] The British house also followed this pattern, but to an even greater degree because their educational institutions were older and had stronger ties to the British gentry. All of the Morgan, Grenfell & Co. partners who entered the firm after the

Table 7 Partners who had family ties to another partner before joining the firm, J.P. Morgan & Co. and Drexel & Co., 1895–1940

Name	Date became partner	Place of birth	Education	Firm before went to JPM	Occupation of father if known	Wife's maiden name[a]	Occupation of wife's father if known
John Pierpont Morgan Sr.	1895	Hartford, CT	University of Gottingen	Drexel, Morgan & Co.	Merchant banker	Amelia Sturges/ Frances Louisa Tracy	Merchant/ lawyer
John Pierpont Morgan Jr.	1895	New York City	St. Paul's; Harvard	Drexel, Morgan & Co.	Merchant banker	Jane Norton Grew	Merchant
George Sullivan Bowdoin	1895	New York City	Private schools; Lawrence Scientific School (Harvard)	Morton, Bliss & Co.	Lawyer	Julia Irving Grinnell	Shipping merchant & collector of the port
Temple Bowdoin	1895	Wolfert's Dell, Irvington, NY	Columbia University	None	Banker	Helen Parish Kingsford	Merchant
James W. Paul Jr.	1895	Philadelphia	Public Schools	James C. Young & Co., Exchange Brokers	Lawyer	Frances Catherine Drexel	Merchant banker
Edward M. Robinson	1895	Philadelphia	N/A	N/A	Banker	Aileen Ivers	Press., insurance co.
W. Pierson Hamilton	1900	New York City	St. Paul's; Yale	Manhattan Trust Co.	Businessman & steel wheel manufacturer	Juliet Pierpont Morgan/ Theodosia S. Carlin	Banker/farmer

Table 7 (continued)

Name	Date became partner	Place of birth	Education	Firm before went to JPM	Occupation of father if known	Wife's maiden name[a]	Occupation of wife's father if known
Elliot C. Bacon	1920	Boston	Groton; Harvard	None (diplomatic service)	Banker	Hope Norman	Banker & senator
Junius Spencer Morgan Jr.	1920	New York City	Groton; Harvard	Brown Bros. & Co.	Banker	Louise Converse	Composer
George Whitney	1920	Boston	Groton; Harvard	Kidder, Peabody & Co.; Markoe, Morgan, Whitney	Banker	Martha Beatrix Bacon	Banker & secretary of state & ambassador to France
Henry P. Davison Jr.	1929	Englewood, NJ	Groton; Yale; Cambridge	None	Banker	Anne Stillman/ Eleanor Sparks	Banker/N/A
Thomas Stilwell Lamont	1929	New York City	Phillips Exeter; Harvard; Trinity College, Cambridge	None	Banker	Elinor Branscombe Miner	Manufacturer (glass/enamel)
Henry Sturgis Morgan	1929	New York City	Groton; Harvard	None	Banker	Catherine Adams	Secretary of navy

[a] Slash indicates more than one marriage; N/A indicates information not available

war and who were related to other partners, apprenticed at J.P. Morgan & Co. All, except American Walter Burns, went to Eton (f. 1440) (see Table 3).

To be sure, private partnerships like the Morgans were hierarchical and every partner was not equal in status. But a partnership was also an ownership stake in the firm, a legally binding and moral obligation between partners to share in the profits and liabilities of their business. It was not, in other words, a salaried position or work for hire. It was a special type of relationship, as Lamont stated, like a marriage. A partnership thus meant assuming the identity of a Morgan partner regardless of one's birth and background. How did the firm create a whole out of different parts? How did they know that non-family members would fit in and become integrated into the culture of the firm? How was confidence built up outside the family structure? Again, the Morgans relied on outside institutions, meaning they recruited partners who had ties to institutions with which they identified.

In his letter to Carter, Lamont suggests that Stanley could fit in, not only because he was from Guaranty, but also because he was a 'Yale man'. His joke about Yale men referred, of course, to the fact that he, Jack Morgan, and George Whitney, who were all partners at that time, were Harvard men. Partnership changes were as much about how the partners saw themselves as they were about a new partner. Implicitly Lamont was affirming the connection between partners through the shared identification with institutions older than the Morgan bank, to which they had deep, and in some cases, lifelong attachments. In the context of the firm, even the historic rivalry between the two universities became something of an inside joke, a shared narrative that they all understood.

Common ties to elite educational institutions were actually a relatively new phenomenon for the Morgan American firms (Pak 2013, 301–302, footnote 11). It was not until the 1920s that a majority of the Morgan partners had a college education, but by this time, university ties played a more significant role in creating a sense of shared identity precisely because the Morgan partners had become more diverse in terms of demographic background. Like they did with firms, the Morgans tended to recruit from select universities. Although there were exceptions, and though non-family members were more likely to attend graduate school, the majority of the American partners between 1900 and 1940 came from four schools: Harvard, Yale, Columbia, and the University of Pennsylvania (within the Drexel firm).

Even more than past firm affiliation, university education allowed the partners to create legacies for themselves from which the firm benefited by association because university ties even connected partners who personally did not attend those elite schools, and family members who did not join the firm. In this regard, Lamont's joke about Harvard and Yale in his letter to Jack Carter is instructive because Carter did not go to Harvard. Carter descended from a colonial Virginia family and was born in Baltimore. His father went to Harvard Law and Trinity College, but he attended Trinity College (CT) and Maryland University Law School. When Carter's son, Bernard, entered the Morgan, Harjes & Co. in 1924, however, he did not follow in Carter's footsteps. Bernard attended Groton and Harvard like Jack Morgan's sons, Junius and Henry. In other words, he looked more like the son of a Morgan banker because he was.

This pattern repeated itself throughout the history of the bank and appeared in the second generation and beyond. Regardless of whether the partners' sons joined the firm or whether they or all of their children attended those universities, Morgan partners participated in that culture. Charles Coster did not go to university, but his son, Charles Coster, Jr., who went into the Foreign Service, went to Groton and Harvard. Henry P. Davison also did not go to college, but his sons, F. Trubee and Henry Jr. (who became a Morgan partner) went to Groton and Yale. (F. Trubee Davison, who also went into public service, even married the daughter of Groton's founder and headmaster, Rev. Endicott Peabody). Nelson Dean Jay went to Knox College in Illinois, but his sons, Nelson Dean, Jr., and Robert Dean, who joined Bankers Trust in New York, went to St. Paul's and Harvard. (A third son, George, was killed in a riding accident in France while he was still a student at St. Paul's). Thomas W. Lamont went to Phillips Exeter and Harvard as did all three of his sons, one of whom, Thomas S. Lamont, joined the Morgan partnership.

A brief genealogical survey of the Morgan partners demonstrates that these kinds of legacies were commonplace, and qualitative analysis of the partners' personal papers and biographies indicate that they saw these choices as an entirely normal reflection of their opportunities and values. For the purposes of this study, these acts of self-interest are important because aggregated, these ties did the work of creating new family lines for the firm while contributing to an image of generational continuity in the absence of direct kinship ties between partners. In other words, the firm benefited from the ways in which the partners sought to create legacies for themselves and their families through elite private schools at the secondary and university level.[22]

Stanley is an exemplary case. In the end, the Morgans did not get him to move to Paris, but they held him in such high esteem that he joined the New York house. Though he moved to Morgan Stanley with Henry Morgan in 1935, the partners, and their firms, retained close, personal relations. Stanley did not have any biological children of his own, and his first wife, Edith, died in 1934. In 1939, however, he married Louise Todd Gilbert, the widow of Morgan partner, S. Parker Gilbert, Jr., whose son, S. Parker Gilbert III, was only five years old when his father died in 1938. Gilbert III, who was known as Parker, followed in Stanley's footsteps, graduating from Hotchkiss and Yale.

In 1960, Parker, who was also Henry Sturgis Morgan's godson, joined Morgan Stanley. He became a partner in 1969 and chairman in 1984. In 1986, he became a pivotal figure in the firm's history when he oversaw Morgan Stanley's first public stock offering after convincing the older members that going public would not change the culture of the bank. Though the story of Morgan Stanley and the late twentieth century history exceeds the limits of this paper, Parker's story is a very familiar one and speaks to the way in which the Morgan banks and their descendants continued to be viewed as family firms. When Parker died in 2015, a former Morgan Stanley colleague and friend remembered him as 'the heart and soul of Morgan Stanley', stating that 'he was born into the firm' and that he was 'the firm's DNA'.[23]

6 Marriage and Society

Though the New York house gained Harold Stanley as a partner, the Paris house still faced the issue of finding a replacement for Herman in Paris. Given the Morgans' history, it should not be a surprise that

Morgan et Cie picked a Harvard man. Benjamin Joy, a former partner at Dillon, Read & Co., was also a Groton School graduate. Unfortunately for the Morgans, Joy did not stay. He left Morgan et Cie. in 1930 and eventually joined Bankers Trust. He supposedly returned to the United States for reasons of 'poor health', but the New York partners doubted that this was the true cause.[24] It was very unusual for partners to leave the House of Morgan before dying. As private partnerships, the attrition rate of the Morgans was generally low (Pak 2013, 60). Morgan et Cie., however, was exceptional because it had several disadvantages as one of the smaller Morgan firms in terms of size and prestige. The partners were, for the most part, American and living permanently in Paris may not have appealed to them. But Joy was also different from the other Morgan partners in one important respect. He was not married, which may have impeded his integration into the firm culture.

Out of the 67 partners in the House of Morgan between 1895 and 1940, the marital status of 60 is known, and only two of the partners were unmarried. Both left the firm well before their deaths. One was Joy. The other was Edward Farley Whitney, another Harvard graduate, who left the New York house in 1910 and died in 1928. The lack of a wife and family distinguished Whitney and Joy from the other partners, and not necessarily in a positive way. As we saw, one of the most tangible benefits of being a Morgan partner was that it conferred an identity and social status regardless of a partner's original background. And it extended that social capital to families, including wives and children who did not become partners, including daughters. The firm's network created opportunities for partners and their children to build relationships in a wider community where they carried on their own family line. And when the firm's partners incorporated new family lines, they also indirectly expanded the network of the firm.[25]

Banking involvement in a wider world beyond the firm was part of the state of doing business for unlimited liability partnerships like the Morgans. Because private banks did not have to share their partnership information with the public, the reputation and behaviour of the partners gave outsiders a way to judge the character and credit of the firm. Most senior partners had substantial ties to the society at large. Active social participation correlated with a partner's status within the partnership (Pak 2013, 75).

The personal nature of private banking meant that the actions of their families also reflected on the bank. The social activities of their wives, the marriages of their children, and the education of their sons were all considered reflections of a partner's trustworthiness and his character.

For the Paris firm, cultural integration was an important indicator of a partner's tenure. In contrast to Joy, Jack Carter, who was also American, was deeply entrenched in life abroad. Even before he joined the bank, Carter had lived in Europe for many years. Between 1894 and 1909, he was the secretary of the American embassy in London (1894–1909), and in 1911 his daughter, Mildred, married the heir of the Earl of Gosford, Viscount Acheson.[26] Carter served as US minister to Yugoslavia, Romania and Bulgaria (1909–1911) before leaving the service, somewhat unwillingly, because of what he felt was a lack of adequate financial compensation.[27] Upon joining the Morgan firm, Carter and his family established themselves as leading members of the American community in Paris.

When Carter's wife, Alice, died in 1933, her obituary stated, 'Mrs. Carter for many years was a leader in the social activities of the American colony in Paris'.[28] His son, Bernard, who assumed his father's seat as the senior member of the Paris house, was also remembered 'as a long-time resident of Paris…one of the best-known Americans [in Paris]…. [with] friendships [that] extended well beyond the large American colony in Paris and included prominent persons of French and other European nationalities'. Bernard trained at both J.P. Morgan & Co. and Morgan, Grenfell & Co. before joining Morgan, Harjes & Co. in 1924. When Morgan, Harjes became a corporation in 1945, he became the company president and later chairman of the board. After J.P. Morgan & Co. merged with Guaranty Trust, he became the head of the European Policy Unit for Morgan, Guaranty, a position he held until his death in 1961.[29]

Bernard had two sons—Bernard S., Jr., who became a painter, and David Ridgely, who went to Groton and Harvard. David also joined the Morgan firm, trained at J.P. Morgan & Co. in New York, and made his career in Paris at Morgan, Guaranty. He retired from the bank in 1999.[30] By the end of the twentieth century then, the history of the Paris firm was identified with three different family lines: the Drexels, the Harjes and the Carters. The point, of course, is not only that the breaks in continuity did not undermine the firm's identity as a family firm or that the firm was able to incorporate new family lines over time, but also that the institutional and cultural ties between the Carters and the American Morgan firms were strong enough that the Paris firm retained its identity as a Morgan firm, even though it was never directly led by a Morgan family member.

7 Conclusion

The deaths of partners like Herman Harjes are events that serve as a window into the historical nature of the House of Morgan as a private family firm, and they offer insight into the mechanisms of decision-taking in situations of high risk, as partnership changes inherently were. Generational change, external pressures, and individual idiosyncrasies caused some names to disappear and others to emerge, but throughout it all the Morgan name persisted. Generations of Morgan partners believed that their shared identity was based on something natural even though the moments when their firms changed, expanded or contracted demonstrated their potential instability. In fact, there were no universal or ahistorical criteria by which one became a member of the Morgan firm. In this way, the House of Morgan was just like the institution of the family because it was a historical institution that saw itself as a natural one.

The process of becoming and being a Morgan partner and winning the confidence of the older partners took place within a larger community, which, in the twentieth century, involved state, educational, and social institutions. The voluntary activities of the partners created ties to outside organisations that benefited the firm's status and were important to its overall identity and cohesion. Confidence was still built up with very similar mechanisms even though kinship was no longer the crucial criterion. Of course, the specific institutions, which established those ties that created confidence, could and did change over time. Schools were not always as important, but they became more so. Though not discussed here due to lack of space, board memberships on certain elite artistic institutions, which were important to Pierpont Morgan like the Metropolitan Museum of Art, have held their sway.

Elsewhere the author has also written at length about the partners' memberships in private men's social clubs, though they declined in significance after the 1960s. All this is to say that it took a village of sorts to build and sustain the identity of the Morgan bank over time. Ties to an institutional historical network allowed the partners to confront generational change, incorporate new family lines and also distinguish the bank from its peers. On this last point, there is much more to say about how the Morgans compared to the partners of other firms. Identity was, after all, not only historical, it was also relative. That, however, remains a story for another time.

Notes

1. 'Articles of copartnership, 1893,' 'Articles of copartnership, 1909,' 'Articles of copartnership, 1927–1928,' 'Articles of copartnership, 1932–33,' Morgan Firms Papers, ARV 131798, Box 5, Pierpont Morgan Library (PML).

   'Hope Harjes, Daughter of Morgan Partner, Is Killed in France While Riding,' *The New York Times*, January 5, 1923; 'Polo Mates Mourn for Herman Harjes,' *The New York Times*, August 23, 1926; 'Harjes, Partner of Morgan, Dies of Polo Injury,' *Chicago Daily Tribune*, Aug. 22, 1926; 'Mrs. Vanderbilt and H.H. Harjes Dead in France,' *The Hartford Courant*, Aug. 22, 1926.
2. 'Articles of copartnership, 1893,' 'Articles of copartnership, 1909,' 'Articles of copartnership, 1927–1928,' 'Articles of copartnership, 1932–33,' Morgan Firms Papers, ARV 131798, Box 5, PML.
3. Francis Drexel had been in the brokerage business for many years before the formal organisation of Drexel & Co. in 1847. 'Anthony J. Drexel is Dead,' *The New York Times*, July 1, 1893. 'J.H. Harjes Dies in France,' *The New York Times*, February 16, 1914.
4. 'Joy to be Partner of Morgan in Paris,' *The New York Times*, December 20, 1927.
5. 'Miss Joan Blake Becomes Engaged,' *The New York Times*, June 15, 1934.
6. The American partners of J.P. Morgan & Co. and Drexel & Co. were bound by the same partnership agreement. The American branches

were partners as firms in the European houses, J.S. Morgan & Co./Morgan, Grenfell & Co. and Morgan, Harjes & Co./Morgan et Cie. see 'Articles of Partnership, 1894–1908' and 'Articles of copartnership, J.P. Morgan & Co., 1916–1939,' Morgan Firm papers, ARC 1195, Boxes 1 and 5; Records of the Morgan firms, Box 5, Folder: Articles of copartnership, 1893, Folder: Articles of copartnership, 1907–9, Folder: Articles of copartnership, 1927–1928, Box 6, Folder: Articles of copartnership, 1931, Folder: Articles of copartnership, 1932–33, Folder: Articles of copartnership, 1934, Folder: Articles of copartnership, 1937, Folder: Articles of copartnership, 1941; Box 3, Folder: Articles of Co-partnership: J.S. Morgan & Co., 1882–1884; Folder: Articles of Co-partnership: J.S. Morgan & Co., 1885–1889; Folder: Articles of Co-partnership: J.S. Morgan & Co., 1898–1899, PML.

7. Franz Schneider, Jr., financial editor of old *New York Sun*, 'Notes regarding Mr. J.P. Morgan: typescript of interviews with Thomas W. Lamont and Dwight W. Morrow,' 1925, Morgan Firms Papers, ARC 131798, Box 1, PML.
8. Letters from Edward Stettinius to Jack Morgan, September 26, 29, 30, 1919; October 1, 1919, Morgan Firms Papers, ARC 131798, Box 3, Correspondence: Edward Stettinius, 1919, PML.
9. There was also a change in the structure of the British house from a partnership to a company in 1918, but the firm retained unlimited liability at that time.
10. Drexel & Co. severed its ties with J.P. Morgan & Co. in order to remain a separate partnership in 1940. 'J.P. Morgan & Co. Will Incorporate as a State Bank,' *The New York Times*, February 16, 1940; 'Bernard Carter, Banker, 68, Dead,' *The New York Times*, November 9, 1961.
11. 'E.C. Bacon, Banker, Dies; Ill Only a Week,' *The New York Times*, September 28, 1924; 'Thomas Lamont, Banker, 68, Dead,' *The New York Times*, April 11, 1967; 'Sons of 3 Partners Enter Morgan Firm,' *The New York Times*, January 1, 1929; Edward White, ed., *The Banking Law Journal*, vol. 36 (New York: Office of Publication, 1919): 302; *Catalogue of Princeton University* (Princeton, NJ: Princeton University, 1922): 205; 'W.C. Stettinius, Baltimore Broker,' *The New York Times*, July 21, 1937.

    For references to Tables 1–4, see:

    For Alan Vasey Arragon: 'Alan Vasey Arragon,' National Archives and Records Administration (NARA); Washington D.C.; NARA Series: *Passport Applications, January 2, 1906 – March 31, 1925*; Roll #: *1114*; Volume #: *Roll 1114 – Certificates: 188000–188375, 13 Mar 1920–13 Mar 1920;* Year: *1910*; Census Place: *Chicago Ward 25, Cook, Illinois*; Roll: *T624_267*; Page: *13A*; Enumeration District: *1035*; FHL microfilm: *1374280;* National Archives and Records Administration (NARA),

Washington, D.C.; *General Records of the Department of State*; Record Group: *RG59-Entry 5166*; Box Number: *126*; Box Description: *1974 AA—BK;* 'Former Chicago Resident is Made Morgan Partner,' *Chicago Tribune*, January 1, 1933, page 5.

For Elliot C. Bacon: *The Grotonian*, vol. 22, no. 4 (Groton, MA: The Groton School, February 1906): 128; *The Grotonian*, vol. 34, no. 16 (Groton, MA: The Groton School, December 1917): 106.

For George Sullivan Bowdoin: *The New York Genealogical and Biographical Record,* vol. XLV (New York: New York Genealogical and Biographical Society, 1914): 105–106.

For Walter Hayes Burns: *The Bankers' Insurance Managers' & Agents' Magazine*, vol. LXIV (London: Waterlow and Sons Ltd., 1897): 763; *Memorial of the Harvard College Class of 1856* (George H. Ellis Co., 1906): 50.

For Walter Spencer Morgan Burns: 'Ruth E.C. Bentinck,' Class: *RG12*; Piece: *1835*; Folio: *72*; Page: *52*; GSU roll: *609694;* Ancestry.com. *1891 England Census* [database on-line]. Provo, UT, USA: Ancestry.com Operations Inc., 2005.

For Bernard Shirley Carter: 'Bernard Carter, Banker, 68, Dead,' *The New York Times*, November 9, 1961; 'Bernard Shirley Carter,' Online publication – Provo, UT, USA: Ancestry.com Operations, Inc., 2007. Original data – Passport Applications, 1795–1905. NARA Microfilm Publication M1372, 694 rolls. General Records Department of State, Record Group 59. National Archives, Washington, D.C.; 'Louise H Thacher,' Year: *1900*; Census Place: *Boston Ward 11, Suffolk, Massachusetts*; Roll: *681*; Page: *3B*; Enumeration District: *1319*; FHL microfilm: *1240681;* 'Louise Hope Thacher,' National Archives and Records Administration (NARA); Washington D.C.; NARA Series: *Passport Applications, January 2, 1906 – March 31, 1925*; Roll #: *237*; Volume #: *Roll 0237 – Certificates: 50711–51580, 12 Feb 1915–23 Feb 1915.*

For John Ridgely Carter: 'John R. Carter,' Online publication – Provo, UT, USA: Ancestry.com Operations, Inc., 2007.Original data – Passport Applications, 1795–1905. NARA Microfilm Publication M1372, 694 rolls. General Records Department of State, Record Group 59. National Archives, Washington, D.C.; 'Bernard Carter,' Year: 1880; Census Place: Baltimore, Baltimore (Independent City), Maryland; Roll: 501; Family History Film: 1254501; Page: 79B; Enumeration District: 108; Image: 0339; Arthur Meredyth Burke, ed., *The Prominent Families of the United States of America* (London: The Sackville Press, 1908): 54.

For Charles Henry Coster: Lyman Horace Weeks, *Prominent Families of New York* (New York: Historical Company, 1898): 139.

For Clinton E. Dawkins: Class: *RG12*; Piece: *18*; Folio: *18*; Page: *30*; GSU roll: *6095128;* Ancestry.com. *1891 England Census* [database on-line]. Provo, UT, USA: Ancestry.com Operations Inc, 2005.

For Thomas Gates: 'Marie Rogers Gates,' Historical Society of Pennsylvania; Philadelphia, Pennsylvania; Collection Name: *Historic Pennsylvania Church and Town Records.*

For Robert Gordon: *The Bankers' Insurance Managers' & Agents' Magazine*, vol. 69 (London: Waterlow and Sons Ltd., 1900): 901; George Austin Morrison, Jr., *History of Saint Andrew's Society of the State of New York, 1756–1906* (New York, 1906): 111; *Guy's Hospital Gazette*, vol. 32 (London: Ash & Co., June 29, 1918): 202.

For Edward Charles Grenfell: 'Edward Charles Grenfell MP,' *The Times*, November 28, 1941.

For William Edward, 2nd Viscount Harcourt: Helmut E. Gerber, ed., *George Moore on Parsassus* (Newark: University of Delaware Press, 1988): 527.

For Herman Harjes: 'Harjes Estate to Family,' *The New York Times*, March 6, 1927; 'Joan Blake Becomes Engaged,' *The New York Times*, June 15, 1934; 'Mrs. Frederica Berwind Harjes,' National Archives and Records Administration (NARA); Washington D.C.; NARA Series: *Emergency Passport Applications, Argentina thru Venezuela, 1906–1925*; Box #: *4535*; Volume #: *Volume 151: Paris, France;* Greg H. Williams, *The Liberty Ships of World War II: A Record of the 2,710 Vessels and Their Builders, Operators and Namesakes, with a History of the Jeremiah O'Brien* (Jefferson, NC: McFarland & Co., 2014): 285.

For John H. Harjes: 'John Henry Harjes,' National Archives and Records Administration (NARA); Washington D.C.; Passport Applications, 1795–1905; Collection Number: ARC Identifier 566612 / MLR Number A1 508; NARA Series: M1372; Roll #: 610; 'Amelia Harjes,' National Archives and Records Administration (NARA); Washington D.C.; Emergency Passport Applications, Argentina thru Venezuela, 1906–1925; Collection Number: ARC Identifier 1244183 / MLR Number A1 544; Box #: 4536; Volume #: 152; 'Mrs. Amelia Hessenbruch Harjes,' National Archives and Records Administration (NARA), Washington, D.C.; General Records of the Department of State; Record Group: RG59-Entry 205; Box Number: 1462; Box Description: 1930–1939 France Fi—Ha; Year: *1860*; 'Am Hessenbrach,' Census Place: *Philadelphia Ward 24 Precinct 7, Philadelphia, Pennsylvania*; Roll: *M653_1175*; Page: *872*; Image: *364*; Family History Library Film: *805175.*

For John H. Harjes, Jr.: 'Mrs. Frederica Berwind Harjes,' National Archives and Records Administration (NARA); Washington D.C.; NARA Series: *Emergency Passport Applications, Argentina thru Venezuela, 1906–1925*; Box #: *4535*; Volume #: *Volume 151: Paris, France;* 'Charles F. Berwind,' Ancestry.com. *U.S. City Directories, 1822–1989* [database on-line]. Provo, UT, USA: Ancestry.com Operations, Inc., 2011.

For Michael Herbert: Class: *RG10*; Piece: *1957*; Folio: *46*; Page: *1*; GSU roll: *830882; Census Returns of England and Wales, 1871.* Kew, Surrey, England: The National Archives of the UK (TNA): Public Record Office (PRO), 1871; Edward Hilliard, ed., *The Balliol College Register, 1832–1914* (Oxford: University Press, 1914): 149.

For Nelson Dean Jay: 'Sarah E. Jay,' Year: 1910; Census Place: Elmwood Ward 4, Peoria, Illinois; Roll: T624_315; Page: 10A; Enumeration District: 0054; FHL microfilm: 1374328; 'Anne Augustine,' Year: *1910*; Census Place: *Carondelet, Saint Louis, Missouri*; Roll: *T624_809*; Page: *26B*; Enumeration District: *0107*; FHL microfilm: *1374822; 'Mrs. Anne A. Jay,'* National Archives and Records Administration (NARA); Washington D.C.; NARA Series: *Passport Applications, January 2, 1906 – March 31, 1925*; Roll #: *1744*; Volume #: *Roll 1744 – Certificates: 85500–85875, 23 Sep 1921–24 Sep 1921; The Social Register, St. Louis* (Social Register Association, 1915): 55.

For Benjamin Joy: 'Charles H. Joy,' Year: *1880*; Census Place: *Boston, Suffolk, Massachusetts*; Roll: *555*; Family History Film: *1254555*; Page: *43B*; Enumeration District: *658*; Image: *0580.*

For Junius Spencer Morgan, Jr.: Edward White, ed., *The Banking Law Journal*, vol. 36 (New York: Office of Publication, 1919): 302; *Harvard Alumni Bulletin*, vol. 17, no. 1 (Boston: Harvard Alumni Association, September 30, 1914): 708; 'F.S. Converse Dies, Leader in Music,' *The New York Times*, June 9, 1940.

For James W. Paul Jr.: Charles Franklin Warwick, *Warwick's Keystone Commonwealth* (Philadelphia, PA, 1913): 309–310.

For Edward Moore Robinson: *Town Topics: The Journal of Society*, vol. 29, no. 2 (New York, January 12, 1893): 1.

For Francis James Rennell Rodd: 'Obituary: Lord Rennell of Rodd, KBE, CB, JP,' *The Geographical Journal*, vol. 144, no. 2 (July 1978): 392–393.

For Randal Hugh Vivian Smith: *Dod's Peerage, Baronetage and Knightage of Britain and Ireland for 1901, including all the Titled Classes* (London: Sampson Low, Marston & Co., 1901): 642; Arthur Charles Fox-Davies,

Ed., Armorial Families (Edinburgh: T.C. & E.C. Jack, Grange Publishing Works, 1895): 741.

For Vivian Hugh Smith: *Dod's Peerage, Baronetage and Knightage of Britain and Ireland for 1904, including all the Titled Classes* (London: Sampson Low, Marston & Co., 1904): 114; 'Honorable William Randal Mcdonnell,' Ancestry.com. *London and Surrey, England, Marriage Bonds and Allegations, 1597–1921* [database on-line]. Provo, UT, USA: Ancestry.com Operations, Inc., 2011.

For George C. Thomas: *Ellis Paxson Oberholtzer, Philadelphia: A History of the City and its People*, vol. 4 (Philadelphia: S.J. Clarke Publishing Company, n.d.): 62–71.

For Harry Ashton Watkins: 'Harry Ashton Watkins,' Ancestry.com. *Florida Marriage Indexes, 1822–1875 and 1927–2001* [database on-line]. Provo, UT, USA: Ancestry.com Operations Inc., 2006; Year: *1920*; Census Place: *South Orange, Essex, New Jersey*; Roll: *T625_1039*; Page: *1A*; Enumeration District: *313*; Image: *348;* 'Charles Cheney,' Year: *1920*; Census Place: *Manchester, Hartford, Connecticut*; Roll: *T625_181*; Page: *11B*; Enumeration District: *138*; Image: *1035;* 'Barbara Cheney Watkins,' Ancestry.com. *Idaho, Divorce Index, 1947–1964* [database on-line]. Provo, UT, USA: Ancestry.com Operations, Inc., 2013; William Richard Cutter, *New England Families, Genealogical and Memorial*, vol. 4 (New England: Lewis Historical Publishing Co., 1913): 1949; 'Watkins-Cheney,' *The New York Times*, May 12, 1929; 'Harry A. Watkins, Certificate of Death,' No: 156-76-109967, Division of Records, Department of Health, City of New York, May 27, 1976.

For Charles F. Whigham: 'British Partner of Morgan Killed,' *The New York Sun*, February 14, 1938; 'Charles Frederick Whigham,' Ancestry.com. *Scotland, Select Births and Baptisms, 1564–1950* [database on-line]. Provo, UT, USA: Ancestry.com Operations, Inc., 2014.

For Edward Farley Whitney: *Eleventh Report of the Class of 1871 of Harvard College* (Cambridge: Riverside Press, 1921): 191.

For Wilfred William Hill Wood: '*Wilfred William Hill Wood*,' London Metropolitan Archives, Chelsea Holy Trinity, Register of Baptism, p74/tri, Item 007; Class: *BT26*; Piece: *1253*; Item: *18*, Ancestry.com. *UK, Incoming Passenger Lists, 1878–1960* [database on-line]. Provo, UT, USA: Ancestry.com Operations Inc., 2008; 'Wilfred W.H Hill-wood,' Ancestry.com. *England & Wales, Marriage Index, 1916–2005* [database on-line]. Provo, UT, USA: Ancestry.com Operations, Inc., 2010.

Unless listed in this paper, for biographical sources, see footnotes associated with Tables 5–10, Susie J. Pak, *Gentlemen Bankers: The World of J.P. Morgan* (Cambridge, MA: Harvard University Press, 2013).

12. 'Nelson Dean Jay,' undated, Thomas W. Lamont papers, Box 112, Folder 112–116, Baker Library, Harvard Business School (HBS).
13. The French house was not in the same position as the British house because most of the partners were actually American, and they were viewed as American representatives in Paris (see Table 4).
14. For original see, TWL, 'J.P. Morgan & Co. and Their Relations to the Public.' TWL papers, Box 110–2, HBS. See also J.P. Morgan (Jr.), Statement of condition, June 16, 1934, TWL papers, Box 110–2, HBS.
15. Memorandum from Russell C. Leffingwell (RCL) to TWL and R.G. Wasson, Dec. 22, 1941, Russell C. Leffingwell papers, MS 1030, Box 4–98, Yale University Library; Copy of letter to Morris L. Ernst from RCL, Feb. 9, 1940, TWL papers, Box 103–22, HBS.
16. Letter to J.R. Carter from Thomas W. Lamont, April 13, 1927, TWL papers, Box 110, Folder 110–9, HBS.
17. Thanks to Martin Kenner for this reference.
18. J.P. Morgan & Co. and Guaranty Trust Co. merged as Morgan Guaranty Trust in 1959. 'J.P. Morgan & Co., Guaranty Merge,' *The New York Times*, April 25, 1959; *The History of JPMorgan Chase & Co.: 200 Years of Leadership in Banking* (New York: JPMorgan Chase & Co.): 12. http://www.jpmorganchase.com/corporate/About-JPMC/document/shorthistory.pdf (November 3, 2015).
19. 'Harold Stanley, 77, Is Dead,' *The New York Times*, May 15, 1963.
20. Syndicate Books, ARC 108–ARC 119, PML.
21. Public school refers to the American public school as opposed to British public school, which was more similar to the American private school.
22. 'F. Trubee Davison Dies at 78,' *The New York Times*, November 16, 1974; 'Endicott Peabody of Groton School,' *The New York Times*, November 18, 1944; 'Robert Dean Jay,' *The New York Times,* July 2, 1998; 'Alida Jay will be Married on Sept. 19 to Thorvald Boye, a Lawyer in Oslo,' *The New York Times,* July 12, 1981; 'Miss Diana Draper Engaged to Marry,' *The New York Times,* November 6, 1935; 'Nelson D. Jay's Son Killed,' *The New York Times,* September 10, 1928. See also 'Francis D. Bartow, Jr.,' *The New York Times,* March 17, 1982; 'Clarence Bartow, Investment Banker,' *The New York Times,* January 26, 1972; 'Philip Key Bartow, Investment Banker,' *The New York Times,* January 15, 1962.
23. 'S. Parker Gilbert, 81, Dies,' *The New York Times*, May 29, 2015.

24. See cable to J.P. Morgan New York from J.R. Carter, Dec. 29, 1930; Cable from J.P. Morgan to N. Dean Jay and Benjamin Joy, Dec. 3, 1930; Cable from Morgan to Benjamin Joy, Dec. 9, 1930; Cable from JPM Jr. to J.R. Carter, Dec. 30, 1930; Morgan Bank European Papers, Personal Name File, A–J, ARC 1221, Box 5, Folder: Joy, Benjamin, 1929–1930, PML.
25. 'Anne Stillman to Wed Henry P. Davison,' *The New York Times*, June 4, 1924.
26. 'Miss Carter Weds Viscount Acheson,' *The New York Times*, June 22, 1910.
27. 'John Ridgely Carter (1862–1944),' Department of State Office of the Historian, https://history.state.gov/departmenthistory/people/carter-john-ridgely (November 3, 2015); 'Ridgely Carter Forced Out,' *The New York Times*, February 22, 1912.
28. 'Mrs. John R. Carter Dies in France at 67,' *The New York Times*, January 31, 1933.
29. 'Bernard Carter, Banker, 68, Dead,' *The New York Times*, November 9, 1961.
30. 'Carter, David Ridgely,' *The New York Times*, September 8, 2009; 'Bernard Shirley Carter Jr., 84,' *The Cape Cod Times*, March 3, 2002 http://www.capecodtimes.com/article/20020303/obits/303039963 (November 8, 2015); 'David Carter,' *Who's Who in France* https://www.whoswho.fr/decede/biographie-david-carter_5614 (November 8, 2015).

References

Allen, F. L. (2014; 1935). *The lords of creation*. New York: Open Road Integrated Media.

Burk, K. (1989). *Morgan Grenfell 1838–1988: The biography of a merchant bank*. New York: Oxford University Press.

Carosso, V. P. (1987). *The Morgans: Private international bankers, 1854–1913*. Cambridge, MA: Harvard University Press.

Cassis, Y. (1994). *City bankers, 1890–1914*. New York: Cambridge University Press.

Horn, M. (2000). A private bank at war: J.P. Morgan & Co. and France, 1914–1918. *Business History Review, 74*, 85–112.

Horn, M. (2002). *Britain, France, and the financing of the First World War*. Montreal: McGill-Queen's University Press.

Jones, G. (2000). *Merchants to multinationals: British trading companies in the nineteenth and twentieth centuries*. New York: Oxford University Press.

Maynes, M. J., & Waltner, A. (2012). *The family: A world history*. New York: Oxford University Press.

Pak, S. J. (2013). *Gentlemen bankers: The world of J.P. Morgan*. Cambridge, MA: Harvard University Press.

Rottenberg, D. (2006). *The man who made wall street: Anthony J. Drexel and the rise of modern finance*. New York: University of Pennsylvania Press.

Steel, R. S. (1999). *Walter Lippman and the American century*. New Brunswick: Transaction Publishers.

Top Careers as a Means of Risk Management in Organisations

Daniel Wylegala

1 Introduction

Depending on the perspective, specific aspects of the far-reaching changes that have taken place both in the economy and in society as a whole since the mid-nineteenth century have to be considered when researching processes of decision-making, the handling of risks and the formation of confidence in banks. With regard to the subject of this chapter, this is particularly the case for the transformation of organisations since that time. The growth of enterprises and the resulting increase of internal organisational complexity in the second half of the nineteenth century were accompanied by the differentiation and shaping of professions and educational pathways leading to professional positions (Kaelble 1983,

D. Wylegala (✉)
Department for History, Heinrich Heine University Düsseldorf,
Düsseldorf, Germany
e-mail: wylegala@uni-duesseldorf.de

K. Schönhärl (ed.), *Decision Taking, Confidence and Risk Management in Banks from Early Modernity to the 20th Century*,
DOI 10.1007/978-3-319-42076-9_3

31–35; Plumpe 2006, 71), also within the banking business (Liefeith 1983, 19–46). This development of modern organisations was fundamental for professional careers and hence, consequently, for top careers. The latter form the focus of this discussion, which examines their function within organisations in the twentieth century. A series of questions are therefore considered: How is decision-making structured in modern organisations? How are decisions, risks and top careers related to one another within such a structure? How do top careers contribute to the establishing of confidence in organisations? The aim is to illustrate the contribution of careers to dealing with the risks that inevitably result from decisions.

One important goal of this volume is to develop methods by which historians can analyse risk management and the decision-making practices of the past. This chapter contributes to this goal by proposing a theoretical model to pursue its objective. The theoretical considerations concerning top careers and their function mainly draw upon Niklas Luhmann's Systems Theory and in particular its organisational theory approach (Luhmann 1984a, 1997, 826–847; 2005b, 2005c, 2006; Martens and Ortmann 2006). The model itself, however, goes beyond the premises of Systems Theory. This model is constructed as an ideal type based on Max Weber's approach (Kocka 1986, 86–89; Weber 1980, 9–11), with the intention of gaining terms for the analysis of top careers. A theoretical concept, in Clifford Geertz (1973, 4) words, 'does not explain everything, not even everything human, but it still explains something'. The choice of a theoretical concept always implicitly involves choosing a specific perspective and concurrently deciding against all other perspectives. The choice of a perspective is inevitable because empirical reality's complexity is not immediately accessible via cognition. Different perspectives are always possible, i.e. the perspective selected is always contingent. According to Hans-Georg Gadamer (1975, 430), a theory is only a tool, here it is viewed as a tool to reduce complexity. Therefore, with reference to Werner Plumpe (2003, 144), one can say that a theoretical model is not a set of rules explaining all empirical phenomena. Each empirical case is unique and requires its own analysis. However, a theoretical model as a tool is useful because it forces the adoption of a very specific focus, far exceeding the dictates of common sense. A theoretical concept does not have to be true in an ontological sense; it only has to prove its viability. The following theoretical concept has done just this during the author's ongoing study of the career of Karl Klasen (1909–1991), the former president of the state central bank in Hamburg (1948–1952), member of the executive board of the Norddeutsche Bank/ Deutsche Bank (1952–1967), CEO of the Deutsche Bank (1967–1969) and president of the Bundesbank (1970–1977).

In the first section the most important premises of Systems Theory, on which the model is based, are presented in broad terms and the context of organisation, decisions and risks are sketched briefly. However, the fundamentals of Systems Theory itself cannot be dealt with here.[1] Based on these concise remarks, the concept of the career is explained in the second section. Theoretical considerations are by their very nature highly abstract. For this reason, empirical examples from the study of Karl Klasen's career are used to give an impression of the diverse empirical forms that can hide behind the abstractness of a theoretical model. The cited empirical examples are not explained in every detail, rather they illustrate how a theoretically focused approach can be useful to structure the analysis of a top career and to highlight interrelationships. These first two steps aim to provide a framework for the discussion of the function of top careers with regard to the context of decision-making, the handling of risks, and confidence in business companies.

2 Organisations, Decisions and Risks

From a historical point of view, organisations in the modern sense are a young phenomenon; their genesis is closely related to the emergence of modern, functionally differentiated society. Resulting from functional differentiation, the function systems of modern society have never been 'organised' as a whole, that is, summarised in only one organisation. Instead, a multitude of organisations has arisen which are primarily oriented towards a functional system-specific code, but cannot represent a functional system by appropriating its function alone. The organisations thereby occur between the levels of the social system or its functional subsystems and the interaction systems. They assume a mediating role by providing the specific performance of a functional subsystem, due to taking over its functional primacy on the one hand, and coordinating interactions through the conditioning of membership roles on the other hand. Their function is, therefore, the reduction of complexity, the absorption of uncertainty, and the 'fixation' of contingency by coordinating actions in a targeted manner via the definition of membership roles. This ability of organisations justifies their importance for modern society (Luhmann 1984a, 1997, 743–776, 826–847; 2005a).

An organisation is the result of decisions, and the fundamental ability to connect new decisions continuously is the condition for the existence of an organisation. In other words, an organisation can only be continuously reproduced on the basis of ongoing decision-making. Decisions can take numerous forms. However, from the perspective of the system, a decision is everything that is considered as a decision by the organisation. Decisions are not simply choices between alternatives. Instead, decisions are events that disappear even at the moment of their creation. As events, they are the unity of the difference between the situation before deciding and the situation after deciding. While any decision fixes the contingency of a situation by establishing one specific possibility and excluding all other possibilities, at the same time new possibilities are always enabled whereby further decision-making is necessary (Luhmann 1984c, 1988, 272–301; 1993, 2005b, 391–397; 2006, 39–80, 123–151). Decision-making based on previous decisions is simply the basic operation of an organisational system. Organisations thus reproduce themselves self-referentially from their own elements. In order to handle these operations in a flexible and coordinated way, a limiting structure is necessary. This structure results essentially from three decision premises, which are the result of decisions and, of course, can also be the subjects of decisions. Firstly, the decision programmes, which in a general way define the conditions for the correctness of decisions. Secondly, the communication paths and the competencies as communicative links between positions, which determine how decisions must be communicated, who can make which decisions or who should be involved in specific decisions. Thirdly, there is the decision premise staff. These three decision premises create the positions of an organisation and, finally, from these positions the structure of the organisation results (Luhmann 1981, 113–116; 2005b, 423–428; 2006, 222–301).

On the one hand, the recursive nature of decision-making leads to redundancy of decisions, that is to say, to decision-making structures that allow a certain routinization of decision-making and thus reduce complexity. On the other hand, concurrent with the constantly changing social environment of organisations, a sufficient degree of variance is necessary for appropriate structural adjustments to respond to environmental changes. As shown above, decisions are fundamental for organisations in general, and thus of course for business companies as well. Risks, understood as the ever-present possibility of decisions having negative consequences, are the result and to a certain extent the product of decisions. Because of the need to make ongoing decisions, business companies are therefore inevitably confronted with risks all the time. As already mentioned above, organisations are not necessarily associated with a functional subsystem of society, but this is usually the case. There is no doubt that business companies are associated with the economic functional system. With regard to their decision-making, the primacy of the economic function is crucial. Therefore, decisions based on economic rationality always aim at least to preserve the ability to pay, and actually—this is clearly the purpose of a business company—to increase it. Payments are the basic communicative actions within the economic system. Whether a payment is made or not is dependent on the price. However, such decisions are not necessarily based on the current best price but are more likely to be oriented towards future expectations concerning cost/benefit considerations. It is therefore necessary for business companies to observe changes in the social environment as changes in prices, and to react to these observations through the continuous adaptation of the decision premises (Luhmann 1988, 13–42, 302–323). Admittedly, the complete information that is necessary for perfectly rational decisions might be conceivable in theory, but is of course never achievable in reality. This is because the necessary information does not exist outside the organisation and hence cannot enter it. Information rather is generated within the organisation and by the corporate structure itself during its observation of its social environment. However, the complexity of the social environment is not altogether observable, so corporate structures are to a certain degree always insufficient. What is not or cannot be observed fails to become information and so remains a blind spot. Because of this lack of information, or these blind spots, which are associated with observations of the past or the present, the basis for decision-making is always uncertain. This uncertainty derives, furthermore, and indeed to a far greater extent, from the fundamental openness and contingency of the future to which decisions are aligned. Even in the improbable case of complete information, future expectations can, in retrospect, turn out to be wrong, no matter how plausible they may have been at the time when a decision was made, which may have negative, and even dramatic consequences. Ongoing decision-making reproduces an organisation, but it also produces risks, which, if realised, may have the ability to destroy the organisation (Luhmann 2006, 56–59, 445–479).

Hierarchies arise whenever the size of an organisation reaches a degree of complexity that requires the definition of paths of communication and the delimitation of competences to ensure the functionality of the organisation. As shown above, the structure of a business company can be represented as a hierarchy of positions or as a hierarchy of persons, but it can also be represented as a decision-making hierarchy. Usually, the more far-reaching and inevitably riskier a decision is, the higher its location in the hierarchy. This is especially true for a decision that cannot be made within decision-making structures that allow redundancy but must be decided outside this framework, thus rendering it a decision about the decision structure itself. As already shown, decisions must, in general, be based on uncertainty. This applies particularly to decisions about decision-making structures, which are made at the top of the hierarchy. The assumption of risks is therefore a fundamental component of the role of leadership positions in business companies. This finally results in the task associated with such positions: to balance the opportunities and risks in decision-making and to decide on the basis of this assessment about the modification of existing structures or the implementation of new ones (Luhmann 1991, 211–215). As James G. March and Zur Shapira put it:

> *In the words of a senior vice-president of one firm, 'If you are not willing to assume risks, go deal with another business.' This link between risk taking and management is less a statement of the measurable usefulness of risk taking to a manager than an affirmation of a role. As the president of an electronic firm said, 'Risk taking is synonymous with decision-making under uncertainty.' In*

> *keeping with contemporary managerial ideology, he might have added that management is synonymous with decision-making.* (March and Shapira 1987, 1409)

Consequently, of course, it is not the structures that decide, but the individuals as 'persons', that is to say, as role holders in the respective leadership positions.

3 Professional Careers: Selection and Socialisation

The fundamental importance of decisions suggests that a mechanism is concealed behind professional careers, one that serves to fill leading management positions with individuals who are suitable with regard to the company's interests. In general, careers consist of past events that in the present allow or obstruct a favourable future development. Based on these events, careers reproduce themselves to some extent, although logically not every career can lead to a top position. Of course, the following considerations relate only to the few top careers, not to the vast majority of other kinds of professional careers that are also more or less successful. In simple terms, the professional careers under consideration consisted primarily of a series of positions in one company or in several companies, finally leading to a top position, which, moreover, was successfully held. In the case of German companies, these top careers largely took place in one company. They were often so-called *Hauskarrieren* (in-house careers) (Bartmann and Plumpe 2003; Faust 2002; Hartmann 2006, 2007, 2008; Joly 2000; Kocka 2002). Analysing such careers as empirical individual cases reveal, for instance, that as individuals ascend the decision-making hierarchy, decisions are less limited by decision-making structures and the need for self-reliant decisions, hence the responsibility and consequently the degree of risk-taking increases. Inspired by Karl Ulrich Mayer's considerations (2006, 465–466), a career in the sense of a series of positions can thus be regarded, on the one hand, as a process of selection and, on the other hand, as a process of socialisation, depending on the perspective selected.

The focus of the selection process lies on proving the reliability of the person in every professional position. Proving their reliability, which in the positive cases results in promotion, depends essentially on three factors: contingency, support, and performance. The decisive factor is contingency or, in reference to successful professional careers, simply fortune or luck. For example, with regard to professional careers, conditions that are beyond the influence of the individual at least facilitate and may even enable important career milestones and should not be underestimated. Certainly, contingency gains importance in the course of ascending the decision-making hierarchy. Thus not only risks—and therefore the degree of risk-taking—increase with increasing responsibility, but obviously also the chance of making the wrong decisions with far-reaching negative consequences for the company, which can end a career. Max Weber (1995, 11) compares careers in science to the gambling game of *Hasard*, and despite all the clear differences this is no less true in other functional systems, or for careers in organisations, which are associated with these other systems. The many forms of contingency become obvious by consideration of Karl Klasen's career.

From 1929 onwards, Klasen studied law in Freiburg, Berlin and Hamburg. In 1931, he completed his studies with the first state examination, in 1933 he received his doctorate, and in 1935 he finished his legal clerkship by passing the second state examination. His professional goal was to pursue a career as a judge and, indeed, he was initially employed as an assistant judge in the civil service.[2] Politically, Klasen was closely linked to the Social Democrats and had been a member of the party since 1931. After the seizure of power by the National Socialists, he was forced to adapt to the new political realities in order to complete his legal clerkship, as the professional training of jurists was reformed along political lines (Gruchmann 1988; Klasen 1982).[3] Although the president of the higher regional court of Hamburg, Curt Rothenberger, who was decisive for Klasen's career, supported him and a successful career was probable, Klasen took the first opportunity to change his professional field of activity for political reasons. In October 1935, a position as second syndic happened to be open in the Hamburg branch of Deutsche Bank. Accordingly, Klasen, who had previously never had dealings with the banking business, began his career at Deutsche Bank by chance (Klasen 1982).[4]

Two authorised signatories worked at the secretariat of the branch in an assistant function for the directorate: Max Martin Heimreich, who was trained commercially, while Karl Ulrich Meyer, Klasen's direct superior, was legally trained.[5] When Meyer died in 1937, Klasen was promoted and received procuration at the age of 28. Henceforth, he was responsible for advising the directorate and for representing the branch in legal matters.[6]

After his military service (1943–1945) and his discharge from his subsequent captivity as a prisoner of war, he returned in June 1945 to the branch of Deutsche Bank, where he began to work in the position of a deputy director.[7] Although his field of activity now increasingly included banking business as well, he also remained responsible for legal matters. This meant that he was at the time especially responsible, firstly, for the implementation of the financial laws of the British Military Government in banking business practice, in consultation with the *Reichsbankleitstelle* in the British Zone, and secondly, he obviously represented the interests of the bank in legal matters *vis-à-vis* the British financial officer and the senate of Hamburg.[8] Finally, in the course of the reorganisation of the West German central banking system in 1948 someone was required to fill the position of president of the state central bank in Hamburg (LZB), and Klasen fitted the profile internally defined by the senate. He was politically unencumbered and was considered politically reliable by the SPD, the party to which the mayor Max Brauer likewise belonged. Furthermore, because of his occupation, he knew the banking business and was known by the senate as well as the military government.[9] Klasen took advantage of this opportunity and moved from Deutsche Bank to the LZB, so that in 1948 he reached his first top position at the age of 39, after having been promoted to director of the branch a short time before. Due to his position, Klasen was also Deputy Chairman of the administrative board of the LZB. Through this activity, he became acquainted with another member of the administrative board, Karl Schiller, the senator for economy and transport in Hamburg.[10]

When in the late 1960s Schiller, federal minister of economic affairs since 1966, was looking for a successor for Karl Blessing, whose contract as president of the Bundesbank was not to be renewed for reasons of age, Klasen was his preferred candidate. Possibly Klasen's party membership played a role because the social-liberal coalition had won the election in 1969. Nevertheless, Klasen was seen as politically independent. More important was that as a former president of the LZB in Hamburg and CEO of Deutsche Bank, Klasen was a proven expert of the Federal Reserve System and the banking business, which he would regulate in his new role in the context of the monetary policy of the Bundesbank. Most significantly, Klasen and Schiller, as shown above, had already worked together in a similar professional arrangement. The close integration of the fiscal policy of the state and the monetary policy of the Bundesbank was of great importance in the context of economic policy, and a corresponding relationship based on mutual confidence was thus necessary. It is therefore not surprising that Klasen's appointment was viewed very positively by the public.[11] Klasen's path from a student of law to the position as president of the Bundesbank, as briefly sketched above, serves as an example of how, over a long period of time, successful careers reproduce themselves from their own elements, and demonstrates the role that contingency plays. On the career path, contingency occurs in various forms: individual decisions, positions becoming vacant at the right time, deaths, coincidental acquaintances, complex developments in society etc. To a certain extent contingency sets the course, i.e. it is decisive.[12]

Support is the second factor. It has two faces, one of which is the allocation of opportunities in the form of tasks or promotion by a superior so that a candidate may prove his/her reliability. However, at the same time, a superior depends on the quality of the execution of his decisions by subsidiary persons in the decision-making hierarchy, especially when those subsidiary persons reached their positions because of a decision about the decision premise staff by their superior. In other words, such relationships are characterised by mutual dependency and support is more likely if there is a basis for confidence.

At the beginning of his career at the Deutsche Bank Klasen was initially supported by Max Martin Heimreich. Thus, Klasen later wrote:

[I only want] to tell you that I owe a lot to you for my personal career. It was especially lucky for me that you were one of the first men who attended to my moulding in the banking business after I joined the bank. Very often when I say something in daily business life about the banking business which

I think is very 'wise', especially towards younger people, I repeatedly notice that I have quoted my old teacher M.M. Heimreich.[13]

Accordingly, Heimreich's support helped Klasen to overcome his initial deficit in terms of business training. Furthermore, after Meyer's death in 1937 Klasen had the chance to take over more responsibility as the authorised signatory and syndic of the branch, after less than two years at the branch and at the age of 28. It can be assumed that this personnel decision was the decision of the branch manager and later executive board member of the Deutsche Bank, Erich Bechtolf. It is worth mentioning in this context that Bechtolf's career began in a very similar fashion to Klasen's. He studied law in Bonn and Berlin and became an assistant judge in Elberfeld in 1920. In 1921, he became an executive director of an employers' association. In 1922, he joined Deutsche Bank and worked as the syndic of the branch in Elberfeld. In 1925, he became director of the branch in Hamm, in 1928 assistant director at the headquarters in Berlin, and in 1932 director of the branch in Hamburg.[14] Given Klasen's limited experience in the banking business and tax law, the main subjects that Klasen had to deal with as the branch's syndic, the decision to make him the authorised signatory and syndic was quite risky.[15] Bechtolf, who could assess Klasen's juridical abilities from his own experience, seemed to have confidence in him and thus gave him the chance to prove his professional reliability. These two short examples show how support sets the course for a successful career by assisting an individual to grow into a new professional role and by the allocation of opportunities. Additionally, Bechtolf's decision to promote Klasen is an example of the above-mentioned mutual dependency, because if Klasen had failed due to his inexperience then this would have been to the detriment of the bank and Bechtholf would have been responsible. This already alludes to the next and final factor.

The third factor is performance. It is, of course, beyond question that skills and motivation are essential. However, from the organisation's point of view performance itself means nothing more than the execution of decisions in the form of appropriate further decisions taken in the organisational interests, that is, in the case of companies, economic interests. Furthermore, the basis for confidence and, ultimately support, results from performance. As in the case of the other two factors, performance may occur in very different forms. However, what these forms always have in common is that they are tasks whose execution requires further decisions and serves the interests of the organisation. Admittedly, these tasks differ in their range, depending on where they are situated in the decision-making hierarchy. Examples from both Klasen's early career and from a later stage of his career illustrate this.

One of the most important of Klasen's tasks at the beginning of his career was the implementation of the deed tax law of 1936. The law caused significant difficulties in terms of practical implementation since it was the content of a deed rather than its drawing up that was decisive for taxation purposes, i.e. only certain legal transactions specified by law were taxed.[16] It was assumed that the legal transactions were unambiguous, but this was often not the case so that the tax obligation was controversial in many instances. The branch in Hamburg was particularly affected by these problems because the financing of foreign trade played a major role and a lot of operations had to be certified in this business, for example, in the documentary credit business.[17] Because of the special position of Deutsche Bank in Hamburg, Klasen's tasks were varied. He coordinated the handling of problematic cases between the banks in Hamburg and he consulted with the legal department of the Berlin headquarters. He also represented the branch's interests towards the tax authorities and instructed the relevant departments about the design of the forms, ensuring that they were both legally impeccable and served the economic interests of the bank, i.e. that, at best, no taxes would be due.[18]

When Klasen became a member of the Norddeutsche Bank's executive board in 1952, the industrial customer business was one of the traditionally substantial business segments (Holtfrerich 1995, 544–578). He was responsible for the most important business customers in the branch areas allocated to him on the executive board (e.g. BP Benzin und Petroleum Gesellschaft mbH, Continental Gummiwerke AG, Howaldtswerke Hamburg AG, etc.). Some of the tasks associated with this business were the granting of credit, assistance in the acquisition of companies, and issuing bonds or shares. On the one hand, he had to assess the risks and then suggest appropriate business conditions that served the economic interests of the bank. On the other hand, however, he was always willing to maintain long-term business relationships or to establish new business contacts, i.e. to weight the importance of commercial short-term interests lower than that of future business activities.[19] As he was an executive board member of the Norddeutsche Bank and later the Deutsche Bank, a further part of his role associated with this business segment was the representation of the bank's interests through the acceptance of supervisory board mandates. Thus, Klasen was part of the specifically German entanglement of banks, insurance companies and large industrial companies commonly referred to as 'Deutschland AG' (Beyer 1996, 1999, 2013; Beyer and Windolf 1995). In 1956, Klasen took over one of the most important mandates from Bechtolf as Deputy Chairman of the supervisory board of the Hamburg-Amerikanische Packetfahrt-Actien-Gesellschaft (Hapag).[20] From 1957 onwards, Klasen increasingly came into conflict with the shipowner Behrend Schuchmann, the majority shareholder and chairman of the supervisory board, because from the perspective of the bank Schuchmann interfered in a disproportionate manner in the work of the executive board, i.e. he acted as if he were the sole owner. In a personal conversation with Schuchmann, Klasen clarified the position of the bank: 'As an absolute ruler, we considered him […], I would have to tell him this quite frankly, dangerous and therefore we were obliged to use the blocking minority to restrict his potential capacities in the Hapag to useful limits. These were, in any case, our interests.'[21] Additionally, Schuchmann abused his majority ownership to his own economic advantage. In September 1957, for example, he refused to agree to further debt-financed orders for the building of new ships. Instead, the Hapag should charter the ships from his shipping company, the Bugsier-, Reederei- und Bergungsgesellschaft mbH & Co. KG.[22] Since the charter costs would have exceeded the cost of credit for two new ships, which would, in the end, have become the property of the Hapag, Klasen rejected this demand vehemently.[23] Klasen declined an offer by Schuchmann to take over the share package of Deutsche Bank, which would have resulted in a high profit.[24] Instead, he used his position to prevent Schuchmann's harmful behaviour for the Hapag. The situation escalated in early 1958. Schuchmann threatened to use his majority shares to replace the executive board, to make himself CEO and to appoint his son as the chairman of the supervisory board. Thereupon Klasen issued a public statement urging the executive board to preserve its independence from Schuchmann. Due to the importance of the Hapag for Hamburg, as well as for the West German economy, this resulted in Schuchmann being criticised by the chamber of commerce in Hamburg, the mayor Max Brauer and the federal ministry of transport for his attempt to extend his power over the company.[25] Due to this pressure, Schuchmann withdrew from the company and sold his share package in September 1958 to Deutsche Bank, whereby the bank became the major shareholder.[26] On the one hand, it was clearly not in the bank's interest to become a major shareholder with a stake in the share capital of temporarily more than 85 percent, i.e. to assume such a great business risk.[27] However, on the other hand, the alternative was to sell their share package to Schuchmann and to let him follow his plans, which would have inflicted serious damage on the bank's reputation. Due to the importance of the industrial customers for the bank and in the context of the 'Deutschland AG' this alternative was never considered, although the decision to refuse Schuchmann's lucrative offer to buy the share package and instead engage in a conflict was against the bank's own short-term interests. To put it in Klasen's words: 'That is precisely what is meant by performance and tradition because the reputation that a bank has to lose is much greater than once missing out on a deal.'[28]

In addition to the perspective of viewing a career as a selection process with the key factors contingency, support and performance, a career can furthermore be described (as part of tertiary socialisation) as a process of professional socialisation during a series of positions. In the course of many years of a professional career, through the successful interplay of the three aforementioned factors of the selection process, an ascent through the positions in the decision-making hierarchy is achieved. Along this career path, increasingly sophisticated tasks have to be managed, which are characterised by increasing responsibility, that is to say, they are progressively less located in the frame of decision-making structures which define the execution of strictly limited redundant decisions. In parallel, the variety or freedom of the decisions that concern the execution of decisions increases and, as a result, decisions regarding decision-making structures increase.

The functional capability of organisations depends on the acceptance of membership terms by individuals, that is to say individuals as persons, as role holders in the frame of the position to which they are assigned. In other words, this acceptance of the membership terms means that the tasks associated with a position are accomplished in line with the decision programmes and under consideration of the communication paths and the competencies. Acceptance is based initially on extrinsic motivation, but can be converted by processes of internalisation and integration into intrinsic motivation (Frost 2005, 271). This process can also be described as the formation of a specific professional habitus, which results from the interplay of performance and support. The socialisation process is effectively a mutual process of habituation to the organisation's interests, which leads to a 'Community of Assumptions' among members of the executive level (Kirsch 2005, 427–428), i.e. among those persons who decide about the adjustment of the organisation to the social environment by deciding about the decision premises.

The success of this socialisation process is the basis for a special kind of confidence because it enables mutually predictable behaviour. Consequently, personal affection is not necessary as a basis and there is no need to hope for appropriate behaviour from individuals. Instead, it becomes possible to be confident that a person will act predictably within certain limits in line with his or her role within the organisation (Luhmann 2000, 27–38, 124–126). Finally, individuals who have proved their reliability by acting successfully as persons within the organisation over a long period, who have passed through the selection and socialisation process and have reached a leadership position, have thus proved that they most probably have the will and ability to make far-reaching decisions in the organisation's interests and to bear the inevitable risks associated with such decisions.

4 Conclusion

The aim of this article was to develop a methodological approach for the research of careers based on archival material. As shown above, an individual career can initially be analysed as a selection process, i.e. using the three factors: contingency, support, and performance. Subject to the appropriate archival sources, in a first step the empirical phenomena that fall within these three categories are relatively easy to identify at any career stage. In a second step, it is then necessary to elaborate their mutual influence. With a rise through the decision-making hierarchy, i.e. in later career stages, the practical form of the factors changes, since now decisions are increasingly about decision premises. Thereby, the other aspect of the career, the process of socialisation, becomes gradually important. To understand the process of socialisation is somewhat more difficult. The development of the professional self-image of the person whose career is under study must be reconstructed in order to address the question of whether the organisation's interests were internalised, i.e. a professional habitus was formed which is finally mirrored in decisions.

Based on Luhmann's organisational theory approach, which is embedded in his theory of society, the model for top careers is constructed as an ideal type offering a high degree of abstraction. This has the advantage that the high level of complexity of empirical reality can be reduced to a few categories, i.e. a career can be analysed by using a simple scheme despite the diversity of the empirical phenomena. The perspective resulting from this theoretical premise on organisations is only one possible view. Admittedly, other approaches are therefore possible. For example, a perspective that takes the biography of the individual or society into account. This would certainly change the focus to concentrate on the question of the importance of a career in the context of the biography or the question of its function in the context of the reproduction of social structures.

The focus of the perspective presented can contribute to the aim of this volume. This focus is on the function of top careers for an organisation. Ongoing decision-making is the fundamental operation that constitutes and continuously reproduces an organisation. However, at the same time decisions inevitably produce risks, i.e. risks cannot be avoided. Therefore, they must necessarily be managed. The selection process means that the individuals who reach the executive level are those able to bear a growing amount of responsibility successfully and at the same time able to demonstrate that they can manage risks. The socialisation process, in the course of which a professional habitus is formed, enables confidence, since the ability to decide in the organisational interests has been proved and thus the future behaviour of those who have also successfully passed through this process is to a certain extent predictable. In other words, a top career is a mechanism to reduce the high risks of far-reaching decisions.

Notes

1. See additionally Luhmann 1997 and id., 1984b.
2. Klasen's matriculation request, 26 April 1929, CampusCenter of the University Hamburg; Klasen's matriculation request, 12 May 1932, CampusCenter of the University Hamburg; Klasen's doctoral certificate, 24 April 1933, owned by the family; Klasen's qualification report by Curt Rothenberger, 27 August 1935, BA Berlin, R3001, 63318.
3. If Klasen wanted to continue his training, he had to join an organisation that was acceptable to the Nazis. First, he became a member of the Stahlhelm, from there he was handed over a few months later to the SA. Questionnaire of the British Military Government, 1 July 1946, StaHH, 221–11, F 1901.
4. Qualification report by Curt Rothenberger, 27 August 1935, BA Berlin, R3001, 63318. After moving to the Deutsche Bank he left the SA. Furthermore, he was never a member of the NSDAP. Information given to the author by the Bundesarchiv in Berlin, 29 October 2013.
5. Legal Department in Berlin to the branch in Hamburg, 11 November 1929, HADB, F002, 1008; Branch in Hamburg to the Legal Department in Berlin, 11 November 1929, HADB, F002, 1008; Legal Department in Berlin to the branch in Hamburg, 12 November1929, HADB, F002, 1008; The Secretariat of the Branch in Hamburg to the Secretariat of the headquarter in Berlin, 1 December 1931, HADB, F002, 1010.
6. Tabular overview of Klasen's career without signature, 18 January 1957, HADB, V003, 0195.
7. Certificate of Discharge, 28 May 1945, owned by the family; Questionnaire of the British Military Government, 1 July 1946, StaHH, 221–11, F 1901.
8. File note by Klasen, 12 June1945, HADB, F002, 2685; File note by Klasen, 22 August.1945, HADB, F002, 2685; File note by Klasen, 31 August 1945, HADB, F002, 2689; Branch in Hamburg to Brauer, 10 February 1948, StaHH, 131–1 II, 1830.
9. Schmedemann to the party executive of the SPD, 4 February 1948, AdSD, SPD-Landesorganisation Hamburg, 304. After his denazification process Klasen was classified in the category V: Entlastungsschein, 19 February 1948, owned by the family. So he was regarded as being completely unencumbered politically. See Zonal Executive Offices Control Commission for Germany (British Element): Zonen-Exekutivanweisung Nr. 54. Kategorisierung und

Behandlung von Kriegsverbrechern und Nazis, 30 November 1946, AdSD, SPD-Landesorganisation Hamburg, 548.

10. Minutes of the meeting, 12 September 1949, StaHH, 371–16 II, 1139.
11. See, for example, 'Eine gute Kombination', in: Handelsblatt, 17 November 1969; 'Hervorragende Kandidaten', in: Stuttgarter Zeitung, 17 November 1969; 'Der beste Mann', in: Die ZEIT, 21 November 1969.
12. The fact that the large German companies recognised the contingency of careers as a problem and responded to it by professionalising the recruitment of executives through the development and implementation of appropriate structures is clearly shown by Reuber (2012).
13. Translation by the author. Klasen to Heimreich, 31 July 1959, HADB, V010, 0002. '[Ich möchte] Ihnen nur sagen, dass ich für meinen persönlichen Berufsweg Ihnen viel verdanke. Es war für mich ein besonderes Glück, dass Sie einer der ersten Männer waren, die sich bei meinem Eintritt in die Bank meiner bankgeschäftlichen Formung annahmen. Sehr häufig, wenn ich im täglichen Geschäftsleben, und ganz besonders jüngeren Menschen gegenüber, über das Bankgeschäft einmal etwas sage, was ich als sehr ‚weise' halte, dann merke ich immer wieder, dass ich meinen alten Lehrmeister M. M. Heimreich zitiert habe.'
14. Bechtolf's curriculum vitae, 16 December 1941, HADB, P1, 3.
15. The subject of Klasen's doctoral thesis was an international law issue (Klasen 1933), as assistant judge he worked in the field of civil law. Klasen 1982; Klasen's qualification report by Curt Rothenberger, 27 August 1935, BA Berlin, R3001, 63318.
16. Deed tax law of 5 May 1936 (RGBL I 1936, pp. 407–434); Eiffler 1937.
17. Report on the meeting of the tax committee of the chamber of commerce in Hamburg on the 31 August 1936, 1 September 1936, HADB, F002, 2734; Minutes of the meeting of the Vereinigung von Hamburger Banken und Bankiers, 2 November 1936, HADB, F002, 2367; File note by Klasen, 9 March 1937, HADB, F002, 2367; Branch in Hamburg to the Vereinigung von Hamburger Banken und Bankiers, 22 April 1938, HADB, F002, 2767; Branch in Hamburg to the chamber of commerce in Hamburg, 30 May 1938, HADB, F002, 2734.
18. Report on the meeting of the tax committee of the chamber of commerce in Hamburg on the 31 August 1936, 1 September 1936, HADB, F002, 2734; Klasen to the departments, 24 September 1936, HADB, F002, 2734; Klasen to the departments, 7 October 1936, HADB, F002, 2734; Klasen to the departments, 24 September 1936, HADB, F002, 2735; File note by Klasen, 13 November 1937, HADB, F002, 2734; Branch in Hamburg to the legal department of the headquarter, 15 January 1938, HADB, F002, 2734; Branch in Hamburg to the legal department of the headquarter, 26 February 1938, HADB, F002, 2734; Legal department of

the headquarters to the Branch in Hamburg, 28 February 1938, HADB, F002, 2734; Branch in Hamburg to the Vereinigung von Hamburger Banken und Bankiers, 22 April 1938, HADB, F002, 2767; File note by Klasen, 12 March 1940, HADB, Bestand F002, 2734; Branch in Hamburg to the legal department of the headquarters, 20 April 1940; HADB, F002, 2735; Branch in Hamburg to the legal department of the headquarters, 30 July 1940, HADB, F002, 2735.

19. File note by Klasen, 5 October 1953, HADB, V10, 0065; File note by Klasen, 16 September 1954, HADB, V10, 0065; File note by Klasen, 12 October 1955, HADB, V10, 0065; File note by Klasen, 1 December 1955, HADB, V10, 0065; File note by Klasen, 17 March 1956, HADB, V10, 0065; File note by Klasen, 15 February 1957, HADB, V10, 0065; File note by Klasen, 28 February 1957, HADB, V10, 0065; File note by Klasen, 16 May 1957, HADB, V10, 0065; File note by Klasen, 6 June 1957, HADB, V10, 0065; File note by Klasen, 3 February 1958, HADB, V10, 0065; File note by Klasen, 10 February 1958, HADB, V10, 0065; File note by Klasen, 5 March 1958, HADB, V10, 0065; File note by Klasen, 17 March 1956, HADB, V10, 0065; File note by Klasen, 19 April 1958, HADB, V10, 0065; File note by Klasen, 1 December 1958, HADB, V10, 0065; File note by Klasen, 20 January 1960, HADB, V10, 0065; File note by Klasen, 19 October 1960, HADB, V10, 0065.
20. Bechtolf to Schuchmann, 2 August 1956, HADB, V10, 0342; Minutes of the meeting of the supervisory board, 8 October 1956, StaHH, 621–1/95 Hapag, 17.
21. Translation by the author. File note by Klasen, 30 June.1957, HADB, V10, 0351a. 'Als unumschränkten Herrscher hielten wir ihn dagegen, ich müsste ihm das ganz offen sagen für gefährlich und uns deshalb für verpflichtet, durch die Sperrminorität seine Wirkungsmöglichkeiten bei der Hapag in den für diese nützlichen Grenzen zu halten. Dies seien jedenfalls unsere Interessen.'
22. Excerpt of the minutes of the meeting of the working committee, 10 September 1957, StaHH, 621–1/95 Hapag, 177.
23. Ibid.
24. File note by Klasen, 11th December 1958, HADB, V10, 0351a.
25. 'Hapag auf gefährlichem Kurs. Berechtigt ein dickes Aktienpaket zur Machtergreifung?', in: Die ZEIT, 20th February 1958; 'Die Deutsche Bank kauft die Hapag frei', in: Die ZEIT, 2nd October 1958; Schubert to the advisory board, 26th February 1958, HADB, V10, 0342.
26. File note by Klasen, 24th September 1959, HADB, V10, 0342.
27. Abs an Kebschull, 19th February 1959, HADB, V10, 0342; Text of Klasen's speech at the annual general meeting 1959, without date, HADB, V10, 0068.

28. Translation by the author. Transcript of the broadcast 'Die Stimme des Volksaktionärs' in the NDR, 7 August 1959, HADB, V10, 0002. 'Darin besteht ja gerade die Leistung und die Tradition, denn der Name, den eine Bank zu verlieren hat, ist viel grösser, als einmal ein Geschäft auszulassen.'

References

Bartmann, W., & Plumpe, W. (2003). Anmerkungen zu den Vorständen der I. G.-Farbenindustrie AG-Nachfolgegesellschaften 1952–1990. In: V. R. Berghahn, S. Unger, & D. Ziegler (Eds.), *Die deutsche Wirtschaftselite im 20. Jahrhundert. Kontinuität und Mentalität* (pp. 153–186). Essen: Klartext.

Beyer, J. (1996). Governance Structures. Unternehmensverflechtungen und Unternehmenserfolg in Deutschland. *Zeitschrift für Betriebswirtschaft*, (supplement 3/1996), 79–101.

Beyer, J. (1999). Unternehmensverflechtungen und Managerherrschaft in Deutschland. *Leviathan. Zeitschrift für Sozialwissenschaft, 27*, 518–536.

Beyer, J. (2013). Die Strukturen der Deutschland AG. Ein Rückblick auf ein Modell der Unternehmenskontrolle. In: R. Ahrens, B. Gehlen, & A. Reckendrees (Eds.), *Die 'Deutschland AG'. Historische Annäherungen an den bundesdeutschen Kapitalismus* (pp. 31–56). Essen: Klartext.

Beyer, J., & Windolf, P. (1995). Kooperativer Kapitalismus. Unternehmensverflechtungen im internationalen Vergleich. *Kölner Zeitschrift für Soziologie und Sozialpsychologie, 47*, 1–36.

Eiffler, K. (1937). *Urkundensteuergesetz vom 5. Mai 1936 mit amtlicher Begründung, Durchführungsbestimmungen und anderen ergänzenden Bestimmungen nebst Einführung.* Berlin/Leipzig: De Gruyter.

Faust, M. (2002). Karrieremuster von Führungskräften der Wirtschaft im Wandel—Der Fall Deutschland in vergleichender Perspektive. *Mitteilungen aus dem SOFI—Soziologisches Forschungsinstitut Göttingen an der Georg-August-Universität, 30*, 69–90.

Frost, J. (2005). *Märkte in Unternehmen. Organisatorische Steuerung und Theorien der Firma.* Wiesbaden: Deutscher Universitätsverlag.

Gadamer, H.-G. (1975). *Wahrheit und Methode.* Mohr/Tübingen: Grundzüge einer philosophischen Hermeneutik.

Geertz, C. (1973). *The interpretation of cultures. Selected essays.* New York: Basic Books.

Gruchmann, L. (1988). *Justiz im Dritten Reich 1933-1940. Anpassung und Unterwerfung in der Ära Gürtner.* München: Oldenbourg.

Hartmann, M. (2006). Vermarktlichung der Elitenrekrutierung? Das Beispiel der Topmanager. In: H. Münkler, G. Straßenberger, & M. Bohlender (Eds.), *Deutschlands Eliten im Wandel* (pp. 440–445). Frankfurt: Campus.

Hartmann, M. (2007). Ausbildungsschwerpunkte und Karrieremuster deutscher Topmanager. Soziale Selektion, Hauskarriere und geringe Internationalisierung. *Personalführung, 17*, 57–59.

Hartmann, M. (2008). Transnationale Klassenbildung? In: P. A. Berger & A. Weiß (Eds.), *Transnationalisierung sozialer Ungleichheit* (pp. 245–252). Wiesbaden: Verlag für Sozialwissenschaften.

Holtfrerich, C.-L. (1995). Die Deutsche Bank vom Zweiten Weltkrieg über die Besatzungsherrschaft zur Rekonstruktion. In: L. Gall et al. (Eds.), *Die Deutsche Bank 1870–1995* (pp. 409–578). München: C.H. Beck.

Joly, H. (2000). Kontinuität und Diskontinuität der industriellen Elite nach 1945. In: D. Ziegler (Ed.), *Großbürger und Unternehmer. Die deutsche Wirtschaftselite im 20. Jahrhundert* (pp. 54–72). Göttingen: Vandenhoeck & Ruprecht.

Kaelble, H. (1983). *Soziale Mobilität und Chancengleichheit im 19. und 20. Jahrhundert. Deutschland im internationalen Vergleich.* Göttingen: Vandenhoeck & Ruprecht.

Kirsch, W. (2005). *Die Führung von Unternehmen. Ausgewählte Studientexte.* München: Kirsch.

Klasen, K. (1933). *Die völkerrechtliche Bedeutung der Anerkennung der Tschechoslovaken während des Weltkrieges*. Hamburg: Schimkus.

Klasen, K. (1982). Warum trat die Regierung sang und klanglos ab? In: R. Italiaander (Ed.), *Wir erlebten das Ende der Weimarer Republik. Zeitgenossen berichten* (pp. 181–182). Düsseldorf: Droste.

Kocka, J. (1986). *Sozialgeschichte. Begriff—Entwicklung—Probleme*. Göttingen: Vandenhoeck & Ruprecht.

Kocka, J. (2002). *Unternehmer in Deutschland seit 1945*. Bochum: Klartext.

Liefeith, H. (1983). Entwicklung der Berufsbildung im privaten Bankgewerbe seit dem 19. Jahrhundert. In: G. Ashauer, H. Liefeith, & K. Weiser (Eds.), *Berufsbildung in der deutschen Kreditwirtschaft. Ein geschichtlicher Überblick* (pp. 19–155). Mainz: v. Hase & Koehler.

Luhmann, N. (1981). *Politische Theorie im Wohlfahrtsstaat*. München/Wien: Günther Olzog.

Luhmann, N. (1984a). Article organisation. In: J. Ritter & K. Gründer (Eds.), *Historisches Wörterbuch der Philosophie* (Vol. 6th, columns 1326–1328). Basel: Schwabe.

Luhmann, N. (1984b). Soziale Systeme. In: *Grundriß einer allgemeinen Theorie*. Frankfurt: Suhrkamp.
Luhmann, N. (1984c). Soziologische Aspekte des Entscheidungsverhaltens. *Die Betriebswirtschaft, 44*, 591–603.
Luhmann, N. (1988). *Die Wirtschaft der Gesellschaft*. Frankfurt: Suhrkamp.
Luhmann, N. (1991). *Soziologie des Risikos*. Berlin/New York: Walter de Gruyter.
Luhmann, N. (1993). Die Paradoxie des Entscheidens. Verwaltungs-Archiv. *Zeitschrift für Verwaltungslehre, Verwaltungsrecht und Verwaltungspolitik, 84*, 287–310.
Luhmann, N. (1997). *Die Gesellschaft der Gesellschaft, 2 Volumes*. Frankfurt: Suhrkamp.
Luhmann, N. (2000). *Vertrauen. Ein Mechanismus der Reduktion sozialer Komplexität*. Stuttgart: Lucius & Lucius.
Luhmann, N. (2005a). Interaktion, Organisation, Gesellschaft. Anwendungen der Systemtheorie. In: id., Soziologische Aufklärung 2. *Aufsätze zur Theorie der Gesellschaft* (pp. 9–24). Wiesbaden: Verlag für Sozialwissenschaften.
Luhmann, N. (2005b). Organisation und Entscheidung. In: Id., Soziologische Aufklärung 3. *Soziales System, Gesellschaft, Organisation* (pp. 389–450). Wiesbaden: Verlag für Sozialwissenschaften.
Luhmann, N. (2005c). Organisation in Wirtschaftssystem. In: id., Soziologische Aufklärung 3. *Soziales System, Gesellschaft, Organisation* (pp. 451–478). Wiesbaden: Verlag für Sozialwissenschaften.
Luhmann, N. (2006). *Organisation und Entscheidung*. Wiesbaden: Verlag für Sozialwissenschaften.
March, J. G., & Shapira, Z. (1987). Managerial perspectives on risk and risk taking. *Management Science, 33*, 1404–1418.
Martens, W., & Ortmann, G. (2006). Organisationen in Luhmanns Systemtheorie. In: A. Kieser & M. Ebers (Eds.), *Organisationstheorien* (pp. 427–461). Stuttgart: Kohlhammer.
Mayer, K. U. (2006). Abschied von den Eliten. In: H. Münkler, G. Straßenberger, & M. Bohlender (Eds.), *Deutschlands Eliten im Wandel* (pp. 455–479). Frankfurt: Campus.
Plumpe, W. (2003). Die Unwahrscheinlichkeit des Jubiläums—oder: warum Unternehmen nur historisch erklärt werden können. *Jahrbuch für Wirtschaftsgeschichte*, (2003/1), 143–156.
Plumpe, W. (2006). Unternehmen. In: G. Ambrosius, D. Petzina, & W. Plumpe (Eds.), *Moderne Wirtschaftsgeschichte. Eine Einführung für Historiker und Ökonomen* (pp. 61–94). München: Oldenbourg.

Reuber, C. (2012). Der lange Weg an die Spitze. In: *Karrieren von Führungskräften deutscher Großunternehmen im 20. Jahrhunder*. Frankfurt: Campus.

Weber, M. (1980). *Wirtschaft und Gesellschaft. Grundriß der verstehenden Soziologie*. Mohr: Tübingen.

Weber, M. (1995). *Wissenschaft als Beruf.* Stuttgart: Philipp Reclam.

Cooperative Governance in Banking: Consequences for Decision-Making Processes

Friederike Sattler

1 Decision-making in Economic Theory and Historians' Criticism

According to modern economic theory, the decision-making of economic players is a question of—obviously more or less experience-based—expectation formation processes. Economic decisions always relate to the future and therefore they necessarily take place under conditions of uncertainty that can only be reduced through the formation of expectations. This is because expectations about future developments, especially about the behaviour of other economic players (and their expectations), help to manage the complexities of decision-making and thus establish one's capacity to act at all. Economic theory has so far developed multiple approaches with regard

F. Sattler (✉)
Department of History, Goethe-University, Frankfurt on the Main, Germany
e-mail: sattler@em.uni-frankfurt.de

K. Schönhärl (ed.), *Decision Taking, Confidence and Risk Management in Banks from Early Modernity to the 20th Century*,
DOI 10.1007/978-3-319-42076-9_4

to the core question of how economic expectations emerge. However, the undeniable value of historical experience for expectation formation has not yet been precisely determined.

The influential models of rational or limited-rational expectation formation assume that economic players are principally oriented towards maximising their own benefit and have at their disposal retrospective as well as prospective information. In the rational model this information can be used extensively in the process of expectation formation and decision-making, whereas in the limited-rational model it can—for financial or cognitive reasons—only be acquired and applied on a limited scale (Biervert and Wieland 1990 for a short, concise overview). These models of rational or limited-rational expectation formation, essentially based on the concept of the *homo economicus*, have developed a strong persuasive power and historical effect, because they can reasonably claim to recognise, describe and explain not only historically specific but almost universally valid interdependencies of economic decision-making. However, exactly for this methodological reason, they show a lack of a 'sense of reality'. They have therefore been increasingly criticised since the 1970s, not least by the representatives of behavioural economics, cofounded by Daniel Kahneman and Amos Tversky. Most behavioural economists do not dismiss the concept of *homo economicus* at all; rather they connect it with approaches of cognitively limited rationality, and try to model their own assumptions about expectation formation much 'closer to reality' by, for instance, including psychological, sociological or legal and scientific findings about human behaviour (Kahneman and Tversky 1979; Thaler 1994; Kahneman 2011; Gigerenzer and Selten 2001; Gigerenzer 2008).

Behavioural scientists have in recent times cooperated increasingly with neuroscientists, trying jointly not only to grasp individual economic expectation formation more realistically, but also to explain overall economically relevant problems supposedly based on 'irrational', often emotionally conditioned collective acting; in other words, they try to explain the 'herd instinct' of human beings. Especially noteworthy in this context is the approach of 'animal spirits' developed by George A. Akerlof and Robert J. Shiller, which tries to explain the economic effects of deeply rooted human instincts (Akerlof and Shiller 2009). They use the examples of prominent forms of expression of such instincts—for instance, the need for fairness, the temptation for corrupt behaviour, the inclination to think in stories—to show their importance in the context of economic expectation formation. Because of the distinct inclination for imitating others, such mental states can goad each other on, resulting in developments on a national economic scale. As a result, experience-based knowledge as well as down-to-earth rational calculation becomes less significant.

Although Akerlof and Shiller failed to draw from their observations clear consequences for a consistent economic-behavioural theory of expectation formation, their findings about the effect of anthropological realities in economic decision-making are nevertheless especially relevant. The tendency for thinking in stories, in other words, in sequences of events with an inner logic and dynamics, for example, is of particular importance for the question about the status of historical experience in expectation formation (Akerlof and Shiller 2009, 51–56). The relevance of one's own life and professional story, events and experiences, self-interpretations and constructions of meaning cannot be overestimated for economic expectation formation, and, according to Akerlof and Shiller, there are many similarities in the history of all kinds of organisations. The stories experienced and retold in corporations and other organisations as a rule contain fictional elements as well as elements related to the future, and they are, as Akerlof and Shiller convincingly demonstrate in several examples, by no means just accompanying symptoms but rather independent economic influencing variables that could fuel, for instance, an economic boom.

In order to improve understanding of expectation formation and decision-making processes, further theoretical and methodological suggestions are offered by the sociological approach of 'fictional expectations', recently presented by Jens Beckert (2013). According to Beckert, decision-making based upon expectations by intentionally rational economic players is always anchored in their fictional thinking, defined as imagined constructs about a future state of the world and (the) causal connections leading up to it. Fictions are not unequivocally connected to empirical facts; they appear as factual anticipations in narrative forms of stories of events, as well as in scientific theories or political ideologies, and find their way into various discourses. They thus serve as a guiding principle for organising decision-making processes. Beckert outlines the possible applications of this new approach, for instance, for choosing corporate strategies, implementing innovations and making investment decisions; he further defines the essential features of connections between rational calculations and future-related fictitious constructs, and subsequently manages to provide instructive suggestions for business and banking historians.

However, even if one succeeded in enriching the concept of a fundamentally, but rationally limited acting *homo economicus* with economic-behavioural or sociological findings, and therefore were able to bring it 'closer to reality', from the perspective of economic history it must be noted that economic expectation formation always depends on concrete historical conditions (Plumpe 2004a, 2004b). From this perspective, it is essential to understand the concept of *homo economicus* and the related concept of 'rational' expectation formation as historical, ever-changing phenomena. The concept of *homo economicus* established itself only during the transition to a modern economy and never raised human aspirations for self-interest to the status of an irrefutable natural law (although to the status of an increasingly accepted behavioural norm); to date such aspirations have rather been subject to 'reasonable' limitations that can only be deciphered in their specific historical contexts (Plumpe 2007).

Thus, from a historical perspective, economic expectation formation and decision-making processes are essentially associated with the core question of the ever-changing, but quite differently shaped concepts and criteria of the rationality of individuals and collectives. It is perfectly obvious that the respective individual and collective experiences, as well as the stories told and constructed on this basis, enriched with both past- as well as future-related fictitious constructs, scientific theories, political ideologies and social discourses, do play a significant role for the changing criteria and concepts of rationality (Karafyllis and Schmidt 2002 as a philosophical perspective with numerous suggestions in the context of plural 'rationality' and 'expectation formation' in science, culture and society).

Nevertheless, how exactly individual and collective historical experiences and the narratives related to them influence the expectation formation and decision-making processes of economic players has largely remained unanswered in historical research too. Some years ago Reinhard

Koselleck pointed out that experience and expectation are two indistinguishable and intertwined cognitive processes that combine the 'present past' with its respective 'future realised in the present' (Koselleck 1979). However, so far historical science has not yet reached beyond this point, other than warning against overestimating the evidence of experiences in the interpretation of future-related behaviour and, consequently, starting to raise the shaping of experiences into an object of investigation (Scott 1994; Tanner 2004, 214–221 for an overview of various research approaches). In so doing, it has become evident that historical experiences have by no means a solid, sharply contoured significance that is equally present at all times in the consciousness of the players, but rather—as Koselleck already pointed out—shift and change dependent on the current level of expectations, in other words of the 'future currently realised in the present' (Seefried 2015). Historical experiences are even able to form themselves anew, for instance through the revaluation of so far neglected or even completely forgotten experiences, whereas experiences that were to date strongly present may become invalidated. However, this branch of historical research remains in its extreme infancy concerning the expectation formation and decision-making processes of both entrepreneurs and enterprises in general, as well as bankers and banks in particular.

Overall, the status of research into the theoretical understanding of experience-based entrepreneurial expectation formation has to be characterised as insufficient. There is no clear notion of experience-based expectation formation and decision-making processes yet, neither with regard to individuals nor organisations. The author would thus like to contribute here at least a first vague idea about how to develop a historically sound model for experience-based expectation formation that focuses on the change of the rationality concepts and criteria of economic players as such. Following this intention, it seems very helpful to use an abstract notion of historical change that is accrued from decisive historical criticism about the concepts of New Institutional Economics (Plumpe 2009, 30–40). Hence, in opposition to the theoretical premises of New Institutional Economics, historical change cannot be explained by the complex structures of institutions alone, to be understood as the multifaceted formal and informal rules and norms of economic players that mutually stabilise their respective expectations. Rather, it is assumed that historical change is caused by the even more complex interplay of, *first*, institutions; *second*, prevailing semantics (to be understood as partly descriptive, partly normative ascriptions of meaning); and *third*, everyday practices (which may distinctively differ from the legally fixed or morally accepted norms). Therefore, historical change may be conceptualised in the abstract—using the vocabulary of Niklas Luhmann—as a recursive, suspenseful, co-evolutionary relationship between three essential driving forces: institutions, semantics and practices. These three drivers of historical change mutually enable and mutually limit each other, but they are not completely taken up in each other. Each of the three drivers is able to gain dynamics on its own (by variation, selection and new stabilisation). In their interplay, the three drivers may complement and reinforce each other as well as contradict and challenge each other. This may result in mutual adaptations. However, in stark contrast, it may also result in frictions, possibly even ruptures, that sharply conflict with simultaneous tendencies of perpetuation, for instance the long-term process of the professionalisation of risk management in banks and the subsequent replacement of the empirical knowledge of individuals, maybe private bankers, by certain functional equivalents of a non-personal, more organizationally related expectation formation in the meaning of Niklas Luhmann, in joint stock credit banks (Luhmann 2002, 2011).

Initial ideas for a model of experience-based expectation formation thus focus on changes in the rationality concepts and criteria of economic players by analysing their practices, the prevailing semantics they used, and the main institutions they agreed to—separately and in their interplay with one another. These notions should be kept in mind as attention shifts to an empirical case study examining the decisions of German universal banks concerning their investments abroad during the late 1960s and 1970s. As will be seen, all the three large German banks decided on a strategy of 'club banking', i.e. cooperative governance. What consequences did this have for their expectation formation and decision-making processes in international banking? Certainly, at this very early stage of research personal expectations should be confined: the main purpose of the following case study is just to identify the most interesting and relevant questions that should be answered by further research—based on (hopefully) rich empirical sources and data. This should then enable the construction of a historically sound model for experience-based expectation formation and decision-making processes with regard to the specific problems of cooperative governance in banking, a model that is applicable for in-depth comparisons between different multilateral banking clubs.

2 Foreign Investment Decisions of German Universal Banks in the 1960s and 1970s

In Germany, the traditionally strong position of universal banks had not been seriously shaken by World War I, nor by the world economic crisis of 1929, or the banking crisis of 1931.[1] Of course, the large German joint stock banks were heavily weakened, they had to write-off all their foreign investments and they lost their position as leading players in international finance after the war, but they managed to survive as universal banks during the years of inflation and the subsequent highly competitive second half of the 1920s. The crisis of 1931, which resulted—at least partially—from the 'hypercompetitive conditions' for banks in the late 1920s, was followed by an intense investigation of the whole banking sector. Surprisingly, and in spite of all the deficiencies in banking practices uncovered by this investigation, the Credit Control Act of 1934 repudiated both the demand for the socialisation of banks as well as the demand for the separation of the banks' deposit and loan activities from their security business. On the contrary, the new legal framework offered welcome protection to the already existing universal banks, among them the 'Big Three': Deutsche Bank, Dresdner Bank and Commerzbank.

Even after the collapse of the Nazi regime, when the Allies tried to smash these banks, they were able to reconsolidate again as universal banks.[2] There are two main reasons for this: first, the managers of the former joint stock banks were extremely good at lobbying for their interests, and second, the large banks were needed for rapid economic reconstruction in the context of the intensifying Cold War. As early as 1952, a German law stopped the decentralisation process launched by the Allies and provided a legal basis for the well-directed re-concentration ambitions of the three banks.[3] Five years later, in 1957, this process was officially completed.[4] Hermann Josef Abs (1901–1994), member of the management board of Deutsche Bank since 1937 and spokesman of the reunited Deutsche Bank from 1957 until 1967, is surely the most prominent personification of this continuity (Gall 2004). From the late 1950s on, the 'Big Three' were able to return to a path of rapid growth.[5] Other banking groups recovered rapidly too, particularly the public savings banks but also the credit cooperatives; and both these types of organisation also increasingly adopted universal banking practices. Consequently, the market shares of the three large universal banks decreased in spite of their successful reconsolidation (see Table 8). The conditions for banking were competitive once again.

These developments in the structure of the West German banking sector reflect far-reaching changes in the West German economy as a whole. Two of these changes are of particular relevance here: first, the locus of savings shifted away from business enterprise towards private households (because of growing incomes and affluence in society, supported by the strong institutions of the expanding welfare state); this was a long-term trend which—initially, during the 1950s and 1960s—especially favoured

Table 8 Market shares of credit institutions in Germany (without foreign branches), in percent

	1950	1955	1960	1970	1980	1989
'Big Three': *Deutsche Bank, Dresdner Bank, Commerzbank*	**19.5**	**14.7**	**11.3**	**10.2**	**9.6**	**9.6**
Regional Banks	12.6	11.6	10.6	10.7	10.6	13.7
Private Bankers	4.6	3.0	2.6	2.5	1.5	1.6
Savings Banks (including *Girozentralen*)	32.0	34.1	35.7	38.5	38.4	36.9
Credit Cooperatives (including *Zentralkassen*)	10.4	8.5	8.4	11.5	15.2	16.5
Mortgage Banks (private and public)	5.8	11.2	17.1	13.7	13.6	13.5
Banks with special functions	11.4	13.1	10.3	8.4	6.4	6.8
Other	3.7	3.8	4.0	4.5	4.7	1.4

Source: Monthly Reports of Deutsche Bundesbank for 1950, 1955, 1960, 1970, 1980, and 1989 (Compilation by author)

the savings banks at the expense of the commercial banks. Second, the 'catch-up growth' so typical for the early post-war decades petered out somewhere between the end of the 1960s and the early 1970s; from then on the economic centre of gravity moved from traditional industrial production, for instance steel, to more service-related and consumer-oriented industries.

In response to these far-reaching changes in the West German economy, the large universal banks developed two lines of strategy: they accepted both the rising importance of retail banking in the context of growing general consumption and the need for an intensification of their international activities in the context of economic globalisation (Wixforth 2010).

Deutsche Bank, Dresdner Bank and Commerzbank, who traditionally saw their field of competence as especially embracing large and medium-sized industrial clients and wealthy private clients, started trying to win new private clients among employees and workers in the late 1950s (Frost 2009). In order to achieve this aim, they designed numerous new products and opened many new domestic branches during the 1960s. This strategy helped them to reduce decreases in their market shares, but it was a very cost-intensive strategy.

With regard to the expansion of their international activities, all three banks acted rather cautiously until the end of the 1960s, compared to the large commercial banks of other Western European countries (Tilly 1993b; Steinke 2000; Institut für bankhistorische Forschung 2003; Ahrens and Wixforth 2010). This low-key approach is usually explained by two factors: first, the utmost importance of the banks' own reconstruction processes in the early post-war decades; second, the twofold loss of all foreign investments as a consequence of the two World Wars. After the currency reform of 1948 and the London Debt Agreement of 1953, all three large German universal banks had systematically re-established connections with their corresponding banks in all countries that supported the West German economic recovery via imports or exports. Besides, all three large German universal banks reopened prestigious offices in Europe and overseas, for instance in South America, in Turkey and the Middle East, in North and South Africa, and, last but surely not least, in Japan. Additionally, all three of them began to acquire minor interests in finance companies in both developing and newly industrialising countries. But as to further international operations, they initially did not act on their own behalf, but rather only as partners of international syndicates, especially of Western European banking clubs, called Europartners, for instance Associated Banks of Europe Corporation (ABECOR) or European Banks' International Company (EBIC) (Regul and Wolf 1974; Steuber 1974, 1977; Institut für bankhistorische Forschung 1994; Ross 1998; Hartkopf 2000; Roberts and Arnander 2001; Ramm 2002).dd

This general picture gives the impression that the expectation formation and decision-making processes of all three large German banks concerning investments abroad produced the very same outcome. All three banks rather hesitantly started to expand their international activities during the second half of the 1960s, supposedly because all three of them were convinced that the intensification of their businesses abroad was still a rather risky option; nevertheless, at the very same time, all three seemed to expect that both their industrial clients and their domestic and foreign competitors in the credit business would intensify their own international activities. In other words, they perceived that intensifying internationalisation was risky, but that it was still necessary. Because of this, the banks searched for a strategy to minimise the risks of foreign investments, and in the end all of them eventually decided to become partners of Western European banking clubs. Consequently, all three had to cope with the cooperative governance structures of these banking clubs in the following years.

However, this is only a very general picture. If one dares to take a closer look at the three banks and their respective strategies for entering specific foreign markets in the late 1960s, for instance the US market, which was without doubt one of the most important for them, it becomes quickly clear that there are significant differences between their behavioural patterns, probably because they were acting on the basis of very different individual and collective experiences and expectations, which influenced their foreign investment decisions *vis-à-vis* specific markets. Of course, all three of them were large joint stock banks and therefore it can be assumed that their decisions were not primarily based on empirical knowledge of individual managers but rather on non-personal, more organizationally related and methodologically advanced factors, i.e. scientifically based techniques of market research, consisting of the three basic elements observation, analysis and prognosis. Nevertheless, the application of these presumably non-personal techniques of market research in the three banks led to different results for the US market. Thus, Commerzbank and Dresdner Bank tried to enter this market on their own behalf much earlier than Deutsche Bank. The two of them decided to use a dual strategy early in the 1970s, which means they entered the US market with European partners on the one hand, and also alone, on the other hand. It was of prime importance for this modification of strategy that the industrial clients of the German universal banks had begun to ask for more complex financing solutions with regard to their own growing international activities. Additionally, by expanding abroad the German universal banks could have hoped to find compensation for real and expected losses on the home markets, especially concerning cost-intensive retail banking. The growing competition of US and other foreign banks entering the German market was a factor too, but for the time being one of only minor importance.[6]

In contrast to Commerzbank and Dresdner Bank, Deutsche Bank hesitated almost a whole decade before they too adopted a dual strategy. Obviously, different historical experiences as well as different expectations about the future are responsible for the different outcomes of these respective decision-making processes. But how and in what way did experiences and expectations differ? In this context, of most interest is whether the envisaged or actually experienced problems of cooperative governance in multilateral banking clubs were pivotal factors that Commerzbank and Dresdner Bank tried to avoid by also entering the US market with branches of their own in 1971/72. Were the experiences of Deutsche Bank with the cooperative management of its own banking club significantly better? What is already known about the general circumstances?

Commerzbank, the smallest of the three large German universal banks, was the very first to try and explore the US market on its own behalf, not just as a partner of a European banking club (Europartners, cofounded in 1970 by Commerzbank and Crédit Lyonnais, later joined by Banco di Roma and Nordic Bank Ltd.) (Commerzbank 1994; Krause 2003). Already in 1971, when the Europartners group launched the mutual investment bank EuroPartners Securities Corporation, Commerzbank also opened a branch of its own in New York City. There had been a prestigious Commerzbank office there from 1927 to 1939, in the good years as it were of the interwar period, and Commerzbank had been able to expand its business activities throughout the US considerably. Quite obviously, in the early 1970s the bank tried to resume the close ties it had enjoyed during the interwar years with the former US president Herbert Hoover, who was a personal friend of Friedrich H. Neuerbourg, a board member of Commerzbank.

Dresdner Bank, which had also been very active in the US market in the interwar period, did not hesitate for long: only a year later, in 1972, it also opened its own banking branch in New York City (Meyen 1992, 260–277). Besides this Dresdner Bank had tried intensively even some years before to get direct access to the New York Stock Exchange in order to benefit from the broad US capital markets. However this proved to be a very difficult undertaking, because the media condemned it as an immoral demand, unworthy of any serious discussion because Dresdner Bank was notorious among the influential Jewish community of New York for closely cooperating with the Nazi regime. Dresdner Bank was flexible enough to avoid further discussion by shifting from New York to Boston and choosing another, more neutral name for its planned brokerage house. The German-American Securities Corporation (GASC), founded by Dresdner Bank in 1968, was the first Western European bank to become a member of a US stock exchange after World War II. Three years later GASC merged with ABD Securities Corporation in New York, which had been mutually established by Dresdner Bank and the other partners of the ABECOR group, among them Bayerische Hypotheken- und Wechselbank, Banque de Bruxelles S.A. and Algemene Bank Nederland N.V. The ABD Securities Corporation soon became the largest foreign brokerage house in the US, active in New York, Boston, Chicago and Los Angeles, as well as other places.

However, in contrast to Commerzbank and Dresdner Bank, Deutsche Bank did not open a branch of its own in the US until the end of the 1970s, to be exact, until the opening of its New York branch in 1979 (Büschgen 1995, 754–756; M. Pohl 1999; Kobrak 2008, 383–485). Before that, Deutsche Bank's presence in the US market was almost exclusively limited to the 'European-American Banking Corporation' and the 'European-American Bank & Trust Corporation' (called the EABs), two joint ventures founded in 1968 together with Banque de la Société Générale de Belgique (Brussels), Amsterdamsche Bank (Amsterdam), and Midland Bank (London).[7] The three partners of this Western European cooperation, which had been born in 1963 with a rather vague concept of cooperation under the name 'European Advisory Committee', decided in 1970 to set up the EBIC located in Brussels. One year later, in 1971, Creditanstalt Bankverein, Vienna, and Société Générale, Paris, joined the group; in 1973 they were followed by Banca Commerciale Italiana, Rome. The main purpose of this truly extensive and varied, but nevertheless close and dense, partnership network was—besides regular consultation, for instance concerning general security and control issues—to place the services of each bank's organization on the domestic and the international markets at the disposal of the clients of the other partner banks in order to lower the costs of transactions (Fig. 1).

Compared to the Europartners and the ABECOR group, the EBIC seems to have worked relatively successfully, especially in regard to the US market, and by the end of the 1970s, the European-American Banking Corporation

Fig. 1 Meeting of the founders of the EBIC-Group in 1963 (C: Deutsche Bank) (Source: Historische Gesellschaft der Deutschen Bank 2011, p. 130)

as the holding company of the two EABs had become the biggest foreign bank in the US and was among the 25 biggest US-American banks overall. One factor contributing to this success was surely that the EABs did not have to start from scratch. The Banque de la Société Générale de Belgique had brought two of its own subsidiaries to bear in the EABs in 1968: the Belgian-American Banking Corporation and the Belgian-American Bank & Trust Corporation. Additionally, in 1974 the EABs had the opportunity to merge with Franklin National Bank, a retail banking company that went bankrupt but left a network of more than 100 branches throughout the city and suburbs of New York to the new investor. In other words: the EABs took the chance to enter the promising US retail banking sector at relatively high costs, and in the end, this risky investment turned out to be worthwhile. At the beginning of the 1980s, the EABs were active in all fields of banking and were seemingly operating quite successfully, at least more successfully than most of the other European banking clubs that were active in the US financial markets with German participation, for instance, Europartners or ABECOR.[8] However, surprisingly, not much is known about the true reasons for this relative success. Obviously, this has to do with the specific problems of cooperative governance for decision-making processes. At least it seems an appropriate hypothesis for further research to assume that Deutsche Bank and the other partners of EBIC were probably able to cope a little bit better with these specific problems than others.

3 Club Banking: Consequences for Decision-making Processes

Building upon this hypothesis, the next step is to analyse the specific problems that resulted from the cooperative governance of decision-making processes. First the great advantage of club banking and cooperative governance has to be emphasised once again, and while the risks of foreign investments could be shared among the partners there were many disadvantages and problems, too.

First of all: from where should top management and trained staff be found? Within the partner banks themselves, in the respective home countries, or in the labour market of the foreign country targeted by the investment? The problems of recruitment, as well as the problems of different languages, mentalities, political, economic and business cultures (ranging from German universal banking to American investment banking) with all the consequences for internal and external communication had to be considered. Rather formal, time-consuming procedures for the preparation of decisions in all areas of business activities were made inevitable by these circumstances. On the other hand, there was strong pressure to find compromises among the different partners with regard to every single decision to be taken, for instance concerning strategic options, the general organisational structures, and the business and official contacts. Another specific problem of cooperative governance for decision-making was to evaluate exactly which partners contributed to the positive or negative results of their common business activities and to what extent. Club banking always had to cope with the danger of moral hazard and lack of confidence between the partners, who, despite their cooperation, were nonetheless competitors. Club banking imposed self-confining restrictions on the partner banks for their individual decisions and business options; it made them more inflexible *vis-à-vis* prospective business partners of their own in the foreign country. Last but not least, there were growing tensions between the partners of banking clubs because some partners turned to dual strategies earlier than others did.

Further research on the consequences of cooperative governance in banking for decision-making processes will have to take all these general disadvantages and problems into account. Additionally—and turning back to the more theoretical and methodical aspects of decision-making processes—there are a few general research questions that are presumably of great interest for the analysis of specific problems of cooperative governance regarding EBIC and the EABs: Which information did the managers of the EABs and EBIC have at their disposal in particular decision-making situations; how did they make use of this information and how did they communicate their interpretations? Did they use special semantics and narratives? What was the role of personal biographies and company traditions *vis-à-vis* the different partner banks? In particular decision-making situations, did the economic players try to improve the information at their disposal by mobilising additional historical-empirical or scientifically based knowledge?

In what way did the partners simply rely on common experience and mutual trust? What did they do to stabilise mutual trust?

Did they routinely employ certain methods of internal cost controlling, and of monitoring prices and markets? Did they actively search for additional information and, if so, at what cost?

How did the managers of the EABs and EBIC try to adjust themselves to anticipated changes in their relevant markets? Did they rely on procedures that they had rather adaptively practically experienced during the two post-war decades? Did they decide to adopt new techniques of observation, analysis and prognosis in particular situations or from certain points in time? If so, which methods precisely? Can they be categorised as methodologically advanced, i.e. scientifically based techniques? Were these techniques designed to work recursively, in other words, did they make systematic use of the results of former cycles of analysis and prognosis?

Did the managers of the EABs and EBIC ask for external consultants, especially for legal advisers, personnel and management consultants? There are as yet scarcely any empirical studies about the interrelations between newly implemented techniques and procedures and the subsequent restructuring on the one hand and enlisted consultations on the other. However, one can reasonably assume that especially the fictitious content of management consultations—for instance, the mere idea of a completely rational corporate organisation—in itself fulfilled an important goal by creating a basis of fictional assumptions about rationality that made management decisions on strategies and structures possible under very complex conditions.

Can a professionalisation of management in the expectation formation and decision-making processes of the EABs and EBIC be observed? Is there any clear evidence that intuitively employed empirical knowledge of the involved individuals was subsequently and systematically replaced by certain functional equivalents of a more 'rationally' oriented, non-personal, organisational expectation formation? Which new practices and routines of expectation formation for decision-making could be cited as proof?

Did the professionalisation of management and the related change of expectation formation processes ever come up against their own inherent limitations during a corporate crisis? Did the managers of the EABs and EBIC employ a sober, level-headed analysis of the quality of their own expectation formation processes in this situation?

Did the managers of the EABs or EBIC consciously fall back on historical-empirical knowledge, dating farther back or extending into other areas, during or immediately after a crisis? And did they still adhere to the recently introduced professional techniques and procedures, perhaps with the intent of optimising them—despite newly acquired knowledge about their limited scope? In the long run, what consequences did this have for the processes of expectation formation and decision-making overall, not only in the EABs and EBIC but also in the partner banks themselves?

Notes

1. On the origins and early development of the German banking system: Pohl, M. 1986; Tilly 1992a, 1992b, 1994; Fohlin 1999; Burhop 2004; Ziegler 2005.
2. On the post-World War II development of the German banks in general: Tilly 1993a, 2005; Pohl, H. 1998. On the history of the 'Big Three', which has been scrutinized much more intensively for the Nazi period than for the post-World War II period: Gall et al. 1995; James 2001, 2003. – Meyen 1992; Bähr 2006; Ziegler 2006; Wixforth 2006; Henke 2006; Ahrens 2007. – Commerzbank 1994; Krause 2004; Herbst and Weihe 2004; Kreutzmüller 2005; Loose 2007. For a recent overview of the state of the art in German banking history: Sattler 2010b.
3. Cf. 'Gesetz über den Niederlassungsbereich von Kreditinstituten', from March 29 1952.
4. Cf. 'Gesetz zur Aufhebung der Niederlassungsbereiche von Kreditinstituten', from December 24 1956.
5. Together, they increased their total assets from 19.6 billion DM in 1957 to 38.5 billion DM in 1965, 143.9 billion DM in 1975 and 324.3 billion DM in 1985. Cf. Monthly Reports of Deutsche Bundesbank for 1957, 1965, 1975, and 1985.

6. Between the early 1970s and 1988 the market shares of foreign banks in West Germany doubled, but did not exceed four percent of the total volume of business. In 1988 there were 280 foreign banks from 50 different countries operating in West Germany. Most of these banks came from the US, Japan and Switzerland. Cf. 'Die Wettbewerbsposition der deutschen Universalbanken im europäischen Binnenmarkt', manuscript of a speech delivered by Alfred Herrhausen (CEO of Deutsche Bank) at the Banking Colloquium of the Johann Wolfgang Goethe-University Frankfurt on the Main, on December 21 1988, in: Historical Archives of Deutsche Bank [HADB] V 30/11.
7. In 1972, Schweizerische Bankgesellschaft and Deutsche Bank cofounded the brokerage house UBS-DB Corporation located in New York. Only when Deutsche Bank acquired the full majority of shares and in 1978 renamed the UBS-DB Corporation, calling it the Atlantic Capital Corporation, did the bank participate directly on its own behalf in the US market.
8. On their further development: Historical Archives of Deutsche Bank (HADB), V 30/416-424, 1109-1254.

References

Ahrens, R. (2007). *Die Dresdner Bank 1945-1957, Konsequenzen und Kontinuitäten nach dem Ende des NS-Regimes*. Munich: Oldenbourg.

Ahrens, R., & Wixforth, H. (Eds.). (2010). *Strukturwandel und Internationalisierung im Bankwesen seit den 1950er Jahren*. Stuttgart: Franz Steiner.

Akerlof, G. A., & Shiller, R. J. (2009). *Animal spirits. How human psychology drives the economy, and why it matters for global capitalism*. Princeton University Press: Princeton.

Bähr, J. (2006). *Die Dresdner Bank in der Wirtschaft des Dritten Reichs*. Munich: Oldenbourg.

Beckert, J. (2013). Imagined futures: Fictional expectations in the economy. *Theory and Society, 42*, 219–240.

Biervert, B., & Wieland, J. (1990). Gegenstandsbereich und Rationalitätsform der Ökonomie und der Ökonomik. In: B. Biervert, K. Held, & J. Wieland (Eds.), *Sozialphilosophische Grundlagen ökonomischen Handelns* (pp. 7–32). Frankfurt: Suhrkamp.

Burhop, C. (2004). *Die Kreditbanken in der Gründerzeit*. Stuttgart: Franz Steiner.

Büschgen, H. E. (1995). Die Deutsche Bank von 1957 bis zur Gegenwart. Aufstieg zum internationalen Finanzdienstleistungskonzern. In: L. Gall et al. (Eds.), *Die Deutsche Bank 1870–1995* (pp. 579–877). München: C.H. Beck.

Commerzbank (Ed.) (1994). *Die Bank—Dienstleister im Wandel. 125 Jahre Commerzbank. 1870–1995*. Frankfurt: Fritz Knapp.

Fohlin, C. (1999). Universal banking in Pre-World War I Germany. Model or myth? *Explorations in Economic History, 36*, 305–343.

Frost, R. (2009). *Wünsche werden Wirklichkeit. Die Deutsche Bank und ihr Privatkundengeschäft*. Munich: Piper.

Gall, L. (2004). *Der Bankier Hermann Josef Abs. Eine Biographie*. Munich: C.H. Beck.

Gall, L., et al. (Eds.). (1995). *Die Deutsche Bank 1870–1995*. Munich: C.H. Beck.

Gigerenzer, G. (2008). *Rationality for mortals. How people cope with uncertainty*. New York: Oxford University Press.

Gigerenzer, G., & Selten, R. (Eds.). (2001). *Bounded rationality. The adaptive toolbox*. Cambridge: Massachusetts Institute of Technology Press.

Hartkopf, C. (2000). *Die Geschäftspolitik amerikanischer Banken in Deutschland, 1960–1990*. Frankfurt: Peter Lang.

Henke, K. D. (2006). *Die Dresdner Bank 1933–1945. Ökonomische Rationalität, Regimenähe, Mittäterschaft*. Munich: Oldenbourg.

Herbst, L., & Weihe, T. (Eds.). (2004). *Die Commerzbank und die Juden 1933–1945*. Munich: C.H. Beck.

Historische Gesellschaft der Deutschen Bank. (2011). *Deutsche Bank 1870–2010*. Munich: Piper.

Institut für bankhistorische Forschung. (1994). *Cooperation and competition of the European banks since the middle of the 19th century*. Frankfurt: Fritz Knapp.

Institut für bankhistorische Forschung. (2003). *Internationalisierungsstrategien von Kreditinstituten*. Stuttgart: Franz Steiner.

James, H. (2001). *Die Deutsche Bank und die "Arisierung"*. Munich: C.H. Beck.

James, H. (2003). *Die Deutsche Bank im Dritten Reich*. Munich: C.H. Beck.

Kahneman, D. (2011). *Thinking, fast and slow*. New York: Farrar, Straus and Giroux.

Kahneman, D., & Tversky, A. (1979). Prospect theory: An analysis of decision under risk. *Econometrica, XVLII*, 263–291.

Karafyllis, N. C., & Schmidt, J. C. (Eds.). (2002). *Zugänge zur Rationalität der Zukunft*. Stuttgart: J.B. Metzler.

Kobrak, C. (2008). *Die Deutsche Bank und die USA. Geschäft und Politik von 1870 bis heute.* C.H. Beck: Munich.

Koselleck, R. (1979). *Vergangene Zukunft. Zur Semantik geschichtlicher Zeit.* Frankfurt: Suhrkamp.

Krause, D. (2003). Die Auslandsniederlassungen der Commerzbank von 1870 bis in die 1960er Jahre. *Bankhistorisches Archiv, 29* (1), 25–46.

Krause, D. (2004). *Die Commerz- und Disconto-Bank 1870–1920/23.* Stuttgart: Franz Steiner.

Kreutzmüller, C. (2005). *Händler und Handlungsgehilfen. Der Finanzplatz Amsterdam und die deutschen Großbanken 1918–1945.* Stuttgart: Franz Steiner.

Loose, I. (2007). *Kredite für NS-Verbrechen. Die deutschen Kreditinstitute in Polen und die Ausraubung der polnischen und jüdischen Bevölkerung 1939–1945.* Munich: Oldenbourg.

Luhmann, N. (2002). *Einführung in die Systemtheorie.* Heidelberg: Carl-Auer.

Luhmann, N. (2011, 3rd ed.). *Organisation und Entscheidung.* Opladen: Verlag für Sozialwissenschaften.

Meyen, H. G. (1992). *120 Jahre Dresdner Bank. Unternehmens-Chronik 1872 bis 1992.* Frankfurt: Dresdner Bank.

Plumpe, W. (2004a). Die Neue Institutionenökonomik und die moderne Wirtschaft. Zur wirtschaftshistorischen Reichweite institutionenökonomischer Argumente am Beispiel des Handlungsmodells der Rationalität. In: C. Wischermann & K.-P. Ellerbrock (Eds.), *Die Wirtschaftsgeschichte vor der Herausforderung durch die New Institutional Economics* (pp. 31–57). Münster: Ardey.

Plumpe, W. (2004b). Perspektiven der Unternehmensgeschichte. In: G. Schulz et al. (Eds.), *Sozial- und Wirtschaftsgeschichte. Arbeitsgebiete, Probleme, Perspektiven* (pp. 403–425). Stuttgart: Franz Steiner.

Plumpe, W. (2007). Die Geburt des „Homo oeconomicus'. Historische Überlegungen zur Entstehung und Bedeutung des Handlungsmodells der modernen Wirtschaft. In: W. Reinhard & J. Stagl (Eds.), *Menschen und Märkte. Studien zur historischen Wirtschaftsanthropologie* (pp. 319–352). Vienna: Böhlau.

Plumpe, W. (2009). Ökonomisches Denken und wirtschaftliche Entwicklung. Zum Zusammenhang von Wirtschaftsgeschichte und historischer Semantik der Ökonomie. *Jahrbuch für Wirtschaftsgeschichte/Economic History Yearbook, 50* (1), 27–52.

Pohl, M. (1986). *Entstehung und Entwicklung des Universalbanksystems.* Frankfurt: Fritz Knapp.
Pohl, H. (Ed.). (1998). *Geschichte der deutschen Kreditwirtschaft seit 1945.* Frankfurt: Fritz Knapp.
Pohl, M. (1999). Die Deutsche Bank in den Vereinigten Staaten 1870–1999. In: Ibidem (Ed.), *Zur deutschen und amerikanischen Identität: Die Deutsche Bank in den USA* (pp. 57–77). Munich: Piper.
Ramm, U. (2002). German banks and the American challenge. In: S. Battilossi & Y. Cassis (Eds.), *European banks and the American challenge. Competition and cooperation in international banking under Bretton Woods* (pp. 177–199). Oxford: Oxford University Press.
Regul, R., & Wolf, H. (Eds.). (1974). *Das Bankwesen im größeren Europa.* Baden-Baden: Nomos.
Roberts, R., & Arnander, C. (2001). *Take your partners. Orion, the consortium banks and the transformation of the Euromarkets.* Basingstoke: Palgrave Macmillan.
Ross, D. M. (1998). European banking clubs in the 1960s: A flawed strategy. *Business and Economic History, 27*(2), 353–366.
Sattler, F. (2010a). *Animal spirits and the beginning of market research activities of West German Banks.* Paper for the 14th EBHA-conference, University of Glasgow, 26–28.8.2010. http://www.gla.ac.uk/media/media_168373_en.pdf
Sattler, F. (2010b). Geschichte der Banken und Finanzmärkte, Version: 1.0. In: *Docupedia-Zeitgeschichte,* 27.7.2010. https://docupedia.de/zg/Geschichte_der_Banken_und_Finanzm.C3.A4rkte?oldid=75714. Accessed 3 Dec 2015.
Scott, J. W. (1994). The evidence of experience. In: J. Chandler (Ed.), *Questions of evidence, proof, practice, and persuasion across the disciplines* (pp. 363–387). Chicago: University of Chicago Press.
Seefried, E. (2015). *Zukünfte. Aufstieg und Krise der Zukunftsforschung 1945–1980.* Berlin: De Gruyter Oldenbourg.
Steinke, K. (2000). *Die Internationalisierung britischer, französischer und deutscher Kreditinstitute aus historischer Sicht. Von der industriellen Revolution bis zur Gegenwart.* Aachen: Shaker.
Steuber, U. (1974). *Internationale Banken. Auslandsaktivitäten von Banken bedeutender Industrieländer.* Hamburg: Weltarchiv.
Steuber, U. (1977). *Internationale Bankenkooperation. Deutsche Banken in Internationalen Gruppen. Europartners, Ebic, SFE/Abecor, Orion.* Frankfurt: Fritz Knapp.

Tanner, J. (2004). "Kultur" in den Wirtschaftswissenschaften und kulturwissenschaftliche Interpretationen ökonomischen Handelns. In: F. Jaeger & J. Rüsen (Eds.), *Handbuch der Kulturwissenschaften, Volume 3: Themen und Tendenzen* (pp. 195–224). Stuttgart: J.B. Metzler.

Thaler, R. H. (Ed.). (1994). *Quasi-Rational economics*. New York: Russell Sage Foundation.

Tilly, R. H. (1992a). An overview on the role of the large German banks up to 1914. In: Y. Cassis (Ed.), *Finance and financiers in European history, 1880–1960* (pp. 93–112). Cambridge: Cambridge University Press.

Tilly, R. H. (1992b). Zur Entwicklung der deutschen Großbanken als Universalbanken im 19. und 20. Jahrhundert. Wachstumsmotor oder Machtkartell? In: S. Pollard & D. Ziegler (Eds.), *Markt, Staat, Planung. Historische Erfahrungen mit Regulierungs- und Deregulierungsversuchen der Wirtschaft* (pp. 128–156). St. Katharinen: Winkel Stiftung.

Tilly, R. H. (1993a). Geschäftsbanken und Wirtschaft in Westdeutschland seit dem Zweiten Weltkrieg. In: E. Schremmer (Ed.), *Geld und Währung vom 16. Jahrhundert bis zur Gegenwart* (pp. 315–344). Stuttgart: Franz Steiner.

Tilly, R. H. (1993b). The internationalization of West German banks, 1945–87. In: G. Jones & G. Schröter (Eds.), *The rise of multinationals in Continental Europe* (pp. 173–183). Aldershot: Edward Elgar Publishing.

Tilly, R. H. (1994). A short history of the German banking system. In: M. Pohl (Ed.), *Handbook on the history of European banks* (pp. 299–312). Aldershot: Edward Elgar Publishing.

Tilly, R. H. (2005). Trust and mistrust: Banks, giant debtors, and enterprise crises in Germany, 1960–2002. *Jahrbuch für Wirtschaftsgeschichte / Economic History Yearbook 46*(1), 107–135.

Wixforth, H. (2006). *Die Expansion der Dresdner Bank in Europa*. Munich: Oldenbourg.

Wixforth, H. (2010). "Global Players" im "Europäischen Haus"? Die Expansionsstrategie deutscher Großbanken nach 1945. In: R. Ahrens & H. Wixforth (Eds.), *Strukturwandel und Internationalisierung im Bankwesen seit den 1950er Jahren* (pp. 97–120). Stuttgart: Franz Steiner.

Ziegler, D. (2005). Das deutsche Modell bankorientierter Finanzsysteme (1848–1957). In: P. Windolf (Ed.), *Finanzmarkt-Kapitalismus. Analysen zum Wandel von Produktionsregimen* (pp. 276–293). Wiesbaden: Verlag für Sozialwissenschaften.

Ziegler, D. (2006). *Die Dresdner Bank und die deutschen Juden*. Munich: Oldenbourg.

Part II

Second Part: Risk Management Techniques

Minimising Risk: Financial Intermediaries and Bond Issuing in London before the Great War

Anders L. Mikkelsen

1 Dark Clouds over the London Stock Markets

> *The City is becoming enveloped deeper and deeper in a baleful mysterious crisis: Day by day thick clouds gather over the Stock Markets, and where they come from, or who is responsible for them, no one has a definite opinion. … Men have got accustomed to whisper to each other ominously, 'There is trouble in the Air'.*[1]

Thus, the Financial Times described the atmosphere in London's financial district on November 15, 1890, the result of over a month of persistent negative rumours centring on the market for the bonds of the River Plate.[2] During the preceding years of boom market conditions for Latin American securities, Argentina alone was estimated to have borrowed an

A.L. Mikkelsen (✉)
BH-DG Systematic Trading LLP and ICBH, King's College London, London, UK
e-mail: anders.mikkelsen@kcl.ac.uk

K. Schönhärl (ed.), *Decision Taking, Confidence and Risk Management in Banks from Early Modernity to the 20th Century*,
DOI 10.1007/978-3-319-42076-9_5

astonishing £90–£100 million in Europe.[3] It was a publicly held secret that part of this sum had not been successfully placed with the investing public but instead was held by the issuing houses that had sponsored the issues. The falling price made it impossible for firms to realise the capital locked up in such bonds and it was whispered that they now hung around the necks of certain unnamed firms like millstones.[4]

The same day, the news broke that 'one of our most respected and leading English houses was compelled to seek outside assistance' and that the Bank of England and the leading firms of the City had arranged a guarantee fund.[5] The house in question was, of course, Baring Brothers & Co, and the fate of this firm was a potent reminder of the dangers associated with issuing bonds without effective methods of dealing with the risks involved. The firm became the most prominent casualty of developments in the international bond market in the 1880s, a decade that had seen issuing houses facing greater competition and risk without a matching development in their techniques for dealing with these new challenges. This chapter will analyse the development of market practices and techniques used by London issuing houses to minimise or eliminate risks associated with issuing sovereign bonds in London in the decades leading up to the Great War. It will analyse how issuing houses reacted to the new challenges they faced due to increasing competition from the 1880s, and how this development was influenced by wider reputational concerns and shocks like the Baring Crisis.

2 The 1880s: A Brave New World of Increased Competition

The international issuing business became far more competitive over the course of the 1880s. Paris re-emerged as an international centre for new sovereign issues following a hiatus caused by the Franco-Prussian War and the subsequent indemnity, and Berlin appeared as a real competitor to London and Paris (Crick and Wadsworth 1964, 308; Klovland 2004, 6, 8–11; Bussière 1992, 3–4; Cassis 2006, 108–110, 113; Pohl 1977, 81–124).[6] London's issuing houses also faced increased competition domestically, as British joint-stock banks started more forcefully challenging the traditional monopoly of merchant banks in the sovereign loan business and foreign banks opened agencies or branches in the City. The impetus for this foreign presence in London was the attraction of the London money market, but it also enabled foreign banks to issue bonds directly in London (Suzuki 1994, 31–44; Pohl and Burk 1998, 13–22, 30–37, 39–41).

Traditionally, governments had confined negotiations for new loans to their usual London bankers and only sought out alternatives if rebuffed here, since shopping around might give the impression that the country was desperate (Jenks 1938, 272–274; Marichal 2011, 81–82). Emboldened by the knowledge that any proposed loan would likely be met with interest from several different houses and financial centres, some countries abandoned this approach in the 1880s. Instead, they invited issuing houses to compete in a process of open bidding or initiated negotiations with several houses simultaneously, allowing them to play houses off against each other (Marichal 2011, 82; Young 1990, 12, 30).[7] Earlier, borrowing countries had refrained from inviting competition out of fear that unsuccessful bidders would talk down the issue (Jenks 1938, 273–274). However, this concern was no longer as pressing because continental banks, in contrast to their English competitors, were willing to buy entire issues outright ahead of the public offering, known as taking it 'firm'. By taking an issue firm, an issuing house assumed the underwriting risk associated with the issue, meaning that the issuing house would be left holding any bonds not taken up by the investing public.[8]

For sovereign bonds issued in London before the mid-1880s, the underwriting risk was normally borne principally or fully by the borrowing government. Especially first-class firms, who until the mid-1880s were often in a relatively strong position to influence the terms upon which they agreed to manage an issue, rarely agreed to assume any share of the underwriting risk (Mikkelsen 2014, Chapter 3). This was perfectly understandable, as the relative size of most sovereign issues and the capital of London issuing houses meant that taking a bond issue firm could mean staking the future of the house on its success (Ferguson 1998, 1043–44).[9] The greater willingness of continental banks to assume the underwriting risk associated with a new issue can be explained by their greater capital, compared with most London issuing houses, making them better able to withstand any potential losses (Suzuki 1994, 43). Moreover, the French Banque de Dépôts were, to an extent, able to lay off this risk, by distributing bonds to their own customers, who generally relied on the banks for investment advice—something which was not possible in London, where issuing houses did not possess the same in-house brokerage capacity (Suzuki 1994, 213–214, note 63; Michie 1988, 63). Given the option, governments naturally preferred the guarantee that they would receive their money irrespective of the success of an issue. According to Marichal and Flores, it was offering to take issues firm that enabled French banks to secure mandates for new Argentine issues ahead of the country's traditional London bankers in the early 1880s (Marichal 2011, 82; Flores 2010, 139, 143). The willingness to incur this risk thus gave the continental banks a competitive advantage and left London houses with little choice but to follow suit—forcing them to find ways of dealing with the new reality of increased competition and heightened underwriting risk (Mikkelsen 2014, Chapter 3).

3 Competition and Reputational Risk

Increased competition also potentially increased the reputational risk incurred by issuing houses when sponsoring new issues, because it weakened their ability to act as effective gatekeepers to the market. Reputation was the most important attribute that a house had when bringing out a new bond issue and whenever a firm sponsored a new issue, to some extent it risked its reputation by lending its standing in the market to the new offering. If an issue proved expensive for the investing public, it could, therefore, have serious reputational repercussions for the responsible issuing house (Withers 1948, 116–117).[10] Therefore, London houses traditionally took into account the long-term interest of a country's credit, and thereby the interest of investors, when assessing the merits of a proposed new issue, safeguarding their own reputations in the process. It was not uncommon for a firm to seek to dissuade a client from making an issue, or in some cases even to outright refuse the client if a proposed issue was considered unwise.[11] The ability of issuing houses to influence the borrowing of clients in this way was, nevertheless, significantly curtailed by competition. In a highly competitive environment, a cautious house could quickly find itself replaced by a more aggressive competitor and a change of issuing house would be less likely to cause concern among investors. A house could therefore easily find itself having to choose between the certain loss of prestige and income associated with the loss of a client and the reputational and financial risk associated with sponsoring an issue that might not prove a complete success. As Flores has argued, it was the erosion of the gatekeeping function of issuing houses which resulted in the accelerated pace of Argentine borrowing in the 1880s and ultimately contributed to bringing down Barings in 1890 (Flores 2010, 130).[12] Competition was thus a major risk factor for issuing houses and one that they did their best to minimise.

4 Dealing with Competition

Financial intermediaries in the pre-1914 period at times used highly restrictive market practices to achieve this objective, practices that today would not be permissible on political and regulatory grounds. Even before the increased competition of the 1880s, London houses had developed a variety of methods to reduce the threat of competition. One such method was to insert a clause in contracts that prohibited governments from making other issues or negotiating with other houses until the final instalment of the current issue had been paid. Since instalments were often spread over a period of close to a year, this could be a very effective short-term method of excluding rivals and ensuring an inside track in future negotiations, if it was believed that the government would have to return to the market within a relatively short period of time. In the early 1870s, when Russia was borrowing at a frantic pace, Rothschilds successfully used such clauses to side-line rivals and achieve an effective monopoly on new Russian government issues.[13] This method nevertheless had two obvious drawbacks. Firstly, it depended on the willingness of governments to accept such clauses, something they would have been unlikely to accept if they believed they could benefit from competition in connection with further issues. Secondly, even if the government agreed to such a clause, it would merely provide temporary relief from competition and was only effective if a client had recourse to the market on a nearly annual basis. The limited utility of this practice was clearly demonstrated by the fact that Rothschilds' success in using such clauses to stave off competition in connection with the Russian bond issues of the 1870s was not replicated by other houses, or by Rothschilds themselves, in the period up to 1914.[14]

The practices of issuing houses coming to mutually beneficial understandings and splitting the world into areas of interest, with individual countries considered as the exclusive preserve of a particular house, were more prevalent and enduring. In 1902, Lord Revelstoke made it clear that, as far as Barings was concerned, 'it is understood, of course, that the preserves of Brazil and Chile will be respected as belonging to our noble friends in New Court' (quoted in Ziegler 1988, 303). This was an understanding that was part of a gentleman's agreement, which also saw Rothschilds respecting Argentina as the preserve of Barings (Young 1990, 5, note 11). Schroders similarly refused '[to] compete or to appear to compete in any way' with Barings for an Argentine mandate in 1911, as the house saw that country as Barings' territory.[15] Even after Barings had lost the mandate and Schroders were asked to handle the issue in London as an agent of a foreign syndicate, they responded, 'it would be disagreeable to them to be publicly connected with a business which up till the present had been associated with [Barings]'.[16] Such agreements had the distinct advantage of not requiring the cooperation of borrowers and could be a very effective way to eliminate competition between established houses. In some cases, they were also respected by other houses where no direct *quid pro quo* existed, due to long-standing relationships in other areas of business. However, in general, such understandings offered no protection from newcomers who had little incentive to respect such arrangements (Joslin 1963, 142; Young 1992, 37, note 13). This is clearly evidenced by the rampant competition for Argentine mandates in the 1880s and Deutsche Bank's success in securing the mandate for the 1887 Chilean issue from under the nose of Rothschilds.[17]

Another method used by issuing houses throughout the period was paying for 'backstairs influence', that is, giving influential people a pecuniary incentive to further the case of the issuing house in securing a mandate.[18] The Brazilian minister in London from 1855–1889 admitted receiving profitable investment advice and no less than £200,000 in gifts from Rothschilds during his tenure (equivalent to about £19 million today) (Graham 1968, 101–102).[19] This practice was by no means limited to New Court, as there are also examples of Barings rewarding influential people through preferential allotment or even indirect payments in connection with Argentine loans.[20] As with exclusivity clauses and informal agreements, buying 'backstairs influence' nevertheless had a significant limitation when it came to preventing competition. After all, similar arrangements could be made by rival houses, making it a useless but expensive provision.

5 Syndicates as a Means of Dealing with Competition

There was nevertheless one practice as old as the issuing business itself which had the potential to act as an effective countermeasure—turning competitors into collaborators by joining forces in an issuing syndicate. Syndicates were a traditional tool for dividing underwriting risk in the minority of sovereign issues where London houses had taken all or part of loans firm before the 1880s, and some houses had also previously used collaboration as a means of avoiding direct competition. Nevertheless, two factors had significantly limited their use before the 1880s and slowed the adoption and development of issuing syndicates into an effective countermeasure to increased competition during this decade. Firstly, London houses generally disliked this form of collaboration, as it meant sharing the prestige and financial rewards accruing from an issue (Chapman 1984, 156–157). Secondly, there was a potential reputational cost associated with the use of any form of syndicate, as in the public mind, they were inextricably linked with sharp practice, indeed at best, or perhaps at worst, with fraud. However, in spite of such concerns, London issuing houses increasingly turned to issuing syndicates as a means of dealing with competition as well as underwriting risk as the 1880s progressed (Mikkelsen 2014, 67–68).

The use of issuing syndicates in connection with Argentine bond issues shows the gradual development of such syndicates as a method of dealing with competition. In the early 1880s, there was normally no collaboration among London houses or with foreign banks in order to minimise the competition for mandates. Collaboration only ensued once the mandate had been awarded, as when a number of City firms acted as the London agents of the French syndicate that won the mandates for the 1881, 1882 and 1884 Argentine issues (Regalsky 1987, 79; Flores 2010, 141, note 54).[21] It was not until later in 1884 that Barings and J.S. Morgan & Co. joined forces with the (slightly changed) French syndicate, secured the mandate for the later aborted Argentine Public Works Loan, and in 1885 also concluded a deal to manage an £8.4 million bond issue brought out in 1886–87. However, in the second half of the 1880s competition again intensified with the emergence of German banks as serious competitors for the business of the Argentine Republic. Two French-German syndicates secured mandates in 1887, the larger of which was issued in London through Barings in the capacity of agent for the syndicate. It was not until the end of the Argentine borrowing frenzy in 1889 that an international syndicate with representatives from Britain, France and Germany was formed to bring out an Argentine conversion loan (Flores 2010, 141–144).[22]

The 1880s did not see the emergence of a stable constellation of London, French and German issuing houses to form a standing issuing syndicate that would collaborate from start to finish in connection with all Argentine issues. Therefore, issuing houses were not able to regain the role of effective gatekeepers during that decade and could exert little effective influence to limit the frantic pace of borrowing that brought the country and Barings to grief in 1890. However, when Argentina returned as a major borrower in European markets in the first decade of the twentieth century, the country's bankers, and above all the reconstituted Barings, had learned their lesson. Determined to avoid free-for-all competition, the leading British, French and German firms with interests in Argentine issues combined to form a standing international syndicate that would negotiate as one with the Argentine government for all future government bond issues up to 1914.[23] When new competitors emerged and were perceived as strong enough to form the nucleus of a serious rival syndicate, they were invited to join the syndicate, as happened with Dresdner Bank in 1905 and Crédit Lyonnais and J. P. Morgan & Co in 1908 (Young 1990, 18–20).[24] Such collaboration was not only considered to be in the interest of the bankers but was also seen as being of benefit for Argentine credit and the investing public. As Barings explained to the Disconto Gesellschaft in 1908:

The continued existence of the old group has the advantage of eliminating undue competition in Buenos Aires and giving us all, as sponsors to our respective public, a better chance of preventing any recurrence of the extravagancies of the late eighties.[25]

The heavy losses suffered by investors because of these extravagancies also appears to have changed how the market viewed the use of issuing syndicates. In the late 1880s, issuing houses still risked being criticised for collaborating, with The Statist in 1888 lamenting how issuing syndicates reduced the extent to which individual houses were liable both in purse and in reputation for what was done.[26] However, after the turn of the century, issuing syndicates became an accepted bond market practice, with collaboration by issuing houses seen as a distinct advantage for the investing public. Ahead of a prospective Argentine issue in 1911, The Standard argued that:

[W]e may rest assured that the European and American Bankers.... will not bid against each other. They will agree as to the best terms that can be offered and probably Messrs. Baring Brothers will alone tender for the loan on behalf of the syndicate, without fear of competition by outsiders.[27]

The history of Chinese bond issues strongly supports the idea that it was the experience of free-for-all competition in the late 1880s that made London issuing houses realise the need to combine in syndicates in order to minimise the risk of competition. Since the 1870s, the issuing of Chinese government bonds had been the preserve of The Hong Kong and Shanghai Bank (the Hong Kong Bank) but from the mid-1880s, both domestic and foreign competitors were anxious to break into the market for Chinese issues. To this end, in 1885, Rothschilds suggested a collaboration between Rothschilds, the Hong Kong Bank and a group of German banks but, as King has argued, this suggestion was premature, as the Hong Kong Bank was not interested in such an arrangement. Yet a decade later in 1895, the Hong Kong Bank struck a deal with Deutsch-Asiatische Bank (on behalf of a German syndicate), very similar to that which had been proposed in 1885 (King 1987, 556–558; Pohl 1977, 122). The deal was sealed with a contract that bound the two parties to collaborate rather than compete in connection with any potential Chinese mandates. That this agreement was a means to avoid competition is supported by the fact that if either party wished to break the arrangement, it would have to give at least one year's notice. Furthermore, the agreement also included explicit provisions for the future expansion of the syndicate. Each party had the right to expand its domestic syndicates with such expansions not affecting the share of the business held by the German and London syndicates respectively. In contrast, the inclusion of banks from any third country would be the result of an agreement whereby each party would cede an equal share of their participation in the syndicate to the third party.[28] During the next two decades the syndicate grew drastically and by 1912 it consisted of no less than five London houses in addition to various German, French, American, Japanese and Russian banks.[29] The collaboration through this syndicate along with the incorporation of potential competitors was likely a crucial factor in enabling the Hong Kong Bank to continue to dominate Chinese bond issues in the London market despite the increasingly competitive nature of the issuing business.[30]

Collaboration, in the form of standing syndicates, did not eliminate competition completely, as evidenced by the Argentine and Chinese syndicates losing mandates to competitors in 1911 and 1912 respectively.[31] However, competing with an established syndicate could be a very risky proposition, not least because the decision of a government to dispense with the services of the strong international syndicate normally associated with its issues could not fail to raise questions.[32] This was an expensive lesson learned by the rival syndicate that secured the 1911 Argentine mandate by offering the government terms that the Barings syndicate was unwilling to match and later found that they were unable to sell the bonds in the market.[33] Successful challenges to the hegemony of large international standing syndicates were quite rare, and collaboration in such syndicates offered a substantial degree of protection from competition. As a result, standing syndicates were largely able to act as effective gatekeepers to European capital markets and exert significant influence over the borrowing policy of their clients, in the interests of the long-term credit of the country, the investing public and syndicate members.[34]

6 Dealing with Underwriting Risk

Issuing syndicates proved to be an effective method of dealing with increased competition but it was a less than perfect solution for dealing with the underwriting risk incurred by issuing houses when taking an issue firm. Any reduction in underwriting risk came with the sacrifice of a commensurate share of the prestige and profit associated with an issue. It did not bring financial intermediaries closer to separating the prestigious and profitable role of issuer from the risky role of underwriter. Before the 1880s, issuing houses had, on rare occasions, formed separate syndicates to guarantee the success of a bond issue, a practice very similar to the underwriting groups that would become common in London in the twenty years leading up to 1914. However, underwriting bore even more of a public stigma than the use of issuing syndicates, as evidenced by one journalist introducing a partial defence of the practice in 1878 by stating that: 'It is by no means clear to me that a syndicate which 'underwrites' a foreign loan is necessarily an assemblage of thieves.'[35] That public perception of underwriting had not dramatically changed by the early 1890s is shown by The Bankers' Magazine's derogatory description of underwriting in 1892 as 'a regular branch of the company promoter's art'.[36] Public knowledge that an underwriting group had been organised in connection with an issue might therefore significantly damage the reputation of the responsible issuing house.

Owing to this reputational risk, issuing houses in the 1880s primarily relied on a more discreet method of subcontracting underwriting risk to other parties. This took the form of offering their 'friends' among other issuing houses a participation in the issue as silent partners (Cottrell 2012, 505).[37] Such participations will here be referred to as 'red list participations' following The Bankers' Magazine, which in 1892 reported that houses like Barings kept 'red lists' containing the names of the friends to which they offered such participations.[38] Red list participations allowed issuing houses to outsource part of the underwriting risk associated with an issue without having to share the prestige of the issue, and the discreet nature of the practice protected them from public criticism. The extent to which this practice allowed issuing houses to divest themselves of the underwriting risk associated with an issue was, nevertheless, limited by the practice being largely confined to a narrow circle of other issuing houses—an Achilles heel brutally exposed by the Baring Crisis of 1890.

In spite of Barings stretching the red list participations to the limit and serving their friends with what The Bankers' Magazine described as an 'indigestible feast' of securities, the house still ended up with £4.16 million in unsold Argentine securities, which by October 1890 hung as a millstone around the firm's neck (Ziegler 1988, 242, 244–245).[39] Even though it was realised that Barings had been imprudent, the embarrassment of Barings likely sent a shiver down the spine of every issuing house in the City (Ford 1956, 134–135; Ziegler 1988, 246).[40] Barings was far from the only house that was weighed down by unsold securities in the late 1880s, with The Statist arguing in July 1889, 'the great houses ... were already carrying a load [of unsold securities] almost as large as they could safely manage'.[41] Other issuing houses would therefore undoubtedly have taken heed. The crisis highlighted the possible consequences of taking loans firm without having recourse to an effective way of outsourcing the underwriting risk.

This lesson caused issuing houses to brush aside reputational concerns and expand the existing system of red list participations into a more formalised practice of forming underwriting groups. These became increasingly common from the mid-1890s and allowed for a wider group of participants and a greater dissemination of underwriting risk.[42] Members of these underwriting groups would each guarantee the placement of a certain part of the issue in exchange for an underwriting commission of normally between one and three percent. If the issue was fully taken up by the public this commission could be pocketed as profit, but if not the underwriters would take up a pro-rata share of the unsold bonds (Singleton 1928, 9, 11).[43] The more formal nature of underwriting groups allowed the inclusion of stockbrokers (and their clients) as well as institutional investors, which drastically expanded the capital available for underwriting. It also meant that underwriting risk could easily be spread to such an extent that no individual member of the underwriting group had to accept a participation that could in any way tie its continued financial solvency to the success of the loan (Cassis 1987, 120; Supple 1970, 332).[44] This in turn effectively allowed the risk to be assessed, priced and traded as a financial commodity in its own right. In fact, underwriting participations came to be in such high demand that after the turn of the century issuing houses often struggled to meet demand and could limit their own exposure to whatever degree they might desire.[45]

While the growing use of underwriting groups by reputable houses undoubtedly made the practice more accepted from the mid-1890s onwards, it continued to be viewed with some suspicion, with The Economist defending it in 1911 as being of distinct advantage when it was not abused.[46] Its acceptance is nevertheless evidenced by the fact that in spite of Lord Rothschild's reported sceptical attitude, Rothschilds started using underwriting routinely in its issues from around 1905.[47] In fact, by the end of the first decade of the twentieth century, the use of underwriting had become the norm to such an extent that choosing not to have an issue underwritten was in itself newsworthy.[48]

7 Conclusion

This chapter demonstrates how London issuing houses developed methods of respectively minimising and eliminating two risk factors which emerged to threaten their business as a result of the increasingly competitive climate of the 1880s. To negate the effects of competition, including the erosion of the ability of issuing houses to act as effective gatekeepers, issuing houses started collaborating in issuing syndicates. In the last two decades before the Great War, this practice developed into the establishment of large standing international syndicates that negotiated as one in connection with all new issues of the country with which they were concerned. This enabled such syndicates to safeguard their client's long-term credit and thereby the interests of the investing public and the reputations of the participating issuing houses.

Issuing houses also developed methods of distributing the underwriting risk associated with new issues, which competition forced them to assume from the 1880s. An initial system of red list participations was developed into a more formal system of underwriting groups which allowed the inclusion of stockbrokers (and their clients) and institutional investors as well as other issuing houses. The result was a system of underwriting that allowed risk to be widely distributed, which in turn transformed how underwriting risk was viewed. Early on it was regarded as a distinct liability to be avoided, but was later effectively transformed into a valuable financial commodity that issuing houses could allocate as a reward to their friends and clients.

It is nevertheless also clear that market conservatism could have a retarding effect on the development of methods for minimising risk. Both the widespread use of issuing syndicates and the development of underwriting groups were held back by the reputational risk associated with their use, a risk that arose from the negative public perception of the two types of syndicates. In the end, the retarding effect of these reputational concerns was only fully overcome when the Baring Crisis laid bare the dangers to issuing houses of unbridled competition and an inefficient method of dealing with underwriting risk.

Primary Sources

Archives

Baring Archive (BA)
HSBC Archive
London Metropolitan Archive (LMA)
Rothschild Archive London (RAL)

Newspapers and Magazines

Truth
The Bankers' Magazine
The Economist
The Financial Times

The New York Times
The Standard
The Statist
The Times

Parliamentary Reports

Report from the Select Committee on Loans to Foreign States; (House of Commons, 1875)

Notes

1. "The Agony", The Financial Times, November 15, 1890.
2. "The Money Market", The Times, October 16 and November 15, 1890. "The Agony", The Financial Times, November 15, 1890.
3. "Argentine Borrowing", The Statist, September 28, 1889.
4. "The Great Houses", The Statist, July 27, 1889. "The Requirements of Argentine Finance", The Economist, November 8, 1890. "The Agony", The Financial Times, November 15, 1890.
5. "The Money Market", The Times, November 15, 1890.
6. "The Rush of New Foreign Loans", The Economist, December 27, 1873. London Metropolitan Archive (LMA) MS19,063/19, Hambros to Gapelet, April 9, 1878. LMA MS28178/003-4, Prospectus for 1881, 1882 Argentine Loans. Contracts for 1884 and 1886–87 Argentine and 1888 Russian loans.
7. RAL XI/144/0, Chilean Letter Copy Book (CLCB), May 27, 1889 and August 22, 1892.
8. For a more detailed description of underwriting risk and its distribution see Mikkelsen 2014, 36–51.
9. The capital of Rothschilds was £6.5 million in 1873 and £7.8 million on the eve of WWI, a figure often surpassed by the size of sovereign bond issues, and Rothschilds were the ones with the largest capital (Ferguson 1998, 1043–44).
10. "The Issuing Houses and the Argentine Crisis", The Statist, October 5, 1889. BA HC 4.13.21; November 16, 1890, letter from Cosmopolitan to Barings. RAL XI/142/10, Brazilian Letter Copy Book, March 3, 1912.

11. LMA 19,063/14, S. L. Anderson to Hambros, June 23, 1876. RAL XI/142/5, 12, BLCB, March 14; November 14, 1890; October 16, 1913.
12. See also BA PF-1909 Argentine Loan, Vol. I, Barings to Disconto Gesellschaft, December 9, 1908, 174.
13. RAL000/401C/ 9/3, 9/12, /15/2, 15/1, contracts for 1870, 1871, 1872, 1873 and 1875 Russian loans. BA HC10.1.372, Stieglitz & Co to Barings 18/30 May, 1871. BA HC10.28, Charles Jutting to Barings, May 14, 1871.
14. See contracts listed in Appendix 4 of Mikkelsen 2014.
15. BA PF-1911 Argentinean Loan, Part I, Barings to Tornquist, June 12, 1911, 279.
16. BA PF-1911 Argentine Loan, Part I, Barings to Banque de Paris, June 19, 1911, 328, 329.
17. RAL XI/144/0, CLCB, May 27, 1889. Guildhall Library, Stock Exchange Loan and Company Prospectuses, prospectus for 1889 Chilean Loan.
18. LMA MS 21802; J. S. Morgan & Co. Private Telegrams no. 12, J. S. M. & Co. to G. W. P., December 12, 1908, 27–29.
19. The modern equivalent is calculated between 1889 and 2012 using the retail price index at http://www.measuringworth.com, if average earnings are used, the modern equivalent would be about £87 million.
20. BA PF-1907 Argentine Loan, Part I, Tornquist to F. Perugia and telegram from Windham Baring, February 20, 1907, 56-57. BA PF-1909 Argentine Loan, Part II, Barings to Don Carlos M. Dominquez, February 24, 1909.
21. LMA MS28178/001, 003-005, Prospectus for the 1881 and 1882 Argentine Loans. BBA 201782, Contract between French banks and Barings in connection with the issue of the 1884 Argentine Loan.
22. BBA 201823, Contract for 1886-87 Argentine Loan. BBA 201825, Contract between Barings and Deutsche Bank. BBA 201824, Contract for 1889 Argentine Loan.
23. See BA partners files relating to Argentina 1900–14.
24. BA PF-1909 Argentine loan, Part I, various letters, 278-279, 290-291, 310-312. BA PF-1911 Argentine loan, Part 1, various telegrams, 202–204. "The New Loan", The Standard, May 28, 1911.
25. BA PF-1909 Argentine Loan Partners File, Vol. I, Barings to Disconto Gesellschaft, December 9, 1908, 174.
26. "The Great Financial Houses At Home And Abroad", The Statist, November 10, 1888.
27. "The New Loan", The Standard, May 28, 1911.
28. HSBC: SHG 149. Agreement between HSBC and Deutsche Asiatische Bank 1895.
29. For later agreements see HSBC: SHG 149.
30. See Appendix 1 in Mikkelsen 2014.

31. See Appendix 1 in Mikkelsen 2014.
32. "The Argentine Loan in Paris", The Financial Times, July 7, 1911.
33. BBA PF-1911 Argentine Loan Part II, pp. 1, 13.
34. "Argentine – Details of The New Loan", The Economist, July 8, 1911.
35. "Syndicates", Truth, October 3, 1878.
36. "The Financial outlook in 1892", The Bankers' Magazine, January 1892, 47. For the bad name of company promoters see Nye 2011, The Company Promoter in London 1877–1914, PhD, King's College, 11, 18–19.
37. LMA MS 21,793, 1, and 2; Loans and Options. BA H.C. 3.126, Morgans to Barings, Dec. 8, 1885. LMA MS 19,063/15, Morgans to Hambros, June 7, 1876; Raphael & Son to Hambros, March 29, 1878. LMA MS 19,063/20, Hambros to Stern Brothers, December 1, 1880; Hambros to Mildred Goyeneche & Co, December 1, 1880; Morgans to Hambros, December 2, 1880 (see also similar letters in above).
38. "The Financial outlook in 1892", The Bankers' Magazine, January 1892, 46.
39. "The Liquidation of the Barings", The Economist, November 22, 1890. "The Financial outlook in 1892", The Bankers' Magazine, January 1892, 46.
40. "Argentine Borrowings", The Statist, October 15, 1887, 429–430.
41. "The Great Houses", The Statist, July 27, 1889.
42. LMA MS 21,793, 1, 2 and 3; Loans and Options. A similar shift to more formal underwriting groups also appears to have taken place in the colonial loan market in the wake of the Baring Crisis. Attard 2013, 107.
43. RAL XI/III/36; Letter to Rothschilds, March 6, 1907. "Underwriters and Subscribers", IMM, 31 October 1910. "Stock Exchange Underwriting", The Economist, June 3, 1911. LMA MS 21,793,1, 2 and 3; Loans and Options
44. "Underwriters and Subscribers", *IMM,* October 31, 1910. "Stock Exchange Underwriting", The Economist, June 3, 1911. RAL XI/III/57; 1913 Brazil Loan, alphabetical list of Underwriters.
45. BA PF-1906 Russian Loan Part I, Barings to Mendelssohns, April 10, 1906; Revelstoke to Cassel, April 15, 1906, 75, 134. RAL XI/III/57; Letters to Rothschilds from Browning, Todd & Co and Wassermann, Plaut & Co. RAL XI/III/57; 1913 Brazil Loan, alphabetical list of Underwriters.
46. "Mr. Seligman Describes Underwriting Methods", The New York Times, April 26, 1906. "Stock Exchange Underwriting", The Economist, June 3, 1911.

47. "Lord Rothschild Memoir", The Times, April 1, 1915. See Rothschild contracts from 1905 listed in Mikkelsen 2014, Appendix 4. The 1895 Brazilian loan was a special case.
48. "Underwriters and Subscribers", IMM, October 31, 1910. "The Chinese Loan Next Week", The New York Times, May 15, 1913.

References

Attard, B. (2013). The London stock exchange and the colonial market: The city, internationalisation, and power. In: C. Dejung & N. P. Petersson (Eds.), *The foundations of worldwide economic integration: Power, institutions, and global markets, 1850–1930* (pp. 89–111). Cambridge: Cambridge University Press.

Bussière, E. (1992). *1872–1992, Paribas: Europe and the world.* Antwerp: Fonds Mercator.

Cassis, Y. (1987). *La City de Londres, 1870–1914.* Paris: Belin.

Cassis, Y. (2006). *Capitals of capital. A history of International Financial Centres, 1780–2005.* Cambridge: Cambridge University Press.

Chapman, S. (1984). *The rise of merchant banking.* London: George Allen & Unwin.

Cottrell, P. L. (2012, 1st ed. 1985). *Investment banking in England 1856-1881. A case study of the International Financial Society* (Vol. II). Abingdon: Routledge.

Crick, W. F., & Wadsworth, J. E. (1964, 3rd ed.). *A hundred years of joint stock banking.* London: Hodder & Stoughton.

Ferguson, N. (1998). *The world's banker: The history of the House of Rothschild.* London: Weidenfeld & Nicholson.

Flores, J. H. (2010). Lending booms, underwriting and competition: The baring crisis revisited. *Law and Contemporary Problems, 73* (4), 192–150.

Ford, A. G. (1956). Argentina and the baring crisis of 1890. *Oxford Economic Papers, New Series, 8* (2), 127–150.

Graham, R. (1968). *Britain and the onset of modernization in Brazil 1850–1914.* Cambridge: Cambridge University Press.

Jenks, L. H. (1938). *The migration of British capital to 1875.* London: Jonathan Cape.

Joslin, D. (1963). *A century of banking in Latin America.* London: Oxford University Press.

King, F. H. H. (1987). *The Hongkong Bank in late imperial China, 1864–1902*. Cambridge: Cambridge University Press.

Klovland, J. T. (2004). Bond markets and bond yields in Norway 1820-2003 (Chapter 4). In: Ø. Eitrheim, J. T. Klovland & J. F. Qvigstad (Eds.), *Historical monetary statistics for Norway 1819–2003* (pp. 99–180), Norges Bank occasional papers 35, Oslo.

Marichal, C. (2011). Rivalry and collaboration: Relations between Buenos Aires Merchant Bankers and European Bankers in the Issue of Argentine Government Bonds in the 1880s. In: L. Quennouëlle-Corre & Y. Cassis (Eds.), *Financial centres and international capital flows in the nineteenth and twentieth centuries* (pp. 71–95). Oxford: Oxford University Press.

Michie, R. (1988). Different in name only? The London Stock Exchange and foreign bourses, C. 1850-1914. *Business History, 30* (1), 46–68.

Mikkelsen, A. (2014). *The market practices and techniques of London issuing houses in connection with Sovereign Bond issues and their role in facilitating access of Sovereign Borrowers to the London capital market, 1870–1914*. Ph.D., King's College London, unpublished.

Nye, J. G. D. (2011). *The company promoter in London 1877-1914*. Ph.D., King's College London, unpublished.

Pohl, M. (1977). *Deutscher Kapitalexport im 19. Jahrhundert*. Frankfurt: Börsen-Zeitung.

Pohl, M., & Burk, K. (1998). *Die Deutsche Bank in London 1873–1998*. München: Piper.

Regalsky, A. M. (1987). Exportaciones de capital hacia los paises nuevos: los bancos franceses y las finanzas publicas Argentinas, 1881-1887. *Revisita de Historia Economica, 5* (1), 73–98.

Singleton, C. C. (1928). *Stock exchange underwriting: Its principles and practice*. London: Underwriting News Ltd.

Supple, B. (1970). *The Royal Exchange Assurance: A history of British insurance 1720–1970*. Cambridge: Cambridge University Press.

Suzuki, T. (1994). *Japanese government loan issues on the London capital market 1870–1913*. London: The Athlone Press.

Withers, H. (1948, 4th ed.). *Stocks and Shares*. London: John Murray.

Young, G. F. W. (1990). Anglo-German Banking Syndicates and the issue of South American Government Loans in the era of high imperialism, 1885–1995. *Bankhistorisches Archiv 16* (1), 3–38.

Young, G. F. W. (1992). German Banking and German imperialism in Latin America. *Ibero-Amerikanisches Achiv: Zeitschrift für Sozialwissenschaften und Geschichte, Neue Folge, 18* (1–2), 31–66.
Ziegler, P. (1988). *The sixth great power. A history of one of the greatest of all banking families, the House of Barings, 1762-1929*. London: Collins.

Financial Centres as Fields: Reflections on Habitus and Risk in the Nineteenth and Twentieth Centuries

Andrew Dilley

1 Financial Centres and Risk: An Undefined Unit of Analysis?

Judgements of risks by banks and other financial institutions are never taken in isolation. The perception of risk, and hence its management, is always shaped by external factors. The purpose of this paper is to delineate these factors and to consider how, and at what spatial level, they might best be understood to coalesce and operate. In particular it is argued that a combination of legal and political considerations, institutional and interpersonal networks, and culture have all made the individual financial centre a meaningful level on which risk was gauged, judged, and—to some extent—managed. There is, indeed, a strong tradition across disciplines of studying financial centres: they are often taken by historians and social

A. Dilley (✉)
Department of History, University of Aberdeen, Aberdeen, UK
e-mail: a.dilley@abdn.ac.uk

K. Schönhärl (ed.), *Decision Taking, Confidence and Risk Management in Banks from Early Modernity to the 20th Century*,
DOI 10.1007/978-3-319-42076-9_6

scientists to be a *de facto* unit of analysis (Michie 1992; Germain 1997; Cassis and Bussière 2005; Cassis 2006; Dilley 2010). This paper seeks to give this empirically rich approach theoretical ballast. It draws on Pierre Bourdieu's generative structuralism to formulate a definition of a financial centre as a discrete 'field' which possessed a distinctive 'habitus' (essentially mindset, but see below) within which ideas of risk were formulated and refined.[1] It then draws on concepts from Douglass North's new institutional economics to argue that a combination of hard (economic and political) and soft (social and cultural) factors collectively gave definition to the financial centre as a field, in turn shaping perceptions of risk. This is not to deny that individual banking or other institutions possessed unique strategies to manage (or mismanage) risk, nor to deny the relevance of other levels of analysis. However, it is argued that locating analysis at the level of the financial centre possesses significant advantages over an exclusive focus on either micro-level (firms, sectors) or other macro-levels (state, globe).

2 The Financial Centre as Field: Habitus and Institutions

Two bodies of theory inform the argument presented here: Pierre Bourdieu's generative structuralism and Douglass North's new institutional economics. It is first necessary to discuss Bourdieu's key concepts of field and habitus in the context of his praxeology, i.e. his 'theory of practice' (Everett 2002, 70f). They can provide us with a fruitful framework within which to re-conceptualise financial centres. A fundamental concern of generative structuralism is to elaborate on the relationship between broader structures and the agency of individual actors without either resorting to crude determinism or an excessive and anarchic individualism. For Bourdieu interactions or 'games' between actors (who may for these purposes be considered to be firms as well as individuals) take place within a 'field': an arena defined by the operation of a unique combination of forces. Fields are not, therefore, geographical spaces *per se*, but meta-arenas within which particular 'games' take place (although these games may in practice be concentrated in a particular geographical location). A space may contain a field, but a field is not simply a geographical space; in any case, geographers increasingly reject simplistic deterministic notions of space (Harvey 2006). Fields are not necessarily hermetically sealed, a point more easily comprehended once the distinction between a field defined by various forces and geographical space is appreciated. It is far easier to conceive of interactions shaped by particular combinations of forces overlapping (Bourdieu 1979, 1990; Mahar et al. 1990). This is an important consideration in applying Bourdieu's conceptual framework to financial centres, which are, after all, intertwined.

Within the field, individual actors (which might be corporate actors as well as individuals) evolve what Bourdieu describes as a 'habitus', a 'system of durable, transposable dispositions which functions as the generative basis of structured, objectively unified practices' (Bourdieu 1979). The habitus is both produced collectively and shapes collective action. It essentially constitutes the 'rules of the game', broadly conceived, which operate within a given field, and is shaped by, but not necessarily wholly dependent on, the broader forces operating with the field. For Bourdieu, habitus constitutes a set of dispositions which operate on a subconscious as well as conscious level, shaping, instigating and constraining action. Habitus is not fixed but evolves through time. In contests within a field mediated through the particular habitus, individuals both possess and compete for capital, which Bourdieu uses not only in an economic or monetary sense but also to highlight various non-economic resources—status, prestige, and the like (or 'social capital' to use a term of Bourdieu's which has gained wider currency). A diversity of individual strategies are pursued within the broader framework of the habitus and field, varying both with the position (level of capital) possessed by individuals and their own dispositions or aspirations—a point which allows for considerable individual agency (Bourdieu 1979, 1990; Mahar et al. 1990). Thus, financial centres might be considered to constitute fields (interlocking, and with overlapping and imprecisely defined hinterlands) within which particular clusters of financial organisations, possessing differing forms of capital and differing strategies, collectively evolve a distinctive habitus through which risk is judged.

If financial centres are conceived of as fields possessing a distinctive habitus through which risk is approached, a further question arises as to how the forces, which collectively distinguish the financial centre *qua* field and shape its evolving habitus might be identified and categorised. To address this question it is possible to draw on Douglass North's work on the role of institutions in shaping economic activity. North argued that economic decisions and the management of economic risk take place within institutions. His definition of the term institution departs from the common usage (as a synonym for organisation), arguing that 'institutions are the humanly devised constraints that structure political, economic and social interaction. They consist of both informal constraints (sanctions, taboos, customs, traditions, and codes of conduct), and formal rules (constitutions, laws, property rights)'. According to this argument a bank (or any other financial intermediary) is not an institution but an organisation (or an organisational form) operating within a set of institutions, i.e. within a given set of 'constraints' (North 1991, 97; see also North 1990). The implication is that the form taken by a particular financial organisation, and hence important elements of its approach to risk, will be the product of the operation of these broader sets of constraints; institutions in the 'Northean' sense. Therefore, it is important not to conflate the everyday meaning of 'institution' with North's more theoretically exact (and exacting) usage.

North's conception of institutions as constraints acting on economic transactions (perhaps intermediated by organisational forms) is close (if not exactly analogous) to Bourdieu's notion of habitus, which also seeks to describe a set of dispositions shaping action. Both portray the forces shaping and constraining actions by economic agents. By exploiting this close (if of course not exact) connection between generative structuralism and the new institutional economics it is possible to develop a refined means to understand financial centres. On the one hand, North's more precise treatment of economic institutions opens the possibility of a more precise treatment of the forces operating in the field to produce the habitus in the case of the financial centre. It leads us to consider the 'soft'/informal and 'hard'/formal constraints shaping action. On the other hand, a broader and more dynamic framework emerges by incorporating generative structuralism, with its concern to understand the nature of a particular field, the contours of habitus, the accumulation of social capital, and the strategies of individual actors. Judgements of risk and the operation of institutions can thus be located in a broader framework.

At the same time, this framework also leads to a consideration of the contours and trajectory of the field and habitus operating in a financial centre at a particular juncture. Judgements of risk thus become the product of a set of historical forces, and history becomes integral to any understanding of financial risk.

3 Financial Centres Reconsidered

Having elaborated the theoretical position, it is now possible to apply this refined approach to the definition of a financial centre. A financial centre will generally possess a concentrated cluster of financial organisations within a demarcated urban space (possessing a possibly extensive hinterland which might overlap with or incorporate a further sub-centre). However, it is not physical location *per se* that distinguishes the financial centre. In essence, a financial centre is a field (in Bourdieu's sense) constituted by a particular set of forces within which a set of financial games are played and in which a habitus evolves through which risk is judged. The point here is not to eschew the usual connection between a financial centre and a city (London, Paris, Berlin, Tokyo, etc.) but to specify what makes those centres both a distinctive level of analysis and worth distinguishing (from each other and from other possible levels) in analysis. Distinctions between these centres (with their geographical monikers) become not the assumed product of geographical location but the specified product of different forces shaping them as respective fields, forces which operate in and are concentrated at these locations.

Thus conceived, financial centres provide a shifting range of financial services to differing but also overlapping hinterlands. The term hinterland will be used throughout this article to describe the broader regions served by and consuming the services of particular financial centres. Just as the notion of field is not exclusive (fields overlap), neither is the notion of the hinterland. While one centre may dominate or hold a monopoly in some regions, elsewhere several centres may compete to serve the same hinterland. Similarly, the hinterland does not necessarily or even normally coincide with the territorial boundaries of a state. The evolution of the hinterland and the financial centre interact in complex ways—the requirements of the hinterland may shape the habitus of the financial centre but equally that centre's habitus, since not determined in the hinterland, will, in turn, create constraints on economic and political activity (debates about London's financial power might be understood in this way, see, for example, Hopkins, 1994).

Different categories of the financial centre may be discerned, based on the extent of their hinterlands and their relationship to other financial centres. Some were truly global in their connections, conducting transactions encompassing the whole globe. Amsterdam (until the nineteenth century), London, Paris, and (by the twentieth century) New York all fall unambiguously into this category. While interconnected, these centres tend to function relatively autonomously in relation to other centres. Others served large regional or national economies, often intermediating between their arenas of operation and the global economy and hence the global financial centres (with which they might have close but at times asymmetrical relationships). Examples in the Anglophone world might include Montreal, Toronto, Melbourne, Johannesburg, or Glasgow (Michie 1988a). The term financial centre is not, therefore, confined here simply to 'Capitals of Capital' (Cassis 2006) but is extended to smaller centres. Indeed the distinctions between the global financial and the lesser centres may well be elaborated through the factors distinguishing approaches to risk (habitus) in particular centres outlined below, in addition to the extent of their hinterlands and the differing relationships with other centres.

The argument of this paper is that the financial centre *qua* field was an important level on which approaches to risk evolved. How though might this argument relate to other possible levels of analysis: the firm, the state and the globe? First, it is necessary to emphasise that the argument here does not suggest that all institutions or categories of institution displayed identical approaches to risk within a financial centre; only that these calculations of risk (or strategies of accumulation, to borrow again from Bourdieu) took place within a common framework (for a discussion of the competing strategies of British merchant banks, see Chapman 1984). In part, this variation might be understood to be the product of different levels of capital (in Bourdieu's broader sense of the term) and of capital accumulation strategies amongst individual financiers and financial organisations. The notion of varying strategy allows for considerable agency at an individual level, while the emphasis below on the historically specific evolution of particular categories of institution in particular financial centres helps to highlight how contrasting approaches to risk within seemingly identical categories of institution emerge in different locations. Neither the contrasting strategies possessed by individuals nor the contrasting approaches of different organisational forms (banks, stock markets, etc.) invalidate the importance of the financial centre as a field with an associated habitus. Quite the converse, these distinctions may be best understood precisely by considering the specific features of that field and habitus within which they operate.

There is also a strong tradition of analysing economic and financial history at the level of the state. The argument presented here does not deny the importance of states in shaping risk: indeed it emphasises the importance of states and politics at several junctures. However, it does question any simple equation of financial systems with nation states (e.g. the German banking system). Financial centres within the same or similar jurisdictions (and hence sharing the same basic legal framework) might nonetheless constitute a distinctive field possessing a unique habitus due to soft institutional factors: the particularities of their social networks and the particular inflections of their cultures. Each centre will, as a result of this unique habitus, possess a distinctive set of functions and distinctive approach to gauging long- and short-term risk. Moreover, because states do not necessarily constitute a distinctive or sealed economic entity (even when this is a policy goal), the financial centre and hinterland will tend, as a level of analysis, to more closely approximate economic space more broadly.

Financial centres served and possessed overlapping hinterlands which could cross national boundaries and at times encompass the globe (Feis 1930; Cassis 2006). No centre was hermetically sealed and all competed by also often complementing one another in terms of function and geographical focus. It might be asked whether it makes sense to distinguish financial centres or whether, in fact, the globe constituted a single field within which approaches to risk evolved. There may be mileage in this approach, and of course, by the late nineteenth century global financial markets were intimately interconnected (O'Rourke and Williamson 1999). Even so, then (as in the twenty-first century) clear distinctions existed between financial centres in terms of business structure, business practices and investment portfolios—consider for example the far greater orientation of nineteenth-century Paris towards continental European investment compared to London (Feis 1930). To view the global financial system as a single field is, in effect, to assume financial markets operated under conditions of perfect knowledge and unrestricted connection. The specificities apparent in even a superficial examination of the operation of financial markets would lead to questioning of this. The existence and persistence of arbitrage, the movements of individuals and institutions from one centre to another, or the differing investment portfolios held in or mediated through particular locations all suggest the need to recognise and consider analytically the factors differentiating locations. It is more helpful to consider how conceptually to delineate and understand these distinctions rather than to emphasise the undoubted similarities and connections between all centres.

The remainder of the paper outlines four vectors which shaped the emergence of distinctive 'habituses' of risk in particular financial centres, not least through interactions with their respective hinterlands. It was the combination and intersection of these vectors which, in combination, defined individual financial centres as fields and shaped their individual habitus or culture of risk at particular historical junctures. Two relate closely to North's hard formal institutions: economic and business structure, and law and politics; the other two to North's soft informal institutions: social and institutional networks, and cultures and discourses of risk. The paper draws on examples largely taken from the Anglophone world, purely by way of illustration; however it is not suggested that the vectors of differentiation would be different were the focus to be placed on, say, continental Europe. The purpose is to elaborate and illustrate the sketch of a general model rather than to make (or indeed refute) any claims about 'Anglo-Saxon' exceptionalism (for a creative analysis along these lines, see Belich 2009).

4 Vectors of Differentiation Between Financial Centres

4.1 Economic and Business Structure

Financial activities ultimately rest upon the particular economies they serve: their hinterlands. The habitus of risk within their constituent financial organisations therefore to some extent reflects these underlying economies. The sectorial balance of the economy, along with cycles of production, shapes demands for credit and, hence, risk management in individual financial centres. Two examples from the British settlement empire illustrate the point. First, the short-term financial practices of major Canadian banks such as the Bank of Montreal and the Canadian Bank of Commerce evolved in the late nineteenth century in response to the need to provide short-term credit to finance the shipment of the burgeoning output of the Canadian west. The early onset of the Canadian winter created a short window within which an enormous amount of produce had to be shipped, in turn generating an enormous financial strain on Canadian banking institutions. Their management of their investment of reserve funds in New York was structured accordingly (Macivor 1958; Denison 1966; Naylor 1975; Ross 1922).

Second, in eastern Australia in the 1870s and 1880s, many Melbourne- and Sydney-based banks departed from British practices to lend on the security of land, emboldened by rising prices in the context of a long boom in the Australian economy. British-owned banks with head offices in London, less exposed to the intoxicating culture of the boom, proved more conservative in their lending strategies. The level of risks incurred became clear when this boom ended in the early 1890s in depression and ultimately, in 1893, in a financial panic which saw many banks suspend payments and seek assistance from colonial states (Boehm 1971; Beaver and Beaver 1988). In both these examples, in different ways, financial institutions in Melbourne, Sydney, Toronto, and Montreal adjusted their approach to short-term and long-term lending in response to the seasonal cycles and long swings of their respective economies.

As well as deeper economic patterns, the historical evolution of business organisation within a region or state also shaped approaches to risk. Through the eighteenth and nineteenth centuries, a plethora of different financial organisations developed in response to local and global financial opportunities provided by local, regional, national, continental, and global economic activities. These organisations were often highly specific in their functions, and even apparently similar organisations could play different roles in different financial centres. Thus the distribution of financial labour, and hence approach to risk, taken by any one category of financial organisation such as banks, in a particular financial centre would be contingent on the historical evolution of that centre and often on the role played by other elements of that centre's financial system. For example, Ranald Michie has argued that the differences between stock exchanges in Britain and the continental bourses had important implications for the evolution of banking. According to Michie, because the London money markets provided a means, through finance bills, to invest banks' short-term funds by proxy in long-term investments, British banks were far less likely than their continental and especially German counterparts to provide direct investment for industry. Thus, for Michie, investment strategy was a product of other elements of the financial system. The differential opportunities for investing money at call provided by the British bill market led many other banks, including major German banks, to establish branches in London. In this instance, these banks then diversified existing strategies already shaped by differing economic and business opportunities available locally (Michie 1988c).

4.2 Politics, Law and the State

The legal framework established by the state and the state's financial activities constitute further formal institutional factors which shaped the habitus of risk in a particular centre. While obvious in some ways, this basic point needs to be stated vigorously. Consider for example how regulation affects the activities of banks: the focus of this collection. The very definition of a bank and the approach to risk management that a bank might undertake depends on the regulatory framework within which it operates. Indeed, some important institutions frequently called banks concentrate on functions that are difficult to reconcile with any definition of deposit banking. Merchant banks (also often called acceptance houses) in London, including famous names such as Rothschilds and Barings, focused on two main activities: accepting (guaranteeing) bills of exchange and issuing stock exchange loans (Chapman 1984). Nonetheless, merchant bankers were prominent on the court of the Bank of England, the institution which occupied the apex of the British banking system as a whole. Even if they were bankers in name rather than practice, they occupied positions of great influence in the banking system (Cassis 1994). Furthermore, banking regulations concerning the issuing of currency or the level and nature of reserve funds could fundamentally shape banking systems and their approaches to risk. One major contrast between American and Canadian banking in the late nineteenth century lay in the heavy restrictions placed upon the operation of branch banking in the US, especially across state boundaries. This meant that Canada evolved a set of transcontinental banking institutions whose scale outstripped their American rivals (Davis and Gallman 2001).

The approach taken by a state to central banking (and the location of that central bank) could also shape the approach to risk in the system. For the second half of the nineteenth century the US had no lender of last resort, a position finally overturned following the 1907 financial crisis in New York (which essentially forced leading financiers orchestrated by J. P. Morgan to act as impromptu lenders of last resort), which led to the foundation of the Federal Reserve Bank in 1913. Elsewhere central banks recognised by but independent from the state, such as the Bank of England and the Bank of France, played important roles in the London and Paris financial market, both in their currency operations as well as providing informal leadership to the entire financial sector (Cassis 1994, 2006).

Legal frameworks do not precede financial systems. The two evolve in tandem, with regulation often precipitated by crises in financial systems or political reactions against financiers and their machinations on the one hand, while on the other hand drawn up in response to pressure from financiers. Thus relationships between finance and policymakers vary between states and across time, depending on a shifting political context. The contrast between Canadian and American banking systems which became so pronounced by the late nineteenth century in part reflected the deep-set suspicion of bankers of US populism and the close relationship between many Canadian bankers and Canada's political classes. As a result, the powerful Canadian Bankers' Association wrote crucial aspects of Canadian banking legislation (Naylor 1975).

Finally, the financial requirements of states themselves were major factors shaping the credit and capital markets. States' short-term borrowings could affect returns in money markets, states' long-term debts were often the staple long-term investment for a host of different institutions, and the order of magnitude of state borrowing could shape the structure of the capital market. The development successively of the Antwerp, Amsterdam, and London capital markets owed much to borrowings by states creating, in the early modern period, an investing class (Neal 1990; Germain 1997). Conversely, as the British state retrenched and reduced its borrowing requirements in the nineteenth century, the price of consols (British government bonds) fell and individual and institutional investors sought to diversify their portfolios, not least into higher yielding colonial and foreign bonds (Edelstein 1982).

States also shaped major aspects of the macroeconomic framework which, in turn, shaped the framework within which risk was judged in a myriad of ways. Perhaps most obviously, the widespread adoption of the gold standard across the world in the nineteenth century (with the exception of major Asian economies) shaped both the judgement of country risk and hence the mixes of assets banks were required to hold (Bordo and Rockoff 1996). Moreover, the management of gold flows by private central banks (with the various players, not least the Bank of England and the Bank of France, taking different approaches) was often effected through the manipulation of interest rates or other mechanisms, which in turn affected money markets and hence both banking returns and the stock markets (De Cecco 1974). The power of states over macroeconomics also interacted in complex ways with conceptions of political economy and hence perceptions of country risk, a factor further discussed below (Ferguson and Schularick 2006; Dilley 2010).

4.3 Networks and Information Asymmetries

Each financial centre possessed a distinctive set of networks, which in turn shaped the habitus of risk by conditioning, creating, and constraining the flow of information and opportunities. Every financier and every financial organisation possessed a distinctive set of connections (Michie 1979; Dilley 2012). In the nineteenth century, individual firms within financial centres were often locked into distinctive clusters through the interlocking interests and interventions of shared directors. In Canada, the twin peaks of Canadian banking—the Bank of Montreal and the Toronto-based Canadian Bank of Commerce—each stood at the apex of a cluster of insurance companies, bond houses, and associated railway and manufacturing concerns (Armstrong and Nelles 1988). This, by the way, adds a further reason for being sceptical about the idea that the risk management strategies of individual financial organisations can be studied entirely in isolation: often these organisations existed within a broader cluster of organisations with a single overarching, if at times loosely articulated, strategy (Wilkins 1988; Jones 2000).

Since individuals and firms possessed distinctive connections within and beyond individual centres, it follows that these connections provided a particular framework within which risk could be managed and judged. The uneven dimensions of these connections necessarily meant that information about particular business opportunities and their attendant levels of risk varied (Magee and Thompson 2010). Since information flowing to individuals and institutions would flow more readily within their particular locale, the asymmetrical networks of individuals generated an asymmetrical level of information at the level of the financial centre (Harvey and Press 1990).

This asymmetry would be further exacerbated by the patchy and partial nature of information flows around the nineteenth-century world, flows which travelled more readily through certain channels than others (Potter 2007). As well as obvious barriers of language, the communications machinery possessed by particular locations inevitably shaped approaches to risk in those locations by conditioning the information milieu within which decisions were taken. This was a major factor which affected the major elements of risk management in those locations: quite simply investment-related decisions depend on the available information that serves as the basis for those decisions and this varies with the available communications infrastructure of a particular centre (Magee and Thompson 2010).

In some ways two successful exceptions, but of different magnitudes, prove the rule. First, the success of the Rothschilds in the nineteenth century depended in part upon the close communications between the various European branches of the family: communications enabled the information available to the Rothschilds often to supersede that available to rivals in individual locations (Ferguson 1998). Conversely, the London partnership of Canadian financier James Dunn and Swiss banker Hirschler Fischer depended on Dunn's superior knowledge of Canadian-run utility companies in the West Indies and Fischer's connections in European capital markets (Michie 1988b). Both exceptional success and extreme specialism conditioned these transnational partnerships, which were a strategy to overcome (indeed to profit from) the patchy information available in any one location and hence the distinctive information milieu shaping the habitus of risk in any one financial centre.

4.4 Cultures of Risk

Finally, the judgement of risk is itself a perception based on a shifting range of ideas and assumptions which, while based on certain and fundamental underlying principles, also gain specific inflections which vary with time and location. Joseph Schumpeter (Schumpeter 1939, 6) put it well:

> *Our businessman analyses whenever new situations arise. He does so himself in a manner which is unscientific but often shrewd, or other people do it for him—his banker, his newspaper, or by any of the services which present current business facts and inferences therefrom by methods which vary as to scientific value from zero up to anything that can fairly be asked in the present state of our knowledge. There have always been some rules by which businessmen formed their judgement about existing business situations and the changes to be expected, ever since business operations extending over time and space came into existence; but with increasing wealth of, and with improving methods of*

> *treating, statistical facts an ever-expanding number of 'indices' which look objective and sometimes are, have come to the assistance of the untutored mind.*

Virtually every aspect of information production and analysis Schumpeter described would be undertaken by different publications in different centres, each of which interacted with particular sets of ideas about political economy. Moreover, as Schumpeter emphasised, the nature of information and the use of information by financial decision makers also varies over time, as well as by location.

Thus the approach taken to judging risk, and conceptions of what is and is not risky, are best understood to be a cultural phenomenon—a culture of risk—with a strong subjective component. This holds true in the late twentieth and twenty-first century, notwithstanding the triumph of 'econophysics' whose achievement is in part to transform earlier rules of thumb into algorithms, and which in the run-up to 2008 created a clearly quite misplaced confidence that risk had been rationalised and tamed (Porter 1995; Cassis 2006). The very confidence in the primacy and power of complex maths to eliminate uncertainty is (or rather was) itself the product of a particular mentality or habitus. While certain elements of risk are fixed, since judging and managing risk ultimately requires a complex set of judgements to be made about an uncertain future, these judgements must ultimately be based on a shifting and necessarily imprecise set of assumptions. If risk, therefore, is in part culturally determined, then its management depends on circulating ideas and discourses on risk, which depend on past and present experiences as combined by individual decision makers.

Here the financial centre constituted a crucial cultural arena within which these discourses could take place and consequently a distinctive habitus evolved (a point at which the urban space occupied by a financial centre becomes in itself one of the forces defining it as a distinctive field). In addition to the ever-shifting indicators provided by prices on the various exchanges, in Belle Epoch financial centres discussions in public forums such as bankers associations or chambers of commerce, in clubs and other private locations, and most importantly through the medium of the financial press, all combined to enable distinctive discourses on risk, as well as on economic matters more broadly, to emerge (Daunton and

Trentmann 2004, 1–23). It was not just that the information available in different locations was different; it was also comprehended and understood in a distinctive way in each financial centre. Each centre possessed a distinctive discourse on risk and judgements of risk differed as a result (for a discussion of Edwardian London, see Dilley 2012).

Networks and habitus combined, for example, to generate preferences in London and Paris for investing in the British and French empires respectively. As well as perceived or actual legal guarantees of fair or favourable treatment (which actually in the British case at least was surprisingly rare), the networks of empire placed greater information about imperial opportunities before investors (Marseille 1985; Magee and Thompson 2010; Dilley 2012). Moreover, Empire became a crucial element in French and British political culture, or, if Bernard Porter is to be believed in the British case, in elite political culture, which is all that matters for the point being made (MacKenzie 1986; Porter 2004; Sèbe 2013). Serving imperial ends could be a means to attract investors, especially if leading politicians or aristocrats lent stature to company boards; a classic gambit played with aplomb by Cecil Rhodes (Galbraith 1974). Canadian railway promoters in London claimed their trans-continentals would help rivet the empire together; and (doubtless) American trans-continentals were equally portrayed as embodiments of manifest destiny (Wilson 1909; Smith 2013). Yet such strategies of promotion should not simply be seen as attempts by promoters to secure capital from the (seemingly surprisingly small) pool of imperially minded investors. Imperial service could also dignify financial acquisition with a higher purpose and, crucially, benefit the social status of those claiming to serve the higher cause of empire (Cain and Hopkins 2001). For some, then, this non-economic return could become a factor in their business strategies, a return which depended on the political culture prevalent in a particular state. Few American financiers would have expected much kudos in the US for serving British imperialism; conversely, successive American managers of Canadian railways like Sir William Van Horne accepted knighthoods which dignified and masked their Republican origins (Vaughan 1926).

Imperial loyalty did not constitute the only way in which such a culture of risk evolved. It simply illustrates how all financial centres would possess their own particular notions of political economy conditioned by the political culture within which they were located. A host of other areas might also distinguish ideas of risk and political economy in different financial centres. For example, differing ideas about the legitimate role of the state or differing attitudes on the legitimacy of protectionism (or the desirability of free trade) might also shape conceptions of political economy and hence attitudes towards risk.

5 Conclusion

The financial centre, rather than the globe, the nation state, or indeed the individual firm deserves to take centre stage as a unit of analysis in the study of finance and risk. This paper has outlined an approach which defines a financial centre as a distinctive field possessing a unique habitus shaping approaches to risk. A financial centre may, indeed will usually, be concentrated in (indeed almost synonymous with) a particular urban space, but it is the forces operating in the field rather than mere physical geography which give the financial centre definition. It has been argued that drawing on Douglass North's description of formal and informal institutions highlights the categories of forces differentiating the habitus of risk operating within a financial centre at particular junctures. Financial centres, it has been suggested, were differentiated by 'hard' factors: their underlying economies and business structures, and the actions of states and legal frameworks; and 'soft' factors: networks and information asymmetries, and cultures of political economy. These all combined to generate and give texture to those distinctions. Financial actors, including banks, formulated individual strategies of accumulation and risk management within this framework, in part as a result of their differing positions (possession of capital in Bourdieu's broader sense of the term) and goals within the field.

The approach to the history of financial centres outlined here suggests a broader research agenda, not least in banking history, the subject of this volume. It implies that if the history of banking and risk management, or indeed the history of finance more broadly, is to be fully comprehended, the particularities of location set in a broader historical context must be considered. At a micro-level, it necessarily requires historians of banking and finance not only to set the actions of individual firms in a broader context, perhaps comparatively, but also to consider those actions as the product of an interaction between the habitus of risk in a particular location and the strategies and aspirations of the individual firm. At a macro-level, it suggests a need for far more detailed comparative study of financial centres to understand precisely how and why they differ at particular historical junctures. For example, historians of banking might follow Michie's lead in considering the distribution of financial labour between banking and other financial agents. Interesting questions also arise as to how different financial centres articulate the relationship between peak-level international financial centres, or indeed between international financial centres and their lesser counterparts. Finally, the notion of a habitus of risk as shaped by the factors outlined here provides a means to reconnect the study of finance to the broader study of political, economic, social, and cultural histories. If finance cannot be omitted from macroeconomics, neither can macro-history be omitted from the study of finance. The history of finance and banking must, in the end, look outwards as well as inwards.

Note

1. See for more detailed explanations also Reitmayer, M. *Considerations of Social Capital and Future Research of Banking History* in this volume.

References

Armstrong, C., & Nelles, H. V. (1988). *Southern exposure: Canadian promoters in Latin America and the Caribbean 1896–1930*. Toronto: University of Toronto Press.

Beaver, A., & Beaver, M. (1988). Henry gyles turner. In: R. T. Appleyard & C. B. Schedvin (Eds.), *Australian financiers: bibliographical essays* (pp. 110–134). Melbourne: Macmillan.

Belich, J. (2009). *Replenishing the earth: The settler revolution and the rise of the Anglo-world, 1783–1939*. Oxford: Oxford University Press.

Boehm, E. A. (1971). *Prosperity and depression in Australia, 1887–1897*. Oxford: Clarendon Press.

Bordo, M. D., & Rockoff, H. (1996). The gold standard as a "Good housekeeping seal of approval". *The Journal of Economic History, 56*, 389–428.

Bourdieu, P. (1979). *Outline of a theory of practice*. Cambridge, MA: Cambridge University Press.

Bourdieu, P. (1990). *The logic of practice*. Cambridge, MA: Polity.

Cain, P. J., & Hopkins, A. G. (2001). *British imperialism, 1688–2000*. Harlow: Longman.

Cassis, Y. (1994). *City bankers, 1890–1914*. Cambridge, MA: Cambridge University Press.

Cassis, Y. (2006). *Capitals of capital: A history of international financial centres, 1780–2005*. Cambridge, MA: Cambridge University Press.

Cassis, Y., & Bussière, E. (2005). *London and Paris as international financial centres in the twentieth century*. Oxford: Oxford University Press.

Chapman, S. D. (1984). *The rise of merchant banking*. London: Allen & Unwin.

Daunton, M.J., Trentmann, F., (2004). Worlds of political economy: Knowledge, practices and contestation. In: Idem (Eds.), *Worlds of political economy: Knowledge and power in the nineteenth and twentieth centuries*. Palgrave Macmillan; Basingstoke/New York, pp. 1–23.

Davis, L. E., & Gallman, R. E. (2001). *Evolving financial markets and international capital flows: Britain, the Americas, and Australia, 1870–1914*. Cambridge, MA: Cambridge University Press.

De Cecco, M. (1974). *Money and empire*. Oxford: Blackwell.

Denison, M. (1966). *Canada's first bank: A history of the bank of montreal*. Montreal: McClelland & Stewart.

Dilley, A. (2012). *Finance, politics, and imperialism: Australia, Canada, and the city of London, c.1896–1914*. Basingstoke: Palgrave Macmillan.

Dilley, A. R. (2010). 'The rules of the game': London finance, Australia and Canada, c.1900–1914. *Economic History Review, 63*, 1003–1031.

Edelstein, M. (1982). *Overseas investment in the age of high imperialism: The United Kingdom, 1850–1914*. London: Methuen.

Everett, J. (2002). Organizational research and the praxeology of Pierre Bourdieu. *Organizational Research Methods, 5* (1), 56–80.

Feis, H. (1930). *Europe the world's banker, 1870–1914*. New Haven: Yale University Press.

Ferguson, N. (1998). *The house of Rothschild*. London: Penguin.

Ferguson, N., & Schularick, M. (2006). The empire effect: The determinants of country risk in the first age of globalization, 1880–1913. *Journal of Economic History, 66*, 283–312.

Galbraith, J. S. (1974). *Crown and charter: The early years of the British South Africa company*. Berkeley: University of California Press.

Germain, R. D. (1997). *The international organization of credit: States and global finance in the world-economy*. Cambridge, MA: Cambridge University Press.

Harvey, C., & Press, J. (1990). The city and international mining, 1870–1914. *Business History, 32*, 98–119.

Harvey, D. (2006). Space as a KeyWord. In: D. Harvey (Ed.), *Spaces of global capitalism* (pp. 119–148). London: Verso.

Hopkins, A. G. (1994). Informal empire in Argentina: An alternative view. *Journal of Latin American Studies, 26*, 469–484.

Jones, G. (2000). *Merchants to multinationals: British trading companies in the nineteenth and twentieth centuries*. Oxford: Oxford University Press.

Macivor, R. C. (1958). *Canadian monetary, banking and fiscal development*. Toronto: Macmillan Co. of Canada.

MacKenzie, J. M. (Ed.). (1986). *Imperialism and popular culture*. Manchester: Manchester University Press.

Magee, G., & Thompson, A. (2010). *Empire and globalisation: Networks of people, goods and capital in the British world, c.1850–1914*. Cambridge, MA: Cambridge University Press.

Mahar, C., Harker, R., & Wilkes, C. (1990). The basic theoretical position. In: C. Mahar, R. Harker, & C. Wilkes (Eds.), *An introduction to the work of Pierre Bourdieu* (pp. 1–26). Basingstoke: Palgrave Macmillan.

Marseille, J. (1985). The phases of French colonial imperialism: Towards a new periodization. *The Journal of Imperial and Commonwealth History, 13*, 127–141.

Michie, R. C. (1979). The social web of investment in the nineteenth century. *Revue Internationale d'Histoire de la Banque, 18*, 158–175.

Michie, R. C. (1988a). The Canadian securities market, 1850–1914. *Business History Review, 62*, 35–73.

Michie, R. C. (1988b). Dunn, fischer and co. in the city of London. *Business History, 30*, 194–214.

Michie, R. C. (1988c). Different in name only? The London stock exchange and foreign bourses, c. 1850–1914. *Business History, 30*, 46–68.

Michie, R. C. (1992). *The city of London: Continuity and change, 1850–1990*. London: Macmillan Academic and Professional.

Naylor, R. T. (1975). *The history of Canadian business, 1867–1914* (Vol. 2). Toronto: James Lorimer.
Neal, L. (1990). *The rise of financial capitalism: international capital markets in the age of reason*. Cambridge, MA: Cambridge University Press.
North, D. C. (1990). *Institutions, institutional change and economic performance*. Cambridge, MA: Cambridge University Press.
North, D. C. (1991). Institutions. *The Journal of Economic Perspectives, 5*, 97–112.
O'Rourke, K. H., & Williamson, J. G. (1999). *Globalization and history: The evolution of a nineteenth-century Atlantic economy*. Cambridge, MA/London: Massachusetts Institute of Technology Press.
Porter, B. (2004). *The absent-minded imperialists: Empire, society, and culture in Britain*. Oxford: Oxford University Press.
Porter, T. M. (1995). *Trust in numbers: The pursuit of objectivity in science and public life*. Princeton/Chichester: Princeton University Press.
Potter, S. J. (2007). Webs, networks and systems: Globalization and the mass media in the nineteenth- and twentieth-century British Empire. *Journal of British Studies, 46*, 621–646.
Ross, V. (1922). *A history of the Canadian bank of commerce*. Toronto: Oxford University Press.
Schumpeter, J. A. (1939). *Business cycles: A theoretical, historical, and statistical analysis of the capitalist process*. New York: McGraw-Hill.
Sèbe, B. (2013). *Heroic imperialists in Africa: The promotion of British and French colonial heroes, 1870–1939*. Manchester: Manchester University Press.
Smith, A. (2013). Patriotism, self-interest and the 'Empire effect': Britishness and British decisions to invest in Canada, 1867–1914. *The Journal of Imperial and Commonwealth History, 41*, 59–80.
Vaughan, W. (1926). *Sir William Van Horne*. London: Oxford University Press.
Wilkins, M. (1988). The free-standing company, 1870–1914: An important type of British foreign direct investment. *Economic History Review, 41*, 259–282.
Wilson, A. J. (1909). *An empire in pawn*. London: Unwin.

The "Reputation Approach" and the Justificatory Function of Economic Calculation. Some Critical Reflections on Monika Pohle Fraser's Analysis of Risk Management Techniques in the Nineteenth Century

Sebastian Knake

1 Introduction

How can bankers decide on investments whose risks or yields are not calculable? This was the central research question of Monika Pohle Fraser's dissertation. To find answers, she worked through numerous nineteenth-century archives of private French and German banks. In her historical analysis of the investment decisions of German and French bankers and banks in the nineteenth century, Pohle Fraser distinguishes three periods that are widely used in nineteenth-century banking historiography especially in Germany (Hans Pohl and Manfred Pohl 1982; Tilly 1980, 1986; Ziegler 2005). In the first period from 1830 to 1850, industrial investment financing was dominated by a small group of private banks. In the next period between 1850 and 1870, the first joint-stock banks were

S. Knake (✉)
Fakultät für Geschichtswissenschaften, Philosophie und Theologie, Universität Bielefeld, Bielefeld, Germany
e-mail: Sebastian.Knake@gmx.de

K. Schönhärl (ed.), *Decision Taking, Confidence and Risk Management in Banks from Early Modernity to the 20th Century*,
DOI 10.1007/978-3-319-42076-9_7

founded for the purpose of financing industrial investment and especially railways. From 1870 onwards joint-stock companies dominated the investment business in Germany and in France.

Pohle Fraser's analysis is based on two different types of sources. The first type comprises official financial statements, reports, balance sheets as well as commemorative publications. What these sources have in common is that they were available to the general public. The other type of sources consists solely of correspondence between bankers. In order to retrieve these sources, Pohle Fraser accessed numerous archives of banks such as Fould, Neuflize, Rothschild, Thuret, Oppenheim, Crédit Mobilier, Deutsche Bank, Disconto Gesellschaft and Berliner Handels-Gesellschaft.

The differentiation of the two types of sources is a central part of Monika Pohle Fraser's methodology (Pohle Fraser 2007). She contrasts the self-portrayals of bankers and their risk management techniques within the official statements with those found in the correspondence (Pohle Fraser 1999). At the beginning of the research period, all sources presented a common picture of how bankers decided on their investments. According to both types of sources, bankers based their decisions on the assessment of the people who were involved in a proposed investment rather than assessing the proposed project itself. If experts were involved in the decision-making process, it was again not their findings, reports or calculations that were observed by the bankers but the experts themselves. Pohle Fraser calls this the 'reputation approach' (Pohle Fraser 1995). Risk management was the same as assessing the reputation of the people involved. The reputation approach was also at the heart of risk spreading. In order to persuade other bankers to participate in an investment, bankers did not rely on calculations of yield. Instead, they appealed to their own reputations and also to 'bourgeois optimism' as part of a special code of conduct among bankers. Yet, from 1850 on, the two different kinds of sources began to show completely different pictures, which were to some extent even mutually exclusive. The official sources started to portray bankers as rational risk-averse 'prudent' actors and their decisions as an outcome of rational risk management techniques. The official statements began to give a lot of credit to reports, data and calculations as a basis for the decision-making process. However, and this is the central result of Pohle Fraser's work, this was only true for the first type of sources. In the correspondence between bankers, the reputation approach was still dominant.

From these findings Pohle Fraser derived three questions: Why do official statements begin to depart from the traditional view of bankers and their decisions? Does the new rational self-portrayal resemble an actual change in the behaviour of bankers and risk management? If not, why did this change in self-portrayal occur? The answer to all three questions is included in the first part of her dissertation title: *Noisy Optimists*.

Noisy Optimists is a reference and in fact a rejection, of the central assumptions of neoclassical risk management analysis. In her dissertation, she confirmed her hypothesis that throughout the nineteenth and early twentieth century, bankers did not decide on long-term investments as rational risk-averse actors. In the face of fundamental uncertainty, they instead continued to decide on the basis of the two pillars of 'traditional' risk management: the reputation approach and bourgeois optimism.

The evidence that Pohle Fraser offers for this conclusion is twofold. The first argument is chronology. She reconstructs the decision-making process by analysing both types of sources and finds that the references to the reputation approach and the belief in 'Fortuna' (fate) within the correspondence predate or are part of the decision-making process, whereas references to the rationality approach tend to lag behind the original decision. This is bolstered by the observation that banks overwhelmingly produced only best-case scenarios without also looking at the worst case. This is a strong hint that these calculations are offered to justify decisions already made in order to avoid 'post-decisional regret' (for this concept see Kahnemann and Tversky 1982).

The reason why banks and bankers began to portray themselves as risk-averse rational actors who listen to financial experts and follow relevant data, is the involvement of other actors in the field of investment financing. These actors were not part of the special code of conduct and therefore did not find the traditional justifications for investments sufficient. With the emergence of joint-stock banks from 1850, non-bankers became increasingly involved in the practices of investment financing. Wealthy private individuals, governments and non-banking companies were among these new actors who demanded 'rational' information for their support. For these actors, banks started to fabricate this kind of information in order to justify their investment decisions to actors outside the banking community. They produced informational 'noise' because it was demanded by the outside world. They did not use this 'noise' themselves because among the community of bankers it appeared to be understood that it was not possible to make estimates concerning the distant future. Pohle Fraser's conclusion is that in general bankers accepted fundamental economic uncertainty as a given. They only pretended to calculate investment risks on a rational basis in order to satisfy non-bankers who believed in this kind of forecast. In the next section why the acceptance of uncertainty is crucial for the analysis of decision-making behaviour will be explained.

2 Noisy Optimists—Against a Rational Model of Risk Management

> *The outstanding fact is the extreme precariousness of the basis of knowledge on which our estimates of prospective yield have to be made. Our knowledge of the factors which will govern the yield of an investment some years hence is usually very slight and often negligible. If we speak frankly, we have to admit that our basis of knowledge for estimating the yield ten years hence of a railway, a copper mine, a textile factory, the goodwill of a patent medicine, an Atlantic liner, a building in the city of London amounts to little and sometimes to nothing; or even five years hence.* (Keynes 1936, 149f.)

If a bank does not know how much it will yield from an investment if it, in fact, does not even know exactly how expensive an investment will be, how does it know if it is worth the money that is required to get it started?

The simple answer given by John M. Keynes is that it cannot. This conclusion has enormous consequences for the understanding of risk management concerning investment decisions because it rules out the rational actor as its driving force. The rational actor—or the 'prudent merchant' or *homo economicus*—of this abstract model of human behaviour is by definition risk-averse. He would only invest if the calculated chance of yield were higher than the calculated risk of losing the invested money. He will therefore generally demand a risk premium. The rational actor would never invest when the yield or the risk of the investment are not calculable because he would always prefer the money or the goods he already owns. Investing in projects whose outcome is not calculable is, therefore, irrational from a neoclassical point of view.[1] The only exception is the gambler. For the gambler, taking decisions under uncertainty itself is maximising his (or her) utility; the results of these decisions are only secondary.[2] In this regard, Keynes and neoclassical writers reach the same conclusion. Keynes also attributes investments in the absence of competitive investment markets to actors of a certain nature: '

> *[I]nvestment depended on a sufficient supply of individuals of sanguine temperament and constructive impulses who embarked on business as a way of life, not really relying on a precise calculation of prospective profit.* (Keynes 1936, 150).

These individuals are guided by 'animal spirits' that provoke decisions based on 'spontaneous optimism rather than mathematical expectations, whether moral or hedonistic or economic' (Keynes 1936, 136). For Keynes, as for Joseph Schumpeter (1926), the entrepreneur is a key figure for progress in capitalistic systems. Monika Pohle Fraser agrees with Keynes' analysis that spontaneous optimism is at the heart of long-term investment decisions. Yet she denies the biological nature of this kind of behaviour. Instead, she understands bourgeois optimism as a part of a special code of conduct of bankers.

The gambler, however, is considered as an irrational figure by Alfred Marshall (1890) and was even seen as immoral by economists of the nineteenth century. Neoclassical economists dodge the paradox that only irrational actors can take investment decisions under uncertainty by simply ignoring the existence of fundamental uncertainty altogether. The central assumption is that uncertainty can always be converted into a risk calculation by procuring sufficient information and translating it into a probability function. To make this assumption one has to take some important premises. First, one has to define information as numerical data so that it can be used in mathematical equations. Second, one has to assume that there is an objective state of the world and that it is accessible by procuring information and separating data from noise, which is useless information. Since there is an objective state of the world, there is also objective information, which means that it can be separated from its provider (Hayes 1993). This definition of information applies also for the most successful alternative economic theories like Information Economics (Akerlof 1970; Rothschild and Stiglitz 1976; Stiglitz and Weiss 1981) or New Institutional Economics (North 1990; Williamson 1975, 2000). Both theories reject the idea of generally available and 'costless' information on prices. Both the search and the processing of information cost time and money, and information is not distributed equally among all market participants. Yet, objective information is accessible and it can be collected and analysed. Hence, investment decisions by banks can be made on the foundation of rational choice.

In her dissertation, Monika Pohle Fraser rejects the neoclassical approach as well as the approaches of Information Economics and New Institutional Economics. Since her focus is on the process of decision-making, the assumption of the possibility of rational decision-making (in the economic sense) is highly problematic given the ex-post perspective of economic history.

Historical research on nineteenth-century banking and finance in Germany has mainly focused on the emergence of the great universal banks and the economic efficiency of the universal banking system (Bongaerts 1985; Borchardt 1977; Burhop 2006; Fohlin 1999, 2010; Neuburger and Stokes 1974; Tilly 1980, 1986; Wellhöner 1989). The great majority of this research uses one of the three economic theories described above. According to Monika Pohle Fraser (2002), most theoretical approaches can be summed up as presenting a functional approach to banking history, which is defined as follows:

> *An investment environment is characterized by problems (here, of information) and solutions. Depending on the nature of the problem one gets different solutions. [...] The environment which brings about universal banking seems to have been identified. It is characterized by asymmetric information and risk aversion. The ideal solution seems to have been identified: Universal banks can cope effectively with asymmetric information inherent in industry finance.* (Pohle Fraser 2002, 256).

The danger of applying neoclassical or Information Economics to the analysis of the decision-making process of banks is to fall into the trap of the ex-post narrative, which leads to a circular argumentation. By assuming the existence of accessible but asymmetrically distributed information on yields and risks of investments and a general efficiency advantage of the risk-averse actor, the essential institutional advantage of universal banks has to be better access to this information. The long-term survival of banks depended on the success of their investments and, according to the functional approach, decisions about investments had to be based on the analysis of information about the yield and risk of investments. In historical research, it is possible to find out most reasons for the success or the failure of investments. Looking at available data over the course of the funding the reason for the failure of investments can be established, yet as a historian, it is not feasible to try to apply this ex-post knowledge to the decision-making process.

> *A study of risk behaviour defining risks ex post on the basis of losses actually incurred is, however, unsuitable for arriving at statements on the decision-making behaviour that led to particular outcomes in the first place. The historian has, as it were, an information advantage, by knowing for instance the long-term development of manufacturing and capital-market data, which he also presumes his study object, the bank to have. Historical studies on banks' investment behaviour mostly look at the risk aspect in the sense: were the banks right in their investment behaviour in retrospect? Thus, the history of banks' success at the same time becomes the history of their risk aversion, while failure reveals the gambler.* (Pohle Fraser 1999, 6).

The question of what the actors knew about the risks of investments at the time of the decision has long been considered irrelevant because according to economic theory it can be derived from the outcome of the decision. If the investment was successful, the information procurement and analysis was sufficient; if it failed it was not. This is the essence of the 'functional approach'.

In a world where fundamental uncertainty is possible or even likely, the historical analysis of investment decisions has to be conducted quite differently. In an uncertain environment, the decision-making process cannot be evaluated by its outcome. A failure can occur due to bad luck, the unintended consequences of the actions of others, or other reasons that could not have been foreseen. This makes it difficult to evaluate the decision-making process at all. However, that was not the aim of Monika Pohle Fraser's analysis. She asked instead how the bankers coped with uncertainty. To her, it did not matter whether the investment decisions were successful or not.

In order to undertake this kind of analysis, she looked at various criticisms of the rational actor model. The major source of inspiration came from risk sociology. The dichotomy of risk and uncertainty can be found here, too, but in a different context. Niklas Luhmann (1991) rejects the idea of converting uncertainty into risks; in fact, he rejects the idea of a calculable future altogether. In this sense, the concept of risk as used by economists is useless because it cannot be made operational. Instead, Luhmann understands risk as a concept to evaluate decisions or people. Risk is something that seems to be controllable so decisions that are said to be taken under risk emanate reliability. What the economists call uncertainty, risk sociologists call hazard. Decisions taken under hazard are unreliable, uncontrollable and unjustified. Here, the conversion of hazards into risks is not part of a rational choice process but is used as a means of justifying the decisions or actions taken.

> *Utilization of classical information procurement and processing cannot, for those who see the paradox, have any effective utility in the case of uncertainty or hazard. Should they nonetheless employ this kind of risk management, it is to be presumed that they wish to portray themselves as acting responsibly vis-à-vis those who do not see the paradox, i.e. those who believe that uncertainty or hazard can be reduced to risk.* (Luhmann 1991, 28–29).

But if risk is a means to justify a decision rather than its basis, there has to be some other procedure for the banks to reduce uncertainty. Otherwise, it would indeed be pure gambling and anyone could try to play. The answer is not to evaluate the project but the people. 'Second-order observation' is a central concept within risk sociology. Working on self-referential systems, Baecker (1991) rejected the difference between information and its provider, since it would be impossible for human beings to gain information independently from the distinctions set by others. To procure information is therefore basically the same thing as observing the provider of the information. From a sociological perspective, guessing the behaviour of distinct people in different scenarios of the future is more realistic than guessing the future using rational calculations. To these findings, Monika Pohle Fraser adds the suggestion that the behaviour of people is more calculable if they are part of the same milieu, believe in the same norms and rules, and behave in the same way. A common code of conduct reduces uncertainty much more than rational calculations.

> *The banker himself and his business partners must be calculable as members of bourgeois society, since business is regarded as scarcely calculable.* (Pohle Fraser 1999, 275).

The purpose of the observation is to find out how a person might react when things do not go as planned. You can put your trust in the wrong people though. The art of banking is to choose the right people for an investment undertaking rather than guessing the outcome of investments. This is another central conclusion of Pohle Fraser's dissertation.

3 Perspectives from Convention Theory

There are two points that derive from Monika Pohle Fraser's methodology which will be reflected on more closely here. The first point is why non-banking stockholders or the government started to demand information that was fit for formal risk calculations. Pohle Fraser did not focus on this question. She mentions stock exchange crashes as an accelerator of change since they affected people outside of the banking community (1999). Outsiders were repelled by the bankers explaining stock exchange crashes simply by referring to bad luck. But why formal risk calculation replaced bourgeois optimism as a justificatory means was not discussed in her dissertation in a sufficient manner. The second point is a question of methodology. Is it, in fact, feasible to make a strong distinction between decision-making and justification as Monika Pohle Fraser did? Doing so would imply that the decision-making process does not contain elements of justification. To reflect on these questions some aspects of the justification theory of the *Économie des Conventions* will be used.

In 1990, the sociologists Luc Boltanski and Laurent Thévenot published a book (2006, 2007) in which they outlined a comprehensive theory of justification. It was based on the combined analysis of philosophical classics like Adam Smith, Jean Jacques Rousseau and Augustine of Hippo and profane everyday advice literature. They found a finite plurality of societally-shared, supreme 'justifying principles' that formed the basis of any attempt of actors to justify their decisions or actions in the context of decision-making situations. These principles are not ahistorical scientific rules but conventions that have evolved historically along with the development of modern societies. They are the following: the market convention, the industrial convention, the state convention, the family convention, the convention of public opinion and the convention of inspiration.[3] By using these shared conventions, actors among themselves are able to construct different 'orders of worth' concerning other subjects and objects and rank themselves and other actors and objects according to the respective convention principle. Thus, they are normative by definition. Conventions are not interconnected and therefore cannot be integrated into one common mode of justification.

Pohle Fraser is also interested in justification practices and she shares the idea of a societally-shared normative convention (though she does not use the terminology). Before 1850 she identified a special merchant code of conduct, which legitimised the reputation approach as the best form of risk calculation among the most important peer group—the banking community. Yet, Pohle Fraser did not identify an alternative code of conduct for the support of formal mathematical risk calculation as the official risk management technique after 1850. Instead, she refers to a general demand for such risk calculations among the new actors in the field of investment. Using the methodology of the *Économie des Conventions* a distinct normative order as the basis for this demand is suggested: the industrial convention (Boltanski and Thévenot 2007, 276–286). This convention emerged from the planning of production processes. Its supreme principle is efficiency. It is based on the assumption of a direct connection between cause and effect. The functioning of the production process allows for the continuation of the present into the future and the possibility of forecast. People at the top of the order of worth are experts and professionals as well as scientists. These experts guarantee the reliability of the production process on which the whole system of forecast relies. When the principle is distanced from its origin it is safe to say that it depends on rationality. In order to appropriate this principle to banking, it is important to understand banking as a production process. Cause-and-effect have to be connected, so the decision to finance industrial undertakings has to be connected to its outcome.

And here lies the flaw in applying the industrial principle to banking. The 'production process' of banking cannot be separated from its environment, as might be true for the production of, for instance, steel. Provided that production continues, that materials are permanently available and that production factors are fixed, forecasting the output of a steel plant is possible. It might not always be accurate but the chances of accuracy are much higher than in other fields of human life. Banking has no such production processes. Its 'production' of wealth depends on the behaviour and the fate of the banks' environment. It is therefore not to be separated from the social world and is hence highly contingent.

From the perspective of justification theory, the process of change within the justification practices of bankers' investment decisions was a successful attempt to apply the industrial order of worth to banking practices. What Monika Pohle Fraser describes was only part of a general expansion of the industrial convention that went along with the industrial revolution. The growing belief in the calculability of the world made the justification of decisions reached by these means more feasible. Interpreting the increasing demand for formal risk calculations as part of the rise of the industrial convention as a dominant form of justification thus strengthens Monika Pohle Fraser's position on rational risk calculation being a form of noise. It was produced in order to justify investment decisions in a way that maximised legitimacy among actors who overwhelmingly believed in the justificatory principle of the industrial convention. Among the original peer group—the banking community—the industrial convention did not dominate because the members of this group understood the precariousness of applying the assumptions of the industrial convention to investment decisions. Accordingly, among themselves, bankers stuck to the reputation approach. Yet, how can one be sure that the reputation approach is, in fact, the basis of investment decisions and not another form of justification carried out among a group that shares a special normative order?

This leads to the question of whether the distinction between justification and decision-making is valid. Pohle Fraser stresses that at the beginning of the nineteenth century bankers did not have to hide their decision-making methods from the public. They used references to bourgeois optimism or second-order observation as justifying arguments in public announcements, annual reports and even court pleas. The decision-making process and the justification of the decision had the same basis. The means of justification used by the banks in the early period resemble the properties of the family convention, as outlined by Thévenot and Boltanski (2007, 228–245). Diaz-Bone (2015) calls it the handicraft convention. Its supreme principle is that of tradition. People are ranked by their heritage. Heritage is expressed by good manners and a certain character which depends on how someone has been brought up. Characteristics that Boltanski and Thévenot assigned to the family principle resemble exactly those qualities that Monika Pohle Fraser found to be subject to the second-order observation of bankers. Punctuality, loyalty and honour are the qualities of a strong character. They cannot be trained but are part of the person who expresses them. The bankers basically made one important assumption that resembles a simple equation: a person of honour is also worthy of being financed.

Yet, like the rationality approach, this assumption is also based on a justifying convention. The correspondence between bankers is not free from justifying practices, nor can it be said for sure that it is the reputation approach on which bankers actually base their decisions. There is the possibility of 'animal spirits' (Keynes 1936) being at the heart of an investment decision. In this case, the reputation approach was just another way to justify the decision because a decision solely based on impulse was not justifiable even among bankers in the nineteenth century (as opposed to Wall Street's 'Masters of the Universe' in the 1980s). The family convention was, therefore, the appropriate mode of justification for investment decisions when the actors involved were bankers, whereas the industrial convention was used after 1850 to justify actions with a public that believed in the possibility of economic forecast.

If more than just one actor is involved, there is no difference between justification practices and the decision-making process (Salais and Storper 1997). In a decision-making situation, actors have to agree on one mode of justification, i.e. one convention. Alternative decisions are weighed against each other by using the appropriate order of worth. Thus a justification process is at work at the heart of every decision that has to be coordinated among different actors. In order to use the *Économie des Conventions* for the analysis of decision-taking processes one has to reject the distinction made between justification and decision-taking processes. Instead, both the reputation approach and the rationality approach must be understood as justification principles of different normative conventions. Both were important for the making and the legitimising of investment decisions. The decision about which of these principles was used depended on the group of actors involved in the respective situations. This is the central difference to Monika Pohle Fraser's point of view in which the reputation approach is seen as the central method of decision-taking, whereas the rationality approach becomes (after 1850) the dominant form of justification.

For most decisions, it is difficult to find any evidence from the decision-making process itself. In most situations, the mode of justification is agreed upon by the actors involved without any discussion because within convention theory actors have the capability to 'read' the justification context of a situation (Dupuy 1989). Historically these are only discovered when actors do not instantly agree either on the right order of worth or the rating of subjects or objects according to the relevant order. In such cases, actors or decision proposals become subject to criticism, which in turn provokes a justification effort. The correspondence between bankers contains justification practices that can be analysed (Salais 2011). Monika Pohle Fraser's methodology involved accessing these sources and enabled her to unmask the rationality approach as a means of justification. Yet in a way she underestimates the power of justification processes to shape the decision-making process.

In order to understand all the effects of justification, one must give attention to its influence on future decision-making processes. The industrial convention that was used by the bankers to justify their decisions to outsiders after 1850 might have come back to haunt them. In the author's own study, there are numerous examples where justification practices used by the bank were picked up by its customers or the government in order to legitimate their claims for funding. Through this backdoor, other justifying conventions can alter decision-making processes substantially. The analysis of this mechanism might have altered Pohle Fraser's findings on investment decisions in the nineteenth century. As for risk-managing practices by banks, there is a rather prosaic conclusion: banks use risk management practices that are accepted by their peers and their customers. When faced with fundamental uncertainty this is probably the best solution, since a banker can still point to the explicit or silent consensus between the actors involved if something goes wrong. And, given the unpredictability of the outcome of long-term investments, something eventually will go wrong.

4 Risk Management in the Twentieth Century: A Case Study

In the case study about the Braunschweigische Staatsbank (Brunswick State Bank) numerous pieces of evidence that Pohle Fraser's findings also apply to twentieth-century banking were discovered.[4] Given that this case is a public bank that has to deal with the local government much more than private banks usually do, the means of justification had to comply with this close relationship. The interaction of justification and decision-taking can be shown in a short example.

In 1954 the Braunschweigische Staatsbank, with a territory that equated to that of the old Brunswick state, found out that the head of its branch in Salzgitter, Mr Bertram, had for years plotted with the largest borrowers of his branch against the bank.[5] He issued them large loans without asking for any collateral. Both the credit volume and the lack of collateral were illegal according to the standards of the *Staatsbankgesetz*, the law serving as the constitution of the bank. In order to hide these illegal transactions, Bertram faked balance sheets, invented imaginary borrowers and exaggerated other credit lines. The bank did not detect this fraud for years, not until they received a secret tip-off from a local businessman who had found out that the main customer—the owner of a car parts factory—was on the brink of collapse.

The scandal put the whole bank at risk because the businesses of the individuals who used the illegal credit lines were all about to default. A total of DM 9 million was at risk, while the bank's total equity only stood at about DM 15 million. The whole issue was discussed at different meetings of the bank's supervisory board, a mixed board where businessmen, customers, politicians, officials and union representatives alike were present. In the first meeting, the question of the responsibility of the directorate was raised. The answers, given by the president of the bank Walter Nickel, are striking.

Nickel first explained the auditing practices of the bank. He admitted that the auditing department had not found anything conspicuous even after the fraud had been detected. The 'book-cooking' activities seemed to have been very professional. Observance of the branches also included observance of the lifestyle of the heads of the branches. Mr Bertram, however, did not show any signs of an 'extravagant lifestyle' that could have led to suspicion. The observance of the private lives of local branch management is a clear sign that the reputation approach was important, not just for investment decisions within banks but also for controlling employees.

The case shows that it was not the inability to control data that had caused the problems. The bank had simply put its trust in the wrong man. The head of the supervisory board, the minister of finance of Lower Saxony, concluded respectively: 'There can be no doubt that the directorate cannot be held responsible. Faced with cooperation between branch management and customers there is virtually no way to ensure complete security.'[6]

This belief in the limits of controlling represents the acceptance of uncertainty in a quite different area than that of the future forecasting of investment profitability.

Regardless of the question of guilt, the fraud of the branch manager forced the directorate to make an investment decision under uncertainty. The bank did not know how much of the DM 9 million was at risk. Regardless of this uncertainty, the directorate had to decide between two alternatives. The first was to call on the loans, immediately sell off all the assets of the bankrupt companies at fire-sale prices and write off the losses. The second was to keep the companies running and sell the assets over a longer time period at market price levels. The first alternative would potentially mean very high losses, but only a brief period of unrest and uncertainty. The bank would not have to get involved in the companies' fortunes and it would not be in danger of throwing good money after bad. Furthermore, the decision not to get involved would be easy to justify. First, the bank could have argued that it was not the job of a public bank to run private companies. Second, the bank had no experience in running industrial companies and therefore could not by itself evaluate the chances of a slow liquidation as opposed to an immediate call on the loans. Third, the directorate could have justified the loss by pointing to the riskiness of industrial financing as the counterpart to the high interest rates of the granted loans. The directorate, however, opted for the second alternative. This meant investing more money in already bankrupt companies, taking on the entrepreneurial risk of running the companies, and an extended period of uncertainty and incalculability for the bank. If the plan failed, the bank would in the end face even greater losses. If the plan worked, however, the losses could be reduced substantially. The greatest problem of the second alternative was the question of justification. The directorate had to convince the supervisory board that there was an actual chance to reduce the losses and they had to demonstrate that the bank would be able to run industrial companies.

The main support for the second alternative came not from specific calculations but from the general director of the Salzgitter AG and member of the supervisory board of the Braunschweigische Staatsbank, Prof. Dr Paul Rheinländer. Rheinländer informed the directorate and the board about the prospects of the two main companies that were involved in this incident. Dr Rheinländer's knowledge about the economic situation in Salzgitter and the prospects of the bankrupt companies could be trusted because the Salzgitter AG dominated the economy of the city and therefore had business connections to all large and medium companies in the area. He confirmed that both companies had a good reputation among the local business community concerning their products and he was optimistic that a turnaround was possible. One of the companies had worked for the Salzgitter AG on a regular basis. His statement was crucial for influencing a modestly sceptical board towards backing the directorate. Thus the initial decision to not instantly liquidate the companies was backed and justified by a process of second-order observation, which is at the heart of the reputation approach.

Yet, the approval of the first decision led to another pending decision between two alternatives. Since the bank had decided to get involved with the fortunes of the companies, the question came up whether it was better to slowly liquidate or to go even further and try to reorganise the companies into profitable businesses. The directorate estimated that even the slow liquidation of the companies would take up to two years due to the existence of supply contracts, the fulfilment of which was mandatory if instant bankruptcy was to be avoided. The fully stocked inventories of the firms gave the bank another incentive to keep up business for a longer time period. As a consequence, the difference between slow liquidation and restructuring was only gradual for the foreseeable future. Yet, the financial consequences of the decision were potentially great. Slow liquidation meant to accept a certain amount of losses. Yet, if the bank would be successful in restructuring, the lurking losses could be diminished or even be avoided completely. This prospect led the directorate to subtly seek the second alternative. In the following month, they developed a double strategy to get approval from the board. The first strategy used the industrial convention and involved external experts. The second strategy used the family convention and directly involved the individual board members.

At the next meeting in October 1955, the directorate informed the supervisory board that it had commissioned two reports in order to find out if it was possible to turn the companies into profitable businesses. One came from the so-called *Rationalisierungskuratorium der Deutschen Wirtschaft* (RDW, Rationalization Board of the German business community) and the other from an independent consultant. Their original task was to find out whether restructuring and rationalisation of the production process would enable the companies to become profitable. However, the reports were not available by the time the meeting took place. Since the question of profitability remained unanswered, the board could not decide whether to slowly liquidate or to restructure the companies. However, the initially modest difference between slow liquidation and restructuring made it possible to delay a final decision. Anyway, the involvement of the RDW had more than one aim. The expertise of the

RDW was necessary because it filled a gap in the justification efforts of the bank. The directorate had to present the board with evidence that they would eliminate the specific risk that stemmed from their own inexperience in running industrial companies. By buying in experts of industrial production the bank did not actually reduce the risk of losing money in the production process. Since they had started the restructuring before the reports were filed, the expertise came too late. They instead reduced the risk of being accused of incompetence. In their (late) reports the experts had come to the conclusion that it was possible to rationalise the production process so that production would be cost efficient. Even before the RDW report was filed, the engineer in charge was redeployed to optimise the production process in one of the factories. Since the same experts were used for both the evaluation and the restructuring of the production processes it was their responsibility that it was carried out successfully. So the function of the experts in this case strongly resembles their functions in Monika Pohle Fraser's case studies. Yet, the involvement of industrial experts went further than justifying a decision that had already been made. The redeployment of the RDW engineer to the Fahrzeugwerke Kanneberg was not only motivated by a need for justification but also became a crucial step for the success of restructuring. Notwithstanding the result of the report, the rationalisation of production was profitable for the bank, because it could drive down costs during the time the companies had to be kept in operation. So instead of waiting for the reports to arrive, they used the expertise of the RDW to start the restructuring process. The use of rationalisation experts was one main way in which the companies could become profitable. Most of the cost reductions were due to layoffs, which were legitimised by the authority of the industrial expert. The bankers in charge had not been able to justify layoffs by means of the industrial convention, simply because they were not accepted as experts.

The second strategy was to acquire enough orders for the company. For this purpose, the bank used the connections of the board members. In the first discussion of the issue at the board in March 1955 the directorate directly asked the members to help with this acquisition and to use their business connections to find customers. They appealed to the board members' responsibility for the bank. Like the involvement of the

RDW, this call for help had two aims, one of which was justification. By connecting the success of the plan with the ability of the board members to acquire orders the directorate directly involved every board member in the running of the companies. If the venture failed because of a lack of orders, the board members could be held responsible as much as the directorate itself. However, the main aim was to actually find work for the production lines of the companies. Through the connections of board members like Christoph Seebohm, minister of transportation in the government of the Federal Republic of Germany, the bank managed to acquire sufficient orders to keep the companies going while the industrial experts tried to reorganise production.

Two years after the beginning of the scandal in March 1955, the most important company—the Fahrzeugwerke Kanneberg—was reporting the first small profit. The potential loss for the bank had been reduced by 50% in the same time period. An actual decision to restructure the companies had never been made, but the economic and legal circumstances blurred the line between the original decision to slowly liquidate and the actual restructuring process. In the end, the decision to run the companies over a long period increased the pressure to become profitable notwithstanding the still pending decision over the ultimate fate of the companies. Once the bank had succeeded in turning the companies into profitable businesses a final decision became obsolete because it would have been nonsense to liquidate profitable businesses. The double strategy to justify and to successfully carry out the original decision by using the reputation approach and the rationality approach simultaneously, but separated into two different fields, had worked very well. In terms of justification, the bank was able to hedge its original decision nearly completely. The directorate had made sure that others would be blamed in almost any failure scenario. In the sense of carrying out the consequences of the decision, the strategy performed even better. The decision to involve the board members with the acquisition provided a continued inflow of orders. The deployment of industrial experts helped bring down production costs. The achievement of profits in the end relieved the directorate and the board from having to decide between long-term liquidation and restructuring. The double strategy had already made the decision for them.

The new goal of the bank was to sell the companies. Yet, since the companies now created profits for the bank, the pressure to exit the business and sell the companies decreased substantially. At the same time and for the same reason the estimated value of the companies kept increasing. The combination of these two factors was responsible for the reluctance of the bank to sell the companies even for prices that would have been unthinkable in the direct aftermath of the scandal.

As a consequence, the largest company, the Fahrzeugwerke Kanneberg (FAKA), was sold only after the Braunschweigische Staatsbank was disbanded due to the founding of the Norddeutsche Landesbank or Nord LB in 1970. For 16 years the company had been the bank's property, hidden from the balance sheet by outsourcing its properties into a holding company.

The initial decision to save the companies from open bankruptcy was not based on any risk calculation but on a feeling of confidence that the direct involvement of the bank would make things better, not worse. The encouraging first results of the initial decision strengthened this initial confidence, while the developed justification strategy ensured that in the case of failure the bank could blame others. Together, the first results and the successful justification of the initial decision reassured the acting bank officials to continue the direct involvement with the companies to the point where the liquidation of the companies was no longer necessary. Thus, the original decision to avoid bankruptcy and wind up the companies in a controllable manner slowly shifted into reorganising the companies and then again into running the companies until purchase offers resembled the estimated (ever-increasing) value. In the end, the initial confidence of the bank was justified, but this judgement can only be made from an ex-post perspective. At the time, when the decision was taken, nobody knew if it was right.

Notes

1. The risk-averse actor is an essential deduction from the mathematical reinterpretation of marginal utility theory by game theory. Marginal utility theory proposes a declining worth of additional gains against those already acquired. Game theory translates this preference into a

decision-taking model. The foundation of the concept of the risk-averse actor is the expected utility hypothesis and its mathematical translation, the 'von Neumann-Morgenstern utility theorem' (von Neumann and Morgenstern 1953). Risk aversion in this context means that a rational actor would not bet on the chance of acquiring an amount of money when the amount he has to put at risk (for example, 100) is the same or less than the product of the chance of winning (for example, 50%) and the amount he could win (for example, 200). So in order to get a rational actor to take the bet, the offering actor has to pay a risk premium that must be high enough to render the outcome of the above equation positive (for the mathematical foundation of the risk aversion hypothesis see Arrow 1965; Pratt 1964). The risk-averse actor is at the heart of the Capital Asset Pricing Model (CAPM), which is the standard model to measure returns on investments in neoclassical economics (Sharpe 1964; Lintner 1964). In order to carry out the equations the risk has to be measurable. When one outcome of a bet is uncertain in the sense of Knight (Knight 1921), a rational actor would most likely choose either the measurable alternative or he would not bet at all. The deviation from the expected utility hypothesis in the case of uncertainty is known as the Ellsberg paradox (Ellsberg 1961). In the case of uncertainty, actors decide not according to the von Neumann-Morgenstern utility theorem, which means that they act irrationally from the standpoint of neoclassical economics.

2. Friedman and Savage (1948) understand the gambler as a person who has an increasing marginal utility for wealth. In contrast to the rational actor, the accumulation of wealth does not satisfy the gambler, but instead increases the utility of the chance to get even more. Jagdish Handa (1971), on the other hand, understands risk taking as a distinct 'good' and the utility function of the gambler as designed to maximise the 'good' risk as well as wealth. She rejects the von Neumann-Morgenstern theorem as the basis for analysing the decisions of a gambler and instead suggests the use of consumer theory.
3. In recent publications (Boltanski and Chapello 2005; Diaz-Bone 2015) it was proposed that at least one more convention exists: the network convention.

4. The author's dissertation is forthcoming. Major empirical findings will be published in: Hagebölling, Lothar (Hg.), 250 Jahre öffentliches Bankwesen im Braunschweigischen Lande, Braunschweig 2016.
5. The following case study is based on research containing the following archival material: Niedersächsisches Wirtschaftsarchiv NWA 5 Zg. 6/2007, No. 91, No. 107, No. 112 and No. 113.
6. Original in German: 'Es unterliegt keinem Zweifel, daß das Direktorium keinerlei Verschulden trifft. Gegen ein Zusammenwirken mehrerer leitender Angestellter mit der Kundschaft besteht praktisch keine volle Sicherungsmöglichkeit.' Protokoll der 60. Beiratssitzung der Braunschweigischen Staatsbank, Braunschweig, den 22. April 1955, in: NWA 5 Zg. 6/2007, No. 91, p. 6.

References

Akerlof, G. A. (1970). The market for lemons. Quality uncertainty and the market mechanism. *Quarterly Journal of Economics, 84* (3), 488–500.

Arrow, K. (1965). *Aspects of the theory of risk-bearing.* Helsinki: Yrjš Jahnsson Foundation.

Baecker, D. (1991). *Womit handeln Banken? Eine Untersuchung zur Risikoverarbeitung in der Wirtschaft.* Frankfurt/Main: Suhrkamp.

Boltanski, L., & Chiapello, E. (2005). *The new spirit of capitalism.* London: Verso.

Boltanski, L., & Thévenot, L. (2006). *On justification. Economies of worth.* Princeton: Princeton University Press.

Boltanski, L., & Thévenot, L. (2007). *Über die Rechtfertigung. Eine Soziologie der kritischen Urteilskraft.* Hamburg: Hamburger Edition.

Bongaerts, J. C. (1985). Financing railways in the German states 1840–1860. *Journal des Economistes et des Etudes Humaines, 14*, 331–345.

Borchardt, K., (1977). Die industrielle revolution in Deutschland 1750–1914. In: Id., Cipolla, C.M. (Eds.), Europäische Wirtschaftsgeschichte, Vol. 4: Die Entwicklung der industriellen Gesellschaften. Fischer, Stuttgart, pp. 135-202.

Burhop, C. (2006). Did banks cause the German industrialisation? *Explorations in Economic History, 43* (1), 39–63.

Diaz-Bone, R. (2015). *Die Economie des Conventions. Grundlagen und Entwicklung der neuen französischen Wirtschaftssoziologie.* Wiesbaden: Springer.

Dupuy, J.-P. (1989). Convention et common knowledge. *Revue économique, 40* (2), 361–400.

Ellsberg, D. (1961). Risk, ambiguity, and the savage axioms. *The Quarterly Journal of Economics, 75* (4), 643–669.

Fohlin, C. (1999). Universal banking in Pre-World War I Germany: Model or myth? *Explorations in Economic History, 36* (4), 305–343.

Fohlin, C. (2010). Asymmetric information, market power, and the underpricing of new stock issues in Germany, 1882–1892. *The Journal of Economic History, 70* (3), 630–656.

Friedman, M., & Savage, L. J. (1948). Utility analysis of choices involving risk. *Journal of Political Economy, 56* (4), 279–304.

Handa, J. (1971). A theory of risk preference in gambling. *Journal of Political Economy, 79*, 1073–1083.

Hayes, R. M. (1993). Measurement of information. *Information Processing and Management, 29* (1), 1–11.

Kahneman, D., & Tversky, A. (1982). The psychology of preferences. *Scientific American, 246*, 160–173.

Keynes, J. M. (1936). *General theory of employment, interest and money.* London: Macmillan.

Knight, F. H. (1921). *Risk, uncertainty, and profit.* Schaffner & Marx, Boston: Hart.

Lintner, J. (1964). Portfolios and capital budgets. *The Review of Economics and Statistics, 47* (1), 13–37.

Luhmann, N. (1991). *Soziologie des risikos.* Berlin, New York: Walter de Gruyter.

Marshall, A. (1890). *Principles of economics.* London et al.: Macmillan.

Neuburger, H., & Stokes, H. H. (1974). German banks and German growth, 1883–1913. An empirical view. *The Journal of Economic History, 34* (3), 710–731.

Neumann, J. V., & Morgenstern, O. (1953, 3rd ed.). *Theory of games and economic behavior*. Princeton: Princeton University Press.

North, D. C. (1990). *Institutions, institutional change and economic performance.* Cambridge: Cambridge University Press.

Pohl, H., & Pohl, M., (1982). *Deutsche Bankengeschichte. Vol. 2 (1806–1913).* Frankfurt/Main: Fritz Knapp.

Pohle Fraser, M. (1995). Risk, information and noise: Risk perception and risk management of French and German banks during the nineteenth century. *Financial History Review, 2* (1), 25–39.

Pohle Fraser, M., (1999). Noisy optimists. Risk management in French and German banks in the 19th and early 20th centuries. Unpublished Dissertation, Florence.

Pohle Fraser, M. (2002). Design or default? Who does housebanking and why? Some impressions from banks' archives. France and Germany, 1800–1915. In: K. P. Kostis (Ed.), *The creators and the creation of banking enterprises in Europe from the 18th to the 20th century* (pp. 255–291). Athens: Alpha Bank.

Pohle Fraser, M. (2007). Personal and impersonal exchange. The role of reputation in banking. Some evidence from nineteenth and early twentieth century banks' archives. In: P. Cotrell, E. Lange, & U. Olsson (Eds.), *Centres and peripheries in banking. The historical development of financial markets* (pp. 177–195). Aldershot et al.: Ashgate.

Pratt, J. (1964). Risk aversion in the small and in the large. *Econometrica, 32*, 122–136.

Rothschild, M., & Stiglitz, J. E. (1976). Equilibrium in competitive insurance markets. An essay on the economics of imperfect information. *The Quarterly Journal of Economics, 90* (4), 629–649.

Salais, R. (2011). Labour-related conventions and configurations of meaning. France, Germany and Great Britain prior to the Second World War. *Historical Social Research, 36* (4), 218–247.

Schumpeter, J. (1926, 2nd ed.). *Theorie der wirtschaftlichen Entwicklung. Eine Untersuchung über Unternehmergewinn, Kapital, Kredit, Zins und den Konjunkturzyklus*. Duncker & Humblot: München/Leipzig.

Sharpe, W. F. (1964). Capital asset prices. A theory of market equilibrium under conditions of risk. *The Journal of Finance, 19* (3), 425–442.

Stiglitz, J. E., & Weiss, A. (1981). Credit rationing in markets with imperfect information. *The American Economic Review, 71* (3), 393–410.

Storper, M., & Salais, R. (1997). *Worlds of production. The action frameworks of the economy*. Cambridge: Harvard University Press.

Tilly, R.H., (1980). Banken und Industrialisierung in Deutschland. Quantifizierungsversuche. In: Idem (Ed.), *Entwicklung und Aufgaben von Versicherungen und Banken in der Industrialisierung*. Berlin: Duncker & Humblot, pp. 163–193.

Tilly, R. H. (1986). German banking 1850–1914. Development assistance for the strong. *Journal des Economistes et des Etudes Humaines, 15*, 113–152.

Wellhöner, V. (1989). *Großbanken und Großindustrie im Kaiserreich*. Göttingen: Vandenhoeck & Ruprecht.
Williamson, O. E. (1975). Markets and hierarchies: Analysis and antitrust implications. In: *A study in the economics of internal organization*. New York et al: Free Press.
Williamson, O. E. (2000). The new institutional economics. Taking stock, looking ahead. *Journal of Economic Literature, 38* (3), 595–613.
Ziegler, D. (2005). Das deutsche Modell bankorientierter Finanzsysteme (1848–1957). In: P. Windolf (Ed.), *Finanzmarkt-Kapitalismus: Analysen zum Wandel von Produktionsregimen* (pp. 276–293). Wiesbaden: Verlag für Sozialwissenschaften.

Investigating Attitudes to Risk in British Banking: A Case Study of Barclays' Branch Banking System, c. 1900–80

Matthew Hollow

1 Introduction

As all who have studied finance or banking will know, risk-taking is both a central and an inescapable feature of the modern business of commercial banking (Lam 2003, 241–255). Deciding how much cash needs to be held in reserve; ascertaining whether or not a borrower is creditworthy; weighing up whether or not to invest in a particular class of security—all of these processes encompass a high degree of risk and need to be carefully managed if a bank is not to become insolvent and fail (Coleman 2011, 88–125; Crouhy et al. 2006).

Given this crucial position that risk-taking occupies in modern banking, it is perhaps surprising that those working in the fields of financial and business history have not given more attention to the manner in which bank's risk management techniques and decision-making

M. Hollow (✉)
York Management School, University of York, York, UK
e-mail: matthew.hollow@york.ac.uk

K. Schönhärl (ed.), *Decision Taking, Confidence and Risk Management in Banks from Early Modernity to the 20th Century*,
DOI 10.1007/978-3-319-42076-9_8

processes have developed and evolved over time (Pohle Fraser 1995, 29). Indeed, prior to the publication of this volume, the subject of risk management was conspicuous only by virtue of its almost total absence from the mainstream historical literature on banking in the USA and Europe.

This paper goes some way towards rectifying this notable blind spot in the historical literature by providing a detailed investigation of how one major British commercial bank—Barclays Bank—went about the inherently risky process of providing loans to small and local businesses in the period between 1900 and 1980. As will be seen, this was an era in which the majority of such lending decisions were carried out through Barclays' extensive network of local branches, with the chief arbiter typically being the local branch manager. Understanding how, and on what basis, these branch managers made their lending decisions will be one of the key aims of this essay. Also investigated will be the issue of how (or indeed if) Barclays tried to ensure that there was some degree of consistency between the decisions that each of these branch managers was making.

2 Background

2.1 Risk Management: Past and Present

Today, most commercial banks employ distinct risk management divisions containing ranks of specialist risk officers and risk analysts who take responsibility for assessing and managing (among other things): the creditworthiness of prospective borrowers, the potential for movements in the markets, and the optimum capital ratios for the bank to function efficiently (Crouhy et al. 2006; Heffernan 2005, 101–144; Lam 2003, 241–255).[1] Yet, it has certainly not always been this way. In fact, the first specially designated risk management department in the banking industry was only established in 1987 (by Merrill Lynch), and it was not until 1992 that the title of 'Chief Risk Officer' was first used in the sector (by James Lam at GE Capital) (Crockford 1982; Dionne 2013, 25; Kloman et al. 2008; Samakovitis 2012).

From a historical perspective, the fact that these sorts of clearly demarcated frameworks for risk management are only a relatively recent phenomenon is naturally of interest. Most notably, it indicates that, prior to the establishment of modern 'professionalised' risk management (replete with its complex algorithms and formulas), banks must have relied on other processes and procedures to manage the many risks to which they were exposed. Establishing what exactly these processes were (and ascertaining how they functioned in practice) is, therefore, the chief issue for any historian working in this field.

2.2 Current Literature

At the time of writing, the (admittedly fairly limited amount of) previous historical research that has been conducted on this topic has mostly been centred on the procedures through which nineteenth-century commercial banks decided whether or not to grant loans to potential borrowers. Characteristic of this particular approach is Pohle Fraser's (1995) influential study of the investment decisions that nine French and German banks made during the nineteenth century. What her research shows is that, in many cases, these nineteenth-century bankers overlooked the so-called 'bed-rock principles of banking' (balance-sheet data, borrowing history, etc.) in favour of more subjective judgements based upon the character and 'respectability' of the prospective borrower(s) (Pohle Fraser 1995). Similar findings have also been made by Newton (2000), who looked at the procedures that nineteenth-century British bank managers went through when assessing the creditworthiness of prospective borrowers. Like Pohle Fraser, she discovered that, in most cases, local banks would first consider the personal reputation of the applicant and his or her 'standing' in the local community (Newton 2000, 188).

From a historical perspective, inquiries such as these have been of immense value to historians (and those interested in the evolution of finance more generally) in the sense that they have helped to give a sense of how nineteenth-century bankers actually went about ascertaining the creditworthiness of prospective loan applicants. What remains less clear, however, is how far this practice of basing lending decisions upon subjective judgements about the character and 'respectability' of the prospective borrower continued into the twentieth century (and, if so, for how long). By looking at the manner in which Barclays went about making loans to small and local businesses in the years between 1900 and 1980, this paper will hopefully go some way towards improving understanding in this respect.

3 Barclays Bank

Like most of the large British banks, what is now known today as 'Barclays Bank' is actually the product of a series of amalgamations and partnerships between various small family-owned private banks (Capie and Rodrik-Bali 1982). From a historical perspective, the most significant of these various amalgamations was the one that took place in 1896 when twenty private banking firms (many connected to the influential Gurney family of Norwich) joined together to form Barclay and Co. Ltd. (Matthews and Tuke 1926).

Following this amalgamation, the newly established Barclays Bank proceeded to expand rapidly, acquiring many more small banks around the country, as well as expanding its own operations, until, by 1920, it had over 2,400 branches spread out across the country—placing it among the top five clearing banks in the UK (Ackrill and Hannah 2001, 59–72). In terms of its business operations, the most important area of business for Barclays, at this time, was its retail banking division, with individual depositors providing the bulk of Barclays' capital in the form of current and deposit accounts (Tuke and Gillman 1972, 22–25).[2] Indeed, thanks in part to some fairly restrictive legislation, deposit-taking banks like Barclays actually had relatively few other sources of potential income open to them (Collins 2012, 20–29).[3]

In order to ensure that they attracted as many potential deposits as possible, retail banks such as Barclays relied heavily upon their extensive network of local branches (Leyshon and Pollard 2000, 205–206; Moran 1986, 40–42). Aside from attracting fresh deposits, the main function of these local branches was to ensure that the bank (in this case Barclays) had a strong and visible presence in the local community.[4] This was important not only in the sense that it allowed the bank to obtain information about local market conditions but also in the fact that it helped them to foster close links with local businesses (Howcroft 1993).

In terms of their internal structure, most of Barclays' local branches were organised along fairly strict and hierarchical lines. At the bottom of the structure were the cashiers and accounts personnel, who served the bank's customers and dealt with the day-to-day administrative aspects of the branch's business. Next in the hierarchy was the chief clerk or accountant, who oversaw the operational running of the branch and made sure that everything was operating smoothly and correctly (Vik 2014, 92–94). And, finally, at the top of the pyramid stood the branch manager, who not only assumed ultimate responsibility for management of the branch but also undertook most, if not all, of the branch's business lending activity.[5]

The remaining sections of this paper will take a more in-depth look at this aspect of the branch manager's job remit in order to try and understand how—and via what practices and processes—they actually went about making loans to local businesses. In addition to this, how (or indeed if) the senior management in Barclays' head office sought to ensure that there was some degree of consistency between the lending decisions that each of these geographically dispersed branch managers were making in their own respective local constituencies will be taken into consideration.

4 Lending Practices

Before looking at the way in which individual branch managers went about making loans to local businesses it is first necessary to appreciate the parameters within which they were allowed to operate. The first and perhaps most important point to note in this respect is that despite their relative seniority within the bank's administrative hierarchy, no branch manager within Barclays was granted complete freedom to make an unlimited number of business loans. Instead, each branch manager was granted a specific lending discretion, the size of which could vary quite considerably depending on the seniority and experience of the particular branch manager.[6] Anything above this discretionary limit would require the branch manager to submit a special application to either the regional or national head office (who would then make the decision on whether or not to grant the particular loan) (Vik 2014, 90–91).

Alongside these discretionary limits, the senior management within Barclays' head office also tried to make sure that they were being kept abreast of all the lending decisions that were being made across their extensive network of branches. To ensure that this was the case, they made it a requirement for each branch manager to fill out a number of documents and forms each time they made a new business loan.[7] Among the most important of these documents was a form known as 'Form 21' that was intended to contain detailed information about the applicant's financial status and 'the whole extent of the manager's knowledge concerning the customer'.[8]

Guidance about how best to proceed when making lending decisions was also provided by Barclays' head office in the form of handbooks, guides and manuals. In almost every case, these guidelines recommended that the first stage in assessing any new loan application should be to obtain as much information about the finances and financial situation of the prospective borrower as possible (something that was usually made easier by the fact that, at this time, most people applied for loans from the institutions with whom they already banked) (Perry 1975, 300–306). To assist in this process it was also recommended that branch managers should try to obtain up-to-date copies of the borrower's balance sheets, trading and profit and loss accounts, the nature of the applicant's assets, and any relevant details about conditions in their respective industry or trade.[9]

Nevertheless, even with these guidelines and procedures in place, it appears as if many branch managers continued to rely heavily on subjective judgments about the character of the prospective borrower, as the following testimonies from one former Barclays' branch manager illustrates:

> *There were never two lending propositions the same … There was always a twist, the difference in the character of the individual, their ethical thinking. Some people would move heaven and earth to repay a loan. They'd rather go without a meal. They'd rather their children go without a meal in order to make sure that they were doing the absolutely honest thing as far as the bank loan was concerned; whereas there were other people who'd say the bank can wait: the children get fed first and so do I. There's a multitude of different attitudes.* (Vik 2014, 136).

Significantly, there also appears to have been a (tacit) acceptance from head office that branch managers would, at times, have to rely on their own initiative and intuition, as the following extract from one internal staff handbook illustrates:

> *It is, however, impossible to provide for every contingency which presents itself in the course of business, and therefore Managers are expected to exercise judgement and discretion in all matters coming before them, and to remember that it may be expedient in some cases to observe the spirit rather than the actual letter of the instructions, always having in view the best interests of the Bank.*[10]

Similarly, it also appears that, just as had been the case during the nineteenth century, many branch managers continued to put a great deal of effort into investigating the lifestyle and social habits of the prospective borrower, as the following quotes from one former Barclays' branch manager indicates:

> *You knew whether someone was spending a lot of time at local bookies or whether they were off with somebody else's wife.*

> *I knew them, I knew what they were capable of repaying. I used to go visit their businesses and see what they did, what they made and how they seemed.*[11]

Again, this continued practice of trying to obtain as much information as possible about the individual borrower and his or her personal circumstances appears to have been something that Barclays' central management was both aware of and willing to accept. Indeed, in one of the handbooks that all branch managers were provided with it was actually recommended that, before making a loan, a branch manager should find out about the borrower's personality (including his or her health, lifestyle, and spending habits) and, above all else, ask himself whether 'in the given circumstances [he] would be prepared to lend his own money (instead of the depositors') in support of the project'.[12] In this respect, therefore, it can clearly be seen that, despite the advances made in the fields of accountancy and bookkeeping during this era (Matthews 2006, 6–34), who one knew and how one acted still counted for much when it came to applying for a business loan from a local Barclays branch.

5 Consistency and Compliance

As just discussed, subjective judgements about a borrower's character and respectability continued to play an important role in commercial banks' lending decisions —just as they had throughout the nineteenth century (Newton 2000; Pohle Fraser 1995). The difference, however, was that whereas in the nineteenth century most commercial banks functioned on a primarily local scale (meaning that the bank's senior management could quite easily maintain control over all lending decisions being made), by the twentieth century banks like Barclays were operating at a truly national level with vast networks of semi-autonomous branches dotted across the UK (Vik 2014, 5–9). What will be explored in this last section, therefore, are the tactics and strategies that Barclays' senior management adopted to ensure that there was some degree of consistency between the lending decisions that each of these geographically dispersed branch managers were making in their own respective local constituencies.

The first and perhaps most important place to start in this respect is with the internal training that Barclays provided to its employees as they worked their way up the organisational hierarchy.[13] For the period upon which this paper is focused, the bulk of this internal training was orchestrated through three main training centres at Ashdown Park (Sussex), Wimbledon (SW London), and Teddington (SW London). Inside these centres, Barclays were able to negate many of the issues related to having such a dispersed workforce by bringing together branch managers from across the country and instructing them in a uniform and standardised manner, often over the course of many days.[14]

To check whether or not its employees were applying what they had been taught, Barclays also set up a fairly rigorous inspection regime in which local branches would be subject to regular visits (both announced and unannounced) by one of the bank's various regional inspection teams (each answerable to a different head office department). As in any organisation, these inspectors were charged not only with assessing the performance of each individual bank but also with ensuring that those employed in these branches were fulfilling the duties expected of them (McKinlay and Starkey 1998; Vik 2014, 92–93). To do this, these inspection teams would investigate a range of individual branch functions, including administrative procedures, customer service provision, the quality of security held for loans, and (perhaps most importantly) compliance with lending procedures and policies, with any indication of noncompliance (or at least deviance from the guidelines laid out in Barclays' many handbooks) being quickly reported back to head office.[15]

In addition to these frequent inspections, Barclays also had a clear framework for conducting annual performance appraisals for every member of staff within its extensive branch network. In most cases, these job evaluations would be conducted by someone from head office (with the assumption being that they would be able to offer a more detached and objective assessment than someone who was a personal colleague of the interviewee).[16] Among the key areas that these evaluators would look at would be the interviewee's performance and progress over the preceding year, as well as their capacity to advance higher up the career ladder. Based upon the answers that they provided, the evaluator would then award points to each employee in a variety of subcategories, including 'initiative', 'effective output', 'accuracy', and 'judgement'—thereby providing head office with an easy and quick way to assess and compare the performance of different branches and branch managers.[17]

When it came to actually dealing with troublesome and/or underperforming employees, the severity of the response from Barclays' head office could vary quite considerably. In some instances, troublesome and/or underperforming employees were in fact sacked or suspended from their positions in the bank (Hollow 2014). However, extreme punishments of this sort tended only to be used in the most serious incidents (e.g. those involving fraud, theft, forgery, etc.). In most cases, the response from head office would be to either reassign the culpable employee to a different branch or department (where, it was hoped, they would be better suited) or to put them under the close supervision of a (trusted) superior in the bank's hierarchy, whose job would be to 'keep an eye' on the respective employee (Vik 2014, 117).

Nevertheless, it should also be acknowledged that, when it came to the issue of encouraging consistency across branches, Barclays' head office did not just rely on strict disciplinary methods; they also made use of a range of 'softer', less draconian assimilation tactics (Nye 1990; Schwarzwald et al. 2004). Among the most significant of these was their deliberate policy of making sure that all employees had a sufficiently wide range of experiences of working in different departments within the bank (including working as part of the regional inspection teams and appraising loan applications in head office). This policy proved particularly important in maintaining Barclays' internal cohesion as it meant that, by the time they reached the level of branch manager, most employees already had first-hand knowledge of the rules and regulations laid out by head office, as well as a clearly defined sense of what head office expected from them (Vik 2014, 144–147).

Slightly less tangible, but no less important, were the various cultural and social activities that Barclays organised for its employees, including sports clubs, reading groups, theatre societies, and so forth (Ackrill and Hannah 2001, 158–160). Such societies and clubs proved particularly valuable to head office not only because they helped to foster a sense of corporate identity among employees, but also the fact that they worked to indoctrinate branch managers and other employees into the culture and history of the bank. Also important in this respect were the bank's various own in-house publications (notably the long-standing staff magazine *The Spread Eagle*), which played a vital role in propagating a particular image not only of the bank, but also of how its employees ought to behave, as the following entry on 'The Perfect Manager' illustrates:

> *His chief role is that of a lender … He is an influential man in his neighbourhood and a familiar figure in suburban society. Treasurer of every local club, he wields his weight in parochial committees.*[18]

Whether or not every branch manager in Barclays was able to live up to these lofty ideals is, of course, a moot point; however, what does seem clear is that, as a result of these sorts of 'soft' tactics, many branch managers within Barclays did feel compelled to regulate their own behaviour in accordance with how they presumed head office would want them to behave, as the following testimony from one former branch manager illustrates:

> *Essentially we were talking about the ethics of a family and, you know, does a family have a rulebook? The kids know how to behave because they see the parents' example and that's the way a family works.* (Vik 2014, 107).

When statements such as this are placed alongside the sorts of regulatory frameworks discussed above, it becomes possible to see how—despite the continuing tendency (at least partially) to rely upon subjective assessments about the applicant's character—Barclays' central management were able to feel confident that there was still a relatively high degree of consistency between the lending decisions that each of their geographically dispersed branch managers were making in their own respective local constituencies.

6 Conclusion

6.1 Changes Post-1980

Before moving on to summarise the arguments put forward in this paper, some of the changes that took place in Barclays' lending practices in the years after 1980 will be briefly outlined. The first and perhaps most important place to start in this respect is with the introduction of centralised credit-scoring systems (first for personal loans in the 1980s and then for business loans in the 1990s). These computerised credit-scoring programmes proved to have a profound effect upon Barclays' lending practices as they were able to provide central management with (supposedly) more objective 'multi-variate statistical analysis to predict the credit performance of consumers' (Leyshon and Thrift 1999, 444). This not only allowed Barclays' head office to get a clearer picture of their potential credit exposure, it also diminished the need for local branch managers to provide detailed information about the applicant's character or background (Wainwright 2009).

The (inevitable) result of this increased reliance upon computerised and standardised credit-scoring systems was that more and more lending decisions gradually started to be made centrally. As a result, the role of the branch manager slowly came to be redefined from one focused on business lending *and* branch management to one focused solely on branch management (Vik 2014, 156–159). Equally injurious to the prestige of the local branch were the emergence of ATMs and online/telephone banking—both of which lessened the need for bank customers to physically visit their local branch (Bátiz-Lazo and Wood 2002). Again, the upshot of this was that the importance of the local branch came to be diminished, with many branches either closing or having the range of services they offered severely cut back (Ackrill and Hannah 2001, 347–349).

7 Summary

As the preceding paragraphs have outlined, this (relatively) recent trend of using computerised scoring systems to centralise all lending facilities contrasts markedly with the manner in which Barclays oversaw its lending to small and local businesses during the period 1900–1980. Instead, what took place during this period was essentially a continuation of the nineteenth-century practice (Newton 2000; Pohle Fraser 1995) of basing lending decisions on a combination of financial considerations (e.g. balance-sheet data, borrowing history, etc.) and subjective judgements about the 'character' and 'respectability' of the prospective borrower—with the upshot being that individual branch managers (who tended to be most privy to this sort of information) came to assume a pivotal role in the lending process.

Based on these findings, this paper then moved on to look at the tactics and strategies employed by Barclays' central management to try and ensure that there was some degree of consistency between the decisions that each one of these geographically dispersed branch managers was making when it came to assessing loan applications. What it showed was that, in addition to conventional disciplinary measures and standard-issued guidelines, Barclays also made great use of more indirect, 'softer', management techniques, such as specific in-house training, staff rotation, and social activities. The effect of this combining of 'hard' and 'soft' disciplinary measures was to produce a network of branch managers who, despite being widely dispersed throughout the country, not only remained well aware of what was expected of them, but also largely 'bought into' the ethos and culture of the bank—thereby making the potentially challenging task of maintaining consistency in lending decisions across the Barclays' branch network that much easier.

Notes

1. To say nothing of the various other nonfinancial risks (such as reputational risk, operational risks, etc.) that they are often also responsible for managing.
2. By 1957, Barclays held approximately $3.912 m worth of deposits on its books, making it the fifth largest bank in the world at that time (Lascelles 2005, 6).
3. Unlike some other countries, deposit-taking banks in Britain did not really engage in mortgage provision (this was largely left to the building societies). Similarly, insurance and investment banking were also largely provided by specialist organisations (Hamnett 1994).
4. In terms of their other duties, they also assumed responsibility for: opening new bank accounts, issuing new chequebooks, monitoring delinquent loans, and settling the day's business (Vik 2014, 84–86).
5. Although this was the typical internal structure of Barclays' branches, it should be noted that not all branches were structured in this way. Some larger branches also employed Deputy Managers and/or Assistant Managers to assist the Branch Manager in his/her duties, whilst some smaller branches did not actually have their own Branch Managers (remaining instead under the control of a larger local full-service branch) (Ackrill and Hannah 2001, 74–79; Vik 2014, 94–95).
6. For instance, those branch managers with less experience were sometimes only given freedom to lend up to £30,000, whilst those with more experience and/or in charge of bigger branches might be granted lending limits of up to £1m (Vik 2014, 130–131).
7. *London & South Western Head Office Instructions to Branch Managers and Clerks* (1909). Barclays Bank Archive, A81.
8. *Staff Handbook* (1955, 105–106). Barclays Bank Archive, 0029–1601. On top of this, Barclays' Head Office also asked for branch managers to fill out, and keep up to date, a document known as 'Information Sheet

Form 210A'. Like Form 21, this form was intended to contain information about the customer's 'character, connections, assets and liabilities'.

9. *Staff Handbook* (1955, 105–106). Barclays Bank Archive, 0029–1601.
10. *London & South Western Head Office Instructions to Branch Managers and Clerks* (1909, i). Barclays Bank Archive, A81.
11. Finlo Rohrer, *Back to ye olden days banking?* BBC News Magazine (21 October 2008). Available online at: http://news.bbc.co.uk/1/hi/magazine/7681842.stm (Accessed: 4 April 2015).
12. L. C. Mather, *The Lending Banker: A Review of the Principles of Bank Lending Unsecured Advances* (London: Waterlow & Sons 1955, 8–12). And, in fact, most branch managers did have a personal interest in the loans they provided as they invariably banked with Barclays (Vik 2014, 115–118).
13. It should be remembered that, at this time, a job in a big commercial bank such as Barclays was very much considered a 'job for life', with the expectation that those who joined the bank at 16 or 18 would work their way up the ladder, with a handful eventually reaching the position of branch manager (Storey et al. 1997; Stovel et al. 1996).
14. Out of these three centres, two (Ashdown and Wimbledon) provided residential facilities, meaning that Barclays was able to attend long (sometimes up to four weeks) intensive training camps. *Staff Training Centres Report* (1980). Barclays Bank Archive, 0300–1017.
15. In addition, they would also carry out formal and informal interviews with various employees in each branch in order to try and find out as much information as they could about the personal circumstances of each employee and whether or not they would be likely to leave in the future. *Newcastle Branch Report* (28 April 1980). Barclays Bank Archive, 1214–0189.
16. *Barclays: Annual Staff Assessment* (1974). Barclays Bank Archive, 1214–0138.
17. *Standing Instructions for Completion of Staff Report Forms* (1974). Barclays Bank Archive, 1214–0138.
18. L. B. Comerford, 'The Perfect Manager' (1929), in: *The Eagle Looks Back: A silver jubilee anthology of twenty-five years' contributions to 'The Spread Eagle,'* the staff magazine of Barclays Bank Limited (Leagrave Press: Luton, 1951, 21).

References

Ackrill, M., & Hannah, L. (2001). *Barclays: The business of banking, 1690–1996.* Cambridge: Cambridge University Press.

Bátiz-Lazo, B., & Wood, D. (2002). An historical appraisal of information technology in commercial banking. *Electronic Markets, 12*, 192–205.

Capie, F., & Rodrik-Bali, G. (1982). Concentration in British banking 1870–1920. *Business History, 24* (3), 280–292.

Coleman, T. S. (2011). *A practical guide to risk management.* London: CFA Institute.

Collins, M. (2012). *Money and banking in the UK: A history* (Vol. 6). London: Routledge.

Crockford, G. N. (1982). The bibliography and history of risk management: Some preliminary observations. *The Geneva Papers on Risk and Insurance, 7*, 169–179.

Crouhy, M., Galai, D., & Mark, R. (2006). *The essentials of risk management.* New York: McGraw-Hill.

Hamnett, C. (1994). Restructuring housing finance and the housing market. In: S. Corbridge, N. Thrift, & R. Martin (Eds.), *Money, power and space* (pp. 281–308). Oxford: Blackwell.

Heffernan, S. (2005). *Modern banking.* New York: Wiley.

Hollow, M. (2014). Money, morals and motives: An exploratory study into why bank managers and employees commit fraud at work. *Journal of Financial Crime, 21*, 174–190.

Howcroft, J. B. (1993). Branch networks and alternative distribution channels: Threats and opportunities. *International Journal of Bank Marketing, 11* (6), 26–31.

Kloman, H. F., Fraser, J., & Simkins, B. J. (2008). A brief history of risk management. In: J. Fraser & B. J. Simkins (Eds.), *Enterprise risk management* (pp. 19–29). New York: Wiley.

Lam, J. (2003). *Enterprise risk management: from incentives to control.* New York: Wiley.

Lascelles, D. (2005). *Other people's money: The revolution in high-street banking.* Somerset: Butler & Tanner.

Leyshon, A., & Pollard, J. (2000). Geographies of industrial convergence: the case of retail banking. *Transactions of the Institute of British Geographers, 25* (2), 203–220.

Leyshon, A., & Thrift, N. (1999). Lists come alive: Electronic systems of knowledge and the rise of credit-scoring in retail banking. *Economy and Society, 28*, 434–466.

Matthews, D. (2006). *A history of auditing: The changing audit process in Britain from the nineteenth century to the present day*. London: Routledge.

Matthews, P. W., & Tuke, A. W. (1926). *History of Barclays Bank Limited.* London: Blades East & Blades.

McKinlay, A., & Starkey, K. (1998). Managing Foucault: Foucault, management and organization theory. In: A. McKinlay & K. Starkey (Eds.), *Foucault, management and organization theory: From panopticon to technologies of self* (pp. 1–13). London: Sage.

Moran, M. (1986). *The politics of banking: The strange case of competition and credit control.* London: Macmillan.

Newton, L. (2000). Trust and virtue in English banking: The assessment of borrowers by bank managements at the turn of the nineteenth century. *Financial History Review, 7* (2), 177–199.

Nye, J. S. (1990). Soft power. *Foreign Policy, 80*, 153–171.

Perry, F. E. (1975). *The elements of banking.* London: Methuen.

Pohle Fraser, M. (1995). Risk, information and noise: Risk perception and risk management of French and German banks during the nineteenth century. *Financial History Review, 2* (1), 25–39.

Schwarzwald, J., Koslowsky, M., & Ochana-Levin, T. (2004). Usage of and compliance with power tactics in routine versus nonroutine work settings. *Journal of Business and Psychology, 18*, 385–402.

Samakovitis, G. (2012). UK banking experts as decision-makers: A historical view on banking technologies. *Journal of Technology Research, 3*, 1–20.

Storey, J., Cressey, P., Morris, T., & Wilkinson, A. (1997). Changing employment practices in UK banking: Case studies. *Personnel Review, 26*, 24–42.

Stovel, K., Savage, M., & Bearman, P. (1996). Ascription into achievement: Models of career systems at Lloyds Bank, 1890–1970. *American Journal of Sociology, 102*, 358–399.

Tuke, A. W., & Gillman, R. J. H. (1972). *Barclays Bank Limited, 1926-1969: Some recollections.* London: Barclays Bank Limited.

Vik, P. M., (2014). *The demise of the bank branch manager: The depersonalisation and disembedding of modern British banking.* Doctoral dissertation, University of Salford, http://usir.salford.ac.uk/32045/ [Accessed 23 Oct 2016].

Wainwright, T. A., (2009). The geographies of securitisation and credit scoring. Doctoral dissertation, University of Nottingham, unpublished.

Between Novelty and Fashion: Risk Management and the Adoption of Computers in Retail Banking

Bernardo Bátiz-Lazo

1 Introduction

Late in 2015, HSBC was host to some 275,000 unfinished retail payment transactions in a single day (Collinson and Bachelor 2015). This was within a month of the day when 600,000 payments were unfulfilled at the Royal Bank of Scotland and its subsidiaries NatWest, Ulster Bank and Coutts (McAteer 2015; Sheffield 2015). Something along the same lines took place almost simultaneously at the Commonwealth Bank in Australia (Mannix 2015). Upgrades of legacy software were to blame in all cases.

Meanwhile, in wholesale markets (also in 2015), a significant reduction in Chinese stock prices was followed by similar moves across the world. These events led international economic commentator Rana Foroohar (2015) to lament about how little had been learned by financial

B. Bátiz-Lazo (✉)
Bangor Business School, Bangor University, Bangor, UK

K. Schönhärl (ed.), *Decision Taking, Confidence and Risk Management in Banks from Early Modernity to the 20th Century*,
DOI 10.1007/978-3-319-42076-9_9

authorities and market participants about computer trading exacerbating a market correction. Foroohar's view was not novel as similar comments had been a regular feature in the media since at least October of 1987 when computer trading emerged as one of the causes behind the so-called 'Black Monday' (Morris 1987; Knight 2013).

Foroohar's comments, developments around 'Black Monday' and developments in retail banking show how at the dawn of the twenty-first-century applications of computer technology are ubiquitous and a fact of life in banking and finance. Indeed, there is some consensus that the most important forms of change in retail finance since 1970 have been associated with the adoption of computer applications, regulatory innovation and/or new ways to assess (and price) risk (Bátiz-Lazo and Woldensenbet 2006; Bátiz-Lazo and Wood 1999, 2003; Williams 2015). The adoption of information technology (IT) and computer applications in particular, plays a crucial role in the strategic expansion of financial institutions. This growth has been reflected in both the size of business and territorial expansion as financial institutions have constructed national and international networks of agents, representative offices, retail branch outlets and fully fledged subsidiaries. The process of adoption of IT began in the mid to late 1950s. Early computer applications in securities trading involved testing whether stock market prices followed a random walk or not; whereas inside financial institutions computers were initially employed around the accounting function (such as payrolls or digitalising ledgers). Throughout the following decades, banking and finance became one of the main consumers of computer applications across the world.

There is a growing body of systematic studies discussing the impact and use of information technology in business and, particularly, financial institutions in Western Europe and North America from an historical perspective. There are several strands to these contributions, dating from the early introduction of mechanical contraptions and computers (Berkeley 1949; Booth 2001; Campbell-Kelly 1989; Campbell-Kelly 1992, 1998; Ellis 1931; Osborn 1954; Rouse 1930; Wardley 2000), to more recent efforts which include, among others, conceptual discussions (Bátiz-Lazo and Wood 2002; Coombs et al. 1992; Lamoreaux et al. 2003; Langlois 2003), the deployment of specific devices (Bátiz-Lazo 2009; McKenney and Fisher 1993; McKenney et al. 1997) and applications (Haigh 2001,

2006; Pardo-Guerra 2011; Stearns 2011), single company and industry case studies (Bátiz-Lazo and Wardley 2007; Billings and Booth 2011; Booth 2001, 2007; Martin 2012; Wardley 2000; Wood and Bátiz-Lazo 1997), as well as the nature of organisational groups (Billings 2007; Maixé-Altés 2014; Scott and Zachariadis 2014) and specific practices (Poon 2011).

In spite of these contributions, and a special issue (Bátiz-Lazo and Boyns 2004) as well as an edited book (Bátiz-Lazo et al. 2011), the study from an historical perspective of how computers have changed risk management decisions in financial markets and institutions remains underexplored. Although historians have published on computerisation in European and North American financial institutions during the late twentieth century, little has been documented on similar experiences in Asia, Africa, Oceania and Latin America.[1] As a result, the field is somewhat underrepresented within the overall history of banking (Colvin 2015). Others such as Frame and White (2009) continue to perpetrate the myth that all innovations in this area have emerged solely from experiences in the USA.

In short, this chapter will focus on how IT applications changed decision-making processes and risk management routines in retail banking. This is important because, first, it focuses not on the devices but on changes in the management of information. Indeed for a while, the glamour and novelty of applications of computer and communications technologies overshadowed research on how organisational processes, procedures and routines changed (or not) following the adoption of mechanical, electromechanical and digital machinery (Cortada 2011). Information is the fundamental component of the modern corporation (Yates 1989, 1997, 2005). Yet focusing on innovations associated with information technology will help to articulate an overview of the evolution of both commercial banking and computing as well as the history of their industrial organisation. This approach thus enables computing to be viewed as a business history (Cortada 1996), and banking to be seen as part of the history of computing (Cortada 2006).

The next section briefly discusses the challenges of researching innovation in banking. The third section offers a broad look at the history of computing in retail banking from the perspective of the business historian. Emphasis is placed on how decisions to adopt general-purpose computing were made. The fourth and final section reflects on the long-term impact of computer technology on banks' risk management while offering a tentative way forward.

2 About Innovation in Banking

Researching computers in banking and finance from an historical perspective requires developing an understanding of different types of innovation in order to ascertain the nature of technological change. At its most basic, innovation is associated with economic growth and depicted, for instance, as an expansion of the production possibilities frontier or a movement along the long-term average cost curve. Empirical validation, however, is often inconclusive, partly because 'innovation' is one of those overused terms in business and economics that has effectively lost meaning.[2] Whether assessing the impact of new regulation, changes in the productivity of individual firms, or the development of new skills or instruments to assess risk, studies of financial innovation have been subject to the same constraints. This thus renders any review that aims to summarise research into innovation in financial markets and institutions either totally encompassing or thoroughly incomplete.

This chapter opts for the latter while aiming to consider broad trends within established and emerging systematic contributions towards the better understanding of technological innovation as related to the application of computer technology within retail financial markets and the institutions that populate them. Specifically, deposit-taking financial institutions will be focused on, with an emphasis on the so-called commercial banks. These are the organisational forms that dominated empirical studies as well as the market for retail deposits in most countries throughout the twentieth century. Of course, this is not an attempt to dismiss other organisational forms that by the end of the twentieth century had populated markets for retail finance including investment banks, savings banks, micro-finance, postal banks, import/export banks, development banks, insurance companies, hire purchase organisations, etc.

A second order of ideas is the duration of technological change in banking. This is a process which can be dated to the origins of retail banking in the late seventeenth century. Since then financial intermediaries working in retail banking markets have undergone a sustained and continuous process of change that has altered their nature, size, structure and behaviour. In the last century or so financial institutions have also been locations of significant technological change—albeit as the locus of the diffusion of new technology rather than the development of novel machinery. Furthermore, in their application of waves of new technology, financial intermediaries have adapted to change both in terms of what they do and of how they do it.

Inevitably, the nature of mechanisation and the type of technology introduced to achieve 'modernity' is a significant part of this chapter. However, this is not a tale of technological determinism. Rather, managers and directors at retail banks endeavoured to assess the costs and benefits associated with the adoption of new technologies and act appropriately given their perceptions of the business environment (Coopey 1999, 2004). A case in point is the adoption of the cash dispenser in 1967. This was novel and untested technology and one of the few examples where banks rather than engineers promoted its conception and development in Britain and Sweden (Bátiz-Lazo 2009; Bátiz-Lazo et al. 2014). The innovation was a direct response to and a potential solution for greater unionisation and spiralling labour costs. Banks in several other countries (as diverse as the USA, France, Spain, Mexico and Israel) promptly followed suit and explored the potential of this device, albeit cautiously by deploying individual or at most a couple of dozen units. Throughout the 1970s the devices evolved as they sought to replicate different forms of transactions otherwise undertaken by a human bank teller. Banks in several countries persevered and continued to invest in this technology as it was until the mid- to late 1980s when 'it came of age' and proprietary networks grew to thousands of units each (Harper and Bátiz-Lazo 2013).[3]

Of course, managers' assessments altered significantly as the economic, social, political and cultural landscape was transformed by a number of factors. These included: the much expanded role of the state as shown by the adoption of British-made ICL by the Post Office and

Trustee Savings Banks, as a result not of a cost/benefit analysis but of the British government's belated policy attempts to develop an indigenous computer industry (Bátiz-Lazo et al. 2014; Billings and Booth 2011); the impact of war as innovations for the military found their way into business, such as IBM translating knowledge developed through inter-continental ballistic missiles into the business applications of computers (Cortada 2006); changing perceptions of gender, as up to the 1970s, women were limited to secretarial and repetitive, labour-intensive jobs (Booth 2008; Wardley 2011); and the development of a large managerial class and its increased professionalism (more below). Although new technology underpins these developments, these additional themes also play a role in this story.

Mechanisation, and later on computerisation, took place on the back of long-established systems of control in the form of an adherence to closely specified practices and protocols. These clearly specified and supervised routines (and accounting systems) determined the organisation and nature of day-to-day business in head offices and retail bank branches.

An illustration of the transformation of these processes relevant to the theme of this edited book is how computer applications changed the location of and responsibilities for assessing the creditworthiness of individual customers. For most of the twentieth century, this was the remit of the manager of the retail branch, who decided on advances to individual customers, or equally importantly, filtered requests to head office. Achieving the status of manager of a retail branch carried great responsibility and offered financial and social rewards because the manager had important standing within his community (Bátiz-Lazo and Wood 2000). The managers were all men, recruited as school leavers (aged 16). They rose through the ranks by proving themselves to be trustworthy, disciplined and cautious (Seltzer 2004). When assessing creditworthiness the usual criteria was not the individual's cash flow or history of liquid balances (i.e. the ability to repay) as much as the nature of the collateral, history at the branch, social standing and reputation. Eligibility thus required a relationship with the manager and access to a current account which, to begin with, was mostly the remit of the well-off and middle-class men. There was, of course, a degree of 'credit rationing'.[4]

Things were to change, at least in part as a result of retailers developing numerical credit scoring (Poon 2009, 2011). Retail banks adopted this system much later, already in computerised form and controlled from head office. This brief example thus illustrates that the result of this and other forms of computerisation was to upset the organisational setting built in the decades prior to World War II by introducing central offices that would replace retail branches as the bank's value creation units (Ackrill and Hannah 2001; Bátiz-Lazo 2009).

3 From Ledger to Laser Beam

A process involving great changes in the equipping of bank offices began in the late nineteenth century and heightened during the first two decades of the twentieth century. New technology, embodied in telephones, typewriters, pneumatic communication tubes, photographic records, steel filing cabinets, paper clips and electric lighting became more common (see Table 9). One such innovation saw the adoption of the adding machine which could undertake many of the essential but routine operations of basic arithmetic that characterised the overwhelming majority of operations undertaken in banks and other bureaucratic organisations (Wootton and Kemmerer 2007). Communication between the specialists managing the bank's accounting function and vendors of mechanical accounting devices (such as NCR, IBM and Burroughs) was important (Cortada 1993). Their interaction cemented long-lasting relationships that would later see accountants[5] spearheading the introduction of computer equipment into some banks as the vendors of mechanical accounting diversified into general application computer equipment (Bátiz-Lazo and Wardley 2007).

Electromechanical tabulators were a second group of important devices (Heide 1994, 2008, 2009). The adoption of these required a special set of skills for their operation which included, among others, a group of people (usually pools of women) transferring handwritten information to punch cards, as well as a group of specialists (usually men) that could reprogram the device for different applications by physically rearranging the wiring (Bátiz-Lazo and Wardley 2007; Booth 2008; Wardley 2011). The latter group would often form the kernel of the operations

Table 9 Selected use of technology in the retail banking organisation

	Early adoption (1770–1915)	Early mechanisation (1916–1955)	Specific application (1956–1971)	Emergence (1967–1982)	Diffusion (1983–2015)
Innovation in service offering	• Reduce inter-market price differentials • Banknotes • Personal cheques	• Detailed (country club) statements • Currency exchange • Safe deposit boxes	• Conversion from branch to bank relationships • Automated bank statements • Cheque guarantee & credit cards • Personal (unsecured) loans	• Growth of cross-border payment • Widespread adoption of ATM • Bank of the 'masses' • New external forms to price risk (Eurobonds, options)	• Supply of non-payment products like insurance, mortgages and pensions • Debit cards • Financial inclusion • E-wallets, digital currencies, mobile payments. • Self-service
Operational function innovation	• Internal forms to price risk (joint stock & permanent BS) • Explore economies of scale (amalgamation) • Correspondence banking • Office equipment	• Increased coordination between head office and branches • Facilitate specific tasks (e.g. accounting and payroll) • Tabulators	• Reduce cost of labour-intensive activities (i.e. clearing system) • Demise of internal labour market • Computerised teller machines and terminals • Mainframe computers	• Automation of branch accounting • Real-time control begins • Teleprocessing • Mini computers at branches	• Growth of alternative distribution channels, such as phone, e-banking and EFTPOS

Source: Bátiz-Lazo and Wood (2002) and Bátiz-Lazo and Wardley (2007)

and methods departments inside commercial banks (Booth 2004, 2007), and, like accountants, would be responsible for advising on the adoption of general-purpose computing.

As is implied above, the directors of commercial banks in the 1950s and 1960s relied on middle managers in accounting and operations and methods departments to make decisions about the adoption of general-purpose computers. But more often than not they had little idea of what was involved in the use of computers. Nonetheless, senior managers were willing to explore and invest in this technology (Martin 2011, 2012). A case in point is that of Sir John Anthony Holt Saunders (1917–2002), chief executive of HSBC between 1962 and 1972 (Bátiz-Lazo and Smith 2016, 58).[6] Saunders came to regard computerisation as vital for the future of the bank after a visit to the USA in the mid-1960s. Saunders returned to Hong Kong convinced of the need to keep up with US banks. In 1964 he set up a Methods & Research (M&R) unit to study the use of computer technologies and assigned the task of supervising computerisation to Norman Howard Talbot Bennett (born 1921). As head of the M&R team Bennett negotiated the bank's first contract for a computer with IBM in December 1965. A key point here is that British-born Bennett had left the United Kingdom and joined HSBC in 1946, well before the British banking industry began introducing electronic computers in the late 1950s. Bennett had, therefore, been isolated from these developments and knew little more than Saunders about computers.[7] Neither did Bennett possess knowledge of any of the disciplines (such as engineering, maths or physics) that would typically gravitate to electronic computing.

This was symptomatic. Immersed in the logic of an internal labour market,[8] bank directors would appoint 'bankers' to learn about computing while mistrusting 'engineers'. As mentioned, this was partly a reflection of the inertia of the systems and procedures related to control, although a lack of knowledge about computers in general also played a part. But keeping up with technological change was demanding and by the early 1970s directors increasingly relied on external consultants (Bátiz-Lazo and Wardley 2007; Kipping and Westerhuis 2014). At the same time, and as was the case in Swedish savings banks, some young managers embraced the technological change agenda early on and eventually moved up to positions of responsibility where they could implement ideas which in the past were seen as far-fetched (Bátiz-Lazo et al. 2014).

There is reason to believe that, at least in the Swedish case, young managers really believed in the new methods. Throughout the 1950s these young managers were under the leadership of Sven G Svensson, director of Sparfrämjandet, who also organised annual conferences in Saltsjöbaden (near Stockholm) to facilitate the meeting of like-minded young managers (Bátiz-Lazo et al. 2014; Thodenius et al. 2011). They were united by the idea that the savings banks had to adjust to social change. Furthermore, they believed that savings banks should meet the challenge of commercial banks not by demanding protection from the state but by introducing better services. Many of the ideas that came out of the conferences at Saltsjöbaden were implemented during the 1960s and 1970s as the attendants reached influential positions within the savings banks. As a result the Swedish savings banks evolved from small-scale savings institutions to 'modern' business-oriented banks.

It is up to further empirical research to determine whether this type of experience was unique to Sweden and, of even more interest, how changes in attitudes towards computer applications permeated banking organisations as the twentieth century came to a close. The fact remains, however, that a chasm was to open inside banking organisations. In the course of the last three decades of the twentieth century banks increasingly relied on applications of IT for more than gaining greater efficiency in everyday business, and 'engineers' and 'bankers' fought for control of the organisation (Fincham et al. 1994). This arm-wrestling prevailed until 'hybrids' or people that could be trusted and also thoroughly 'speak' the language of both banking and engineering rose through the ranks and came to dominate banking organisations in the late 1990s (Bátiz-Lazo and Wood 1999, 2003).

4 In Summary: Bankers, Risk and IT

This chapter has focused on the role of technicians and computer specialists in the introduction of computerisation in banking. It has discussed how financial institutions in general and retail deposit-accepting banks in particular, adopted mechanical, electromechanical and then digital devices. Initially, the aim was to gain greater efficiency in operations. But at the same time, the introduction of these labour-saving devices brought about changes (perhaps Tayloristic in nature) within the banking organisation where customer-facing staff lost their skill set.

Evidence of this is the manager of the retail bank branch losing social standing within his immediate community. Algorithms inside computers rather than managers of retail bank branches would make ultimate decisions about loans and other types of advances. This was not a linear process: technology changed but so did bankers and the society around them. In the long-term, it is difficult to distinguish cause from effect as these factors were intimately intertwined. For instance, banks' active recruitment of female university graduates rather than male school leavers is yet another sign of change in banks' practices and in society.

In any case, new practices and new technologies brought about new challenges, such as keeping up with technological change and the creation of new communities of practice, that would bid for the ultimate control of the banking organisation. Thus a legacy of technological change in the late twentieth century was that computer technicians and computer engineers had a hand in influencing and shaping banks' risk management techniques. Initially they were seen as a separate and distinctive group, but the jury is still out as to whether the early twenty-first century saw a new breed of banker-technician (such as John Reed at Citibank) or whether key computer applications remain the remit of a handful of people (*ergo*, there is no deep understanding of computer systems by senior managers).

This chapter has emphasised retail markets and the adoption of hardware. The latter is relatively easy to follow given the large capital investment and lifespan involved. There is still much to be learned about smaller devices (such as mini- and personal computers) and, as noted by Gandy (2013), the role of software in shaping practices, procedures and recruitment.

Meanwhile, and with notable exceptions (Kyrtsis 2010; Pardo-Guerra 2011; Scott and Zachariadis 2012, 2014), there is a dearth of studies of the computerisation of wholesale financial markets from an historical perspective. This is in sharp contrast to the attention that the sociology of finance has given to these markets and institutions (McKenzie 2005; Millo and McKenzie 2009; Pardo-Guerra 2010). Broadly speaking, this field argues that computer networks are built to replicate social connections rather than to influence or be shaped by those practices. Whether economic and business historians share this view is yet to be seen. But this literature certainly offers a place to initiate a conversation. There is also a body of literature around the history of computers and computing that often touches on banking applications, published in outlets such as *IEEE Annals in the History of Computing*, *History & Technology*, and *Technology and Culture*.

In addition, there is of course, the work of information system academics and their various outlets, who also regularly deal with issues within financial service organisations.

Finally, and given the large lacuna in this area, it is hard at the start of the twenty-first century to ascertain the extent to which computers took over risk management from human beings to shape technological change, or whether human beings imposed it on themselves. Hopefully, this chapter will enthuse others who will help shed light on this question.

Notes

1. Notable exceptions include Bátiz-Lazo and Smith (2016), del Angel (2011) and Rishi and Saxena (2004).
2. For an interesting yet brief critique on the culture of innovation in business and management see Lepore (2015).
3. The ATM Industry Association expected there to be three million ATMs across the globe by the end of 2015 and the total number of global cash withdrawals from ATMs to rise to above 8.6 billion per year (Morrison 2014).
4. In their seminar article, Stiglitz and Weiss (1981) define 'credit rationing' as an excess demand for loans where individuals of the same credit standing have been denied an advance either randomly (i.e. an internal deficiency of the bank) or as a result of 'redlining'. Redlining was originally coined in the USA to describe the practice of denying services, either directly or through selectively raising prices, to residents of certain areas based on the racial or ethnic makeup of those areas.

5. The trajectory of accountants inside retail financial institutions remains largely unchartered. They certainly do not seem to have achieved the same level of influence as their counterparts in manufacturing (Matthews et al. 1998).
6. Unless otherwise stated the remainder of this paragraph borrows freely from Bátiz-Lazo and Smith (2016, 56–59).
7. HSBC was not totally blind in the navigation of its first adoption as key appointments on Bennett's team were British expatriates who had firsthand programming experience with computers (Bátiz-Lazo and Smith, 2016, 59).
8. Internal labour markets required the implementation of career structures and, most important of all, the designation of power and authority within a retail branch network (Seltzer 2004; Wardley 2000).

References

Ackrill, M., & Hannah, L. (2001). *Barclays: The business of banking 1690–1996*. Cambridge: Cambridge University Press.

Bátiz-Lazo, B. (2009). Emergence and evolution of ATM networks in the UK, 1967–2000. *Business History, 51*, 1–27.

Bátiz-Lazo, B., & Boyns, T. (2004). The business and financial history of automation and technological change in 20th century banking. *Accounting Business and Financial History Journal, 14*, 225–232.

Bátiz-Lazo, B., & Smith, A. (2016). The changing industrial organization of epistemic communities during Hong Kong's progression towards a cashless society (1960s–2000s). *IEEE Annals in the History of Computing, 38*(2 (Apr–Jun)), 54–65.

Bátiz-Lazo, B., & Wardley, P. (2007). Banking on change: Information systems and technologies in UK high street banking, 1919–1969. *Financial History Review, 14*, 177–205.

Bátiz-Lazo, B., & Woldensenbet, K. (2006). Product and process innovations in banking. *International Journal of Financial Services Management, 1*, 400–421.

Bátiz-Lazo, B., & Wood, D. (1999). Management of core capabilities in Mexican and European banks. *International Journal of Service Industry Management (Special issue on Service Management in Latin America), 10*, 430–448.

Bátiz-Lazo, B., & Wood, D. (2000). Effects of regulatory change on European banks: A case study on the strategy and stock market performance of Lloyds Bank 1980–1993. *Journal of European Financial Services, 4*, 31–63.

Bátiz-Lazo, B., & Wood, D. (2002). An historical appraisal of information technology in commercial banking. *Electronic Markets – The International Journal of Electronic Commerce & Business Media, 12*, 192–205.

Bátiz-Lazo, B., & Wood, D. (2003). Strategy, competition and diversification in European and Mexican banking. *International Journal of Bank Marketing, 21*, 2002–2016.

Bátiz-Lazo, B., Maixé-Altés, J. C., & Thomes, P. (2011). *Technological innovation in retail finance: International historical perspectives*. London and New York: Routledge.

Bátiz-Lazo, B. and A. Smith (2016). "The Changing Industrial Organization of Epistemic Communities During Hong Kong's Progression Towards a Cashless Society (1960s-2000s)." IEEE Annals in the History of Computing 38(2 (Apr-Jun)): 54-65.

Bátiz-Lazo, B., Karlsson, T., & Thodenius, B. (2014). The origins of the cashless society: Cash dispensers, direct to account payments and the development of on-line real-time networks, c. 1965–1985. *Essays in Economic and Business History, 32*, 100–137.

Berkeley, E. C. (1949). *Giant brains or machines that think*. New York: Wiley.

Billings, M. (2007). Corporate treasury in international business history. *Business and Economic History On-Line*. The Business History Conference.

Billings, M., & Booth, A. E. (2011). Techno-nationalism, the Post Office and the creation of Britain's National Giro. In: B. Bátiz-Lazo, J. C. Maixé-Altés, & P. Thomes (Eds.), *Technological innovation in retail finance: International historical perspectives* (pp. 155–172). London: Routledge.

Booth, A. E. (2001). British retail banks, 1955–70: A case of 'Americanisation'? In: M. Kipping & N. Tiratsoo (Eds.), *Americanisation in twentieth century Europe: Business, culture, politics* (pp. 309–323). Lille: Université Charles de Gaulle.

Booth, A. E. (2004). Technical change in branch banking at the Midland Bank, 1945–75. *Accounting, Business and Financial History, 14*, 277–300.

Booth, A. E. (2007). *The management of technical change: Automation in the U.K. and U.S.A. since 1950*. Basingstoke: Palgrave.

Booth, A. E. (2008). Technological change and gender in the labour policies of British retail banks, 1945–70. In: J. Melling & A. E. Booth (Eds.), *Managing*

the modern workplace: Productivity, politics and workplace culture in postwar Britain (pp. 101–124). Aldershot: Ashgate.
Campbell-Kelly, M. (1989). *ICL – A business & technical history*. Oxford: Claredon Press.
Campbell-Kelly, M. (1992). Large-scale data processing in the Prudential, 1850–1930. *Accounting, Business and Financial History, 2*, 117–139.
Campbell-Kelly, M. (1998). Data processing and technological change: The Post Office Savings Bank, 1861–1930. *Technology & Culture, 39*, 1–32.
Collinson, P., & Bachelor, L. (2015, August 28). HSBC to process 275,000 delayed payments overnight. *The Guardian*, London.
Colvin, C. (2015). *The past, present and future of banking history, Queen's University Centre for Economic History*. Belfast: The Queen's University of Belfast.
Coombs, R., Knights, D., & Willmott, H. (1992). Culture, control and competition: Towards a conceptual framework for the study of information in organizations. *Organization Studies, 13*, 51–72.
Coopey, R. (1999). Management and the introduction of computing in British industry, 1945–70. *Contemporary British History, 13*, 59–71.
Coopey, R. (2004). A passing technology: The automated teller machine. In: P. Lyth & H. Trischler (Eds.), *Wiring prometheus: globalisation, history and technology* (pp. 175–192). Aarhus: Aarhus University Press.
Cortada, J. W. (1993). *Before the computer: IBM, NCR, Burroughs, and Remington Rand and the industry they created, 1856–1956*. Pinceton: Princeton University Press.
Cortada, J. W. (1996). *Information technology as business history: Issues in the history and management of computers*. Westport: Praeger Publishers.
Cortada, J. W. (2006). *The digital hand* (Vol. 2). New York: Oxford University Press.
Cortada, J. W. (2011). *Information and the modern corporation*. Cambridge, MA: The MIT Press.
Del Angel, G. (2011). Computerization of commercial banks and the building of an automated payments system in Mexico, 1965–1990. In: B. Bátiz-Lazo, J. C. Maixé-Altés, & P. Thomes (Eds.), *Technological innovation in retail finance: International historical perspectives* (pp. 92–117). London: Routledge.
Ellis, F. J. (1931). New lamps for old: Part I. *The Spread Eagle, 6*, 404–407.
Fincham, R., Fleck, J., Procter, R., Scarbrough, H., Tierney, M., & Williams, R. (1994). *Expertise and innovation: Information technology strategies in the financial services sector*. Oxford: Oxford University Press.

Foroohar, R. (2015). A market rout carries echoes of the 2008 crash. What hasn't been fixed? *Time Magazine*, New York, NY, 7–8.

Frame, W. S., & White, L. J. (2009). *Technological change, financial innovation, and diffusion in banking*. Altanta: Federal Reserve Bank of Atlanta.

Gandy, A. (2013). Book review: Technological innovation in retail finance. *Economic History Review, 66*, 1227–1228.

Haigh, T. (2001). The chromium-plated tabulator: Institutionalizing an electronic revolution, 1954–1958. *IEEE Annals of the History of Computing, 23*, 75–104.

Haigh, T. (2006). 'A veritable bucket of facts': Origins of the data base management system, 1960–1980. *ACM SIGMOD Record, 35*, 73–88.

Harper, T. M., & Bátiz-Lazo, B. (2013). *Cash box: The invention and globalization of the ATM*. Louisville: NetWorld Media Group and ATM Industry Association.

Heide, L. (1994). Punched-card and computer applications in Denmark 1911–1970. *History and Technology, 11*, 77–99.

Heide, L. (2008). Punched cards for professional European offices: revisiting the dynamics of information technology diffusion from the United States to Europe, 1889–1918. *History and Technology, 24*, 307–320.

Heide, L. (2009). *Punched-card systems and the early information explosion, 1880–1945*. Baltimore: The Johns Hopkins University Press.

Kipping, M., & Westerhuis, G. (2014). The managerialization of banking: From blueprint to reality. *Management & Organizational History, 9*, 374–393.

Knight, L. (2013). *A dark magic: The rise of the robot traders*. London: British Broadcasting Corporation.

Kyrtsis, A. A. (2010). *Financial markets and organizational technologies: System architectures, practices and risks in the era of deregulation*. Basingstoke: Palgrave-Macmillan.

Lamoreaux, N. R., Raff, D. M. G., & Termin, P. (2003). Beyond markets and hierarchies: Towards a new synthesis of American business history. *American Historical Review, 108*, 404–433.

Langlois, R. N. (2003). The vanishing hand: the changing dynamics of industrial capitalism. *Industrial and Corporate Change, 12*, 351–385.

Lepore, J. (2015). *The disruption machine: What the gospel of innovation gets wrong*. New York: The New Yorker.

Maixé-Altés, J. C. (2014). ICT the nordic way and European Savings Banks. *MPRA Paper* No. 58252, posted 8 September 2014, https://mpra.ub.uni-muenchen.de/58252/ (accessed 18 October 2016).

Mannix, L. (2015, September 11). Customers stranded at supermarkets, servos as CommBank hit by tech outages. *Sydney Morning Herald,* Sydney.

Martin, I. (2011). Britain's first computer centre for banking: What did this building do? In: B. Bátiz-Lazo, J. C. Maixé-Altés, & P. Thomes (Eds.), *Technological innovation in retail finance: International historical perspectives* (pp. 37–70). London: Routledge.

Martin, I. (2012). Too far ahead of its time: Barclays, Burroughs and real-time banking. *IEEE Annals of the History of Computing, 34*, 2–16.

Matthews, D., Anderson, M., & Edwards, J. R. (1998). *The priesthood of industry: The rise of the professional accountant in British management.* Oxford: Oxford University Press.

McAteer, O. (2015, June 17). NatWest, RBS, Coutts and Ulster Bank customer payments are 'missing' after technical glitch. *Metro*, London.

McKenney, J. L., & Fisher, A. W. (1993). Manufacturing the ERMA banking system: Lessons from history. *IEEE Annals of the History of Computing, 15*, 7–26.

McKenney, J. L., Mason, R. O., & Copeland, D. G. (1997). Bank of America: The crest and trough of technological leadership. *MIS Quarterly, 21*, 321–354.

McKenzie, D. (2005). *An engine, not a camera: How financial models shape markets.* Cambridge, MA: MIT Press.

Millo, Y., & McKenzie, D. (2009). The usefulness of inaccurate models: Towards an understanding of the emergence of financial risk management. *Accounting, Organizations and Society, 34*, 638–653.

Morris, B. (1987, October 22). Probe into computer trade. *The Times,* London.

Morrison, D. (2014). *3 million ATMs worldwide by 2015: ATM Association.* Credit Union Times. http://www.cutimes.com/2014/07/28/3-million-atms-worldwide-by-2015-atm-association. Accessed 24 Sept 2015.

Osborn, R. F. (1954). GE and UNIVAC: Harnessing the high-speed computer. *Harvard Business Review, 32*, 99–107.

Pardo-Guerra, J. P. (2010). Creating flows of interpersonal bits: The automation of the London Stock Exchange, c.1955–1990. *Economy & Society, 39*, 84–109.

Pardo-Guerra, J. P. (2011). The automated house: The digitalization of the London Stock Exchange, 1955–1990. In: B. Bátiz-Lazo, J. C. Maixé-Altés, & P. Thomes (Eds.), *Technological innovation in retail finance: International historical perspectives* (pp. 197–220). London/ New York: Routledge.

Poon, M. (2009). From new deal institutions to capital markets: Commercial consumer risk scores and the making of subprime mortgage finance. *Accounting, Organizations and Society, 34*, 654–674.
Poon, M. (2011). Historicizing consumer credit risk calculation: The Fair Issac process of commercial scorecard manufacture, 1957–circa 1980. In: B. Bátiz-Lazo, J. C. Maixé-Altés, & P. Thomes (Eds.), *Technological innovation in retail finance: International historical perspectives* (pp. 221–245). London: Routledge.
Rishi, M., & Saxena, S. (2004). Technological innovations in the Indian banking industry: the late bloomer. *Accounting, Business and Financial History, 14*, 339–353.
Rouse, H. L. (1930). Mechanisation in the banks. *Journal of the Institute of Bankers*. Meetings of the British Bankers' Association and the Committee of London Clearing Banks, London.
Scott, S. V., & Zachariadis, M. (2012). Origins and development of SWIFT, 1973–2009. *Business History, 52*, 462–483.
Scott, S. V., & Zachariadis, M. (2014). *The Society for Worldwide Interbank Financial Telecommunication (SWIFT): Cooperative governance for network innovation, standards, and community*. London: Routledge.
Seltzer, A. (2004). Internal labour markets in the Australian banking industry: Their nature prior to the Second World War and their recent decline. *Accounting Business and Financial History, 14*, 237–256.
Sheffield, H. (2015, June 19). RBS completes 600,000 delayed payments three days after they were due. *The Independent*, London.
Stearns, D. L. (2011). *Electronic value exchange: Origins of the VISA electronic payment system*. London: Springer.
Stiglitz, J. E., & Weiss, A. (1981). Credit rationing in markets with imperfect information. *American Economic Review, 71*, 393–410.
Thodenius, B., Bátiz-Lazo, B., & Karlsson, T. (2011). The history of the Swedish ATM – Sparfrämjandet and Metior. In: J. Impagliazzo, P. Lundin, & B. Wangler (Eds.), *History of nordic computing 3: Revised selected papers*. Berlin: Springer.
Wadhwani, R. D., & Jones, G. (2014). Schumpeter's plea: Historical reasoning in entrepreneurship theory and research. In: M. Bucheli & R. D. Wadhwani (Eds.), *Organizations in time: History, theory and methods* (pp. 192–216). Oxford: Oxford University Press.
Wardley, P. (2000). The commercial banking industry and its part in the emergence and consolidation of the corporate economy in Britain before 1940. *Journal of Industrial History, 3*, 71–97.

Wardley, P. (2011). Women, mechanization and cost-savings in twentieth century British banks and other financial institutions. In: M. Richardson & P. Nicholls (Eds.), *A business and labour history of Britain, Case studies of Britain in the nineteenth and twentieth centuries* (pp. 32–59). Basingstoke: Palgrave Macmillan.

Williams, J. (2015, 3rd ed.). Electronic banking. In: Cooper, C. L. (Ed.), *The Blackwell Encyclopaedia of Management – Vol. IV Finance*. Oxford: Blackwell Publishing.

Wood, D., & Bátiz-Lazo, B. (1997). Corporate strategy, centralization and outsourcing in banking: Case studies on paper payments processing. *International Association of Management Journal, 9*, 33–57.

Wootton, C. W., & Kemmerer, B. E. (2007). The emergence of mechanical accounting in the U.S., 1880–1930. *The Accounting Historians Journal, 34*, 91–124.

Yates, J. (1989). *Control through communication: The rise of system in American management*. Baltimore/London: The John Hopkins University Press.

Yates, J. (1997). Early interactions between the life insurance and computer industries: The Prudential's Edmund C. Berkeley. *IEEE Annals of the History of Computing, 19*, 60–73.

Yates, J. (2005). *Structuring the information age*. Baltimore: The Johns Hopkins University Press.

Part III

Third Part: Methodological Tools for Historians: Network-Theory, Principal-Agent-Relationship, Behavioural Finance and Social Capital

Social Capital Versus Commercial Profits: The Impact of Networks on Decision-Making in Early Modern Banks

Nadia Matringe

1 Introduction

The concept of decision-making is especially pertinent to the study of banks during a period characterised by what Lucien Febvre (1956, 244) once called a 'transfer from sky to earth', when, for the first time, humankind was conceived as capable of governing the course of events. This change would have been promoted by the development of a merchant culture dominated by calculation. How did businessmen, who supposedly played a decisive role in dismissing fatality, use their freshly acquired freedom to make decisions? Examining this question is not only important to understand the functioning of early modern financial markets, but also, ultimately, the course of the global economy which, then just as much as today, largely depended on the strategies of this social group.

N. Matringe (✉)
Department of Accounting, London School of Economics, London, UK
e-mail: nadiamatringe@gmail.com

K. Schönhärl (ed.), *Decision Taking, Confidence and Risk Management in Banks from Early Modernity to the 20th Century*,
DOI 10.1007/978-3-319-42076-9_10

It is no coincidence that the notion of decision-making underlies most studies of the organisation of exchanges and the evolution of financial markets in the context of the rise of the Western model. In the 1950–60s, studies based on the extensive use of business archives, especially business letters, promoted by Fernand Braudel through the series '*Affaires et Gens d'Affaires*', offered thorough analysis of how businessmen made their decisions according to economic circumstances (Lapeyre 1955; Da Silva 1956, 1959; Vazquez de Prada 1960; Ruiz Martín 1965). These studies, however, were less concerned with conceptualising decision-making and risk management than understanding the functioning of credit and exchange markets. In the more recent monographs on early modern firms, decision-making has been analysed through management problems—authors being concerned with who the real decision makers were, and ascertaining the degree of autonomy of agencies' managers (Goldthwaite 2009, 80–82; De Roover 1963, 86–96). Such studies, however, remain marginal. Culturist and institutionalist approaches that continue to dominate recent historiography, leaving aside the figure of the Schumpeterian entrepreneur, tend to focus on the contexts of productions of decisions, with particular focus on mechanisms of regulation and monitoring (Ogilvie 2011; Gelderblom 2013).

Decision-making, while seldom named and conceptualised in all this literature, has thus been considered from both the perspective of individual firms and large-scale economic, political and sociocultural trends. Examination of archives dating from the sixteenth and seventeenth centuries, however, discloses an absentee: networks. In themselves, networks have been the object of many studies and debates among historians of the Early Modern Age. Although their fundamental importance for early modern commercial life has frequently been underlined, their impact on decision-making has never sufficiently been examined. Yet, a close look at early modern firm archives reveals the growing importance of commission trading, that is, the trade led on behalf of commercial partners and, to a lesser extent, third parties outside the business world. How did the development of this operational mode at a very large scale, first in the Mediterranean and then in North-Western Europe, impact on decision-making in these firms? Assuming that businessmen's decisions were determined by the perception of profit, how did their intense reliance on networks in the commission trade influence their conception of profit?

This paper addresses this question by examining the archives of one of the banks that first specialised in commission trading: the Salviati bank of Lyons in the sixteenth century. Settled in the *Cité du Rhône*—at that time the nerve centre of international trade—since the beginning of the century, the Salviati evolved from commodity trading in silks which they mostly conducted on their own account, to a banking business constituted of exchange and deposit transactions performed on commission. From the 1540s onwards, specific books of accounts were devoted to their commission business, which was also the case in other Italian banks active in Lyons in the second half of the sixteenth century (Capponi, Martelli). In the other great marketplaces of the time, mainly Antwerp and London, Italians were also heavily involved in the commission business, which enabled them to respond to the intense demand for goods and capital of such marketplaces, without putting their own assets at risk (Brulez 1959, 53–55, 106–108, 363–365, 580–581; Bratchel 1978/1996). When putting forward the negative consequences that the regulation of the exchange conceived by Thomas Gresham would have on the London market, representatives of Italian businessmen in London started to describe the functioning of their businesses by pointing out that 'the chiefest living and maintenance that we have is upon the commissions that are sent unto us of our friends from beyond the seas' (Bland et al. 1914, 421).

The Archivio Salviati (A. S.) provide an invaluable window on the vital importance of commission networks as manifest at different levels in decision-making. The social capital paradigm is useful to understand these mechanisms. While this concept has been the object of several competing definitions since its inception, this paper adopts the classical definition established by Bourdieu (1980, 2), i.e. 'the sum of the resources, actual or virtual, that accrue to an individual or a group by virtue of possessing a durable network of more or less institutionalized relationships of mutual acquaintance and recognition.' The network of commercial partners at the origin of all transactions executed by the Salviati was in itself a precious asset, which conditioned the economic activity and the profits made by the bank. Indeed, while business networks were the principal medium of dissemination of information for economic decision-making, they also constituted, in themselves, a central object of the deliberation characterising the decision-making process. This is clear from the fact that the reputation of commercial and banking houses was one of the recurrent details in information communicated through business letters. More fundamentally, the particular care that merchant bankers devoted to maintaining their network impacted on their conception of profit. This conditioning reveals itself at three different levels: in the first place, at a formal level, in the design of the accounting system. The value of this accounting system in decision-making lay not so much in facilitating the calculation of profit and assessment of investment alternatives, but in providing a clear overview of the financial position of third parties with reference to the Salviati. The importance of networks also manifests itself at the level of transactions, in the implementation of business strategies: the second part of this paper addresses the extent to which social capital limited the level of interest rates in banking transactions. At times the Salviati accepted financial losses in order to favour some partners. Finally, instances of opportunistic decision-making were not uncommon, but always remained within limits acceptable to the network of committents.

2 Accounting for Social Capital

Early double-entry bookkeeping (DEB) has long been at the core of an intense debate on the origins of capitalism, initiated by the writings of Werner Sombart (1916/1953) and Max Weber (1947/1964). As far as they were concerned, DEB was used in early modern business to measure profit and make rational decisions accordingly and, in this perspective, DEB constituted a crucial factor in the rise of modern capitalism. On the opposite side, Yamey (1949, 1971) claimed that DEB's potential for the calculation of the rate of return was not used for a very long time. Ever since, accountants, economists and economic historians interested in early accounting methods and the management of early modern firms, have tried to position themselves in this debate, mostly by assessing whether or not early DEB enabled entrepreneurs to perfect decision-making on the basis of a critical reading of prior choices. Interestingly, in this debate, the authors who refuted, nuanced or called into question the Sombart-Weberian perspective on accounting based their observations on

English and Flemish account books and manuals (Yamey 1949, 1971; Winjum 1971; Robertson and Funnel 2012), while specialists of medieval and early modern Italian businesses, notably F. Lane (1945, 1977) and F. Melis (1962, 1972), unanimously endorse the views of these luminaries of capitalism. According to them, medieval Tuscan accounting accomplished crucial progress in the evolution towards modernity by introducing a clear distinction between the capital share of the company and the private wealth of each participant, enabling the remuneration of partners at the end of a partnership deed. Do these differing views indicate that the men who invented and diffused DEB across Europe had developed more sophisticated, more modern accounting techniques than their northern counterparts, which enabled rational decision-making based on profit calculation? The Salviati case does not seem to confirm this view. Instead, it reveals the necessity to introduce the notion of network when conceptualising the relation between accounting and decision-making in early modern firms.

Indeed, the most striking feature of the Salviati's accounting system is not its modernity or its efficiency in optimising the quest for financial profits, but rather the priority given to networks in the conceptualisation of business. The Salviati books do not provide any vision of sectoral or global profit enabling the shaping of further strategies. Instead, they focus on the financial and functional position of each individual in the firm's network. Before illustrating this, however, it is necessary to provide an overview of the functioning of the Salviati firm as a whole.

In the middle of the sixteenth century this firm was composed of five main merchant-banking companies: two in Florence and one each in Pisa, Lyons and Antwerp. Although juridically independent, functionally these companies submitted to the supreme control of the directors (*maggiori*), the brothers Averardo and Piero Salviati, settled in Florence, who were the principal investors in all five companies. While some branches were more oriented towards banking (Lyons, Florence) and others, such as Pisa, tended towards the commodity trade, the Salviati did not use an integrated accounting system to reflect the functional complementarity of the components. Each company had its own independent set of ledgers, replicating the typical Tuscan tripartite accounting plan practised since the Renaissance. Narrative memorials and specialised notebooks were completed by a set of ledgers of current accounts, showing debtors and creditors. Between these two levels, 'journals' continued the recordings of memorials while incorporating elements for transfer to the ledgers, that is, the accounts to debit and credit. This layout is similar to that of other Tuscan firms active in Europe in the sixteenth to seventeenth century, whose archives have been preserved (Capponi, Martelli, Saminiati). However, it was neither standardised nor definitively fixed. It was subordinated to spatial variations depending on the specialisation of each company, which, in itself, was determined by the structure of commercial centres.

Examination of the methods used for registering profit shows that the system was not used for decision-making on the basis of the comparative profitability of different sectors. First of all, profit was not divided into sectors (such as banking and merchandise) or specific categories of product (such as silks and spices), but calculated after each specific commercial venture. This was true not only for the profit made on the merchandise trade—which often involved long distance commercial operations that needed to be followed through their duration—but also for the profit made on exchange. In the case of merchandise, profit was calculated after completion of the sales of an entire lot. Similarly, profit on arbitrages was not registered when closing an exchange account but calculated upon the return of each individual or series of remittances or drafts issued on the same day, and followed a similar arbitrage itinerary through Europe. For example, in October 1544, the Lyons Salviati remitted 10,000 crowns to the Castilian fairs through three bills of exchange, which they repatriated on Lyons via Antwerp. Profit was posted after the return of the last Antwerp remittance. Thus Gain and Loss accounts showed a series of gains from specific commercial ventures, but did not render sectoral profitability visible. Moreover, some income and expenditures passed through a transitional account, where they were mingled together, before being transferred under Profit and Loss heads, where they were no longer distinguishable. For example, in the ledgers of the Lyons company, the Deposit account contains several entries normally expected to appear in the Gain and Loss account, such as the result of arbitrages, discount of commercial titles, deductions for the anticipated payment of merchandise, and diverse fees (for transports and brokerage).

Ultimately, the Deposit account's balance was transferred to Gain and Loss, but all these economic results appear to arise from deposit operations, while in fact they were related to other sectors of the firm's activity. Similarly, commission fees on exchange and merchandise were merged together in a Commission account before being transferred to Gain and Loss, a practice that is also followed in the account books of other Florentine companies (e.g., Gondi, Martelli, Capponi). In the Salviati case, the Commission account also comprises 'consul fees' deducted on each transaction by the consul of Lyons's Florentine nation. Thus, even a detailed analysis of Gain and Loss accounts does not facilitate reconstruction of profit distribution according to sources of income—which would be possible only by following each operation in all its stages through the different entries.

The accounting system used by the Salviati also did not enable them to make long-term decisions on the basis of global profits at the end of a fiscal year. The main impediment was the businessmen's habit of registering anticipated income and expenditures on ongoing exchange and merchandise operations. The expected profit on arbitrages was thus recorded *before* the last bill was honoured. Gains on merchandise sales were recorded *before* payment was received, in a context where most merchandise was sold on credit. In the same manner, commission fees on transactions executed on behalf of third parties were transferred to the Gain and Loss account before the end of operations. While firms such as those of the Salviati, located in great international centres, benefitted from a rather safe and organised commercial environment, several events could supervene between the incurrence of debt and its settlement. Discounts could be negotiated, ships sunk or seized, partners or clients could die, etc. Such unexpected events could occur months or even years (in the case of long-distant trade) after beginning an operation, and often lead to rectification in the Gain and Loss account because of objectives unattained or (more rarely) surpassed. Consequently, the Salviati would have needed to analyse their long-term accounts over years before they could have assessed their profits during specific periods.

However, even this kind of long-term approach would be disqualified because of the imprecise characterisation of profit that emerges in the Salviati books, although this firm was one of the biggest of its time (Matringe 2016) and its managers were specialised in the conduct of complex financial operations. Gain and Loss accounts indeed contained several entries unrelated to commercial activity: for example, gifts,[1] household expenditures[2] or rent received from subtenants[3]—usually artisans renting the ground floor of the Salviati bank. This porosity of distinction between the domestic or property sphere and the commercial is related to the ambiguous perception of the commercial site itself—which was often gained through inheritance and was deemed a mere extension of the family palace. Never visiting Lyons did not prevent the directors of Florence, noblemen and entrepreneurs, from considering their Lyons branch as their '*casa di Lione*'. While sources of revenue external to strictly defined commercial profit appeared in Gain and Loss accounts, some gains were not included. For example, the Drapery Book of the Salviati's Lyons company contained a specific account dedicated to the commissions on the sales of raw silk, the balance whereof was directly transferred to the balance sheet without passing through the Gain and Loss account.[4] Thus Gain and Loss accounts obviously did not provide the measure of profit.

Clearly investment decisions did not flow from an examination of profit and loss reports. Partners did not really seem interested in evaluating their own share of profit—even if profit is broadly defined. The Salviati books did contain Capital accounts, where the initial contribution of each participant was recorded. Their respective share of profit, however, was usually not transferred thereto, but left undistributed and directly transferred into the Gain and Loss account of the next ledger. This practice reflected the systematic reinvestment of profits into the company, since the partners remained constant over extended periods of time through successive renewal of the partnership contract. It was also not uncommon for Gain and Loss accounts to remain unbalanced on closure of the books.[5] Thus, Profit and Loss accounts were used not for optimizing the quest for profit, but for addressing the need for clearing up other accounts—which neatly accords with B. Yamey's findings on early modern manuals and sixteenth-century English records.

Examination of the balance sheets confirms the Salviati's disinterest in DEB for decision-making on the basis of economic result evaluation. Indeed balance sheets provided neither a basis for evaluating the solvency of the business, nor a clear view of its relationship with its various commercial partners. Based on DEB, the Salviati could neither gauge the financial health of their business nor assess the need for changing or maintaining their business strategies.

To understand how balance sheets were established, it is necessary to consider the accounting system in its temporal dimension. Partnership agreements were usually for three years, and renewed indefinitely as long as the company continued to exist—even if some partners withdrew or died. Like all Tuscan businessmen of the time, at each renewal, the Salviati opened a new set of books, similar to those mentioned above (memorials, journals, ledgers). The successive sets were alphabetically classified from the opening until the definitive closure of the company, that is, from A to (potentially) Z. When a company survived longer than 78 years (26 letters × 3 years), double lettering (i.e. AA, BB, CC,) would be used to identify the new sets of books. This linear progression reflected the durability of the commercial house, independent of human reconfigurations.

Inside the different sets of ledgers, two types of balance sheet could be found. Some were recapitulations drawn up on loose sheets at the end of the year, or after the end of a fair in the case of Lyons. Others were established at each partnership renewal and opening of a new set of books. In books that were being closed, this second type of balance sheet would bear the title of the new ledger where they would be transferred in an account opened in the name of the previous ledger. Each ledger, whether general or specialised, opened on the balance sheet from the previous ledger, and closed with a balance sheet bearing the name of the following ledger. For example, the balance sheet of Ledger 1 (*libro grande segnato A*), entitled 'Ledger 2' (*libro grande segnato B*), was transferred to Ledger 2 under the name 'Ledger 1' (*libro grande segnato A*).

While the poor state of conservation of the flying balance sheets does not facilitate determining whether they were drawn up regularly (such as every year, or after each fair), the second type of balance sheet was clearly related to the need to transfer the remaining debts of a partnership when it was renewed and a new book opened. Whether drawn up on a loose sheet or at the end of a ledger, balance sheets were similarly structured. The credit side contained the value of goods that the company used for an extended period of time in the framework of its activity, such as bonds and liquidities, or business assets like merchandise and equipment. The debit side contained the balances of the associates' accounts (capital and deposits), long-term and short-term debts contracted towards different stakeholders (clients, commercial partners, tax authorities, etc.). In principle, any discrepancy between the two sides should represent the deficit or excess of the company's budget at any given time, thus enabling the Salviati to evaluate their business performance and, thereupon, develop future strategies.

However, all the elements mentioned above were not systematically included. Some accounts were not settled when opening a new account book. For example, in the Lyons ledger entitled O, the balance sheet of which was established in 1539, some accounts remained active until 1552 and were not balanced before this date. Similarly, in the ledger titled V, open until 1549, some accounts were settled in 1564, while the balance sheet was established in 1552. No common trait could be found between the different accounts that remained in use in some ledgers after the end of a partnership agreement. This type of bookkeeping seems all the more incongruous as it constrained the Salviati to use different ledgers simultaneously, while correspondence between successive sets of books could have spared them this trouble.

Recurrent unbalancing of accounts prevented balance sheets from accurately reflecting holdings at any specific time. Like Profit and Loss accounts, balance sheets too seemed to be composed in order to verify the accuracy of accounting records—when drawn up during a partnership—and related to the necessity of opening of a new set of books at the end of a partnership agreement.

Judging from the account books of a major Italian bank based in the greatest international commercial centre of sixteenth-century Europe, early modern DEB did not help businessmen make rational decisions based on their accounting knowledge of the profitability of previous investments. What then was at stake in their accounting system? Did it still support decision-making and, if so, in what way? The answer seems to lie in the value attached to assessing the correspondent's financial health and reliability. In fact, while the credit of commercial houses appeared as one of many factors to evaluate in the business letters (together with the trends of marketplaces, the price of commodities, exchange rates, etc.), the financial position of correspondents was the primary focus of the accounting discourse.

A simple glance at early modern Italian account books already reveals the overwhelming majority of personal accounts over real accounts and nominal accounts. There were no proper merchandise accounts in the Salviati books, as merchandise was always connected to the merchant on behalf of whom it was bought or sold. The Salviati used, for example, an account titled 'silks of the Strozzi from Valladolid' for the silk they sold on behalf of the Strozzi of Valladolid. This practice was widespread among Italian firms. In the 1540s, personal accounts and personalised accounts represented 95% of accounts in the Lyons bank's ledger (544/573),[6] 98% of accounts in the Florentine bank's ledger (514/526),[7] and 94% of the Antwerp's bank accounts (586/623).[8] The mere distribution of accounts thus already discloses much about the focus of the accounting system: the network.

This preoccupation with the network appeared at a macro level, in the structuring of the system of books, and at a micro level, inside each ledger, in the organisation and the designation of accounts. The construction of ledgers already referred to the functional and financial position of correspondents and clients *vis-à-vis* the Salviati firm. One distinction concerned the location of the different stakeholders, which often determined their relations with the Salviati. The Fair Books (*Libri di Fiere*) in Lyons and the Assignment Books (*Libri di Assegnazione*) in Antwerp mostly contained the accounts of clients and commercial partners located at the same marketplace, who bought and sold bills of exchange to the Salviati and performed clearance with them through book transfers. Foreign commercial partners, whether principals, commission agents or both, usually had their accounts in the main ledgers.

Within each ledger, the designation of personal and personalised accounts enabled the Salviati to both identify the nature of the credit relationship they had with their respective accountholders, and to keep track of the different stakeholders with interest in commission transactions. The primary categorisation distinguished between business conducted on one's own account (*nostro* account) from business conducted on commission (*vostro* accounts). A merchant's *nostro* account in the ledger of his partner corresponded to the *vostro* account his partner held for him in his own ledgers, and vice versa. For example, the Affaitadi's *nostro* account by the Salviati was the equivalent of the Salviati's *vostro* account by the Affaitadi, and contained exchange operations conducted on commission by the Affaitadi on behalf of the Salviati. In the Lyons bank, *nostro* and *vostro* accounts were registered in separate ledgers. Specific Books of Committents, i.e., 'Books of Principals', also to be found in the archives of big other Lyons banks, contained all *vostro* accounts, revealing the growing importance of commission trading in the course of the sixteenth century.

Titles of accounts also reflected the chains of commission relating to each transaction. The Antwerp branch, for example, was very much involved in the import-export of English cloth to Italy. Accounts registering these operations indicated the names of the sender, the recipient, and the committent(s) on behalf of whom the export was organised, and regrouped under a title such as: 'goods sent from London by Stefano de Gradi to ship to Ancona to Giovani di Gondola, on behalf of Francesco de Gradi [of Ragusa]'.[9] While the type of merchandise (here, kerseys) was usually not specified, the network of agents and principals handling the business was carefully noted. The Salviati seemed to care less about what they transported than about the directions of merchandise flows and the stakeholders involved in the different territories covered by the operations. The same principle applied to exchange operations. These were recorded only in personal accounts, not impersonal accounts highlighting, for example, the nature of the activity ('Drafts and Remittances' accounts) or its geographical inscription ('Paris exchange', 'Antwerp exchange', etc.). Here too, the credit relationship between the Salviati and their correspondents prevailed over any other type of consideration.

In the ledgers of the banking companies, titles of exchange accounts not only provided information about chains of commission—as in the case of merchandise, but also reflected the debtor-creditor relationship of some clients *vis-à-vis* the Salviati. Such was the case of *a l'ordine di* (at the order of) and *sopra di* (on top of) accounts. Transactions recorded in these accounts concerned credit operations performed for third parties through bills of exchange (De Roover 1953, 50–55). They involved round-trip exchange operations between two markets, and brought into play partner banks of the Salviati located at foreign marketplaces, as well as clients of these partner's banks. As shown by the commercial correspondence, the Salviati never communicated directly with their partner's clients. Their partners indeed played the role of brokers between their own clients and the Salviati. When a partner's client wished to place capital on the exchange through a round-trip of remittances involving Lyons, the designation of his account in the Salviati ledgers would be his name, followed by the formula *a l'ordine di* and the name of the broker. When a client wished to borrow money through a round-trip of drafts, his name was followed by *sopra di* and the name of the broker. Both expressions were related to the intervention of an intermediary, whose primary function was to ensure the communication between his clients and the Salviati. *A l'ordine di* could indicate that the broker was the one conveying orders. However, in such a case, his name would instead be expected to stand before *a l'ordine di*, which would be followed by the name of his client. Such a formulation would indeed make clear that the broker was acting on behalf of his client. It seems more likely that *a l'ordine di* was employed in a literal sense, meaning that the bills drawn in favour of the client were 'payable to' the broker.

The reason why drafts were registered in *sopra di* accounts also seems to lie in what was written on bills, which referred to a specific custom of guaranteeing bills. The Salviati books indeed offer several examples of interior bills or promissory notes circulating from one French city to another, which were guaranteed by third parties. In the accounts, if A is the drawer and B the guarantor, the transaction was registered as follows: 'We must have 100 crowns for a bill drawn by A *sopra di* or *alla sottoscrizione di* (underwritten by) B *come principale* (as principal)'—that is to say, the one ultimately responsible for the bill to be honoured. When the Salviati encashed a payment made by a partner's client who remitted capital on Lyons, they did not risk anything. On the other hand, when they paid a bill sent by a partner's client, and subsequently sought to be reimbursed by drawing on him, they could not be sure of payment. Under such circumstances, it would be only natural to expect the broker to guarantee the payment due from his own client. And, when addressing the brokers, the Salviati would, in fact, clearly state that the debt would be discharged only after they had secured payment of the counter-bill (or second draft).[10] Recourse to *sopra di* most likely referred to the signatures on the bills of exchange, where the name of the client was written above that of the guarantor.

Consequently, it was possible for the Salviati to identify the chains of commission and to distinguish lenders from borrowers by simply scanning their ledger index. The Salviati accounting system thus enabled the close monitoring of capital circulation according to the position of the different stakeholders doing business with the firm. Transactions were less defined by the nature of the activity that produced them than by the type of credit relationship in which they were embedded. These views are confirmed by the work of P. Gervais on eighteenth-century merchant account books and textbooks from Great Britain and France (Gervais 2014). Knowing who owed what and who paid their debts, seemed far more important to these firms than the precise measure of global profit or comparison of the profitability of different types of investments. Assuming that accounting did influence decision-making—and was already in itself the result of a decision—early modern banks, when elaborating their strategies, were primarily concerned with the reliability of the stakeholders with whom they dealt.

3 Interest Rate Determination

3.1 Balancing Immediate Profits and Social Capital

Analysis of the Salviati books shows not only how networks took precedence over financial profits in the way the business was conceived, evaluated and controlled through accounting, but also how networks actually limited interest rates on banking transactions. To illustrate this phenomenon, two main examples will be taken from the primary fields of activity of the Salviati bank: deposit and exchange, mostly performed on commission. In these two sectors, the Salviati frequently resolved to lower the level of their profits in order to maintain good business relations with their partners. The need to look after their social capital did not, however, prevent them from exploiting balances of power and taking advantage of their clients whenever they could afford so to do without significant protest.

In the deposit business, two categories of operators benefitted from favours: partner banks in Lyons and the wealthiest clients: a Catalan banker from Avignon, Bartolomeo de Paretes and an international Jewish business firm, the Mendes. Before explaining the sacrifices the Salviati accepted for them, it is necessary to recall the main source of their profit in the deposit business. As credit intermediaries, the Salviati lent to some the money borrowed from others, from one fair to the next, that is, every three months (Matringe 2015). The discrepancy between the rate of remuneration of the deposits and the rate of interest on loans determined a minor part of their profit—the rate spread being, on average, only 0.05 percent per fair. In fact, the Salviati drew most of their revenues from the commission fees which they received on deposits and loans. Examination of the rate variations and the policy concerning commission fees reveals the influence of social capital on decision-making. Between deposits of equal duration, individual variations in rates frequently occurred. The less attractive rates applied to merchants of modest status, essentially active in the trade of commodities. Bankers had an undeniable ascendancy over this category of stakeholders, who relied on them to keep their business running. On the other hand, especially low interest rates on borrowing were common among Lyons banks, who also exempted each other from commission fees. These practices signified the deep interdependency between these banks, working together within the same organic system. Lyons banks organised the exchange market as well as regional and international clearance, bought and sold bills to each other, and assigned debts to each other through book transfers. Any difficulty encountered by one of them would have direct consequences for the others. Being located in the same area (the St. Jean quarter) of the same city, they could not, even temporarily, conceal their financial situation from each other. This combination of physical proximity and economic interdependence was a key feature of the relations between these banks and, despite inevitable rivalries, explained the *de facto* cohesion of this financial group. The Salviati also accorded special treatment to their most important depositors. In the winter of 1546, an unprecedented episode of abundance of money on the marketplace (*larghezza*) forced them to retain some 60,000 crowns in the till. Rather than deceive the Mendes and the Paretes, whose investments in the 1540s represented almost 60 percent of deposits received, the Salviati[11] offered them about 1 percent compensation. Consideration for senior clients was all the more necessary since the Salviati often relied on their recommendations to find new clients.

Examples of the voluntary sacrifice of interest rates were also to be found in the exchange business. In March 1544, the Salviati ordered a fund transfer from Spain to Lyons via Rome to one of their correspondents in the Eternal City: the Cavalcanti & Giraldi. These were supposed to draw on Medina del Campo at the rate of 416 *maravedi* per Roman ducat (*ducato di camera*) and to remit the sum so acquired on Lyons at the rate of 60 ducats per Lyons unit of exchange (*écu de marc*). Application of these rates would lead to a loss of 11% compared to a direct transfer from Medina to Lyons via draft from Lyons on Medina at the prevailing market rate of 399 *maravedi/écu de marc*, and a loss of 13.5% compared to a direct transfer via remittance from Spain on Lyons at the current rate of 390 *maravedi/écu de marc*. In principle, arbitrages were intended to take advantage of the differences in exchange rates in order to yield profits. In this case, the Salviati voluntarily chose an unprofitable route for their capital. The Cavalcanti & Giraldi account shows that the arbitrage was finally executed in a slightly different fashion, through remittances from Spain on Rome followed by a draft from Lyons on Rome, representing a loss of 6–8% compared with a direct transfer. Why did the Salviati need to transfer funds from Spain to Lyons, and why did they want to operate an unprofitable detour via Rome? A close examination of accounts provides an indication of the possible reason for this operation. The Castilian remitters (or buyers of the Castilian bills on Rome) were the Affaitadi. The Salviati did not order the first remittance on their own account, but on behalf of the Mendes, whose name was concealed under the cover name *Della Casa aparte D* (Matringe 2015). At that time, the Mendes assets were at risk since Charles V was trying to seize them (Roth 1948/1990, 35–76). The Affaitadi happened to be friends and associates of the Mendes in Antwerp and in the Iberian Peninsula (Denucé 1934, 8, 20–22, 69). It would not be surprising if, through this operation, the Affaitadi and the Salviati were helping the Mendes to extract capital from Charles V's cupidity and to safely transfer it to Lyons. In this context, the detour via Rome could help cover the tracks of the real transfer. To satisfy their wealthiest depositors, the Salviati did not hesitate to operate arbitrages at a loss. It is important to note here that arbitraging at a loss was, most of the time, driven by strictly economic objectives. The anticipated loss was a factor in the overall evaluation of risk and the temporal dimension of profit. Thus the Salviati would often choose the alternative that combined the highest profit with the shortest tying up of capital, despite anticipating loss in the case of unexpected rate variations. In such case, they would indicate to their agents the maximum limit of loss acceptable to them (on the assumption of quick recovery of capital). They could also afford a loss in one segment of an entire arbitrage, against the expectation of compensation in the next. Unfavourable arbitrages related to social pressures were less common, but did occur occasionally, demonstrating the Salviati's determination to maintain, even at monetary loss, their reputation in the circles of high finance. Displays of largesse indeed reflected positively on their standing and enabled them to maintain an image not only of business expertise, but also of being socially elite, thereby rendering them more attractive to wealthy and powerful clients.

3.2 Social Capital and Self-regulation of Opportunistic Behaviour

Analysing the pressure of networks on decision-making finally raises the question of their limits. To what extent did the Salviati disregard their partners' interests when conducting their business and, instead, prioritised their own? The notion of asymmetrical relations between principal and agents, and the correlated conflicts of interest, has occasioned abundant literature on the role of institutions in early modern trade. This section assesses these discrepancies and shows the primary function of networks in the self-regulation of opportunistic behaviour.

During the 1540s, the Salviati never entered into serious dispute with any of their correspondents and always avoided judicial recourse. This does not mean they were not tempted to take advantage of their clients and committents—but they did so only on a very small, acceptable scale. In the field of exchange, this exceptional deceitful behaviour concerned the fixation of rates. The fair accounts contain entries referred to as 'advantage on exchange', which appear to be related to the selling or buying of bills on commission at a rate different from the one written on the bill of exchange—and required by the correspondent. For example, in December 1544, the Sommaia & Gagliano bought, on behalf of the Salviati, a bill on Antwerp for 2500 crowns, at the rate of 73 *gros* (Flemish exchange unit) per *écu de marc*, in order to receive 182,500 *gros* in Antwerp. The bill, however, was issued by the Bonvisi bank at the rate of 72.75 *gros* per *écu de marc*, and in fact yielded only 181,875 *gros* in Antwerp. The notification letter sent by the Salviati to the Affaitadi, on behalf of whom the remittance had been executed, confirms that the rate appearing on the bill was that of 72.75 *gros* per *écu de marc*. The difference of 625 *gros* was debited from the account of the drawer, and converted into local money of account before being credited as 'advantage on exchange' in the Deposit account where profits and losses on commercial transactions were sometimes transferred. This meant that the Bonvisi had agreed to compensate for the difference between the rate they agreed upon privately with the Sommaia & Gagliano (on behalf of the Salviati), and the rate actually stipulated on the bill, which was the one the drawee would take into account when making the payment in Antwerp. In the end, the Salviati bought the bill at a better price than the Affaitadi expected, but kept the surplus without informing their committents. This discrete opportunistic behaviour was not directly detrimental to the partners' business, but clearly shows that the Salviati did not always act with their committent's best interest in mind, and that the standard formula used in the commission business in the early modern age, that merchants would 'treat their correspondent's business as if it was their own', did not always apply. However, only eight cases of similar transactions have been found in the Deposit account between 1544 and 1549, a period during which the Salviati conducted almost ten thousand exchange transactions on commission.

Other instances of the margin of decision-making autonomy available to agents are available in the Salviati's deposit business. As appears from their business letters, bankers were bound to follow their clients' directives concerning markets of investment. Yet gains on money secretly invested in the exchange market and in government loans do appear in the Salviati's Deposit account. Exchange operations took the form of round-trips of bills between two marketplaces. In such cases, the funds were not immobilised longer than the interval between two fairs, and could be reimbursed to clients on schedule. Speculation on the exchange market could also involve movement of coins with differing values on different marketplaces. For example, the Salviati could ask their Antwerp governor to carry Italian ducats to Paris before having them remitted by bill of exchange on Lyons, where they were worth more. Finally, the variations of the suncrown's rate between Lyons and Paris enabled the Salviati to make profits on fund transfers between both places. Such forms of private speculation with depositors' funds significantly increased the level of profit on each operation. Where the average rate of client remuneration was 2%, the Salviati earned 0.3% when they reinvested the money on the exchange, and 2% when they reinvested in government loans—in either case, much more than the 0.05% they usually made by reinvesting the money on the deposit. However, their prudence led them to place only 1.5% of total deposits on the exchange, and 0.8% in government loans.

Thus, if the Salviati sometimes made opportunistic decisions regarding their principals, this propensity remained under control: it was limited by their awareness of the necessity to maintain good relations with commercial partners and clients. While the Tribunal of Conservation did protect the interests of merchants frequenting the Lyons fairs,[12] committents operating from abroad were not so well shielded against fraud. However, the risk of losing their reputation and hence commissions (their main source of income), restrained commission agents from excessive opportunistic behaviour. Since businessmen usually traded on behalf of each other, in all likelihood most clients and committents were aware of the above-mentioned minor frauds. Salviati documentation, however, does not provide any evidence that they were ever criticised for contravening the orders of their principals when performing exchange or deposit transactions. These small secrets seem to have been an integral part of business. They were, in this sense, collectively accepted deviances.

4 Conclusion

Analysis of the Salviati archives thus enables assessment of the complexity of the notion of profit in the decision-making process of early modern merchant banks involved in the commission business. While it remains indisputable that merchant bankers did seek profit when making decisions, profit was not limited to quantifiable monetary gains, but included social considerations about the long-term profitability of social capital.

Indeed, it appears that merchant bankers were more concerned with controlling and maintaining their network of correspondents rather than precisely measuring their profits and maximising benefits on each and every transaction. Double-entry bookkeeping, which, in principle, could have been used to calculate the precise amount of profits and to compare investment alternatives, was mainly used to control commercial partners and clients. Furthermore, merchant bankers accepted some losses and additional work in order to maintain good business relations with their most important clients and partners. Socially induced losses amounted to investments, enhancing trustworthiness and promoting durable credit relations which, in turn, would ensure the steady flow of capital and information. Even when they indulged in 'opportunistic' decisions, disregarding their commitment towards their principal, the Salviati did so only within limits—never jeopardising the cohesion of their networks.

Networks, in fact, were both upstream and downstream of the decision-making process. In a context where the roles of principal and agent were interchangeable, not only did correspondents provide the commissions that, according to the Italian merchant bankers of London, were the mere source of their living, but they were also the only source of information about the situation of foreign markets and the reputation of potential agents. The decisions each banker made were grounded on advice offered by his correspondents. Once decisions were made, correspondents were in charge of implementing them. In light of the tardiness of communication and the relatively rapid swings of financial markets, bankers often had to rely completely on their correspondents for carrying out arbitrages. Indeed, when decisions were made on the basis of information that ceased to be true at the time of their execution, only the skill and reliability of correspondents could save the bankers from loss.[13] Networks thus played a decisive role in managing risk: another aspect of the decision-making process. This was also apparent in the habit of risk sharing in government loans (Drelichman and Voth 2014, 96), or in the practice of guaranteeing commercial bonds (Van der Wee 1993, 157; Lapeyre 1955, 307–308). Such was the multifaceted and overwhelming importance of networks in the shaping of business strategies. In early modern banks, decision-making was not a disembodied process based merely on numbers, but a complex configuration of choices strongly influenced by social capital.

Notes

1. A. S., I, 561, f. 369 (jam sent to a family member in Paris).
2. These were recorded in a specific expense account referring to the 'cost of living' (*spese del vivere*), mostly concerned with wine consumption, whose balance was regularly transferred to the Gain and Loss account (A. S., I, 561, f. 9, 94, 212, 307).
3. A. S., I, 561, f. 209, 241.
4. A. S., I, 568, f. 39.
5. See, for example, the Gain and Loss account of the Lyons ledger opened in 1549 (A. S., I, 588, f. 282). The total sums of the values registered there (952 crowns in debit and 6729 crowns in credit) are not even totalled.
6. A. S., I, 561.
7. A. S., I, 830.
8. A. S., I, 582.
9. A. S., I, 582, f. 211.
10. '*Sopra di voi abbiamo pagato li marchi 4 d'oro trattone Gasparre De Becari e con le nostre spese ce ne vagliamo da lui in voi. Fateveli pagare e sarete disobligo e avisate*'. (Letter to Francesco Bellotti of Milan, A. S., I, 565, f. 61r).
11. This was true while the Salviati had a hundred other depositors, which gives an idea of the importance of these two clients. Matringe, ibid.
12. This fair institution was controlled by Italian merchants. Any merchant who did not show up at the Payments was considered failed and excluded from the fairs, while those who could not pay their debts were severely punished through torture (Brésard 1914, 294–322; Gonthier 2008, 38).
13. For example, in November 1548, the Affaitadi were to draw approximately 10,000 crowns on the Salviati Lyons bank, before remitting them on the Castilian fairs. A few weeks later, however, having learnt that payment periods in Castilla had been extended and, consequently, anticipating *larghezza* (abundance of money), the Salviati, through an urgent written missive to the Affaitadi, cancelled their commission. This unforeseen event jeopardised the profitability of

their arbitrage and even threatened losses. The Affaitadi received the cancellation order too late, after having drawn and remitted the money from Antwerp. However, they took the liberty of slightly modifying the 'route' planned by the Salviati, remitting part of the money drawn on Lyons not from Antwerp but from London, where they both had agents. Resultantly, even though the profit was less than initially expected, the Salviati nevertheless still managed to make the best of their money in the circumstances.

References

Bland, A. E., Brown, P. A., & Tawney, R. H. (dir.). (1914). *English economic history.* Select documents. London: G. Bell & Sons.

Bourdieu, P. (1980). Le capital social. *Actes de la recherche en sciences sociales, 31*, 2–3.

Bratchel, M. E. (1978/1996). Italian merchant organization and business relationships in early tudor England. In: S. Subrahmanyam (Ed.), *Merchant networks in the early modern world* (pp. 1–28). Aldershot, Brookfield: Variorum.

Brésard, M. (1914). *Les foires de Lyon aux XVe et XVIe siècles*. Paris: A. Picard.

Brulez, W. (1959). *De Firma della Faille en de internationale handel van vlaamse firma's in de 16e eeuw*. Bruxelles: Paleis der Academien.

Da Silva, J. G. (1956). *Stratégie des affaires à Lisbonne entre 1595 et 1607. Lettres marchandes des Rodriguez d'Evora et Veiga*. Paris: Sevpen.

Da Silva, J. G. (1959–1961). *Marchandises et finances: lettres de Lisbonne, 1563–1578* (Vol. 3). Paris: Sevpen.

Denucé, J. (1934). *Inventaire des Affaitadi, banquiers italiens à Anvers, de l'année 1568. Texte de l'inventaire dressé par Jean-Baptiste Affaitadi*. Anvers: De Sikkel.

De Roover, R. (1953). *L'Évolution de la Lettre de Change*. Paris: Armand Colin.

De Roover, R. (1963). *The rise and decline of the Medici Bank*. Cambridge, MA: Harvard University Press.

Drelichman, M., & Voth, H.-J. (2014). Lending to the borrower from hell. In: *Debts, taxes and default in the age of Philip II*. Princeton: Princeton University Press.

Febvre, L. (1956). Pour l'histoire d'un sentiment: le besoin de sécurité. *Annales, Économie, Sociétés, Civilisations, 2*, 244–247.

Gelderblom, O. (2013). *Cities of commerce: The institutional foundations of international trade in the low countries, 1250–1650*. Princeton: Princeton University Press.

Gervais, P. (2014). Why profit and loss didn't matter: the historicized rationality of early modern merchant accounting. In: P. Gervais, Y. Lemarchand, & D. Margairaz (Eds.), *Merchants and profits in the age of commerce, 1680–1830* (pp. 33–52). London: Pickering & Chatto.

Goldthwaite, R. (2009). *The economy of renaissance florence*. Baltimore: The John Hopkins University Press.

Gonthier, N. (1993). *Délinquance, justice et société dans le Lyonnais médiéval, de la fin du XIIIe siècle au début du XVIe siècle*. Paris: Éditions Arguments.

Lane, F. C. (1945). Venture accounting in medieval business management. *Bulletin of the Business Historical Society, 19*(5), 164–173.

Lane, F. C. (1977). Double entry bookkeeping and resident merchants. *Journal of European Economic History, 6*(1), 177–191.

Lapeyre, H. (1955). *Une famille de marchands, les Ruiz*. Paris: Armand Colin.

Matringe, N. (2015). *Credit reallocation and trade finance in the early modern age: The fair deposit*. Data available at: https://hal.archives-ouvertes.fr/hal-01152952/document/ (accessed at 12 Dec 2015).

Matringe, N. (2016). *La banque en Renaissance. Les Salviati et la place de Lyon au milieu du* xvie *siècle*. Rennes: Presses Universitaires de Rennes.

Melis, F. (1962). *Aspetti della vita economica medievale. Studi nell'Archivio Datini di Prato*. Florence: L. S. Olschki.

Melis, F. (1972). *Documenti per la storia economica dei secoli XIII–XVI*. Florence: L. S. Olschki.

Ogilvie, S. C. (2011). *Institutions and European trade, merchant guilds, 1000–1800*. Cambridge/New York/Melbourne: Cambridge University Press.

Robertson, J., & Funnell, W. (2012). The Dutch East-India Company and accounting for social capital at the dawn of modern capitalism 1602–1623. *Accounting, Organizations and Society, 37*, 342–360.

Roth, C. (1948/1990). *Doña Gracia Nasi, trad. de l'anglais par C. Bonnafont*. Paris: Liana Levi.

Ruiz Martín, F. (1965). *Lettres marchandes échangées entre Florence et Medina del Campo*. Paris: Sevpen.

Sombart, W. (1916/1953). Medieval and modern commercial enterprise. In: F. C. Lane & J. Riemersma (Eds.), *Enterprise and secular change* (pp. 25–40). Homewood: Richard D. Irwin.

Van der Wee, H. (1993). Antwerp and the new financial methods of the 16th and 17th centuries. In: H. Van der Wee (Ed.), *The low countries in the early modern world* (pp. 145–166). Aldershot: Variorum.

Vázquez de Prada, V. (1960). *Lettres marchandes d'Anvers* (Vol. 4). Paris: Sevpen.

Weber, M. (1947/1964). *The theory of social and economic organization*. London: Collier-Macmillan.

Winjum, J. O. (1971). Accounting and the rise of capitalism: An accountant's view. *Journal of Accounting Resarch, 9* (2), 333–350.

Yamey, B. (1949). Bookkeeping and the rise of capitalism. *The Economic History Review, New Series, 1* (2/3), 99–113.

Yamey, B. (1971). Accounting and the rise of capitalism: Further notes on a theme by Sombart. *Journal of Accounting Research, 2* (2), 117–136.

Risk Management, Credit and the Working of Merchants' Networks in Early Modern Banking

Daniel Velinov

1 Introduction

The device taken from Michael Schirmer's poem on 'The rules a young merchant's conduct should respect in order to avoid perdition' attributes a decisive role in commercial success to a merchant's credit and reputation. Alongside trust and trustworthiness, these notions also play an important role in the literature on medieval and early modern trade organisation. Economics and economic history mobilise these ideas to explain how

Als wie ein Auge/so bewahre dein Gerüchte/
Credit und Namens-Lob/daß man dich nicht vernichte/
Bis zu Grunde gehst
Like the apple of your eye/ guard your reputation/
Credit and praise of your name/so that you shall not be destroyed/
Until you perish
Georg Nicolaus Schurtz, Nutzbare Richtschnur der löblichen Kauffmannschafft (…), Nürnberg, Johann Andreä Endters seel. Söhne, 1695; passage taken from a poem preceding Schurtz's manual; no pagination.

D. Velinov (✉)
LARHRA, CNRS, Lyon, France
e-mail: daniel.velinov@ish-lyon.cnrs.fr

K. Schönhärl (ed.), *Decision Taking, Confidence and Risk Management in Banks from Early Modernity to the 20th Century*,
DOI 10.1007/978-3-319-42076-9_11

medieval and early modern merchants coped with one of the main problems that—according to the literature—they faced: the absence of legal institutions capable of enforcing contracts on an international scale. The apparent severity of this problem contrasts, however, with the remarkable intensity and geographical extension of early modern trade. The literature accounts for this ambiguity by recourse to the notion of merchant networks. Networks compensate for the relative lack of regulation, control and enforcement 'from above' (courts, states) with mechanisms and procedures of self-governance and auto-regulation. Familial, city-based, regional, national, ethnic or religious affiliations, whether individually or in combination, are most commonly considered as constituting the social glue that made merchant networks work. This form of organisation provides incentives for the different merchant groups to discipline their members and to ensure contract enforcement, thereby reducing the risk of opportunistic behaviour and enhancing confidence (Greif 1993, 2006; Gelderblom 2013; Studnicki-Gizbert 2003; Court 2004; Trivellato 2003, 2009).

While this view builds on studies of trade in commodities, the present paper analyses the working of merchant networks based on trade in bills of exchange. This perspective leads, first, to a reconsideration of the nature of the principal-agent relationship, which underlies the entire debate on the working mechanisms of merchants' networks. The focus on trade in bills of exchange leads, second, to the drawing of attention to established practices in commission trading designed to mitigate risk. The analysis of these safeguards inherent to the system introduces an element to the debate on the working mechanisms of merchant networks that has previously received little attention. Third, the close study of the criteria used by operators to establish their colleagues' creditworthiness sheds light on the operators' understanding of credit, reputation and honour.

From a methodological point of view, the focus on common risk-management strategies offers the advantage of putting the analysis of the working of merchant networks on firmer empirical ground. If the logic of sociological analysis and game theory suggests the importance of reputation, personal credit and confidence in the operations of merchants' networks, the available archival material offers little that explicitly shows these parameters at work. Confidence or trust—a notion that is omnipresent in the literature on merchants' networks—is for instance hardly ever mentioned in business correspondence. Instead, merchant letters are explicit about a variety of provisions that aim to mitigate risk in commission trading.

The accounting books and business correspondence of commercial firms represent the most suitable source material to address issues involving principal-agent relationships and risk-management strategies. This source material provides direct insights into the business organisation of firms and allows the analysis of merchants' network structures on the micro-level of how transactions are actually operated. This approach is based on the archive of the seventeenth-century Antwerp banker Jean-Baptiste de la Bistrate, whose business ledgers for the period from 1654 to 1674 are kept in the Plantijn Museum in Antwerp. De la Bistrate is an example of a businessman who specialised in the trade of bills of exchange. His correspondents therefore qualify him as a banker, in accordance with the contemporaneous definition. In the early modern period, banking was indeed less a deposit than an exchange activity.

2 Principal-Agent Relationships: A Matter of Perspective

The study of some representative exchange transactions involving de la Bistrate highlights the interchangeable position of financial market participants. Different configurations represent but a snapshot of a particular stage in a given transaction and thus make it a matter of perspective whether an operator is to be considered as a seller or as a buyer, as acting on his own account or on behalf of principals, as a player, an agent or an intermediary. The exchange transactions that de la Bistrate conducted with his most important client, Brunschweiler & Co. from Basel, illustrate this issue.

Throughout the whole period, de la Bistrate transfers, on behalf of Brunschweiler & Co., funds from Antwerp to Brunschweiler's correspondents in Lille, Valenciennes, Tournai and Mons. These transfers were destined to refund Brunschweiler's correspondents for acquiring

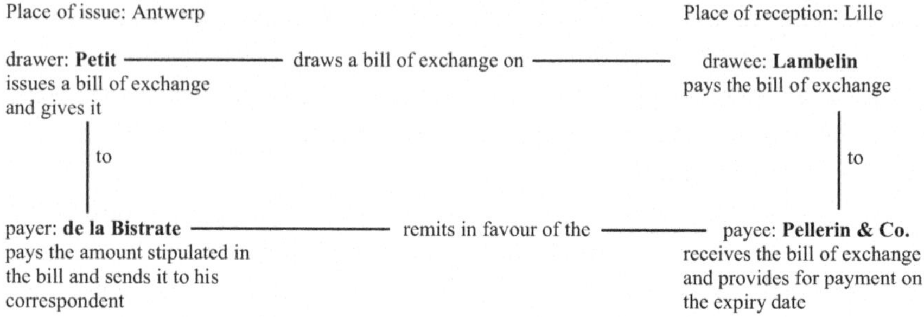

Fig. 2 Principal or agent (1)? Buying a bill on one's own account, selling it on someone else's

and sending Flemish textile products to Basel. The great majority of these transfers were operated by means of bills of exchange. Consider the following example involving a transfer from Antwerp to Lille.

On 11 February 1670, shortly after having received the order to do so from Pellerin & Co., Brunschweiler's correspondent in Lille, de la Bistrate carried out a remittance in favour of the Lille-based firm on the account of his Swiss principals. He remitted at par, a bill of exchange of 136 pounds Flemish drawn by François Petit on Garcia Lambelin. Since Petit had initially issued the bill payable to de la Bistrate, the Antwerp banker carried out this remittance by endorsing the bill in favour of Pellerin & Co. (Fig. 2).[1]

Whereas the distribution of roles between principal and agent is unequivocal with respect to this remittance, the situation turns out to be more complex when the entire history of the bill is considered. A closer look at de la Bistrate's accounting records reveals that de la Bistrate had acquired the bill on his own account from Petit four months earlier on 11 October 1669, at the bill's date of issue. At that moment, he had paid Petit 2% less (133 pounds 6 shillings and 8 pence Flemish) than the face value of the bill (136 pounds Flemish), payable four months later in Lille and at the same time the amount that he would later charge his principals Brunschweiler & Co. (remittance at par). This operation thus yielded a profit of 2 pounds 13 shillings and 4 pence Flemish, resulting from the implicit interest rate included in exchange rates. Thus, de la Bistrate bought the pound Flemish payable in Lille from Petit more cheaply than he sold it to Brunschweiler & Co. Purchasing bills on one's own account and reselling the same bills on somebody else's account is operating neither solely as an agent nor on one's own account. Rather, both modes of intervention go together and determine one another.

The interrelation between agents and principals in exchange transactions appears most strikingly when drawer and payer are the same person, but act on different accounts. Consider the exchange transactions that Giovanni Druyvesteyn, a Venetian trader of Dutch origin, operated with his Antwerp agent de la Bistrate between 1654 and 1658. Apart from Venice and Antwerp, these arbitrage operations mainly involve London. Whereas de la Bistrate either sent Druyvesteyn Antwerp remittances on Venice or honoured Venetian bills on Antwerp, in return he mainly received Venetian remittances on London, which he sold in Antwerp before their expiry date.

Relevant in the context of this topic is the way Druyvesteyn operated his remittances on London. Indeed, in a great number of his remittances on London Druyvesteyn appears as payer *and* as drawer. Consider for instance a bill of 1137 ducats and 3 *grossi* drawn by Druyvesteyn on Thomas Rastel in London on 25 August 1656. The bill was drawn at 55 shillings sterling per ducat at usance, which corresponds to a term of three months between Venice and London. Rastel was thus supposed to pay 260 pounds 11 shillings and 10 pence sterling in London on 25 November. In his role as payer, Druyvesteyn remitted this bill on his own account in favour of de la Bistrate (the payee), who received it by mail on 8 September. On the Antwerp exchange, de la Bistrate then sought to sell this bill at the price limit set by his Venetian principal. He succeeded on 7 October, securing 34 shillings and 7 pence Flemish per pound sterling. Consequently, de la Bistrate credited Druyvesteyn with 450 pounds 12 shillings and 1 penny Flemish (Fig. 2).

In the letter that de la Bistrate sent to Druyvesteyn to inform him of this transaction, he omits to mention the name of the buyer. This is normal and does not constitute an exception in de la Bistrate's correspondence with Druyvesteyn. After all, the identity of the buyer of his bills in Antwerp is of no importance to Druyvesteyn. The buyer's name, however, is revealed in de la Bistrate's accounting books: it is none other than de la Bistrate himself. Thus, this resale transaction was purely ficti-

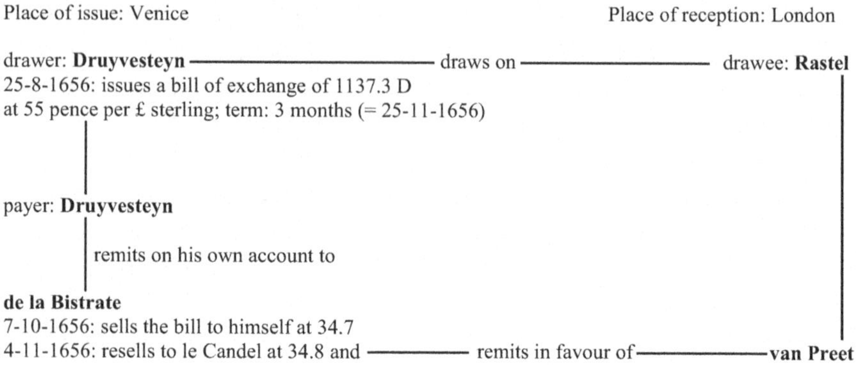

Fig. 3 Principal or agent (2)? Drawing a bill one one's own account, remitting it on someone else's

tious and did not result in any endorsement, because de la Bistrate was already—from the date of issue—the payee of the bill. After having sold to himself the bill without Druyvesteyn's knowledge on 7 October at 34 shillings and 7 pence Flemish per pound sterling, he waited until 4 November when he resold the bill at the more favourable exchange rate of 34 shillings and 8 pence Flemish. As in the previously discussed transaction involving Pellerin & Co. in Lille, the profit that de la Bistrate drew from this exchange operation reflects the time value of money: bills normally appreciate as their maturity approaches.[2] De la Bistrate conducted this second resale-operation with Louis & Robert le Candel, who asked him to endorse the bill to Adrian van Preet, presumably their correspondent in London (Fig. 3).

If it becomes clear from de la Bistrate's accountancy that Druyvesteyn acted here as payer on his own account in the context of an arbitrage operation, the context in which Druyvesteyn acted in this transaction also as drawer is unclear. A hint comes from the accounts that de la Bistrate holds with the drawee, Thomas Rastel, who was perhaps not coincidentally also a correspondent of de la Bistrate. These accounts reveal that Rastel was an English importer of Italian and Levantine products and raw materials, above all silk. This is precisely the commodity that Druyvesteyn was trying—however unsuccessfully—to sell to de la Bistrate. It is thus likely that Druyvesteyn drew the bill on Rastel for silk that he sent for him to

London. De la Bistrate's business correspondence contains more evidence that the reason for at least part of the bills drawn by Druyvesteyn on his various correspondents in London was to mobilise payments for commodities that Druyvesteyn exported from Italy to England.

Druyvesteyn's bills on London thus feature a constellation of exchange transactions where principals and agents were not only interconnected but also identical. On his own account, Druyvesteyn remitted to de la Bistrate; in the same transaction, however, he acted as drawer on the account of London correspondents.

3 Risk Mitigation in Principal-Agent Relations

In his famous manual *Le parfait négociant*, Jacques Savary illustrates this interdependence with an analogy, comparing the commission agent to a guardian and the principal to a pupil. Analogous to this relationship, a commission agent who 'prefers his private interests to those of his principal, enriches himself and ruins [his principal]; if he prefers entirely the interests of his principal to his own ones (what happens very rarely), he ruins himself'. However, Savary reminds his readers, 'It cannot rain on one of them, without dripping off on the other'. He therefore recommends that the guardian 'balances so well the interests of his pupil with his private interests, that neither one of them suffers any loss'. Or, to put it positively, 'The interests of both of them should be in line with each other, so that both profit equally therefrom' (Savary 1675, 151, 163).

Savary's metaphor is noteworthy not only because it reverses the commonly accepted power relation between commission agent and principal (comparing the former with a guardian, whereas associating the latter with a mere pupil), but also because it stresses that the commission agent bears as much risk as the principal in this relation. The 'profession' of commission trading, states Savary, 'is very dangerous, for the agents just as for the principals'. This analysis reminds us that doing business on the account of others is by no means a risk-free endeavour. Savary finds it therefore 'necessary to outline the maxims that commission agents should have in their profession, for the sake of their own security as well as for the security of their principals'. These rules of behaviour and the risk-management procedures that were at the disposal of seventeenth-century merchants will be discussed based on de la Bistrate's exchange business, referring specifically to the exchange operations presented above. Operating exchange transactions are precisely the type of commission trading that Savary considers 'the most tricky and dangerous' activity, 'in particular for the commission agents'. He warns that 'One learns these matters only after a long period of time, and often the hard way, as commission agents sometimes ruin themselves by making one single mistake' (Savary 1675, 143, 158, 169–170).

An important issue that commission agents face in operating exchange transactions is how to hedge risks that come from trading bills of exchange. The two exchange transactions discussed above illustrate the different kinds of risk exposure. In both transactions, the risk that de la Bistrate runs derives from his endorsements, which may make him liable for the payment of the bills. He endorses the first one on behalf of Brunschweiler & Co. in favour of Pellerin & Co. in Lille, and the second one on behalf of Louis & Robert le Candel in favour of Adrian van Preet, presumably in London. Thus, if drawees refuse to pay the bills, the beneficiaries may have recourse to de la Bistrate by virtue of his endorsement. With regard to the first transaction, Savary considers that this recourse would be licit, even though de la Bistrate carried out the remittance in his capacity as commission agent. Savary argues that if an agent endorses on behalf of a principal a bill that he previously bought on his own account, he can then be held liable for its payment. This indeed applies to the bill de la Bistrate endorsed in favour of Pellerin & Co. If, however, the agent endorses a bill that he acquired the same day and only on the account of his principal, then he would not have to face any risk of recourse (Savary 1675, 173–175).

In order to prevent 'this risk [that] a commission agent is running when he remits a bill of exchange', Savary comes forward with the following recommendation. He suggests that,

> *If the person who provides the bill is not the drawer and if the bill is payable to the provider or to his order, [the agent] should ask the provider to endorse it to his [i.e. the agent's] principal or to his [i.e. the agent's principal] order* (Savary 1675, 172).

This is precisely how Louis & Robert le Candel conducted their remittance to their London correspondent Adrian van Preet in the second exchange operation. They asked de la Bistrate, who was the provider of the bill without being the drawer, to endorse it directly to van Preet. In this way, the le Candels do not figure as endorsers on the bill and therefore could not be held liable for its payment. De la Bistrate and his correspondents observed the same safeguard when operating remittances on the account of their principals. They systematically avoided appearing as endorsers or endorsees on the bills they remitted as commission agents. This holds also for bills that they acquired not—as in the previous case—from beneficiaries-endorsers, but directly from the drawers. They thus again followed one of Savary's precepts, specifically that commission agents should ask the drawer 'to issue [his bill] payable to the principal or to his order' (Savary 1675, 172). The rare examples of de la Bistrate operating in a different fashion provide explicit proof that the seventeenth-century exchange dealer had taken this rule completely to heart. Consider a transaction that de la Bistrate operated on the account of Antonio Nieugaert in Amsterdam. He remitted to Nieugaert a bill that the drawers, Jean-Baptiste & Pierre Paulo Borckens, had initially issued payable to him (i.e. de la Bistrate). This means that he carried out the remittance by endorsing the bill in favour of Nieugaert. However, he did not acquire this bill previously on his own account—in contrast to the bill that he endorsed in favour of Pellerin & Co. on the account of Brunschweiler & Co., as discussed above. Therefore, there was no significant time lapse between the date that he bought the bill from the drawers (6 September 1667) and the date that he sent it by mail with his endorsement to his principal in Amsterdam (8 September 1667). In his letter accompanying the bill, he makes clear to Nieugaert that 'This remittance occurs without my prejudice or obligation, notwithstanding that I endorsed the bill; and if you understand it differently, I shall keep the position for myself'.[3] Clearly, de la Bistrate, as commission agent, is aware of the risk that he faces resulting from his endorsement. He therefore disclaims any liability from the very start of this exchange transaction that he conducts on the account of Nieugaert. If Nieugaert will not accept this, then de la Bistrate would claim the bill back. He indeed reasonably believes that if he has to bear the risk of the drawer's and/or the drawee's default, he should also be entitled to pocket the potential profits that this bill might yield.

Another risk-mitigating procedure to which commission agents resort when conducting remittances is to do so in their own bills. This means that the agent himself issues a bill that he draws either on his own account or on behalf of a principal; and that, at the same time, he remits to another principal. By means of this amalgamation of functions, the agent discards any risk resulting from his eventual endorsement in the event the bill is not paid. Indeed, if the bill is not honoured by the drawee and returns protested to the place where it was issued, the agent—in his capacity as remitter and possibly endorser—can be sure that the drawer will reimburse him of the bill's value since the drawer is nobody other than the agent himself.

The agent's twin function is also appreciated by principals who seek to shield themselves from losses resulting from what Savary calls '*l'évenement de la lettre*', i.e. the non-payment of bills (Savary 1675, 172). De la Bistrate indeed regularly urged Druyvesteyn, who might also have acted as his commission agent, to remit his outstanding positions from Venice 'in your own [bills], if possible, [...] so that I do not run any risk of bills'.[4] Asking agents to remit preferably in their own bills was characteristic not only of the relation that de la Bistrate maintained with his Venetian commission agent, but runs through de la Bistrate's entire business correspondence. On 30 July 1660, for instance, de la Bistrate acknowledged receipt of the remittances that his Parisian commission agent Louis Froment had sent him, thanking him for having done this return consignment in his own bills and asking him to continue to do so in the upcoming remittances.[5] Indeed, as principals entrusted to their commission agents part of their exchange dealings, it comes as no surprise that they also found their agents' bills trustworthy. Commission agents were well aware of their principal's preference and were all the more motivated to cater for it, as remitting in their own bills was also in their interest.

The facility of commission agents to operate remittances in their own bills could even become a condition for maintaining the exchange business. This becomes clear, for instance, from the following order that de la Bistrate gives to Druyvesteyn. In his letter from 4 April 1656, de la Bistrate commissioned his Venetian agent to remit bills on London worth 5–6000 Venetian ducats, 'provided that you can remit in your own bills'. He orders, 'You should rest the matter there if you cannot do it in your own bills, unless you shall find bills that are entirely satisfactory'. Interestingly, he links up the reason for giving this restrictive order with his appraisal of the exchange rate movement. 'Because of the very uncertain outcome of this arbitrage operation [i.e. selling in Antwerp Venetian bills on London], one must do it with bills of entire satisfaction.'[6] Clearly, de la Bistrate pondered risk and gain expectation. The increased risk of making a poor profit or even of losing money in this arbitrage scheme increased his demand for safe bills. Often, Druyvesteyn cannot meet this requirement and passages like the following run through his letters to de la Bistrate: 'I would have carried out your commission, but I did not find any bills to my satisfaction and I did not have any occasion [to draw] in my own bills'.[7] That the cessation or initiation of arbitrage operations depends on the availability of remittances in one's own bills also becomes clear in the exchange business that Druyvesteyn operated in his capacity as a principal. Statements like 'If I have the opportunity of [drawing in my] own bills, I shall continue with remitting' point clearly to this dependence.[8] And when Druyvesteyn expressed his satisfaction with the price that de la Bistrate obtained on the Antwerp exchange for his Venetian bills on London, he regrets that he did not remit more bills, 'but this did not happen because I did not have any more occasion [to draw] in my own bills'.[9] The risk-mitigating procedure of remitting in one's own bills not only secures the exchange business but may also become a precondition for this business to exist.

Another widespread procedure to mitigate risk in the exchange business is to dissolve the principal-agent relation and to operate on equal terms, the dealers sharing risks and profits. Instead of de la Bistrate and Druyvesteyn holding separate accounts for each other, this would result in the fusion of the two accounts into a single one. This, however, was not de la Bistrate's preferred mode of operating. Just as he proceeded with Druyvesteyn, he preferred to operate with his correspondents separately, at the same time acting both as principal and as commission agent. An exception to this is his correspondence with Thomas Massillion from Liège, with whom he operated a joint-arbitrage business involving his brother-in-law Jean Desplanches in Amsterdam, the latter acting as their commission agent.[10] Another example of operating by means of joint accounts provides the correspondence between Henri-François Schilders, de la Bistrate's stepson, and the Parisian firm Maillet & Pocquelin. The example of this correspondence shows, however, that the establishment of a joint account does not impede the partners from operating based on a reciprocal principal-agent relation at the same time. Schilders may, therefore, operate transactions on his own account, on the account of Maillet & Pocquelin, or on their joint account. Logically, the Parisian firm had the same options. Note that this complex account structure cannot be explained by the different natures of transactions that are recorded on the different types of accounts since all of the accounts overwhelmingly record arbitrage operations, which moreover involve the same financial centres (Lyon, Venice and London).

The reason that Maillet & Pocquelin invoked for operating by means of '*compte à moitié*' or '*à demy*' was the saving of commission fees. According to the Parisian firm, these fees 'most frequently annihilate all the profit [...] in the exchange business'.[11] Another, if not the main motive for exchange dealers to operate by means of joint accounts is undoubtedly that this way of organising business provided a strong incentive for correspondents to do their utmost to reduce the risk of bills. This concern runs as a *leitmotiv* through the dealers' correspondence. For example, de la Bistrate asks his agent in Valenciennes, Noël Picquet, to 'watch out to [do the remittances] in good bills, so that my mind is put at rest'.[12] When giving de la Bistrate the order to remit to their agents in Lille, Amsterdam and Leiden, Brunschweiler & Co. begged him 'to search for very safe bills in order not to run any risk'.[13] Also Savary's manual echoes this concern. According to Savary, one of the maxims of a commission agent's good conduct is to remit his principal's assets in 'good bills of exchange'. Agents are required to watch out,

> *that those who draw, or those who provide the bills, have the reputation of being good and solvent, so that if the bills happen not to be paid punctually on their expiry date and return protested, the agents could be easily reimbursed by the drawers or by the endorsers* (Savary 1675, 162–163).

In order to sleep peacefully without having to worry about the soundness of the remittances they receive, principals may have even accepted to incur extra costs. Indeed, they frequently reminded their agents not to hesitate to make concessions with respect to the exchange rate, if thereby the agent can obtain safer bills. For example, de la Bistrate ordered his Parisian agent Louis Froment that, when transacting the remittances, he 'should not be concerned to spend ¼ penny Flemish more per French écu in order to get satisfactory bills'.[14] Operating on joint accounts provides powerful incentives to both correspondents to take these guidelines seriously because the assets of both correspondents are equally at stake. These incentives are undoubtedly stronger than the mere threat of losing his principal's commissions that faces a negligent agent. In any case, expressions that agents use frequently to reassure their principals such as, 'We will act as for ourselves', should not be overrated and should be filed instead under conventional rhetoric formulas (Savary 1675, 149).[15] What matters are the incentives for particular behaviour, which depend on what is at stake for the different operators.

The custom called '*del credere*' in Italian or '*du croire*' in French is another important safeguard that commission trading provides in order to shield exchange dealers from the risk of bills. Savary explains this procedure by referring to the trade in commodities. If a commission agent agrees to stay '*du croire*', he vouches for the solvency of those operators to whom he has sold his principal's commodities. With respect to the exchange business, this means that the agent makes himself liable towards his principal for the payment of the bills that he remitted him, even though he neither drew nor endorsed them. This, of course, has its price. Savary indicates that it amounts normally to the commission fee, which means that an agent who stays '*du croire*' in total receives the double commission fee from his principal (Savary 1675, 159; Lapeyre 1955, 307). This is precisely what Brunschweiler & Co. pay to their Parisian agents van Kessel & Coevorden, who vouch for the bills that they remit on behalf of their principals.[16] Operating with agents that guarantee the payment of their remittances manifestly constitutes a general business strategy of Brunschweiler & Co., as they point out in one of their letters: 'In different places, our people stay '*del credere*' when they remit; and we do not find it advisable to hazard anything'.[17] The '*du croire*' agreement reached between Schilders and Maillet & Pocquelin presents the peculiarity that it is reciprocal. Reciprocity was indeed the condition that the Parisian firm set for conceding the '*du croire*'.[18] This means that Schilders guaranteed the payment of the remittances that he operated on the account of Maillet & Pocquelin and *vice versa*. Interestingly, the reciprocal '*du croire*' arrangement applies also to the account discussed above on which both operators share risks and profits.[19] With respect to this joint account, both operators consequently benefit from dual protection.

If the '*du croire*' arrangement reduces, on the one hand, the risk run by the principal, it increases, on the other hand, the risk run by the agent. In the eyes of Savary, this justifies accordingly that 'The principals pay a higher commission fee to the commission agent, because of the great risks that they run' (Savary 1675, 159). Remarkably, and contrary to many of his colleagues, de la Bistrate never operated on the '*du croire*' basis when acting as commission agent. Avoiding this risk, while being satisfied with the ordinary commission fee, was clearly part of de la Bistrate's business strategy, since he observed the same behaviour throughout his twenty-year career as an independent dealer on the Antwerp exchange. He consequently declined every request from his principals to guarantee the payment of any bills or debts that he transacted on their behalf. 'I do not want to stay '*du croire*', because I do not do this for anybody', de la Bistrate informed his Swiss principals.[20]

The risk that any '*du croire*' arrangement involves for a commission agent becomes evident as soon as a case of damage occurs. Happy then are those agents who had refused to agree to any such arrangement. On these occasions, de la Bistrate did not hesitate to make it very clear to his principals that they could not hold him liable for the payment of any debt that he contracted on their account. He does so, for example, when the Antwerp-based merchant Dominico Schuteyser delays the payment of the gold thread that de la Bistrate had sold him on the account of Brunschweiler & Co. As de la Bistrate reminds his Swiss principals unmistakably, 'All debt payments that I am supposed to receive [from Schuteyser] are on your account and risk'.[21]

Conversely, de la Bistrate's manifest reluctance to rely on '*du croire*' arrangements was to his disadvantage when he faced cases of damages occurring in the context of dealings that he operated on his own account. This is the case with a bill drawn by Jacques Heron from Paris on Claude Blot in Amsterdam, which Maillet & Pocquelin had remitted to de la

Bistrate. Unfortunately, both Heron and Blot went bankrupt and the bill remained unpaid. On this occasion, Maillet & Pocquelin, who did not commit themselves to a '*du croire*' arrangement, deployed the same tough talk with their principal de la Bistrate as the latter did in his capacity as commission agent with Brunschweiler & Co. They may well have written that they were 'angry about the loss' that he may have incurred in this affair and they may well have 'pray(ed) God to compensate' him for this misadventure, they may have also assured him that they were 'glad' to have learned that the drawer, Heron, apparently disposed of sufficient assets to reimburse him. 'But this—they ultimately conclude—is of no concern to [us]'.[22]

4 Credit, Creditworthiness and Credit Rating

Significantly, Savary treats the general issue of how to assess an operator's character and conduct in his section on the exchange business. The very first, and developed at length, maxim of this section is precisely 'to know one's principal well'. This order of reasoning clearly implies that, according to Savary, the danger of the exchange business comes from the risk of misjudging one's principal. For an agent, the most difficult aspect here is assessing a principal's 'capabilities' ('*facultez*'). Savary appeals to young and inexperienced traders not to be 'mistaken' by 'outward appearances'. The 'prudent merchant always doubts whether those things that appear outwardly are true or not'. Savary reminds his readership that most of the merchant bankers that went bankrupt in the past twenty years in the kingdom's major commercial centres all 'had considerable property from their fathers & mothers and from their wives, as well as through important inheritances, and did commerce in commodities and money that looked as if it was very lucrative' (Savary 1675, 170–171). However appropriate these general warnings are, Savary nonetheless provides hardly any criteria and instructions on how to assess an operator's capabilities. The reading of Savary's manual will, therefore, be supplemented with a close analysis of de la Bistrate's business correspondence, which provides valuable and first-hand insights on this issue. Apart from showing how exchange dealers assessed their respective creditworthiness, this analysis aims to elucidate notions that are omnipresent in the literature on credit markets and merchant networks, such as an operator's 'reputation' or 'credit'. Specifically, this analysis aims to shed light on the meaning and significance of these notions for the operators themselves.

First of all, it should be pointed out that whereas the terms 'confidence' and 'trust' are ubiquitous in the literature, they are absent in de la Bistrate's business correspondence. This, however, is not true for 'credit', 'respectability' and 'reputation'. Disposing of credit is the condition *sine qua non* for operating as a merchant. This becomes clear from de la Bistrate's report on one of his former colleagues who 'is no longer a merchant [and who now] lives in the countryside [:] the lack of credit has made him abandon trade'.[23]

Respectability appears in association with an operator's compliance with commercial practices and customs. Indeed, when describing one of his fellow operators as 'little respected', de la Bistrate justifies his judgement by stating that this is 'because of a chicanery'.[24] This is in line with Savary's instruction to watch out not to deal with merchants that 'like to trick ['*chicanner*'] and to go to court' (Savary 1675, 170). De la Bistrate echoed this concern when, in his capacity as commission agent, he found it necessary to inform Brunschweiler & Co. that he had 'absolutely no differences' with anybody, a situation for which he praises the Lord.[25]

Finally, an operator's reputation is a general attribute ('he enjoys a good reputation') that is spread and known throughout the international merchant community ('[I know him] only through his reputation because he is friend of my friends', states Froment from Paris about Michel Chauwin from Cambrai).[26] Reputation can also be lost. In de la Bistrate's correspondence, this threat appears in association with illicit trade activities. When asked by Brunschweiler & Co. to trade the gold coins that they are about to send him in Antwerp, de la Bistrate answered that because this trade is against the local ordinances, he does not want to get involved in it, even though it could yield 4 percent profit. If he was caught, 'It would go totally against my reputation,' he argued, because this trade is 'dangerous', especially for 'persons of quality'. It therefore 'suits only persons that have nothing to lose'.[27]

Credit, respectability and reputation thus do appear in the business correspondence. However, seventeenth-century merchants refer to these notions much less frequently than the literature on merchant networks does. One reason for this may be that they are too general to be of use in assessing the creditworthiness of individual operators. The credit of a merchant rests on an array of different, very specific features. Operators, therefore, need to differentiate the notion of credit. The question that they face on a daily basis is not if someone has or does not have credit, but how much credit someone has. As will be seen, operators may be assessed as creditworthy, but only to a certain extent. What are the criteria, what are the rating scales that de la Bistrate and his correspondents apply to assess the capabilities of their fellow exchange dealers?

The most basic condition for dealers to engage in mutual exchange transactions is to have knowledge of each other. Therefore, if the bill's buyer happens not to know the bill's seller, he at first refuses to grant him any credit. Consider the bill drawn by Jan Pierre Destordeix from Amsterdam on Cornelis de Wael from Antwerp that the Amsterdam merchant Antonio Nieugaert remitted to his agent de la Bistrate. Nieugaert informs his Antwerp agent that since he does not know the drawer, he agreed with him to wait for the payment of the bill's value until he has acceptance in due form from the drawee. He asks de la Bistrate to procure the acceptance by the drawee and to tell him what he thinks of the drawee's creditworthiness.[28] The precautions that the credit provider may take in the event of not knowing the borrower (i.e. the drawer) can even go further. Whereas in the former example the buyer pays the bill's value only after the drawee has *accepted* the bill, in the following example he pays it only after the drawee has actually *honoured* the bill at its expiry date. When remitting a bill of 100 écus to de la Bistrate, Maillet & Pocquelin asked him to inform them as soon as he had received payment for the bill. They had not yet given any money to the seller of the bill, 'because this is a person that we do not know'. They are bound to pay him the money only once they have received notice of the bill's payment in Antwerp.[29]

The remitter's discomfort in not knowing the drawer corresponds to the beneficiary's discomfort in not knowing the drawee. One senses the beneficiary's concern through what Louis Froment writes of Jean Trippart, the drawee of one of the bills that his agent de la Bistrate remitted to him. 'I do not know well this Mister Trippart,' writes Froment, 'but I believe that you know the drawer'. From this comment, de la Bistrate indeed understood that his principal had second thoughts since in his answering letter he believes it necessary to assure him that this bill is entirely safe.[30] Conversely, when Froment operated remittances on the account of de la Bistrate, the Antwerp banker wrote of Claude Auvray, the drawee of one of the bills: 'He is a stranger here and not well known, this is why I have enough remittances on him'.[31] Clearly, being known—either among individual merchants or on the exchange as a whole—is a criterion for creditworthiness.

The most important means for reputation to spread are merchants' letters. Their analysis reveals the remarkable variety of different features and aspects to which dealers resort in order to inform their correspondents about the capabilities of fellow exchange operators. A rather general criterion of creditworthiness is the ease with which a dealer succeeds in selling his bills on the exchange. 'I consider these bills as good, at least everybody takes [i.e. buys] them', reports Froment with respect to two bills that he remitted on the account of de la Bistrate.[32] As this quote suggests, however, operators feel uncomfortable when blindly following the general opinion of the exchange. Indeed, their letters show that they also have an opinion of their own on such issues. For example, Maillet & Pocquelin assess one of their colleagues in the following way: 'We judge him safe and we never refuse his bills'.[33] Referring to other colleagues, the information that 'For more than a year we have not wanted to take any of their bills' means, on the contrary, that they denied them any creditworthiness.[34]

Another aspect that operators refer to when reporting on their colleagues is the history of the merchant houses and here especially the family background. Froment linked the good reputation of Charles & Gilles Chelot (they are 'esteemed as good merchants') to the fact that they have 'a good business in the rue St. Denis [i.e. in one of the main commercial streets of early modern Paris] that has been passed from father to son'. He therefore was sure that they would accept the bills that de la Bistrate had sent him.[35] De la Bistrate reasons similarly. Referring to Eduard Butler, he considers him 'a very honest person, who came here 5 to 6 months ago to replace his brother Jean, who passed away'. Therefore, he has no doubt that once Butler has accepted the bills that Froment remitted him, Butler will pay them immediately.[36] Clearly, intergenerational continuity of economic activity warrants creditworthiness. De la Bistrate's assessment of Robert Lalleman of Valenciennes confirms this finding by inverse inference: 'As his father has left Valenciennes, his son has little credit'.[37] Here the disrupted family cohesion affects the estimation of capability. Note that at least for de la Bistrate, being of young age—as we may assume is the case with Robert—is not *per se* a synonym for low capability.[38]

The way operators conduct business may also serve as an indicator of creditworthiness. For example, de la Bistrate thinks that Deccort 'conducts a fairly honourable business', whereas Maillet & Pocquelin reported on Messrs. Bays that they did not 'like the way [they] were doing business'. This is the reason why they had refrained from buying their bills.[39] While these two comments on business conduct remain rather general, others relate to more specific aspects. Jean-Baptiste Guyot from London 'has the reputation of being a very diligent person'. Similarly, Abraham Otger, also based in London, whom his principal de la Bistrate describes as 'a very safe person', operates 'prompt return consignments' of the remittances that he received from Antwerp.[40] Other comments refer to the operators' payment practices. When appraising his own practices, de la Bistrate clearly links speedy payment to creditworthiness. Indeed, he explains to his principals Brunschweiler & Co. that although bills are normally paid only fourteen days after their expiry date on the Antwerp exchange, he and 'other persons of quality' pay them 'promptly' as soon as they fall due.[41] A contrast to de la Bistrate's self-assessment is found in Maillet & Pocquelin's opinion of Jean-Henry Baudry, whom they consider 'a very bad payer'. The Parisian firm complains that Baudry gave them light gold coins to the amount of 500 pounds *tournois* in payment for a bill that was drawn on him, promising to exchange these coins later. However, he 'mocked' them, making them lose more than ten écus.[42]

The relationship between the volume of affairs that a merchant shoulders and his estimated actual capabilities is another indicator that operators take into account when monitoring their colleagues' business conduct. Consider the assessment of Guillaume Carbonnel that de la Bistrate sent to Brunschweiler & Co. in response to their request to inform them about the creditworthiness of this London-based merchant. Carbonnel 'lets himself sometimes be charged by his friends from France', reports de la Bistrate.[43] This means that Carbonnel operates as a commission agent on the account of principals based in France. In itself, of course, there is nothing objectionable in operating on the account of others. Being commissioned by other merchants is rather a sign of trustworthiness. For example, one of the aspects of de la Bistrate's positive evaluation of the London-based merchant Jean-Baptiste Guyot is that 'he has commissions from several operators from this [i.e. the Antwerp] exchange'.[44] However, an agent's creditworthiness could suffer if his colleagues have the impression that his risk exposure towards his principals is about to become excessive. This risk of being excessively charged by his principals is what de la Bistrate diagnoses with respect to Carbonnel: 'Several people from Paris draw on him and he should not accept that'.[45] As Savary explains, the danger here comes from the risk that agents may accept too many bills without disposing of sufficient assets to pay them, 'in the hope that [their principals] will provide them with remittances in time'. Principals, however, 'may fail to do so', and this could cause the agent's bankruptcy (Savary 1675, 163, 172). Based on de la Bistrate's assessment, Brunschweiler & Co. therefore considered very carefully whether they should entrust any commissions to Carbonnel. They refused to do so with respect to Robert Lalleman, following de la Bistrate's judgement. Manifestly, they took seriously their Antwerp agent's warning that young Robert had little credit, not only because he was deprived of his father in Valenciennes but also because 'he is undertaking too much'.[46]

An obvious criterion of an operator's creditworthiness is whether he accepts and pays the bills that are drawn on him. This is a common subject of inquiry among merchants, who frequently wish to be informed on the matter. On Antonio Nieugaert's question whether certain traders active on the Antwerp exchange recently refused to pay bills that were drawn on them, de la Bistrate assured him that he had not heard 'of any bills that would have been protested on their expense'. However, he acknowledged that the Antwerp exchange was suffering a momentary 'inconvenience', which he attributes to a situation of 'little credit' on the exchange.[47] Louis Froment reports from Paris that Michel le Clerc, the drawee of one of de la Bistrate's remittances, refused to accept the bill.

Moreover, one of Froment's friends holds another non-accepted bill on le Clerc, according to what he heard on the exchange.[48] The negative consequences of protested bills on creditworthiness become explicit with respect to a remittance operated by Hoste & Co. from Middelburg to de la Bistrate on the account of Nieugaert in a bill on Balthasar Schoof from Antwerp. When receiving the protested bill from de la Bistrate, Hoste & Co. are 'surprised' that Schoof 'cares so little about [the bill's] respect', all the more as he had previously accepted it. According to them, Schoof's refusal to pay 'will leave him with little credit from his people [i.e. the drawers] here [in Middelburg]'.[49]

A bill's non-acceptance and non-payment, however, not only has repercussions on the drawee's creditworthiness, but also on the drawer's one. This is why Robert Lalleman begged de la Bistrate to pay the bills that he drew on him, so that they would not 'return protested'.[50] The potential danger that this eventuality represents for every exchange dealer's creditworthiness becomes clear from the way de la Bistrate answers Julio Pestalossy's (Paris) question about whether the Antwerp-based merchant Gisbert Coosman does 'good business' and whether he enjoys 'good credit'. 'For quite some time now,' de la Bistrate reported, 'I have not done any business with him because I have noticed that several of his bills returned unaccepted'.[51] Andrea Martens faces the same consequences for his bill drawn on his Venetian correspondent Justo van Eyck, which was returned unaccepted. Indeed, Giovanni Druyvesteyn, on whose account de la Bistrate had remitted the bill, subsequently asks his Antwerp agent 'not to give any more to Martens' on his account. Accordingly, de la Bistrate informs him that he has 'made a note' of not buying any more bills issued by Martens.[52]

Because of the fatal consequences that exclusion of access to credit has for every merchant, Savary devotes an entire paragraph to explaining the mechanisms at work when bills return protested. According to Savary, exchange dealers draw two conclusions concerning those who sold them bills that return protested. First, their correspondents did not pay the bills because they 'did not owe them anything and did not receive any assets from them before the expiry date to provide for the payment of the bills'. Second, which results from the first, their correspondents 'do not do well in their business'. Both conclusions cast a cloud over the bill provider's business situation. Consequently, 'all purses are closed for them'. This could 'ruin the principals and at the same time the commission agents'. Note that the terms that Savary uses in this context to designate what both stand to lose is not 'creditworthiness', 'trust' or 'confidence', but 'reputation' and 'honour' (Savary 1675, 163).

De la Bistrate's business correspondence provides an eloquent example illustrating that according to the understanding of the early modern merchant community, exchange operations engage the honour of a merchant. For de la Bistrate and his correspondents, 'honouring a bill' is a synonym for 'paying a bill'.[53] In the event that the drawee declines to honour a bill, the honour of all of the other operators involved in the transaction is at stake. The efforts that they deploy to provide for the bill's payment, notwithstanding the drawee's refusal, and the expression used for designating the procedures at hand, reveal explicitly that the concept of 'honour' is at the heart of the exchange system. Specifically, the custom of assigning a third party with the payment of a bill 'for the honour of the drawer' or 'for the honour of the endorser' provides drawer and endorser with the possibility of saving their honour in the context of a protested bill. This is what Louis Froment requests de la Bistrate to do with regard to a bill that he had drawn on Jean-Baptiste van Eyck, who refused payment: 'I ask you to satisfy it for my honour'.[54] An example of a payment made by a third party on behalf of the endorser is provided by a bill drawn on Jean-Henry Baudry that de la Bistrate had acquired from Pierre Oudaert before remitting it on his account to Maillet & Pocquelin. His Parisian agents reported that Baudry had refused to honour the bill, but that they nonetheless received payment from Mister Verspreet 'for the honour of the endorser [i.e. Oudaert]'.[55] It is finally noteworthy that the non-payment of a bill not only affects the honour of all of the operators that are involved in the exchange operation, but also of their families and even their in-laws. Concerning the above-mentioned protested bill on van Eyck, Jean Desplanches, an Amsterdam-based correspondent of the bill's drawer, Louis Froment, urged de la Bistrate 'to represent to Mister de Man [i.e. a relative of van Eyck] the consequence and the impertinence of this affair'.[56] He also assumes that as soon as the bill's remitter (i.e. Jean de Launay from Paris) takes legal action against van Eyck via his representative in Antwerp, van Eyck's father-in-law van der Mandoere 'will give order to satisfy [the remitter] for the sake of the preservation of his honour and of his family'.[57]

The return of protested bills is but one indicator for assessing an operator's credit by means of his correspondents' business behaviour and state of affairs. The event that is most likely to trigger dealers' alarm bells is the news of a correspondent's bankruptcy. For example, with respect to a remittance that his London agent Abraham Otger had carried out of a bill issued by Arnaut van der Becke on Jean Gille from Flushing, de la Bistrate was worried about the creditworthiness of van der Becke, because he had learned that van der Becke's correspondent in Amsterdam, Leonart van Ceulen, had gone bankrupt.[58] Manifestly, de la Bistrate is concerned that van Ceulen's insolvency may affect van der Becke's financial capabilities. The risk here is that if the bill were to return protested to London, the drawer might no longer be able to provide for its reimbursement to Otger. Because Otger had conducted the remittance in his capacity as commission agent, de la Bistrate would have to suffer any loss resulting from the payment default. This threat appears again with respect to a remittance that de la Bistrate had undertaken on his own account to Maillet & Pocquelin of a bill drawn by Jean de Neufville from Amsterdam on Jacques de Kessel & Co. Fortunately de la Bistrate's Parisian agents gave the all clear. De Kessel & Co. were 'not interested' in the insolvent de Neufville, i.e. they did not have any outstanding debts with him. Therefore, Maillet & Pocquelin considered them 'safe' and that de la Bistrate should not worry about the payment of his remittance.[59]

The shadow that every correspondent's bankruptcy may cast on one's own credit is undoubtedly the reason why operators find it necessary to reassure their agents and principals when this event occurs. For example, when de la Bistrate's Parisian correspondent Julio Pestalossy goes bankrupt, de la Bistrate informed his Parisian agents Maillet & Pocquelin that he had no stake in Pestalossy's business. Manifestly relieved, Maillet & Pocquelin replied that they were 'very pleased' about this.[60] In turn, Maillet & Pocquelin assured de la Bistrate that they had no 'interest' in any one of the numerous bankruptcies that had occurred recently in Paris.[61] If an operator happens to admit that he has outstanding debts with an insolvent correspondent, he normally indicates the exact amount. It comes as no surprise that in all instances observed, this amount is sufficiently insignificant to allow any doubt to be cast on the operator's creditworthiness. For example, Maillet & Pocquelin informed de la Bistrate that they, unfortunately, had stakes in the bankruptcy of Jacob Aboab from London, but that these stakes amounted to only 500 écus. Their Parisian colleagues Sadocq, Jacques de Kessel and van Kessel & Coevorden, however, 'are deeply involved'.[62]

The procedure of assessing an operator's credit based on his correspondents' credit becomes even more subtle when the chain of correspondents taken into account is extended. A telling example for assessing an operator's credit by considering not only the credit of his correspondents, but also that of the correspondents of his correspondents, is provided by a remittance that Louis Froment conducted on the account of de la Bistrate of a bill drawn by Bobiere & Preubze[63] from Paris on Jacques Pincquet from Antwerp. The case is interesting because Froment deals with the Parisian drawers of the bill also on his own account. When he buys the bill from them, he still has an outstanding debt with them for goods that they had sold him. He hesitates to settle this account because he has doubts about the creditworthiness of Bobiere & Preubze's Antwerp correspondent and drawee of the above-mentioned bill. These doubts prove justified, as de la Bistrate considered Pincquet 'not very solid', especially as he was involved with approximately 1200 pounds Flemish in various bankruptcies that had occurred in Lille. 'The loss is great' judged de la Bistrate, who finishes his report by adding that he had just learned about the bankruptcy of Jacques Croquet, another Lille merchant with whom Pincquet was also doing business. He therefore advises Froment not to settle his account with Bobiere & Preubze until Pincquet has paid their bill in Antwerp.[64] Clearly, Bobiere & Preubze's credit in Paris depends on that of their Antwerp correspondent's correspondents in Lille.

The ultimate goal for exchange dealers in their constant consideration of all of the above-discussed criteria and indicators is to know to whom they can provide how much credit. These very concrete questions require precise answers. From reading de la Bistrate's business correspondence, there is the impression that dealers have a virtual list in mind of every one of their colleagues on the exchange, and attribute to each a certain amount up to which they deem them trustworthy. For example, de la Bistrate considers the Antwerp firm Martin & Jean Jacobs very safe and would entrust it with the enormous sum of up to 20,000 écus.[65] In contrast, he would give not more than 150 to 200 pounds Flemish on his own account and as much on the account of his principals to another of his colleagues on the Antwerp exchange, although he considered this colleague 'a friend' who 'does fairly good business'.[66] He holds a similar opinion of Geert van Beurcken, whom he considers 'an honest man' but one who has no important financial resources. Therefore, he would not grant him more than 200 Reichsthalers.[67] His rating of Jean Adriansen Happart's credit was also rather conservative. Replying to Jean Desplanche's inquiry about whether one could entrust Happart with 1000 pounds Flemish, he asserted that he 'would not make any difficulty about giving him 400 to 500 pounds Flemish for bills of exchange'.[68]

These examples suggest that for seventeenth-century exchange dealers, credit is not a 'soft' sociological, anthropological or cultural category. This understanding could not have provided them with the concrete analytical tools that they needed to cope with the daily challenges of the exchange business. For them, credit is a measurable, quantifiable category. According to their understanding, credit does not depend exclusively on friendship, honesty or conducting good business. Credit depends even less on kinship, religion or ethnical affiliations. Credit is the sum of observable features that all relate to conventional business practices.

5 Conclusion

Focusing on the working mechanisms of the exchange business, i.e. on what banking was about throughout the early modern period, has brought to light several findings that delineate starting points for future research. These findings concern the overall question of what made long-distance trade possible and how it was organised and secured. The analysis of de la Bistrate's accountancy and business correspondence supplements, and indeed questions parts of the narrative that runs through the literature on early modern trade and raises issues that have not yet received a lot of attention.

First, the analysis suggests reconsidering—at least with respect to exchange transactions—the commonly accepted principal-agent model. The idea that underlies this model, i.e. that transactions carried out on a commission trade basis involve one principal and one agent, does not prove useful when applied to the trade in bills of exchange because it fails to account for the complexity of exchange transactions. Indeed, in one and the same transaction, a principal may become an agent and *vice versa*. This twin function is also made apparent by the operators' propensity to hold accounts with their correspondents both in their capacity as principals and as agents. Therefore, the principal-agent relationship does not describe a unilateral dependency, as the basic model implies, but an interdependency. Consequently, it is not only the principal who faces business risks, but also the agent.

Second, the analysis of de la Bistrate's business correspondence does not provide any evidence for the operation of risk-mitigating mechanisms related to group affiliations, which are widely accepted in the literature. In their letters, de la Bistrate and his correspondents never even mention the religious or ethnical affiliation of any of their colleagues and specify their origins only on very rare occasions. Instead, this analysis has shown the overwhelming role played by a remarkable variety of risk-mitigating customs, techniques and procedures that were inherent to the system of commission trading. It is these practices that both principals and agents relied on to shield themselves from potential risks.

Third, the limited role of kinship, religious or ethnical affiliation, as well as origin, is also obvious from the way operators assess their respective creditworthiness. This is also true of the role of confidence and trust, two other notions that are omnipresent in the literature but never occur in de la Bistrate's business correspondence. This, of course, does not mean that they do not exist in the operators' minds. However, their absence from the analysed source material suggests that they are not applicable to how exchange dealers determined the financial capabilities of their colleagues. They are inappropriate analytical categories not only for the twenty-first-century scholar of early modern banking but undoubtedly also for the seventeenth-century exchange operator. They are too general and vague to serve them as guidelines in their daily operations. While exchange dealers may consider a fellow colleague as generally creditworthy, they may still find at times that he accepts and sells bills that exceed his capabilities. Credit is no absolute category, but one that needs to be constantly reassessed and quantified precisely. To this end, dealers monitor each other's business conduct very carefully. As for the risk-mitigating procedures, the criteria that operators consider for assessing their colleagues' creditworthiness almost exclusively relate to mechanisms that underlie the exchange business and commission trading.

Finally, the analysis does not confirm the role that courts or public institutions allegedly played in reducing risk and enhancing business confidence. On the contrary, de la Bistrate prides himself on not being involved in any lawsuits, as if this were proof of his credit. Indeed, neither de la Bistrate files suit against any of his agents, nor do any of his principals against de la Bistrate. After all, this is only logical, since by far the greatest risk for every exchange dealer is the non-payment of his remittances due to the bankruptcy of the drawer and possibly also of the endorsers. All of the risk-mitigating procedures deployed by exchange dealers are intended to shield them from precisely this eventuality. To be sure, bankruptcy cases are of course heard, disputed and negotiated in courts and other public institutions, and de la Bistrate and his colleagues were involved in such cases. Yet, however widespread, developed and bestowed with legal competence courts and public institutions may be, they cannot protect exchange dealers from bankruptcies. This is as true in the early modern period as it is today.

All of these findings point to the central role played by commission trading in early modern trade. As Savary states, 'There is nothing that sustains commerce as much as the commission agents' (Savary 1675, 143). Savary's testimony accords with the way de la Bistrate and his correspondents organised their business activities throughout Europe: seventeenth-century trading was intimately bound up with commission trading. Issues that are central to the understanding of early modern trade—such as the working of merchant networks, and risk management or creditworthiness—therefore all need to be related to commission trading. This is precisely the case for the techniques and procedures that de la Bistrate and his correspondents deployed to carry out and secure their exchange business, which are all inherent to the system of commission trading. Where, when and how did these techniques develop? Where, when and why did commission trading develop? When did the first traders appear that specialised exclusively in operating on a commission basis? Recently, N. Matringe has come forward with interesting suggestions on the history of commission trading. She links the development of commission trading to the development of fairs in general (Lyon, Medina del Campo), and to specialized exchange fairs in particular (Bisenzone) in the 16th century. The significant increase of exchange activities would have stimulated the demand for services provided by commission agents. The birth of commercial firms specializing in commission trading materializes in the appearance of accounting books dedicated exclusively to the business that these firms operated on the account of principals ('*libri dei committenti*'). This is what N. Matringe observes with respect to several Italian firms active in Florence and Lyon in the 16th century (Salviati, Gondi, Capponi, Martelli): see *id.*, 2016, 38, 137, 161–173, 335 and the chapter written by the same author in the present volume.

At the current state of research, these questions remain unresolved, as the history of commission trading remains to be written.

Notes

1. Museum Plantijn, Economisch Archief [henceforward: MP/EA]. All transactions quoted are recorded in de la Bistrate's ledgers n°1306 (1642–1657), n°1336 (1657–1664), n°1347 (1664–1672), n°1366 (1672–1674), and journals n^{os}1305, 1335, 1348, and 1368, which correspond to the same time intervals.
2. At an exchange rate of 34 shillings and 8 pence, the bill's value amounts to 451 pounds 13 shillings and 8 pence Flemish. With respect to the bill's purchase price of 450 pounds 12 shillings and 1 penny, this corresponds to a profit of 1 pound 1 shilling and 7 pence that de la Bistrate makes within 28 days, i.e. between 7 October, when he bought the bill, and 4 November, when he resells it. The profit that de la Bistrate draws from this transaction increases by 1 pound and 10 shillings Flemish, which corresponds to the commission fee that the Antwerp banker charges for his services. The fee amounts to 1/3% of the value of each of the bills that he draws, remits, endorses or honours on the account of his principals.
3. MP/EA, n°1354, de la Bistrate [henceforward: LB] to Nieugaert, 8 September 1667.

4. MP/EA, n°1333, LB to Druyvesteyn, 22 November 1658.
5. 'Po[ur] mon avance me remettes 2300 [écus] en vostre lettre sur Amsterdam, [...] vous remerciant que m'aves fait le retour en vostre lettre' (MP/EA, n°1339 [1]).
6. MP/EA, n°1328, LB to Druyvesteyn, 4 April 1656.
7. MP/EA, Druyvesteyn to LB, 2 June 1656.
8. MP/EA, Druyvesteyn to LB, 28 December 1657.
9. MP/EA, Druyvesteyn to LB, 1 January 1658.
10. See, for instance, de la Bistrate's letter to Desplanches of 7 November 1655: 'I received a letter from Massillion, by which he informs me of having drawn on you on the account we share with each other ("po[ur] compte de luy et moy à ½") 460 pounds Flemish' (MP/EA, n°1328).
11. MP/EA, Archive of Henri-François Schilders, incoming correspondence, Maillet & Pocquelin to Schilders, 3 April 1665 and 12 November 1666.
12. MP/EA, n°1326, LB to Picquet, 10 December 1654.
13. MP/EA, Brunschweiler & Co. to LB, 25 September 1666. The Swiss firm repeats this order in its letter of 2 October 1666: 'Sur tout il vous plairra cherger des bonne lettres tout assuré pour ne point courrir risque' (*ibid.*).
14. MP/EA, n°1333, LB to Froment, 26 April 1658. Note that the exchange rate between Paris and Antwerp is quoted in a variable number of Flemish pennies for one French écu.
15. The occurrences of this classic formula in de la Bistrate's correspondence are countless. See, for example, Maillet & Pocquelin to LB, 19 March 1666: 'Nous avons fait comme pour nous mesme'; same to same, 3 March 1667: 'Soies certain que nous fairons plus que pour nous-mesmes'; same to same, 13 April 1668: 'Nous agirons comme p[our] n[ou]s' (MP/EA, de la Bistrate's incoming correspondence). The maxim is echoed in Savary's manual: 'Les commissionnaires [...] doivent [...] agir comme si les achats estoient pour leur compte propre'. Variants of this formula are commonly used also in the 16th century: Matringe, 2016, 161–162.
16. 'Van Kessel nous respondent pour les lettres et nous sont bon moyenant la double provision que leur donnons' (MP/EA, Brunschweiler & Co. to LB, 24 June 1672).

17. MP/EA, Brunschweiler & Co. to LB, 31 July 1666.
18. 'Vous demeurerons du croire des lettres que vous remetrons, pourveu que vous faites une condition reciproque pour celles que pourrez remetre à l'advenir pour nostre compte' (MP/EA, Schilders's incoming correspondence, Maillet & Pocquelin to Schilders, 3 April 1665). Interestingly, also the Salviati from Lyon stipulate reciprocity as a condition for conceding the '*du croire*' to the Affaitadi from Antwerp in 1544 (Matringe, 2016, 166 and footnote 105).
19. 'Nous demeurons d'accord de demeurer du croire des lettres que nous vous remetrons pour compte à demy, comme vous demeurez aussy du croire de celles que vous nous remetrez pour mesme compte, sans que les uns ny les autres soient obligés de payer aucune provision' (*ibid.*, Maillet & Pocquelin to Schilders, 12 November 1666).
20. MP/EA, n°1339 (2), LB to Brunschweiler & Co., 5 June 1664. For refusals of previous requests, see de la Bistrate's letters to his Swiss principals from 7 July and 10 August 1662 (*ibid.*, n°1339 [1]).
21. MP/EA, n°1328, LB to Brunschweiler & Co., 21 July 1656.
22. MP/EA, Maillet & Pocquelin to LB, 25 March 1667.
23. MP/EA, n°1339 (2), LB to Julio Pestalossy, 21 September 1663.
24. MP/EA, n°1369, LB to Brunschweiler & Co., 14 December 1673.
25. MP/EA, n°1328, LB to Brunschweiler & Co., 24 November 1656.
26. MP/EA, n°1328, LB to Brunschweiler & Co., 21 July and 29 September 1656; Louis Froment to LB, 16 October 1665.
27. MP/EA, n°1354, LB to Brunschweiler & Co., 6 May 1666 and 29 December 1672. With respect to a similar request, see also de la Bistrate's letter to Jean Hooghen from Ghent as of 13 January 1655: 'Dan alsoo het selve een dangereuse handel is, principalyck voor persoenen van qualityt […]" (*ibid.*, n°1326).
28. MP/EA, Nieugaert to LB, 18 May 1668. For another example of this procedure, see also *ibid.*, Nieugaert to LB, 17 September 1668.
29. MP/EA, Maillet & Pocquelin to LB, 21 August 1671.
30. MP/EA, Froment to LB, 27 November 1665; *ibid.*, n°1339 (2), LB to Froment, 11 December 1665.
31. MP/AE, n°1333, LB to Froment, 28 December 1657.
32. MP/AE, Froment to LB, 30 November 1657.
33. MP/AE, Maillet & Pocquelin to Schilders, 30 October 1665.

34. MP/AE, Maillet & Pocquelin to Schilders, 29 May 1665.
35. MP/AE, Froment to LB, 25 August 1656.
36. MP/AE, n°1354, LB to Froment, 23 April 1666.
37. MP/AE, n°1354, LB to Brunschweiler & Co., 14 July 1667.
38. Whereas de la Bistrate is rather sceptical towards Carbonnel of London ('a fairly young French merchant'), he thinks of Deccort however—'a young man that came here a while ago from Spain'—that he is a 'good acceptant' (MP/AE, n°1326, LB to Noël Picquet [Valenciennes], 8 April 1655; *ibid.*, n°1354, LB to Brunschweiler & Co., 25 November 1666).
39. MP/AE, n°1326, LB to Noël Picquet, 8 April 1655; *ibid.*, Maillet & Pocquelin to Schilders, 5 May 1665.
40. MP/AE, n°1339 (2), LB à Brunschweiler & Co., 26 February 1665.
41. MP/AE, n°1339 (1), LB to Brunschweiler & Co., 25 May 1662.
42. MP/AE, Maillet & Pocquelin to LB, 2 February 1668.
43. MP/AE, n°1354, LB to Brunschweiler & Co., 25 November 1666.
44. MP/AE, n°1339 (2), LB to Brunschweiler & Co., 26 February 1665.
45. MP/AE, n°1354, LB to Brunschweiler & Co., 28 October 1666.
46. MP/AE, n°1354, LB to Brunschweiler & Co., 14 July 1667.
47. MP/AE, n°1354, LB to Nieugaert, 3 October 1667.
48. MP/AE, Froment to LB, 4 August 1656.
49. MP/AE, Hoste & Co. to LB, 4 November 1667.
50. MP/AE, Lalleman to LB, 29 May 1667.
51. MP/AE, Pestalossy to LB, 14 September 1663; *ibid.*, n°1339 (1), LB to Pestalossy, 16 March 1663.
52. MP/AE, Druyvesteyn to LB, 29 September 1656; *ibid.*, n°1328, LB to Druyvesteyn, 13 October 1656.
53. For example, the Rouen branch of Maillet & Pocquelin thanks Schilders for having 'honoured' their drafts (MP/AE, Maillet & Pocquelin [Rouen] to Schilders, 26 March 1666). Robert Lalleman asks de la Bistrate to 'honour' the bills that he ordered Joachim Endelin to draw on him from Paris (*ibid.*, Lalleman to LB, 1 February 1666).
54. MP/AE, Froment to LB, 13 July 1667.
55. MP/AE, Maillet & Pocquelin to LB, 20 April 1668.
56. MP/AE, Desplanches to LB, 25 July 1667.
57. MP/AE, Desplanches to LB, 26 August 1667.

58. MP/AE, n°1354, LB to Otger, 17 March 1668.
59. MP/AE, Maillet & Pocquelin to LB, 5 December 1669.
60. MP/AE, Maillet & Pocquelin to LB, 22 April 1671.
61. *Ibid.*
62. MP/AE, Maillet & Pocquelin to LB, 19 December 1669.
63. The spelling of the firm's name is unclear. 'Bobiere & Preusxe' was also found.
64. MP/AE, Froment to LB, 19 April 1658; *ibid.*, n°1333, LB to Froment, 26 April 1658.
65. MP/AE, n°1333, LB to Froment, 28 December 1657.
66. MP/AE, n°1354, LB to Pestalossy, 30 July 1666. In his letter, de la Bistrate omits to spell out the name of this colleague, undoubtedly for reasons of confidentiality.
67. MP/AE, n°1328, LB to Willem Engelbrecht (Hamburg), 6 February 1657.
68. MP/AE, Desplanches to LB, 25 July 1667; *ibid.*, n°1354, LB to Desplanches, 28 July 1667.

References

Court, R. (2004). *Jenuensis ergo mercator*: Trust and enforcement in the business correspondence of the Brignole family. *Sixteenth-Century Journal, 35*, 987–1003.

Gelderblom, O. (2013). *Cities of commerce. The institutional foundations of international trade in the Low Countries, 1250–1650.* Princeton: Princeton University Press.

Greif, A. (1993). Contract enforceability and economic institutions in early trade: The Maghribi traders' coalition. *American Economic Review, 83*, 525–548.

Greif, A. (2006). The birth of impersonal exchange: The community responsibility system and impartial justice. *Journal of Economic Perspectives, 20*, 221–236.

Lapeyre, H. (1955). *Une famille de marchands: les Ruiz. Contribution à l'étude du commerce entre la France et l'Espagne au temps de Philippe II.* Paris: A. Colin.

Matringe, N. (2016). *La Banque en Renaissance. Les Salviati et la place de Lyon au milieu du XVI*e siècle, Rennes: Presses Universitaires de Rennes.

Savary, J. (1675). *Le parfait negociant, ou instruction generale pour ce qui regarde le commerce [...]*. Paris: Louis Billaine.

Schurtz, G. N. (1695). *Nutzbare Richtschnur der löblichen Kauffmannschafft [...]*. Nürnberg: J.A. Endters seel. Söhne.

Studnicki-Gizbert, D. (2003). La „nation" portugaise. Réseaux marchands dans l'espace atlantique à l'époque moderne. *Annales Histoire Sciences Sociales, 58*, 627–648.

Trivellato, F. (2003). Juifs de Livourne, Italiens de Lisbonne, hindous de Goa. Réseaux marchands et échanges interculturels à l'époque moderne. *Annales Histoire Sciences Sociales, 58*, 581–603.

Trivellato, F. (2009). *The familiarity of strangers: The Sephardic diaspora, Livorno, and cross cultural trade in the early modern period*. New Haven: Yale University Press.

The Role of Group Psychology in Behavioural Finance: A Research Starting Point for Banking, Economic, and Financial Historians

Victor Ricciardi

1 Introduction

Banking, economic, and financial historians would benefit from gaining a stronger grasp on the psychology inherit within the financial markets and a better understanding of the decision-making process applied by all types of economic participants. However, most historians have never been made aware of the existence of the various biases that are present each day within the financial markets. Behavioural finance offers a new perspective on finance by examining the cognitive issues (rules of thumb or mental mistakes) known as heuristics and emotional biases. In various laboratory experiments and questionnaire-based studies within the social sciences and business fields, findings have demonstrated that all types of individuals—including both novices and experts—tend to be influenced by these different types of biases. Historians would enhance their

V. Ricciardi (✉)
Business Management Department, Goucher College, Baltimore, MD, USA
e-mail: victor.ricciardi@goucher.edu

K. Schönhärl (ed.), *Decision Taking, Confidence and Risk Management in Banks from Early Modernity to the 20th Century*,
DOI 10.1007/978-3-319-42076-9_12

research by exploring the role of group behaviour associated with themes of behavioural finance. This involves addressing issues of overconfidence, herd behaviour, the psychological aspects of speculative behaviour, and investor group behaviour in organisational settings (e.g. group polarisation and groupthink) as potential causes of various events and time periods within banking, economic, and financial history. These considerations can open up new perspectives on historical sources and stimulate new narratives. Of course it is still open to question whether these biases can be applied to actors in the past.

2 What Is Behavioural Finance?

Behavioural finance is an interdisciplinary field based on theories, biases, and research methods from the diverse decision-making sciences of psychology, economics, and neuroscience (Ricciardi 2006). Behavioural finance focuses on the role of mental factors and emotional influences on individuals, groups, organisations, and markets. These biases are not only accidental types of behaviour; on the contrary such outcomes are rather systematic missteps that individuals have a propensity to repeat time after time (Baker and Ricciardi 2014a). The following provides an overview of some important themes of financial behaviour, including:

- Investors' unwillingness to admit bad judgement or mistakes;
- Individuals exhibiting severe levels of loss, worry, and regret;
- Individuals using cognitive tools or mental shortcuts known as heuristics, during the decision-making process;
- Investors revealing excessive levels of pride, greed, and overconfidence;
- Investors experiencing a loss as being twice as painful as an equivalent gain;
- People being afraid of making a mistake and then appearing irrational to others;
- Investors failing to measure their investment time horizons accurately; and
- Individuals having a desire to be a part of the crowd, which is based on the need for social belonging and the myth that groups always make better decisions.

The decision-making process involves developing, assessing, and selecting between a series of choices or alternatives, a judgement that involves a degree of risk and uncertainty (Ricciardi and Rice 2014). In a rational environment, individuals decide upon the optimal choice, however, if quantitative complexity is too intense then cognitive assessment occurs in many instances. This type of decision-making may result in effective outcomes, however throughout human history habitual errors have been made. Behavioural finance is based on the assumption that investors are often irrational or only quasi-rational (known as bounded rationality), and that people are frequently inconsistent in their financial decisions, straying from the strict rationality of the notion of economic man (Baker and Ricciardi 2015). Researchers from the fields of psychology, sociology, and neuro-economics have conducted studies that have shown that humans are constantly illogical in terms of their money, personal finances, financial planning, and investments (Baker and Ricciardi 2014b).

The next two sections discuss the prevalent concepts in behavioural finance that influence the actions of individuals and groups, especially during panics and crashes, but also in terms of everyday speculation within the stock market.

- In the first part (3.), some biases concerning the individual actor are introduced, like overconfidence, representativeness, grandiosity, anchoring, worrying, and herd behaviour.
- In the second part (4.), decision-making processes within groups are explained.

3 A History of Speculation: The Behavioural Aspects of Bubbles, Panics, and Crashes

Speculation, panics and crashes of the past are very suitable fields for the study of the investment behaviour of historical actors. Examples in financial history are the Tulip Mania in the 1600s, the South Sea Bubble in the 1700s, the internet bubble of the late 1990s, and the financial crisis of 2008. The list can be expanded. According to Schwartz (1995) two major examples of historical bubbles are the stock market crashes of 1929 and 1987. The Dow Jones Industrial Average (DJIA) declined nearly 12% on 29 October 1929 and almost 23% on 19 October 1987 (Schwartz 1995). These two stock market crashes demonstrate the inefficiency of stock prices and the irrational behaviour of investors. When speculative bubbles occur the situation is always similar: they develop when a stock market has extreme valuations above historical averages, e.g. the overvalued real estate market during the early 2000s, a real estate bubble that burst during the financial crisis of 2008. In this most recent stock market crash the DJIA peaked above 14,000 points in October 2007 and decreased to a low of approximately 6600; the equivalent of over a 50% decline during this time period.[1]

Many historical examples of a speculative frenzy involved declarations either of a 'new technology', like the 'internet economy' of the late 1990s, or of a 'new investment philosophy' in which new models were used to value internet stocks with no profits. In the bubble phase, the traditional investment tools or ideas of the past such as value investing, earnings performance or dividend stock valuation models no longer mattered. Why did actors seem to jettison all rationality in their decision-making? In order to understand these historical events historians should consider certain aspects of the psychology of speculation such as overconfidence, representativeness, grandiosity, the anchoring bias, the notion of worrying, and herd behaviour.

3.1 Overconfidence

Investors demonstrate a predisposition to overestimate their skills, capabilities, and forecasts for success. Many investors think they are above average in intellect, overall judgement, and financial expertise (Ricciardi 2008).

Overconfidence is a bias that pertains to how well people understand their own abilities and the limits of their knowledge. People who are overconfident about their abilities think they are better than they actually are. People who are overconfident about their level of knowledge think they know more than they actually know. (Shefrin 2005, 6).

Pressman (1998, 415) further elaborates on the significance of overconfidence:

The human disposition toward overconfidence gets rewarded and reinforced by the typical format of a financial fraud. Normally, large gains are paid to initial investors to generate overconfidence. There is a great deal of psychological evidence that people frequently make misjudgments when looking at events that term purely by chance. Instead of attributing these events to chance, people develop some rationalization for these events. One rationalization is a belief that they are better than others or luckier. Thus is born the belief in the 'hot hand' ... even though good statistical analysis and arguments point to the conclusion that the hot hand is not a real phenomenon.

An extensive amount of academic literature has documented that this overconfident behaviour has an important influence on investment decisions. Individuals exhibit overly positive beliefs in their capabilities to control investment returns or predict the performance of stock markets. For example, Chuang and Susmel (2011) examined the trading performance of individual and institutional investors in Taiwan and reported that both groups reveal overconfident behaviour, although individual investors demonstrated a higher level of overconfident trading behaviour than the institutional investors. In another study Pan and Statman (2012) conducted an online survey of more than 2500 individuals, and reported that investors with higher levels of risk tolerance are more likely to exhibit overconfident behaviour, have higher levels of trust, and are prone to maximisation (e.g. the requirement for above-average investment returns).

A historical example of overconfident behaviour is the internet bubble of the late 1990s. Based on overconfidence, high levels of enthusiasm, and the role of crowd psychology, investors were naive about the price valuation of the initial public offerings (IPOs) of internet and dot.com technology stocks. The major reasons for this historical event were that individuals had access to online trading accounts for the first time, traders had excessive margin loans outstanding, and many novice investors were drawn into the 'fad of investing' in the stock market. The stock market bubble resulted in a bear market in the years 2000 to 2002. In October 2002, the value of the NASDAQ stock market stood at below 1150, down from the high of above 5100 that it had reached during the bubble only two and half years earlier. This represented a more than 75% decline in stock prices during this time period.

Economic historians should contemplate the overconfidence bias in analysing investors' behaviour. There is evidence that actors within financial markets in the past were influenced by this bias as much as actors today. Considering the phenomenon from this perspective can therefore guide historians in studying their historical sources and developing new reasons or uncovering the causes for historical events.

3.2 Representativeness, Grandiosity, Anchoring and Worrying

Investors also often suffer from the 'representativeness bias' during the early stages of a bubble. The representativeness bias is based on the idea that investors are inclined to hold a skewed belief about a financial event and then overestimate how much this circumstance is similar to others in the past. Basing their belief system on the representativeness bias rationalises the behaviour of investors who purchase stocks at the time of the bubble when prices are increasing, because these individuals become even more bullish about the future of stock prices. This representativeness bias escalates the herd behaviour to even higher levels of crowd psychology.

Investors exhibit high levels of 'greed' when the bubble is expanding and desire to be a member of the group. Investors also experience the affective state of 'grandiosity' (Lifton and Geist 1999). Lifton and Geist describe grandiosity: 'when prices continue to escalate, investors feel like Icarus—they feel increasingly excited and capable of flying higher and higher' (1999, 24). This euphoric mindset of grandiosity gives individuals a feeling of invincibility combined with excessive excitement about financial wealth; investors make unreasonable forecasts and predictions of stock market returns and completely disregard risk and uncertainty (Ricciardi 2008). Investors lose all notions of realism and instead substitute a 'euphoria condition' so that they experience unrealistic optimism about investment gains in the foreseeable investment time horizon.

A speculative bubble continues to inflate until it can no longer maintain the unrealistic increase in stock prices at which point the bubble bursts. For instance, the stock market bubble of the late 1990s is now a classic example:

From 1982 to 1999, the U.S. experienced an impressive bull market. Especially towards the latter half of that time period, much of the growth in market equity was due to the proliferation and rapid growth of technology and internet firms. As the Dow Jones Industrial Average increased tenfold over 17 years, the NASDAQ composite index, teeming with tech stocks, increased thirty-fold... (Adams and Finn 2006, 48)

The aftermath of the stock market bubble in 2000 was that the NASDAQ bottomed out in October 2002, losing the equivalent of more than 75% of its market value from its historical high of 5100 to below 1200. A clear indicator of the exorbitant valuations of many NASDAQ stocks were the price-earnings ratios (P/E ratios) and the market-to-book ratios (M/B ratios), which were well above historical norms. These types of financial ratios should have acted as warning signs to investors that the stock market bubble was to burst within a matter of months. Other potential risk indicators were that many of these firms had unworkable business models, very little revenue, and a very high probability of failure. Interestingly, individuals experienced herd behaviour after the bubble burst and stock market prices severely declined. This herd of investors then all tried to sell their stock positions and found no buyers in the market (see Section 3.3 for a more extensive discussion of herd behaviour).

Malmendier and Nagel (2011) investigated the influence of macroeconomic shocks on individual investor and risk-taking behaviour, using data from the Survey of Consumer Finances (SCF) for the time period of 1960 to 2007. Individuals who realised low investment returns in the stock market over their lifetimes revealed a lower motivation or tendency for taking financial risks, were less likely to invest in the stock market, allocated a lower percentage of their liquid securities to stocks if they participated in the market, and were less enthusiastic about future stock returns. For safer securities such as bonds, individuals who previously had lower returns in bonds were less likely to hold bonds within their portfolio. Investor experience that is attributable to more recent investment performance has a stronger influence on individual judgements and decisions (also known as 'recency bias'). 'Risk estimates become anchored on recent events. Overemphasis on recent events can also produce disaster myopia during a market crisis as instruments are priced as if another crisis will occur' (Rizzi 2014, 440). For example, Bricker et al. (2011) investigated the influence of the financial crisis in 2008 on families, using survey data from the SCF before and after the financial crisis. Interviews held from mid-2009 to early 2010 revealed a change towards much more cautious financial behaviour among families after the economic shock. Families demonstrated a reduction in tolerance for taking investment risk, and a higher degree of precautionary savings (i.e. a greater demand for safer cash securities combined with a preference for reducing total spending behaviour in the household).

The two major behavioural finance biases that investors experience after a bubble burst are the 'anchoring bias' and high levels of negative emotions such as worry or depression.[2] 'Anchoring' is the predisposition to hold on to a viewpoint and then apply it as a subjective reference point for making decisions in the future. Investors often base their assessments on the first piece of information which they are shown and have difficulty adjusting or revising their beliefs to new information. Many people still apply a 'negative anchor' to the financial crisis of 2008. As Ricciardi (2012) states, this results in higher levels of worry, which causes individuals to under-weight stocks within their portfolios as investors are overly risk-averse since the bubble burst. Also, investors still experience high levels of depression, regret, fear or worry years after the financial crisis of 2008. Worry, for instance, educes memories and visions of future crashes that alter an individual's judgement about investing in the stock market in the future. Based on a survey of more than 1700 individual investors in 2011, Ricciardi reports that a much larger percentage of individuals associate the term 'worry' with common stocks (70% of the sample) compared to bonds (10% of the sample). People with higher levels of anxiety or worry about stocks increase their perceived risk and lower the degree of risk tolerance among individual investors. This higher level of worry and the anchoring bias related to the financial crisis of 2008 increase the likelihood that some investors will not purchase stocks or stock mutual funds for many years after the crisis. Economic historians should apply this research finding to investigate whether similar effects can be shown for financial crises of the past as well.

3.3 Herd Behaviour

Another significant topic regarding investor psychology is herding or herd behaviour. Individual investor biases such as overconfidence, excessive risk-taking behaviour, representativeness, anchoring, and worry have an inclination to increase the herding effect of groups. Within the investor domain, herd behaviour explains how irrational investors act cooperatively in very large groups on an aggregate level such as a financial marketplace or setting. The size of the herd may eventually grow to include thousands of individuals trading the same stock or stocks for an extended period of time. Often this herd behaviour is driven by external forces such as media coverage of a new investment trend or idea. This type of herd behaviour is contrary to the notion of rationality and the efficient market hypothesis (EMH) espoused by the standard (traditional) finance school. The EMH is based on the premise that financial markets are efficient in the sense that individuals within these markets process information instantaneously and that stock prices completely reflect all existing information.

Herding occurs when a group of individuals, including both novice investors and investment professionals, all make the same financial judgements on a specific piece of information, while at the same time the entire group overlooks other relevant information such as economic news or revised company data. For example, experts compare their selection of financial choices and investment performance to each other as a benchmarking exercise in which under-performers (loser stocks) may chase the superior returns of the over-performers (winner stocks). The individuals exhibiting herd behaviour within the group also overemphasise or over-weight the positive aspects of price performance and then draw inaccurate conclusions about markets continuing to have upside price increases for years to come.

Matt Siegel describes the motivation for joining the herd: 'it's better to fit in with the crowd—even if the crowd is wrong—than to risk being off on their own' (1998, 230). Norton explains investor behaviour from a similar perspective: 'the herd minimizes risks and prevents loneliness … the result of herd behavior on stock prices is that they get bid higher or lower without regard to valuation' (1996, 43). Rizzi (2014, 444) explains herd behaviour in more detail:

Herding occurs when a group of individuals mimics the decisions of others. Through herding, individuals avoid falling behind and looking bad if they pursue an alternative action. Herding is based on the social pressure to conform and reflects safety by hiding in the crowd. In doing so, someone can blame any failing on the collective action and maintain his reputation.

Santacruz (2009) explores the role of risk tolerance of individual investors and the financial mood during times of different stock market cycles. The study reveals that economic mood does not influence the risk tolerance of individual investors. Thus, the author suggests that modifications to an individual's risk tolerance profile are not vital in accounting for overall changes in market investor sentiment or the business cycle. However, Santacruz notes that a positive link might exist between an individual's risk tolerance and overall economic mood because of herd behaviour. This herd behaviour may cause individual investors to purchase risky financial assets such as common stocks in bullish market cycles and sell these assets during bearish market downturns, resulting in lower investment performance.

Herd behaviour can frequently occur over different time periods such as weeks, months or years. An example of herd behaviour during a bubble is when individuals purchase stocks on price momentum while ignoring all other factors, especially financial information, basic historical valuations, and economic conditions. When the bubble bursts, panic occurs and people demonstrate 'herding' by selling all the stocks in their portfolio due to high levels of worry, fear, and panic. An example of speculation and crowd psychology is apparent in the historical event 'Tulip Mania'. Charles MacKay in *Extraordinary Popular Delusions And The Madness Of Crowds* explains,

tulips, in the fourth decade of the seventeenth century in Holland, became the object of such insane and unreasoning desire that a single bulb—about the size and shape of an onion—could fetch a small fortune on any of the several exchanges that had sprung up to trade them (1980, IX–X).

This herd behaviour happens on both the upside (over-buying of an asset in the form of manias and bubbles) and downside (over-selling of an asset resulting in panics and crashes) within financial markets when investor sentiment is driven by large groups of investors influenced by crowd psychology and thus moving in the same direction. Financial history has the propensity to repeat itself with episodes of herd behaviour such as bubbles, manias, panics and crashes. This is only a brief introduction to the notion of irrational herd behaviour and is limited to investor psychology within the financial markets.[3]

So individuals are often not rational in their decision-making processes. But the classically trained economist would counter that this is unimportant when considering stock markets as a whole because based on the efficient market theory these irrational elements neutralise one another in large groups. However, behavioural finance is able to demonstrate that decision-making processes within groups are sometimes irrational at the aggregate level (e.g. the stock market) based on the notion of herd behaviour. The central focus for the remainder of this paper will therefore emphasise a more detailed discussion of group behaviour pertaining to the topics of group polarisation and the groupthink premise. The next section provides a brief overview of the role of groups and the reasoning behind forming groups.

4 The Role of Groups

Groups have been around for thousands of years; however, it is only within the last hundred years that formal studies have been conducted on groups and group behaviour. A group is a collection of two or more people who are aware of each other and interact together. In theory, groups should be more successful than individuals because they use the collective skills, knowledge and attributes of a variety of people. By combining a diverse set of skills, successful groups should ensure higher accuracy and efficiency, and generate better outcomes than an individual. However, 'working in groups may not always improve performance.

Group members may affect one another in ways that worsens individual performance' (Warneryd 2001, 212).[4]

4.1 Why Formulate Decisions in Groups?

Everyday people make collective decisions through a group process rather than on an individual basis. The line of reasoning is that group decisions are thought to be more effective due to:

- Additional expertise, more brainstorming, better feedback;
- Enhanced opinions from group members and an improved capacity to avoid mistakes;
- The provision of a set of guidelines and principles for assessing different options that result in a final decision;
- An ability to avoid individual responsibility.

Research exploration in behavioural finance has been undertaken in the area of group behaviour and the social sciences, especially the field of social psychology. The topics of group polarisation (which is the augmentation of the 'risky shift' effect—see below) and the theory of groupthink have abundant research prospects for scholars in banking, economic, and financial history. In most cases, group polarisation and groupthink are both types of group behaviour that take place within a formalised organisational structure such as a corporation, non-profit organisation or a government agency. The members of these groups communicate with each other directly and have specific management responsibilities. A small group is in the range of five to ten members while larger groups might have nearly 40 members. The next sections will present an overview of each topic and an initial literature review.

4.2 An Overview of the Concept of Group Polarisation

James Stoner first established the concept of 'risky shift' in 1961 in his master's thesis, extending the concept in 1967 with his doctoral thesis

The Effect of General Values on Cautious and Risky Shifts in Group Decisions (today the current adaptation of the concept is known as group polarisation). Individuals in a group situation frequently make choices that are somewhat different from the decisions they would make on an individual basis. A group discussion might result in a riskier or more cautious shift depending on a person's specific viewpoint or opinion. For instance, many studies have shown that groups make riskier decisions than individuals. This concept is known as the 'risky shift phenomenon'. This risky shift has been associated with historical events such as the NASA decision to blast-off the space shuttle Challenger before its explosion in 1986 and the attack on Afghanistan by the Soviet Union. In 1972, Paul Slovic, in a seminal behavioural finance paper, identified the 'risky shift effect' as a form of important group behaviour within an investment management setting. The problem with this type of change in decision-making by group members is that it usually results in a questionable and sometimes illogical final judgement being made by the group. Behavioural finance researchers have found that groups sometimes choose an option that has a larger

payoff but a lower probability of attainment. If a group and its individual members were to place bets on a horse, for example, the group would more likely bet on 100-to-1 shot than would any of the individuals deciding alone (Fisher and Ellis 1990, 55).

James Stoner (1977, 337) further elaborates on the concept of the risky shift effect:

It is popularly assumed that groups are more conservative and cautious than individuals. Considerable evidence shows, that in some situations groups make riskier decisions than individuals. In those situations group solutions tend to represent 'risky shifts' from solutions that might be offered by individual group members. For example, in dealing with a hypothetical case in which an individual must decide whether to stay in a secure job or leave for one that is less secure but offers a higher salary, groups have been more likely than individuals to recommend the riskier option.

The first studies incorporating the risky shift phenomenon (Stoner 1961; Wallach et al. 1962), as well other studies on risk-taking behaviour (Kogan and Wallach 1964), were based on a standard 12-question survey known as the Choice Dilemma Questionnaire (CDQ). This questionnaire was designed to test subjects by having them review narrative case scenarios in which an imaginary person had to select between a predetermined number of choices. In each hypothetical situation, the option that offered the more attractive rewards was additionally the course of action least likely to be carried out successfully.

The participants completed the Choice Dilemmas Questionnaire (CDQ) at the beginning of the experiment, after discussing the stories with a group of four to six subjects, and again alone. In some cases, individuals repeated the questionnaire several days or weeks after the experiment. When responses to the questionnaire were compared, the testers concluded that the participants generally supported riskier choices in groups than as individuals. This group shift (choice shift) continued when they gave their confidential answers following the group dialogue. This change in risk-taking behaviour became known as the risky shift phenomenon (Wallach et al. 1962).

During the 1960s and 1970s, over 200 research studies and articles in the area of risky shift or group polarisation were published in social science journals such as the *Journal of Experimental Social Psychology, Journal of Abnormal and Social Psychology, Organizational Behavior and Human Performance, Journal of Personality, and Social Psychology, Psychological Reports,* and *Psychological Bulletin.* In a paper entitled 'The Relevance of Kahneman and Tversky's Concept of Framing to Organizational Behavior', Max Bazerman (1984, 340) comments on this issue:

Although the risky shift, using the CDQ, has been remarkably stable across a wide variety of experimental settings and types of experimental subjects, the shift for the various items of the CDQ differ substantially both in direction and magnitude. Some items consistently produce risky shifts, some items produce no significant shift, and two items regularly generate cautious shifts (i.e. the groups are less risky than individuals) ... Added questions concerning the risky shift paradigm were provided by contradictory research in real situations (e.g. studies of investors, juries, consumers) and laboratory research that did not employ the CDQ. Sometimes a risky shift occurred, sometimes a cautious shift occurred, and sometimes no shift occurred.

During the early 1970s, the concept of 'risky shift' was transformed into its current variation known as 'group polarisation'. Myers and Lamm (1976) extended this phenomenon over a broader spectrum, establishing the term 'group polarisation'. They demonstrated that after group discussion the average group response would tend to be more extreme but in the same direction as the average pre-discussion answer of individual members. There are two underlining themes regarding group polarisation:

- The group decision-making process associated with this concept involves the enhancement or augmentation of the original beliefs of the group's members;
- The inclination for group conversation or debate to create 'shifts' in the direction of the more extreme attitudes or risky decisions among members of the group.

Researchers started to discover that even though group conversation (debate) frequently produces a shift or change in individual viewpoints, such a swing or move does not always transpire towards a tendency of greater risk. 'It has been shown that, if the initial opinions of the group tend toward conservatism, then the shift resulting from group discussion will be toward a more extreme conservative opinion' (Wrightman and Deaux 1981, 466). An underlying theme of the group polarisation premise is that groups can move in two different directions: they may shift towards either 'extremely risky choices or behaviour' (known as a risky shift) or 'very risk-averse behaviour' (known as a cautious shift). The cautious shift demonstrates that some group decisions result in a more conservative selection than individual decisions, contradicting the original findings of Stoner's risky shift concept.

In a study by Burton et al. (2006) on investor behaviour it was revealed that people who hold the most excessive price views will influence the market to a greater degree than people who hold the most conservative viewpoints. These findings also imply 'that participation in a market will accentuate risk preferences so that good news produces a cautious shift in prices (i.e. towards lower prices) whereas bad news produces a risky shift (i.e. towards higher prices)' (Burton et al. 2006, 107). Historians should, therefore, pay greater attention to the group behaviour of the actors of the past and consider how it may have heavily influenced the decisions of the different actors.

4.3 An Overview of Groupthink Behaviour

In 1972, Irving Janis first introduced and pioneered the notion of groupthink behaviour. Groupthink is typically associated with a specific historical event in which group members do not want to disturb group consensus or unity by revealing a 'different viewpoint or perspective'. The decision-making perspective of 'organised groups' is sometimes made difficult by the intense fear or extreme optimism of the overall group. This was first noted with President Kennedy's decision to take military action against Cuba in the incident known as the 'Bay of Pigs' invasion. Most of President Kennedy's foreign-policy team were against his decision but were hesitant to express a contrary assessment. Janis (1971, 44) provides this description of the groupthink effect:

The symptoms of groupthink arise when the members of decision-making groups become motivated to avoid being too harsh in their judgments of their leaders' or their colleagues' ideas. They adopt a soft line of criticism, even in their own thinking. At their meetings, all the members are amiable and seek complete concurrence on every important issue, with no bickering or conflict to spoil the cozy, 'we-feeling' atmosphere.

Janis's theory was originally applied to important political events of the past; however since its inception this topic area has been examined in other disciplines, including behavioural finance, psychology, and organisational behaviour.

4.4 The Causes and Symptoms of Groupthink

Researchers in banking, economic, and financial history should be aware of certain 'major themes' or 'warning signs' that are associated with the groupthink effect in order to identify and apply this concept to past historical events. The following are some of the most common signs and behaviours associated with groupthink:

- *Biased perceptions:* During a groupthink incident, group members react to individuals who contest their ideas with distrust, suspicion, and resentment.

- *Status quo behaviour:* Participants take it for granted that everything is functioning flawlessly and adhere to the status quo behaviour or (inertia) of the group decision-making process.
- *Faulty decision-making approaches:* Groups practising groupthink use defective strategies when the group makes final decisions. Groups might be presented with information overload, incorrect facts or imperfect information that contributes to their faulty decision-making outcomes. The usual pattern of behaviour is not that members of the group make a few small errors in judgement; instead, the group commits numerous mistakes throughout the entire decision-making process.
- *Conformity pressures:* Conformity is a normal and essential characteristic of the dynamics of a group. Asch (1952) found that divergences of viewpoints resulted in a tendency to search for accord (agreement) so that individuals can relieve emotional feelings of angst. According to Janis (1982), during a groupthink event the pressure and high level of anxiety to conform become overpowering, resulting in pressure for all members to agree to the overall group decision. Each individual member of the group experiences a personal unwillingness to deviate from the overall group consensus viewpoint or majority decision.
- *Excessive overconfidence and optimism*: The mutual acceptance of all group members, the presence of excessive levels of confidence, overly optimistic individuals, and a feeling of harmony lead the group to reject everything that might be taken as evidence or viewpoints that contradict the group decision. In particular, a leader with a strong and aggressive personality may influence the overall risk-taking behaviour of the entire group (Shefrin 2008). The result of this misguided convention is known as the risky shift phenomenon discussed above.

4.5 A Behavioural Finance Perspective on Groupthink

The role of group behaviour can be seen throughout financial history in the form of speculative behaviour. Stock market bubbles and crashes, herd behaviour, group polarisation and the groupthink effect all have certain common attributes because each involves an emotional response within a group and the characteristics of crowd psychology. For example, Nofsinger (2014) attributes the real estate bubble of 2001 to 2006 as a groupthink event: 'Real estate became thought of as a speculative and tradable asset for some people, instead of an investment' (Nofsinger 2014, 135). In the classic book *Psychology and the Stock Market,* David Dreman (1977, 100) connects groupthink and stock market behaviour:

> *[T]he mindless conformity and the excessive risk taking that Janis describes in smaller groups are precisely the major symptoms that Le Bon pinpoints in larger crowds. Curiously enough, these symptoms, and the relaxed, chummy atmosphere often found in cohesive group decision making were also found to a significant degree in [...] speculative bubbles.*

Interestingly, a historical event may involve a groupthink effect among a smaller group of individuals that then spreads over time to a much larger group of investors within the financial markets as they start to follow the herd, as alluded to by Dreman (1977). Historical groupthink events occur within formal business settings in all different types of organisations. Within behavioural corporate finance, Shefrin (2005) sees groupthink behaviour as a major cause of the historical accounting scandals and bankruptcies of Enron and WorldCom. Both portfolio management teams (Cici 2012) and mutual fund managers (Puetz and Ruenzi 2011) have been seen to descend into groupthink behaviour, whereby expert group members reached consensus without strictly reviewing investment recommendations or financial information. Wright and Schaal (1988, 42) describe the relationship between groups and individual decision makers within a formal organisational environment:

> *An investment committee will have a series of norms and attitudes that may be called 'current policy'. This includes views on economic conditions and the course of the markets. The more important the group is to the individual, the greater the likelihood each professional believes the policy is correct. He or she is not simply complying … but has internalized the committee policies so they are now the professional's own.*

Among such members of an investment committee, a person's own viewpoint might be influenced by the majority opinion. An individual could, therefore, be inclined to support the 'current policy' rather than to state their individual objection; this will result in the maintenance of the status quo decision of the group.

In the publication '*Who's Minding the Store?*' Robert Shiller, a behavioural finance expert, provides a perspective on groupthink theory to institutional investors. Shiller argues that a possible groupthink situation may occur in a formal setting because the decision-making process of big organisations is often flawed owing to the overly bureaucratic nature of these corporations (i.e. they possess a traditional management structure) that suppresses innovative processes. Shiller (1992, 74–75) provides this analysis about institutional investors:

[G]roup-decision difficulties [...] may be mitigated to some extent by the fact that their objective performance has always been observed on a regular basis [...] getting feedback on the success of their investment strategies. But, of course [...] the short-run immediate feedback on their quarterly investment performance may not awaken a bureaucracy to long-term strategic issues; there is room for 'groupthink' to arise.

Within many organisations there are 'groupthink events' and 'mistakes in judgement' by different categories of groups that historians should consider as potential past, present or future causes of banking, economic, and financial events.

5 Conclusion

Behavioural finance offers an opportunity for banking, economic, and financial historians to explore and consider additional issues as possible causes of severe economic events.[5] The decision-making process incorporates the cognitive errors and the emotional issues that investors exhibit as individuals or groups within the financial markets. This paper provides a discussion of some major behavioural finance themes that focus on how investors process information and behave within a group setting. The topics of group polarisation and groupthink have been widely studied within the social sciences. The behavioural finance research literature on herd behaviour is abundant. However, in the areas of group polarisation and groupthink, the behavioural finance academic literature is very limited and researchers have much more work to explore on these two issues. Of course, this is only a small selection of the potential objects of investigation for behavioural finance.

Can these results be applied to past historical events? It is not self-evident that the biases described, as investigated in psychology and the social sciences over the last few decades, can be applied to actors of former centuries. The author does not want to claim that there are anthropological constants which do not change over time. However, these themes within the social sciences have the potential to open up new perspectives on events of the past for historians in banking, economics, and finance.

Notes

1. The following sample of books provides an overview of the behavioural aspects of historical bubbles and crashes: Chincarini (2012), Cohen (1997), Cooper (2008), Dale (2004), Fox (2009), Kindleberger and Aliber (2005), Taleb (2007) and Vogel (2009).
2. For a wider discussion of behavioural biases see the following sources: Baker and Ricciardi (2014a, b, 2015), and Ricciardi (2008).
3. See Fairchild (2014) for a much deeper discussion that examines the academic literature of irrational and rational herding in finance.
4. Herd behaviour is a good example of this issue, as previously discussed.
5. See Korinna Schönhärl 'Behavioural finance as a methodological approach for historians? A field report concerning the construction of the Canal of Corinth in nineteenth-century Greece' in this volume.

References

Adams, B., & Finn, B. (2006). *The story of behavioral finance*. New York: iUniverse.

Asch, S. (1952). *Social psychology*. New York: Prentice-Hall.

Baker, H.K., & Ricciardi, V., (2014a, February–March). How biases affect investor behaviour. *European Financial Review*, pp. 7–10. http://ssrn.com/abstract=2457425 (Accessed 29 Jan 2016).

Baker, H. K., & Ricciardi, V. (Eds.). (2014b). *Investor behavior: The psychology of financial planning and investing*. Hoboken: Wiley.

Baker, H. K., & Ricciardi, V. (2015). Understanding behavioral aspects of financial planning and investing. *Journal of Financial Planning, 28* (3) http://ssrn.com/abstract=2596202 (Accessed 29 Jan 2016).

Bazerman, M. (1984). The relevance of Kahneman and Tversky's concept of framing to organizational behavior. *Journal of Management, 10*(3), 333–343.

Bricker, J., Bucks, B., Kennickell, A., Mach, T., & Moore, K., (2011). Surveying the aftermath of the storm: Changes in family finances from 2007 to 2009. *Working Paper, Federal Reserve Board*. https://www.federalreserve.gov/pubs/feds/2011/201117/201117pap.pdf (Accessed at 3 May 2016).

Burton, F. G., Coller, M., & Tuttle, B. (2006). Market responses to qualitative information from a group polarization perspective. *Accounting, Organizations & Society, 31* (2), 107–127.

Chincarini, C. B. (2012). *The crisis of crowding: Quant copycats, ugly models, and the new crash normal*. Hoboken: Wiley.

Chuang, W., & Susmel, R. (2011). Who is the more overconfident trader? Individual vs. institutional investors. *Journal of Banking and Finance, 35* (7), 1626–1644.

Cici, G. (2012). The prevalence of the disposition effect in mutual funds' trades. *Journal of Financial & Quantitative Analysis, 47* (4), 795–820.

Cohen, B. (1997). *The edge of chaos: Financial booms, bubbles, crashes and chaos*. Chichester: Wiley.

Cooper, G. (2008). *The origin of financial crises: Central banks, credit bubbles, and the efficient market fallacy*. New York: Vintage Books.

Dale, D. (2004). *The first crash: Lessons from the south sea bubble*. Princeton: Princeton University Press.

Dreman, D. (1977). *Psychology and the stock market: Investment strategy beyond random walk*. New York: AMACOM.

Fairchild, R. (2014). Emotions in the financial markets. In: H. K. Baker & V. Ricciardi (Eds.), *Investor behavior: The psychology of financial planning and investing* (pp. 347–364). Hoboken: Wiley.

Fisher, B. A., & Ellis, D. (1990, 3rd ed.). *Small group decision-making: Communication and the group process*. New York: McGraw Hill Publishing Company.

Fox, J. (2009). *The myth of the rational market: A history of risk, reward, and delusion on Wall Street*. New York: HarperBusiness.
Janis, I. (1971). Groupthink. *Psychology Today Magazine, 43–46*, 74–76.
Janis, I. (1972). *Victims of groupthink: A psychological study of foreign-policy decisions and fiascoes*. Boston: Houghton Mifflin Company.
Janis, I. (1982, 2nd ed.). *Groupthink*. Boston: Houghton Mifflin Company.
Kindleberger, C., & Aliber, R. P. (2005). *Manias, panics and crashes: A history of financial crisis*. New York: Wiley.
Kogan, N., & Wallach, M. (1964). *Risk taking: A study in cognition and personality*. New York: Holt, Rinehart and Winston.
Lifson, L. E., & Geist, R. A. (1999). *The psychology of investing*. New York: Wiley.
MacKay, C. (1980). *Extraordinary popular delusions and the madness of crowds*. New York: Crown Publishing Group.
Malmendier, U., & Nagel, S. (2011). Depression babies: Do macroeconomic experiences affect risk taking? *Quarterly Journal of Economics, 126*, 373–416.
Myers, D. G., & Lamm, H. (1976). The group polarization phenomenon. *Psychological Bulletin, 83* (4), 602–617.
Nofsinger, J. R. (2014). *The psychology of investing* (5th ed.). Boston: Pearson.
Norton, P. (1996, May 20). The outliers: Refusing to run with the herd can be dangerous, but can pay off. *Barron's*, 43–44.
Pan, C. H., & Statman, M. (2012). Questionnaires of risk tolerance, regret, overconfidence, and other investor propensities. *Journal of Investment Consulting, 13* (1), 54–63.
Pressman, S. (1998). On financial frauds and their causes: Investor overconfidence. *American Journal of Economics and Sociology, 57* (1), 405–421.
Puetz, A., & Ruenzi, S. (2011). Overconfidence among professional investors: Evidence from mutual fund managers. *Journal of Business Finance & Accounting, 38* (5/6), 684–712.
Ricciardi, V. (2006). A research starting point for the new scholar: A unique perspective of behavioral finance. *ICFAI Journal of Behavioral Finance, 3* (3), 6–23 http://ssrn.com/abstract=928251 (Accessed 29 Jan 2016).
Ricciardi, V. (2008). The psychology of risk: The behavioral finance perspective. In: F. J. Fabozzi (Ed.), *Handbook of finance: Volume 2: Investment management and financial management* (pp. 85–111) . Hoboken: Wiley.http://ssrn.com/abstract=1155822 (Accessed 29 Jan 2016).

Ricciardi, V., (2011). *The financial judgment and decision making process of women: The role of negative feelings.* Third Annual Meeting of the Academy of Behavioral Finance and Economics. http://ssrn.com/abstract=1936669 (Accessed 29 Jan 2016).

Ricciardi, V. (2012). Our 3-year market hangover. *MoneySense.* http://www.moneysense.ca/2012/05/09/our-3-year-market-hangover (Accessed 29 Jan 2016).

Ricciardi, V., & Rice, D. (2014). Risk perception and risk tolerance. In: H. K. Baker & V. Ricciardi (Eds.), *Investor behavior: The psychology of financial planning and investing* (pp. 327–345). Hoboken: Wiley.

Rizzi, J. V. (2014). Post-crisis investor behavior: Experience matters. In: H. K. Baker & V. Ricciardi (Eds.), *Investor behavior: The psychology of financial planning and investing* (pp. 439–455). Hoboken: Wiley.

Santacruz, L. (2009). Effect of general economic mood on investor risk tolerance implications for financial planning. *JASSA: Finsia Journal of Applied Finance, 1*, 35–42.

Schwartz, E. (1995). *ECON 101 ½*. New York: Avon Books.

Shefrin, H. (2005). *Behavioral corporate finance: Decisions that create value.* New York: McGraw-Hill/Irwin.

Shefrin, H. (2008). *Ending the management illusion.* New York: McGraw-Hill.

Shiller, R. (1992). *Who's minding the store? The report of the twentieth century fund task force on market speculation and corporate governance.* New York: Twentieth Century Fund Press.

Siegel, M. (1998). What analysts and cattle have in common. *Fortune, 138* (4), 230.

Slovic, P. (1972). Psychological study of human judgment: Implications for investment decision making. *The Journal of Finance, 27* (4), 779–799.

Stoner, J. A. F. (1961). *A comparison of individual and group decisions involving risk.* Unpublished master's thesis. Massachusetts Institute of Technology, School of Industrial Management, Cambridge, MA.

Stoner, J. A. F. (1967). *The effect of general values on cautious and risky shifts in group decisions.* Unpublished doctoral thesis. Massachusetts Institute of Technology, School of Industrial Management, Cambridge, MA.

Stoner, J. A. F. (1977, 2nd ed.). *Management.* Englewood Cliffs: Prentice-Hall.

Taleb, N. N. (2007). *The black swan: The impact of the highly improbable.* New York: Random House.

Vogel, H. L. (2009). *Financial market bubbles and crashes.* New York: Cambridge University Press.

Wallach, M. A., Kogan, N., & Bem, D. J. (1962). Group influence on individual risk taking. *Journal of Abnormal and Social Psychology, 65* (2), 75–86.
Warneryd, K.-E. (2001). *Stock market psychology: How people value and trade stocks*. Cheltenham: Edward Elgar Publishing.
Wright, J. P., & Schaal, D. (1988). Groupthink: The trap of consensus investing. *Journal of Financial Planning, 1* (1), 41–44.
Wrightman, L., & Deaux, K. (Eds.). (1981, 4th ed.). *Social psychology in the 80s*. Monterey: Brooks/Cole Publishing Company.

Behavioural Finance as a Methodological Approach for Historians? A Field Report Concerning the Construction of the Canal of Corinth in Nineteenth-Century Greece

Korinna Schönhärl

Abstract Historians investigating the risk perception of bankers and the decision-making processes in banks could consider the behavioural finance approach to investigate their sources. In this chapter, this is illustrated using a case study concerning the financing of the construction of a maritime canal at Corinth (1882–1893). It can be shown that the risk perception of the French bank *Comptoir d'Escompte* can be analysed following the model of Joseph A. Litterer. The bankers' investment decision was influenced by two biases described by behavioural finance as 'belief in experts' and 'overconfidence'. The analysis of the way these biases came about and worked allows banking, political and cultural history to be combined in a coherent narrative.

K. Schönhärl (✉)
Historical Institute, University Duisburg-Essen, Essen, Germany
e-mail: korinna.schoenhaerl@uni-due.de

K. Schönhärl (ed.), *Decision Taking, Confidence and Risk Management in Banks from Early Modernity to the 20th Century*,
DOI 10.1007/978-3-319-42076-9_13

1 Behavioural Finance and Historical Research

How do bankers make their decisions? Which factors influence their risk perception? These questions are of special relevance in case studies where the rational choice approach does not offer much guidance, for example in emerging markets with high risks but limited expectations of profit. Why did bankers nevertheless invest in such environments? The wish to maximise gains seems to be only one of several motives, and bankers mention others in their ego-documents. The behavioural finance perspective, as described by Victor Ricciardi in this volume, opens new perspectives on historical sources and helps to construct narratives for empirical research.

Especially helpful is the model of perception formation by Joseph A. Litterer (1973, 106–132). The model shows how perceptions of risk are produced and how they affect the behaviour of financial actors (Ricciardi 2008, 89f). Thus the model demonstrates how an overwhelming amount of information, much more than the decision maker can use at one time, can impact an individual in financial decision-making situations. The individual has to focus on certain pieces of information and neglect others to avoid information overload. 'Some facts enter our consciousness very quickly and easily, and others, because of their high thresholds, enter only with difficulty, if at all' (Litterer 1973, 106). Important information can be lost in this process for example, due to the pressure of time. In a second step, the selected information is interpreted by the decision maker, a very distinct process. The same stimulus may be interpreted completely differently by different actors, depending on their past experiences and their value systems. In the last step, the closure mechanism characterises the tendency of actors to form a 'complete picture' of the decision situation. In this step information that is not available may therefore be assumed to achieve a consistent and significant picture of the situation which makes sense and can be used as a basis for the decision-making (ibid.).

Both the selection of information and its interpretation can be influenced by certain biases, as Ricciardi describes in this volume. The two focused on in this case study are the 'belief in expert knowledge' (Ricciardi 2008, 103; LeBoeuf and Shafir 2012, 315) and 'overconfidence' (Ricciardi 2008, 98; Glaser and Weber 2010).

2 Investment in Nineteenth-Century Greece from the Behavioural Finance Perspective

The case study by which this methodological approach is put to the test forms one chapter of nineteenth-century Greek financial history: the construction of the Canal of Corinth (1882–1893).[1] Fifty years had passed since the foundation of the Greek Nation State (1830) when the French *Société internationale du Canal Maritime de Corinthe* (SICC) started the construction work. Two state bankruptcies (1825, 1843) occurred during this period in Greece (Dertilis 2009, 195–199, 212–216). International capital reined in its first enthusiasm for the newly installed kingdom in the 1830s, when the serious financial problems of the state became obvious and its industrialisation was delayed (Agriantoni 2010, 21–40). After the foundation of the National Bank of Greece in 1841 by the Swiss philhellene Jean-Gabriel Eynard (Historical Archives National Bank of Greece 1999), international investment stopped nearly completely for several decades. Some isolated cases like the silver and lead mines of Lavrion, financed by an Italian and a French entrepreneur in the 1860s, are rare exceptions (Dermatis 2003).[2]

After the Congress of Berlin in 1878, the situation changed completely. Greece not only won new territory (Thessaly and parts of Epirus) from the collapsing Ottoman Empire (Zelepos 2014, 71–75), she was also able to settle her older debt from the 1820s, which reopened the way to the international stock exchanges (Levandis 1944, 25ff.). In a period when international capital was looking for employment abroad, the Balkans as a whole became an attractive investment market. So within the next 15 years, Greece was able to issue seven international loans with an overall value of 640 million francs (Iliadakis 2011, 56). Investment in private projects also started again, for example, in railway lines (Papagiannakis

1982) and in the drainage of wetlands (Papadopoulos 1997). In this context, the plans for the canal at Corinth emerged again, plans that had been repeatedly considered by various rulers since antiquity (Werner 1993). The completion of the Suez Canal by Ferdinand de Lesseps at the head of the *Compagnie Universelle du canal maritime de Suez* in 1869 had fuelled the enthusiasm of international capital for big maritime canal projects. The French attempt to open the seaway between North and South America via the Panama Canal was undertaken at the same time (McCullough 1977).

Within this historical context, the behavioural finance approach helps to focus the research: what were the reasons for the Paris-based *Comptoir d'Escompte* (CE) to issue the shares of the SICC in 1882? How did the bankers try to obtain information about the project, and what information was available? What was the individual cultural background of the bankers? What did their value system look like? What was the cultural and political background to their risk perception? What images of Greece were common among contemporaries? How did the bankers interpret the pieces of information that they selected, and which ones did they omit? Can a 'closure' of perception formation as described in Litterer's model be observed? Of course, the sources do not answer all these questions, contrary to what modern psychological test series promise to do, but the questions enable the construction of a narrative through the great variety of handed-down sources.

3 Case Study: The Canal of Corinth (1882–1893)

Behavioural finance requires taking on the perspective of the bankers to research their decision-making process and risk management. The archives of CE preserve the first letter by István Türr to the bank concerning the Corinth Project.[3] Türr as concessionaire of the Greek Government for the canal project asks the bank to issue shares to the amount of 30 million francs, divided into 60,000 shares of 500 francs each for the foundation of an international canal building company. The idea was to cut off the Peloponnesus from the Greek mainland by a canal, saving ships from travelling the 340 km around the peninsula. Türr offered the CE a commission of one million francs. The only document attached to his letter is the expert report of the French engineer Guillaume-Vincent Dauzat, which calculates the proposed costs at 25 million francs.

3.1 Expert Knowledge

From a behavioural finance perspective, this expert report shows how the risk perception of the bankers worked. In his report, Dauzat expatiated at length on the mineral constitution of the soil, geological questions and technical difficulties and needs. For the bankers, most of these scientific details must have been incomprehensible, as they are for the nonprofessional reader today. The bankers therefore turned to a second-order observation and evaluated the reputation of the engineer Dauzat. This was excellent: Dauzat had been head of the works at Suez, and he also participated in the plans for the Canal of Panama (Société des anciens élèves des écoles nationales d'arts et métiers 1885). So the bankers relied on the expertise of Dauzat, although he had not even travelled to Corinth himself but worked on the basis of material provided by Türr's engineer Bela Gestner on behalf of Türr. The bankers did not take offence at this practice. They relied on the expert knowledge without further checking, a procedure that behavioural finance describes as a typical bias that can influence investors' risk perception. This practice had become very common in banking circles during the nineteenth century: expert surveys were used to make a decision or just to prove the bankers' elaborate risk management to their customers or the bank's shareholders. Even if the bankers themselves did not rate the significance of this expertise for their decision-making particularly highly, this tool became more and more common with the growing 'trust in numbers' (Porter 1995; Pohle Fraser 1995, 34).[4]

Türr realised the importance of this scientific expertise and did everything to locate his project within the geological scientific discourse of his time, presenting the Corinth Project not only to the *Académie des Sciences* in 1881 but also at several international congresses and conferences, for example the *Congrès géographique* in 1881, the *Exposition Internationale des*

Sciences géographiques in 1884 or the *Congrès international de Navigation intérieure* in 1886.[5] The acclamation of the scientific community was highly relevant to the project's acceptance by its financiers. Later on, the company also tried to popularise the technical details for a broader public in its advertising material, by including little diagrams showing how much of the excavation had already been completed (Fig. 4).

3.2 Available Information

The very limited material in the archives of CE suggests that there were oral negotiations prior to the above-mentioned letter. The speed with which the bankers managed to organise a syndicate for the issuance of the company's shares to share the risk on several strong shoulders[6] is also evidence of this. During these preceding discussions, the bankers surely checked up not only on the expert Dauzat but also on the applicant

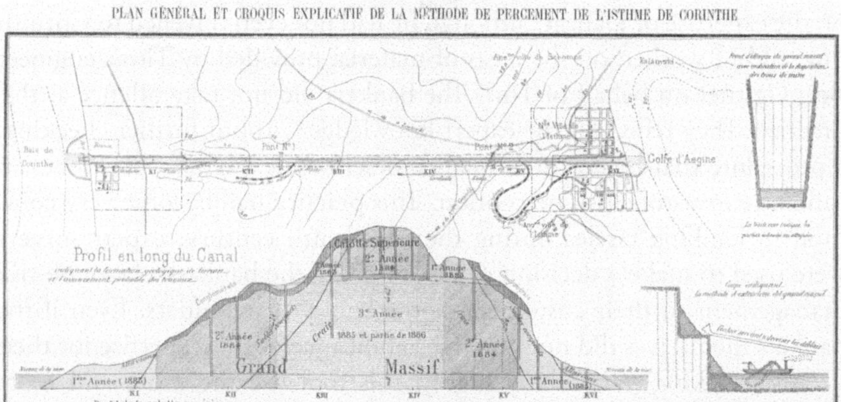

Fig. 4 Plan Général et croquis explicative de la méthode de percement de l'Isthme de Corinthe, Assemblée général du 28. Juin 1884 (BNP Paribas Archives & Histoire, DS 068)

Steven Türr himself and his reputation. Probably much of the following information was available to them.[7]

István (or Steven) Türr was born on 10 August 1825 in Baja in Hungary as the son of a hardware dealer. He interrupted his studies in 1842 to join the Austrian Army. In January 1849 Türr deserted to join the revolutionary Hungarian troops. There are rumours that he did so to avoid a disciplinary enquiry because of a breach of trust concerning money. After the end of the revolution, Türr travelled through Europe and encountered the Italian *Risorgimento* movement. He joined the *Risorgimento* troops fighting for the unification of Italy. When unification was achieved in 1861, he became a general in the official Italian army. He was also instructed to conduct diplomatic negotiations with the Balkan states with the aim of achieving a so-called *Confédération danubienne*. In this context, he came into contact with Greece, for example with Markos Renieri, later to be director of the Greek National Bank. In 1861 Türr married Adeline Wyse-Bonaparte, a grandchild of Lucien Bonaparte, the brother of Napoleon. The marriage ensured him a high reputation and good relationships with the French elite. He also published some articles to bolster his reputation as a convinced liberal and protagonist for the freedom of the people of Europe: 'I am liberal. All my life is dedicated to trying to ensure that liberalism and progress triumph'[8] (Türr 1878, 25).

In 1863 he was dishonourably dismissed from the Italian army. Again misappropriation of funds was mentioned as the reason. One year later he successfully applied for the concession to build the Canal of Corinth, together with Ferdinand de Lesseps, the promoter of the Canal of Suez. But the project was not started at that time as de Lesseps was completely occupied by the Suez Canal. Türr returned to Hungary in 1867 and entered the diplomatic service. He busied himself with certain infrastructure projects in Hungary, among them smaller canal projects. He also negotiated on the Suez building lot, but obviously in a subordinate position.

In 1876 Türr applied as chief of the *Société Civile Internationale du Canal Interocéanique de Darien* for the concession to build the Canal of Panama—and was once again successful. He was able to sell the concession to Ferdinand de Lesseps, who paid Türr's syndicate 10 million francs and transferred him his share part in the concession of Corinth

(McCullough 1977, 101). Türr was now the only concessionaire of Corinth, and he had plenty of capital. The concession was renewed in 1881 by the Greek government for 99 years.

3.3 The Background of the Bank and Its Decision Makers

To sum up, Türr seemed to be a reliable partner, providing the rumours about his careless handling of money in military positions are neglected. This is something the bankers might not have known—or they may simply have ignored this information in order to achieve a more harmonious picture of the decision situation. The fact that rumours about Türr's honesty were published in contemporary newspapers (Wurzbach 1883, 102) make the second alternative likely. Türr's experiences in the famous Suez Canal project may have counted for as much as his good relationships to elite circles in Paris and in Athens. His reputation as a liberal protagonist might also have been attractive for the bank, which could itself look back on a republican history. The history of the foundation of the bank is important from a methodological perspective because it explains the value background and the past experiences of the bank, meaningful factors influencing the interpretation of the available information. The CE was founded after the February Revolution of 1848 when the French banking system threatened to break down. The idea was to rebuild confidence within banking circles by granting business loans. The capital was provided in equal shares by the state, the communities and shareholders at the stock exchange, a model which was considered to be explicitly democratic. The CE was able to expand in the following decades, as well as in the French colonies. Its capital in 1870 amounted to 100 million francs (Stoskopf 2002). This democratic tradition remained a key element in the self-concept of the bank, and this certainly influenced its perception of the 'freedom fighter' Türr and his canal project.

The bank was interested in the Mediterranean, and especially in Greece as the vice-director, Antonios Dimitrios Vlasto was a native-born Greek. He published investment guidelines for Greece (Vlasto 1885), advertising the Greek financial market in the warmest colours. Even if the sources offer no proof in the matter, most probably a Greek investment project found an earnest advocate in his person.

3.4 The Political and Cultural Background of the Decision-Making Situation

This corresponded very well with the interests of the French government in infrastructure projects in Greece. France was anxious to ensure its market share in its trade with Greece, and thus extend its influence in this strategically important part of the Mediterranean, especially in competition with Great Britain.[9] The important role played by France in the proclamation of Greek independence fifty years earlier was stressed in this context. The French government thus accepted an invitation from the Greek government to send a *Mission Française de travaux publiques* to Greece to hunt out promising infrastructure projects and ensure jobs for French industry (Papagiannopoulos 1989, 49). The Greek market was considered very promising, and the trade in this area as having a high potential for growth. The *Société International de Canal des Corinth* expected an annual passage of 5.9 million tonnes of shipping. It planned to charge 1 Franc or 50 centimes per tonne, depending on the starting harbour of the transfer. So a dividend of 5% per share during construction works and of 11% afterwards, once the canal was operational, was predicted.[10] This was very inviting compared with the earning prospects of investment in France at this time.

The competitive situation between France and Great Britain was intensified in 1876. With the support of the Rothschild bank, the British Government was able to take over the majority of the shares in the Suez Canal Company, which had been finished in 1869 mostly due to French capital (Bonin 2010). This takeover was highly relevant for the establishment of formal British imperialism in Egypt thirteen years later. The consequent growth in the influence of Great Britain was a sensitive issue for France, particularly in view of her imperial interests. The idea of compensating for this defeat by the construction of another canal in the area was therefore popular in France. In this situation, the Canal of Corinth project was seen in close connection with both the Suez and the Panama projects. The SICC did everything to advertise the Corinth Canal as the 'little sister' of the two other, much bigger projects. Accordingly, the company mentioned its honorary president, *le grand Français* Ferdinand de Lesseps, in every possible manner in its advertising material. Even if Great Britain had been able to take over one of these important projects and to surpass France in terms of economic performance, the glory of having built the Suez Canal was reserved for France. Only French technical knowledge had been able to achieve such glories over non-human nature:

> *Marco Polo has mapped out our mission, Gentlemen: it is to practise good in our endeavours, to bring our knowledge to the aid of all peoples less intelligent and less knowledgeable, and to help them: to bring all peoples closer together, and, as our presidents Ferdinand de Lesseps and the Prince of Téano have said, thus to banish the last relicts of barbarism on earth. The scholars divide the world in two realms: the natural and the animal. Let's force them to admit, Gentlemen, that there is, separate from the latter, also a human realm.*[11]

This nationalistic dimension goes beyond the common nineteenth-century belief in progress. It has to be taken into consideration when analysing the bankers' decision to get involved. However, the competition between France and Great Britain concerning Greece was not limited to economic and political issues. It was also an issue of cultural history. Since the seventeenth century, the question of the true heir and successor to ancient Greek heritage had been discussed in both nations (Zabel 2016). In the nineteenth century, this discussion was extended because ancient Greek and classical texts from Homer to Thucydides and Plato became an indispensable part of the curricula of the elite schools. Classical Greece became a cultural model to be emulated. In Great Britain, shaken by heavy social unrest, the Homeric epics facilitated the attempt of the elite to reassure itself that its position was justified by performance. And in the Third French Republic, the history of the Attic Democracy was perfect to support the identification process (Turner 1989, 63f; Bowen 1989, 161; Jenkyns 1989).

The ancient dimension of the project, also a unique selling point compared with Panama and Suez, was therefore strongly emphasised by Türr and the SICC. It was easy for Türr to open all of his lectures on the project by referring to ancient history: the first *diolkos* over the isthmus already existed in early antiquity, and all the ancient governors of the region made plans to cut through the isthmus: Periander and Poliorcetes, Caesar and Caligula. Indeed Emperor Nero started to build the canal, even if he was far from completing it (Werner 1993, 12, 27f., 32f.). The SICC cited this ancient history in all the advertising material, and Türr did so in all his presentations and lectures. The *Bulletin* of the company often published pictures of the ruins of Corinth, and the company shares were designed accordingly (Figs. 5 and 6):

Some French newspapers took this impulse up enthusiastically:

Fig. 5 Acro-Corinthe et Ancienne Ville de Corinthe, in: Bulletin de la Société Internationale du Canal Maritime de Corinthe, No 2, 18.11.1882 (BNP Paribas Archives & Histoire, DS 069)

Fig. 6 Société Internationale du Canal Maritime de Corinthe, Obligation au Porteur à cinq cents francs, 8.3.1888 (BNP Paribas Archives & Histoire, DS 068). The design is identical with the shares of 1882.

> *Corinth! What classical reminiscences this name calls up. Corinth, physically and morally located between Sparta, the puritanical capital of the Peloponnesus, and Athens, the graceful city of Attica! Corinth is like the core of Greece, like the soul of this little country, situated on this slender strip of earth that links the two parts of ancient Hellas, the homeland of our civilization.*[12]

A satire from the year 1893, entitled *The Canal of Corinth* shows the close connection between the nationalist and the antique dimensions of the project (Durocher 1893). The satire deals, in contrast to its title, with the Panama Canal project and the scandal provoked by the breakdown of the constructing company in 1889 after huge sums had been embezzled and members of parliament bribed. The French government had to resign due to the scandal. All the actors of the satire can easily be identified as those involved in the Panama project, for example, de Lesseps and de Reinach, the financial expert of the Panama Company (but also of the SICC) (Mollier 1991). The sense of distance is produced through a transfer into antiquity: the paying public is located in ancient Athens (instead of contemporary Paris) and the building slot in Corinth (instead of Panama). This opens rich potential for alienation: The oracle of Delphi recommends the Company pay for a newspaper campaign, and some newspapers resistant to its donations are suspected to have been bribed by Sparta (Durocher 1893, 13, 17). All doubts concerning the technical feasibility of the project are parried: 'impossible, that's not Greek' (ibid., 26)[13]. Sophie Basch describes this attitude in her study on the perception of Greece in France as very common: to speak about Greece, but rather and at the same moment about France (Basch 1995, 245). Both levels seem to overlap here.

The satire mocks the attitude of the French elite in completely overvaluing itself, in terms of its technical knowledge and ability to remodel nature, and also in terms of its imperial power and glorious position as heir to ancient Greece. It is this contemporary value system of the bankers that influenced their interpretation of the available information on the Corinth Canal project. As described by Litterer, they did not struggle to get additional information, but on the contrary omitted pieces of available information which did not fit within their harmonious and positive image of the decision situation. Behavioural finance would describe this bias as an expression of bounded rationality and overconfidence, and would emphasise its elements of groupthink. Obviously, the decision of the bankers in the financial sphere can only be interpreted against the background of cultural history.

3.5 The Works at Corinth

At the time when Durocher published his satire, the Corinth Canal project had failed in its first instance, like that of Panama. The preliminary works had cost more time and money than the experts had estimated, not least due to the railway line for the transport of material and excavation, the accommodation for the workers, indeed the construction of two entire little cities at both ends of the projected canal.[14] Furthermore, during the works a deposit of marlstone was detected. The engineers were afraid that this would cause the canal to cave in when it was flushed out by the sea. So the canal had to be protected by additional walls, at high extra costs.[15] In 1888 the SICC had to issue obligations to gain the necessary money. This sent the shares of the SICC crashing. As its bank, the CE was asked to organise the issuance of the obligations to get additional capital, with a commission for the bank of 15 francs per obligation.[16] There was no alternative for the bankers that allowed them to save face towards their customers on the one hand, and to save the SICC as their debtor on the other hand. It could also be argued that the bankers did not see any alternative because they did not want to leave the existing structured problem space to avoid further responsibilities (Sarasvathy *et al.* 1998, 218).[17] However, the archive material shows that little remained of the reckless confidence so abundant at the start; this time several experts and an entire commission of professionals were asked to judge the necessity of the additional capital. The bankers tried to control the risks by continuing their second-order observation: notwithstanding their doubts about the necessity of the additional arrangements they attested that the specialists were all highly reputed and trustworthy, and so the bankers decided to believe their expertise and to save the SICC from liquidation.[18]

The bankers clearly saw that the issuance would be a delicate issue. Again several partners were engaged in sharing the risk.[19] Only one-third of the obligations was offered to the public at the stock exchange, while the rest remained in the hands of the CE. As early as spring 1889 the SICC found itself unable to pay out its dividends to the shareholders (Glasemann 2010, 10). In March the situation became even worse, because the CE itself collapsed due to severe financial problems (the SICC was only one of its minor problems) (Hautcoeur *et al.* 2014), as a result of which the value of SICC shares dropped. Türr tried to find additional capital by negotiating with several European governments, but he failed, even though four-fifths of the work was already complete.[20] Not even the Greek government was willing to help: the contract stated that in the case of its non-fulfilment the building site with all its material would become the property of the Greek state, so why should it intervene?[21]

In the end, the shareholders did not lose everything. A new company in Greece was founded thanks to the initiative of the Greek banker Andreas Syngros and the Eprio-Thessalian Bank. This *Société Hellénique Canal de Corinth* was able to obtain the necessary capital and to finish the canal in 1893 when it was ceremonially inaugurated. The shareholders of the old French company were supposed to receive three-quarters of the predicted earnings.[22] That it was not possible to achieve these earnings in the following years and decades due to deficiencies in the construction, changes in trade channels and other problems is beyond the subject of this chapter. It must, however, be stated that for the shareholders of the SICC the construction of the Canal of Corinth remained a loss-making business (Glasemann 2010, 16).

4 Conclusion

The aim of this chapter was to test the applicability of behavioural finance as a methodological tool for economic historians. Indeed the behavioural finance perspective helped to develop several questions which enabled sources to be analysed, even if it cannot be assumed that actors of the nineteenth century can be described in a similar way to modern subjects. Nevertheless, they seemed to tend to 'close' their perception of the decision situation like Litterer described in his model, omitting information that did not fit. Two main biases could be found which influenced the risk perception and decision-making of the bankers. First, is the belief in expert knowledge, which prevented the bankers from collecting additional information and expertise on the project. Instead, they simply trusted in *one* technical expert report because of the good reputation of the engineer responsible, a typical case of second-order observation. And, second, is overconfidence as the inclination of investors to 'overestimate their skills, capabilities, and forecasts for success' (Ricciardi in this volume). In the case of the Corinth Canal this overconfidence was caused not only by confidence in the technical feasibility of large-scale projects typical for the second half of the nineteenth century. It was also fuelled by the competition between France and Great Britain in the age of imperialism, not only in the fields of technical knowledge, political power in the

Mediterranean and economic success but also in the sphere of intellectual ambition concerning the succession to the glories of ancient Greece. It was not possible for the contemporaries to reason about Greece without considering its famous ancient history. All these factors influenced the bankers in their decision to finance the Corinth Project, from which they did not benefit in the end. The behavioural finance perspective thus offers a good and manageable tool for the historical researcher, one which allows banking, political and cultural history to be combined.

Archives

BNP: BNP Paribas, Archives & Histoire, Paris.
AN: Archives nationales de France, Sites de Paris et de Pierrefitte-sur-Seine
BAR: German Bundesarchiv, Berlin-Lichterfelde

Notes

1. The case study is part of the broader study 'Financer's desired spaces. European bankers and Greece in the 19th century', forthcoming. It includes an extended version of this chapter.
2. For an overview of foreign investment in Greece in the nineteenth century see Giannitsis 1977. Concerning the investments of French banks see Bonin 2013.
3. Kohn Reinach & Cie, Türr, an Compoir d'Escompte, 13.4.82, in: BNP DS 070.
4. See also Knake 'The "reputation approach" and the justificatory function of economic calculation. Some critical reflections on Monika Pohle Fraser's analysis of risk management techniques in the nineteenth century' in this volume.
5. Bulletin de la SICC, No 14, 30.6.1884, 1; Bulletin de la SICC, No 38, 12.8.1887, 1f.
6. Participants of the syndicate were, among others, the Greek National Bank, Crédit Industriel à Athènes, Oscar de Reinach, Hentsch Lutsches & Cie, Banque d'Escompte de Paris, Hottinguer, Kohn,

Reinach & Cie, Banque de Paris & des Pays Bay, Lullin & Cie, Hoskier, Banque Franco Egyptienne (see also Bonin 2013, 45, 47).

7. See for the following information Schwarz 1868; Wurzbach 1883; Werner 1993, 41f.; Fornaro 2004.
8. '*[J]e suis libéral; toute ma vie a été employée à tâcher de faire triompher la cause de libéralisme et du progrès.*' (Translation by author).
9. Note statistique sur le commerce de la Grèce, undated, probably at the beginning of the 1860s, in: AN F12 2670.
10. Bulletin de la SICC, No 1, 21.9.1882.
11. '*Marco Polo nous a ainsi tracé notre mission, Messieurs : c'est de pratiquer le bien dans nos explorations, de venir en aide, avec nos connaissances, à tous les peuples moins intelligents et moins instruits, et par la de nous faire aimer d'eux : de raprocher [sic!] en général entre eux tous les peuples, et, comme l'ont si bien dit nos présidents, Ferdinand de Lesseps et le Prince de Téano, faire ainsi disparaître les derniers vestiges de la barbarie de la terre. Les savants divisent le monde en deux règnes : le végétal et l'animal. Forçons-les à admettre, Messieurs, que, bien distinct de ce dernier, il y a aussi le règne humain.*' (Translation by author). Speech by Türr on occasion of the Congrès géographique in Venice in 1881, cited in: Bulletin de la SICC, No 27, 15.5.1886, 4.
12. '*Corinthe! Que de souvenirs classiques ce nom ne rappelle-t-il pas! Corinthe, c'est le lieu physique et moral entre Sparte, l'austère capitale du Péloponnèse, et Athènes, la gracieuse cité de l'Attique. Corinthe, c'est comme le noyau de la Grèce, comme l'âme de ce petit pays, placé sur cette bande étroite de terre qui lie les deux parties de l'ancienne Hellade, le berceau glorieux de notre civilisation.*' (Translation by author). A. de Lorquin, Le canal de Corinthe, in: France Industrielle, 12.7.1886, cited in: Bulletin de la SICC, No 29, 6.
13. '*Impossible, n'est pas grec.*' (Translation by author)
14. Bulletin de la SICC, No 14, 30.6.1884, 3.
15. Bulleto in de la SICC, No 28, 30.6.1886, 5.
16. SICC, Situation, BNP DS 068.
17. This study points out that entrepreneurs of today tend to maximise their profits at a given level of risk which seems to be acceptable to them, framing the investment decision with personal values, which involves a higher level of responsibility. Bankers, instead, 'use target

outcomes as reference points and operate by attempting to control risk within the existing structured problem spaces, avoiding situations where they risk higher levels of personal responsibility' (Sarasvathy et al. 1998, 218). It was interesting to investigate whether these results could be proved in historical research.
18. Situation, 1.1.1887, in: BNP DS 068.
19. List of subscribers, 8.3.1888, in: BNP DS 068.
20. Bulletin de la SICC, No 55 17.7.1889, 2.
21. German embassy at Athens to German Foreign Ministry, Berlin, 14.1.1889, in: BAR R 901-9531AA.
22. Liquidateur Philis to CEP, 23.6.1890, BNP DS 070, folder: Rapports, prospectus, extraits de journaux.

References

Agriantoni, C. [Αγριαντώνη, Χ.] (2010). *Οι απαρχές της εκβιομηχάνισης στην Ελλάδα τον 19ο αιώνα [The beginnings of industrialization in Greece in the 19th century]* (2nd ed.). Athens: Κατάρτι [Katarti].

Basch, S. (1995). *Le mirage grec. La Grèce moderne devant l'opinion française depuis la création de l'École d'Athènes jusqu'à la guerre civile grecque (1846–1946).* Paris: Hatier.

Bonin, H. (2010). *History of the Suez Canal Company 1858–1960. Between controversy and utility*. Genève: Droz.

Bonin, H. (2013). *French Banks and the Greek "Niche Market" mid-1880s–1950s.* Genève: Droz.

Bowen, J. (1989). Education, ideology and the ruling class: Hellenism and English Public Schools in the nineteenth century. In: G. W. Clarke (Ed.), *Rediscovering Hellenism. The Hellenic inheritance and the English imagination* (pp. 161–186). Cambridge: Cambridge University Press.

Dermatis, G. N. [Δερμάτης, Γ. Ν.] (2003). *Λαύρειο το μαύρο φως. Η μεταλλευτική και μεταλλουργική βιομηχανία στο Λαύρειο 1860–1917: Ελληνική και ευρωπαϊκή διάσταση [Laurion the black light. The metallic and metallurgical industry in Laurion 1860–1917. Greek and European dimension].* Athens: Τεχνολογικό Πολιτιστικό Πάρκο Λαυρίου (Ε.μ.Π.) [Technological and Cultural Park of Lavrion (E.M.P.)].

Dertilis, G. B. [Δερτιλής, Γ. Β.] (2009). *Ιστορία του ελληνικού κράτους 1830–1920 [History of the Greek State 1830–1920]* (5th ed.). Athens: Εκδόσεις της Εστίας [Estia Publishing House].
Durocher, L. (1893). *Le percement de l'isthme de Corinthe*. Paris: H. Simonis Empis.
Fornaro, P. (2004). *István Türr: una biografia politica*. Messina: Rubbettino.
Giannitsis, A. K. [Γιαννίτσης, Α. Κ.] (1977). Οι ξένες άμεσες επενδύσεις και η διαμόρφωση της νεοελληνικής οικονομίας (1830–1939) [The foreign direct investments and the formation of the Greek economy (1830–1939)]. *Επιθεώρηση Κοινωνικών Ερευνών [The Greek Review of Social Research], 80*, 234–253.
Glasemann, H.-G. (2010). *Die Finanzgeschichte des Kanals von Korinth. Historische Wertpapiere 1882–1977*. Norderstedt: Books on Demand GmbH.
Glaser, M., & Weber, M. (2010). Overconfidence. In: H. K. Baker & J. R. Nofsinger (Eds.), *Behavioral finance. Investors, corporations, and markets* (pp. 241–258). Hoboken: Wiley.
Hautcoeur, P.-C., Riva, A., & White, E. N. (2014). Floating a "Lifeboat": The Banque de France and the Crisis of 1889. *Journal of Monetary Economics, 65*, 104–119.
Historical Archives National Bank of Greece. (1999). *Jean-Gabriel Eynard. Visionary and architect of the establishment of the National Bank of Greece*. Athens: National Bank of Greece.
Iliadakis, T. [Ηλιαδάκης, Τ.] (2011). *Ο εξωτερικός δανεισμός στη γένεση και εξέλιξη του Νέου Ελληνικού Κράτους 1824–2009 [The foreign loans and their role in the formation and development of the modern Greek State 1834–2009]*. Athens: Εκδόσεις Ν. & Σ. μπατσιούλας [N. & S. Batsioulas].
Jenkyns, R. (1989). *The Victorians and ancient Greece*. Oxford: Blackwell.
LeBoeuf, R. A., & Shafir, E. (2012). Decision making. In K. J. Holyoak & R. G. Morrison (Eds.), *The Cambridge handbook of thinking and reasoning* (pp. 301–321). Cambridge: Cambridge University Press.
Levandis, J. A. (1944). *The Greek foreign debt and the great powers 1821–1898*. New York: Columbia University Press.
Litterer, J. A. (1973, 2nd ed.). *The analysis of organizations*. New York: Wiley.
McCullough, D. (1977). *The path between the seas: The creation of the Panama Canal, 1870–1914*. New York: Simon and Schuster.
Mollier, J.-Y. (1991). *Le scandale de Panama*. Paris: Fayard.

Papadopoulos, A. G. (1997). The socio-economic effects of the drainage of Lake Copais. In J. L. Bintliff (Ed.), *Recent developments in the history and archaeology of central Greece*. Proceedings of the 6th international Boeotian conference (British archaeological reports, Vol. 666, pp. 365–377). Archaeopress, Oxford.

Papagiannakis, L. [Παπαγιαννάκης, Λ.] (1982). *Οι Ελληνικοί Σιδηρόδρομοι (1882–1910). Γεωπολιτικές, οικονομικές και κοινωνικές διαστάσεις [Greek railroads (1882–1910). Geopolitical, economic and social perspectives]*. Athens: Μορφωτικό Ίδρυμα Εθνικής Τραπέζης [Educational Institution of the Greek National Bank].

Papagiannopoulos, E. [Παπαγιαννοπούλου, E.] (1989): Η διώρυγα της Κορίνθου: τεχνικός άθλος και οικονομικό τόλμημα [The Canal of Corinth: Technical Feat and Economic Adventure]. Athens: Πολιτιστικό Τεχνολογικό Ιδρυμα ETBA [Cultural Technological Institution ETBA].

Pohle Fraser, M. (1995). Risk, information and noise: Risk perception and risk management of French and German banks during the nineteenth century. *Financial History Review, 2* (1), 25–39.

Porter, T. M. (1995). *Trust in numbers. The pursuit of objectivity in science and public life*. Princeton: Princeton University Press.

Ricciardi, V. (2008). The psychology of risk: The behavioral finance perspective. In F. J. Fabozzi (Ed.), *Handbook of finance. Vol. 2: Investment management and financial management* (pp. 85–111). Hoboken: Wiley. Data available at http://ssrn.com/abstract=1155822. Accessed 6 May 2015.

Sarasvathy, D. K., Simon, H. A., & Lave, L. (1998). Perceiving and managing business risks: Differences between entrepreneurs and bankers. *Journal of Economic Behavior & Organization, 33* (2), 207–225.

Schwarz, H. J. (1868). *Stefan Türr. Zeitgemälde aus Oesterreichs jüngster Vergangenheit.* Wien: Albert Last.

Société des anciens élèves des écoles nationales d'arts et métiers. (1885, avril). Dauzats, Guillaume-Vincent. *Bulletin administratif, 1111* (245), XXI–XXVI.

Stoskopf, N. (2002). La fondation du Comptoir national d'escompte de Paris, banque révolutionnaire (1848). *Histoire, économie et société, 21* (3), 395–411. Data available at, http://web/revues/home/prescript/article/hes_0752-5702_2002_num_21_3_2310. Accessed 6 May 2015.

Turner, F. M. (1989). Why the Greeks and not the Romans in Victorian Britain? In: G. W. Clarke (Ed.), *Rediscovering Hellenism. The Hellenic inheritance and the English imagination* (pp. 61–81). Cambridge: Cambridge University Press.

Türr, I. (1878). Observations sur la guerre. Publié dans le Journal des débats à Paris le 7 octobre 1870. In: I. Türr (Ed.), *Solution pacifique de la question d'Orient* (pp. 25–30). Paris: Published by the author himself.

Vlasto, A. D. (1885). La Grèce en 1884. *Nouvelle Revue, 34*, 263–289.

Werner, W. (1993). *Der Kanal von Korinth und seine Vorläufer* (Das Logbuch: Sonderheft). Brilon-Gudenhagen: Arbeitskreis historischer Schiffbau e.V.

Wurzbach, C. (1883). Türr, Stephan. In: *Biographisches Lexikon des Kaiserthums Österreich* (Vol. 48, pp. 91–102). Wien: Kaiserlich-königliche Hof- und Staatsdruckerei.

Zabel, C. (2016). *Polis und Politesse. Der Diskurs über das antike Athen in England und Frankreich, 1630-1760*. Berlin: De Gruyter Oldenbourg.

Zelepos, I. (2014). *Kleine Geschichte Griechenlands. Von der Staatsgründung bis heute*. München: C.H. Beck.

Considerations of Social Capital and Future Research in Banking History

Morten Reitmayer

1 Innovation in Methodology and the Problem of Connectivity

One of the aims of the workshop from which this chapter is derived was to stimulate discussion about methodological innovation in the field of banking history with the idea that banking history might thus become more interesting for general history. The contribution here not only explains the concept of social capital but also identifies fields of research where social capital could function as a bridge between innovative banking history and the interests of general history.

The scene is set in this way to enable commentary on the basic assumption underlying the aim of this volume, after which some sociological elements of social capital and the possible relevance of social embeddedness for an up-to-date banking history will be explained. In the last part, a few

M. Reitmayer (✉)
Department for History, University Trier, Trier, Germany
e-mail: reitmayer@uni-trier.de

K. Schönhärl (ed.), *Decision Taking, Confidence and Risk Management in Banks from Early Modernity to the 20th Century*,
DOI 10.1007/978-3-319-42076-9_14

ideas about fields of research where banking history and contemporary history could meet will be outlined.

However, the first consideration is about the relationship between methodological innovation in banking history on the one hand, and the interests and demands of general history (if there is a 'general history' at all) on the other hand. One particular problem that is anticipated is the possibility that instead of building new bridges, methodological innovation in banking history could actually lead away from general history—thus achieving the opposite of what this workshop intended. This is seen as a risk because the kind of innovation under discussion implies a form of professionalisation, and in consequence a step towards a banking history that solely defines its own interests, fields of research, methods and theories. The whole debate on 'what is business history, what is it good for, and what are its methods and interests', which emerged in Germany around the year 2000 (Pierenkemper 1999a, 15–31; 1999b, 33–53; 2000, 158–166; Plumpe 2003, 143–156; Hesse et al. 2002; Berghoff 2004b, 131–148; Erker 1997, 321–365; 2002, 557–604; 2006, 605–658; Berghoff 2004a; Schröter 2000, 30–48; Pohl 1999, 150–163) produced exactly this side-effect. This was not very helpful for the academic standing of economic and business history in Germany, and the seizure of academic chairs is still ongoing. Interestingly enough, since a lot of economic history professorships in Germany are located within economics departments and not within philosophical faculties (where the history departments—'general history'—are found), the debate helped at least to save some of these chairs. At that time it seemed necessary to professionalise business history, to find its own methods, theories and research fields. These chairs were officially assigned to 'economic and social history' and, as everyone claimed to do social history, this academic luxury was increasingly questioned. There can be no doubt that professionalised business history lost ever more connection to the demands of general history and more and more academic resources.

Given this risk, it is hoped that slipping into a situation where one has to decide between professionalising banking history and finding overlapping interests with general history is avoided. So, what conclusions can be drawn from these considerations?

First, the idea that methodological innovation *per se* in banking history, or indeed in any historiographical sub-discipline, will attract the benign attention of general history is seriously doubted. In this respect, the years between about 1965 and 1985 represented an exceptional era in the history of historiography, characterised by the high tide of an economically informed social history with strong political implications, which was bound to modernisation theory (Raphael 2003; Kocka 2002). The unity of discussion at the time resulted from a common interest in the historical roots of democratic failure in Germany. This interest united not only more conservative and more lib-lab researchers, but also historians with expertise in political, social, economic, and even cultural history. However, this former unity is now fragmented. Nowadays, historians on all sides pay more attention to new fields of research than to new methods. This is not to say that there is no methodological innovation, nor that banking history or business history in general, should not operate in a state-of-the-art fashion, but innovations in methodology as such do not create bridges between sub-disciplines. During the process of its professionalisation, economic history fell into the arms of economics but after a short period of happy enthusiasm economic historians had to realise that economic departments would not hesitate to close economic history chairs and convert them into a fourteenth or fifteenth chair of marketing. Economists did not return the economic historians' love. On the other hand, the process of professionalisation only led to non-communication between general and business history, and to mutual indifference. And, what is more, some methodological refinements, especially those involving large amounts of quantitative data, sometimes met with disinterest and open rejection on the part of general history, particularly in the wake of its cultural and linguistic turns.

Second, those figurations and situations where and when economic and business history really met the demand and interest of general history can be observed. For example, one encounter happened when both history as an academic discipline and the wider public were interested in Nazi 'Aryanisation' of Jewish private enterprises, stolen gold, the whereabouts of Jewish accounts and assets during the Third Reich and World War II, and in the purge of Jewish managers from the boards of large enterprises (Feldman 1999, 2001; Henke 2006; Buchheim 2006,

351–390). None of the examinations, books and articles in question became famous for their methodological innovation. The interest was rooted in new demands for knowledge on the economic dimensions of Nazi rule throughout the whole of Europe, including neutral countries like Switzerland, on the personal and economic continuities of all those involved, and on the relationship between the economic and Nazi elite. Once the Cold War was over and the Soviet empire fell, the blockade on questions like this was broken and access to firms' archives was permitted because suspicion of Soviet influences on these investigations vanished. Under these circumstances and at this moment, the specific competencies of economic and business historians, especially experts in banking history (and only their unique competencies!) could meet the demand of general history and a wider public.

The only conclusion that can be drawn from this observation is that business historians should have a closer look at those more or less public debates where their expertise is needed. To this end, after a short consideration of the concept of social capital, some ideas about fields of research where business and especially banking historians can satisfy such interests will be discussed.

2 Social Capital: Concept and Meaning

Concepts of reputation and trust are not alien to business history (Reitmayer and Marx 2010). Already the early historiography of the 1950s, in exploring the success of banks and bankers of distinct minority origin—especially but not only Jews—was looking for social ties which established mutual trust and could explain economic outcomes in times of huge uncertainty (Schnee 1953-1967; Rachel and Wallich 1934-1938; Schwarz 1958, 300–310). However, although reputation may be a result of social capital, the relationship between both concepts is complex.

Social capital is a concept developed by the French sociologist Pierre Bourdieu (Bourdieu 1992, 49–79).[1] For Bourdieu, social capital stands in line with three other forms of capital: economic, cultural and symbolic capital. Capital here is just another word for 'social energy', but this social energy can be invested, accumulated, bequeathed and transferred.

Though economic capital underlies all other forms of capital, these other forms cannot be reduced to economic capital. Social capital is therefore embedded into a whole social economy, which is why the concept of social capital can be of great value for a renewed business history.

Social capital encompasses the totality of resources which are tied to a certain group. The total amount of capital possessed by the members of the group lends creditworthiness—in a wider sense—to all of them. The amount of one's social capital depends on two factors: the extent of social relations which can actually be mobilised, and the totality of one's economic, cultural and symbolic capital. This network of social relations is the product of continuous work; work that is necessary for the production and reproduction of enduring and useful connections, which result in material or symbolic profits. In other words, the network is the product of individual and collective strategies of investment, which are directed in a conscious *or unconscious* way to establish or preserve social relations that promise immediate benefits sooner or later. But the extent of one's social relations is not to be understood in a purely quantitative way as if the mere number of contacts determines one's social capital. Instead, the value of an agent's social relations depends on the amount of the economic, cultural and symbolic capital of the whole group he/she belongs to, and on the amount that can be mobilised. It thus follows that social capital exerts a multiplier effect on the total amount of one's capital.

Social capital takes effect only within a certain field of action. Therefore, Bourdieu's concept of social fields must be more closely examined. Regrettably, Bourdieu was unable to complete his 'general theory of fields'—he sometimes also refers to a 'general theory of the economy of fields' —before his death (Bourdieu 1997, 59–78; 1996, 124–147). One must, therefore, revert to compiling Bourdieu's explanations and the individual studies made in various different places (especially those in the fields of the French 'elite universities' and entrepreneurship) (Bourdieu 1981, 2004; Id., 1988). A social field, as conceived by Bourdieu, has a double character. On the one hand, it represents a structure, i.e. a system of permanent relations, within which each relevant agent and each group of agents finds his, her or its position. This position is defined by the possession of 'capital', i.e. of those means of power and influence that can be effective in each field. In a company, these are primarily rights of control, rule, participation and disposal, ownership of shares in the company capital, relevant information about products and production processes, dependence on or towards suppliers, customers and creditors, etc. On the other hand, such a field represents an arena of confrontations, a battlefield on which agents wrestle in accordance with their respective interests—conceived in the manner in which they themselves perceive and define their interests, and not according to external theories, which are often economically reductionist—for the field-specific profits that have been collaboratively earned. When transferred to corporate history, this means that an analysis of the company as a field (i.e. a place of production of material goods and acquisition of material profits) examines the confrontations between all of these groups, their means of power, their interests and motives, especially to the extent that they refer to decisions on the products to be manufactured, the organisation of their production and the structure of their working relationships, and thus the continuation of this field (i.e. the company) with the purpose of reconstructing the specific logic of the actions of its agents. At the end of such an analysis it should hopefully be clear, firstly, that this procedure allows systematic comparisons (mainly, but not only, between individual companies), and, secondly, that the value of universal theories of the company 'as such' is clearly relativised in favour of genuine historical findings.

Stressing the importance of social relations furthermore relates the concept of social capital to a different strand of sociological theory: the analysis of social networks (Jansen 2003). Like reputation, the concept of social networks is familiar to most business historians. What is lacking, however, is the connection between these concepts.[2] And it is very questionable whether it is reasonable or even possible to use only one of these concepts without taking into consideration the relationship between them. In short, the network of social relations can be seen as the structural element, while social capital is circulating within this structure in different manifestations: trust, reputation, information, obligations, access to institutions, and groups of immaterial goods. Vice versa, in order to analyse, for example, the flow of technical knowledge within one firm or between firms it is also necessary to explore the structure of that network.

Lastly, focus will be placed on three problems connected to the concept of social capital, all of which are neglected in current research in business history. First, social capital does not fall into the agent's lap. Although it is possible to acquire social capital by heritage or by delegation, it is necessary to invest time, money and labour to accumulate and maintain social capital. This work has to be undertaken continually to protect one's social capital from dissipating. How do businessmen and corporations work to preserve their social capital? A recent biographical study of the German steel magnate Paul Reusch demonstrated the immense expenditure of time and resources necessary to keep a widespread network operational (Marx 2013). Banking history has maybe underestimated this expenditure, following the (auto-) biographical sources which suggest the ease and effortlessness of the networking done by some extraordinary successful bankers (Reitmayer 1999; Augustine 1992, 161–185; Wallich 1978).

Second, what are the institutional resources of social capital, and where are the nodes located, that is, where do different ties join together? In other words, what are the places where the social capital of business and corporations is concentrated? German banking history has focused on (cross-) board memberships and found some extraordinarily important results (Wixforth and Ziegler 1994, 5–25; Id., 1997, 205–235). For obvious reasons, British banking history has undertaken much more research on different institutions from the social world of the City, for example—besides board memberships—London clubs and the honours system (Cassis 1984, 1987, 1994; Scott 1982, 1991). And what is the value of family and family ties, especially during the twentieth century when all business was rationalised, to the disadvantage of traditional patterns?[3]

Third, both network analysis and the concept of social capital stress the point that social ties depend on reciprocity. So what are and have been the return services rendered when managers and corporations deploy their social capital to do their jobs or promote their careers? Until recently in-house careers dominated in German corporations (Freye 2009; Hartmann 2007). The way in which these careers function and the impact of this type of entrepreneurial reproduction on managerial decisions still remain unexplored.[4]

3 Debates and How to Use Them

Maybe the most vibrant current debate in Germany where historians' expertise is badly needed is the controversy about the history, present and future of 'democratic capitalism', which has been aroused by Wolfgang Streeck in his book *Buying Time* (Streeck 2014a). A summary of the book will not be provided here (Priemel 2014, 30–36; Rischbieter 2014, 37–43; Plumpe 2014, 44–52; Tooze 2014, 53–60; Wingert 2014, 61–70; Tanner 2014, 71–79; Streeck 2014b, 299–316), but Streeck claims that nearly all Western societies have left the path of what he calls 'democratic' or 'consensus capitalism' behind. He argues that for about 40 years, ever since 'capital' began to desert from that consensus, the fertile tension between capitalism and democracy has been in crisis. Under the auspices of neo-liberalism, he suggests, the balance of power between both sides (as well as between capital and labour) has shifted more and more towards a barely regulated global capitalism. Apart from some comment in the 'debate' columns of a number of journals (remarkably enough, journals of general history), historians have, to date, left the whole debate to authors from the social sciences, mostly sociologists and political economists. This reluctance seems strange since one can see at least one critical point within Streeck's argument which is genuinely historical: the erosion of consensus capitalism and the rise of neo-liberalism since the 1970s.

Interestingly enough, this very process—from consensus capitalism, or to put it more broadly, the era of consensus, to neo-liberalism—is the focus of three or four loosely connected debates to which banking historians could easily contribute.

The first discussion concerns the end of 'Fordist' modes of regulating the economy in Western Europe and the USA. This debate finds its empirical basis in examinations of the global automobile industry and was very much driven by French researchers originating from the so-called (post-Marxist) regulation school (Boyer and Saillard 2002; Freyssenet et al. 1998; Freyssenet 2009; Boyer and Freyssenet 2002; Crouch and Streeck 1997; Hancké 1999). In Western Europe and the USA, the 1970s saw the end of the standardised mass production of durables by a readily available semi-qualified workforce with more or less consensual industrial relations, driven by increasing wages and supported by an expanding welfare state, the latter centred around the male worker. At the same time, old industries like mining, steel production, textiles and shipbuilding came under pressure from a new international division of labour. Although a great deal of research has since been conducted in this field, business history in Germany was slow to explore the years and decades after the post-war boom (Reitmayer and Rosenberger 2008; Rosenberger 2008). Most promising, therefore, are research projects that transcend the 'border' of the 1970s and analyse the history of corporations from the 1960s up to the 1990s.[5] One question is whether social capital in one or more of its different manifestations, for example, trust between employers and employees, helped firms to cope with the long economic crisis (Reitmayer forthcoming).

The second debate circles around the social consequences of neoliberalism as the most influential economic theory worldwide since the early 1970s. These consequences are seen both as an opening for new opportunities (not only for businessmen), and as a threat for established ties, for example, the guarantee of social security. As a whole, this debate focuses on the vulnerability and the 'resilience' of societies towards neoliberalism and is conducted by Canadian researchers, namely Peter Hall and Michèle Lamont (Hall and Lamont 2013). Interestingly enough, although the concept of 'resilience' is widely discussed among social scientists, business history has not yet really begun to use it. But there are some considerations on the embeddedness (Grabher 1993) and the social capital of firms in rapidly changing local and regional contexts, which deserve to be expanded because such research explores part of the invisible assets of corporations (Neumann 2008, forthcoming; Gerstung forthcoming; Bonaldo forthcoming).

The third debate to mention here was launched by the sociologist Paul Windolf and focuses on the end of German corporatism. Windolf considers the rise of what he calls 'financial market capitalism' in general, and the dissolution of the so-called 'Deutschland AG' in particular, referring to the tightly woven network of board memberships between large corporations and the specific role of banks and insurance companies at the centre of this network (Windolf 2005, 2006, 191–222; Krenn 2012). Windolf claims that this network, which was established during the late nineteenth century, dissolved during the late 1990s, and that since then investment funds have acquired a dominant role in controlling large corporations; a role formerly held by the three universal banks in Germany.[6] Of the above-mentioned discussions, the dissolution of the network of board memberships and cross-investments may be the best known among German historians (Wixforth and Ziegler 1997). This network of board memberships represented a form of highly institutionalised social capital. Taking care of it required a large amount of time and work. The dissolution of this network has therefore reduced the costs of what had been regarded as an integral part of the German corporate governance model. The open question is not why the large corporations suspended the network, but why they left it so late to do so. For how long was this network really useful and necessary? There is much literature on the ineffectiveness of the bank-industry relations within that network (Ahrens 2013, 195–220; Wellhöner 1989). Very obviously, social capital played a very ambivalent role in this structure of social (and capital) relations. At the time when the network structure was established during the last third of the nineteenth century, board memberships were a proper way for banks to control firms in debt. But the more firms grew, and the more complex their organisations became, the less possible it was to exert proper control. The early 1930s demonstrated the lack of information held about the condition of many large corporations even by their board members. The answer was not only to legally regulate the number of board memberships one person was allowed to take on but also to professionalise auditing. The externalisation and professionalisation of methods of obtaining sufficient information on the condition of corporations was about to make the dense network of board memberships needless, at least with regard to control. So perhaps the dissolution of the network just liquidated the practice of a form of social capital that had become obsolete?

The last line of discussion to be referred to here concerns the outlines of the 'After-the-Boom' research group at the universities of Tübingen and Trier. This group focuses on the interactions between changes in the political economy, new intellectual movements, educational expansion, the welfare state, modes of consumption and other topics of contemporary history, in order to identify the characteristics of the era between the end of the golden boom years following 1945 and the present. Some of the individual research projects have already been mentioned above.[7] The focus of the After-the-Boom research group is to identify the nature, the driving forces and the period of the structural breach that distinguished the boom-era from the decades since.

These four loosely interconnected debates form a context and could function as an arena waiting to be filled by economic and business historians who can introduce their expertise—if they succeed in identifying fields of research which are of sufficient interest beyond the borders of economic history, and providing they can produce answers to questions posed by a wider (academic) public. This should not be impossible, given the fierce public debate surrounding Streeck's warnings that the democratic control of capitalism is in danger or has even vanished. Here, that debate is interpreted as a hint that there is a wide demand for knowledge about the history and future of democracy, capitalism and society. Economic and business history can and should contribute to and profit from this demand.

4 Fields of Research

Lastly seven fields of research in which questions of social capital can be used as a tool to break down such problems, and at the same time help to meet the demand to individuate business history are distinguished. These fields of research are:

1. The dissolution of the Deutschland AG. Windolf claims more or less openly that the importance of social capital declines as the network erodes. Even if he is right, the question is what has replaced the now redundant social capital.
2. In Germany at least, large corporations with widely spread shareholdings are looking for investors (or for one single, friendly and patient investor) who can act as an 'anchor' *vis-à-vis* rapid floating shares and the threat of hostile takeovers. Windolf states the systemic importance of hostile takeovers. Does social capital function as the cement in the alliance between anchor investors and corporations?
3. For historical reasons, German corporations are not as oriented to the stock market as British or American corporations. In what way does

social capital structure the connection between non-stock market listed corporations (which include the vast majority of German corporations) and financial institutions like banks and saving banks?
4. What kind of social capital is needed for the successful financial support of very wealthy private customers—a very profitable and traditional business activity of banks (in the past, private banks)?
5. Lobby groups on national and European levels have successfully blocked the closer regulation of financial markets during the current crisis when political initiatives tried to include banks in financing the costs of rescuing system-relevant institutes and to prevent future financial crises. What kind of social capital do lobby groups use for their activities?
6. Especially in Germany, nearly every second top manager spends his whole career within one corporation (in-house careers). What is the relevance of social capital, and what is the nature of this social capital, in a successful manager career? Currently, the sociology of business elites has no answer to this question, but it has also not even looked for one.[8]
7. Lastly, the current political controversy on Greece's remaining within the Eurozone introduces the question of what kind of social capital Prime Minister Alexis Tsipras and his former Secretary of the Treasury Yanis Varoufakis lack when they talk to the European establishment of governments, central banks, economists and so on. Is social capital the link between the members of the European power elite—if this elite really exists?

Notes

1. The concept of Bourdieu is used by Dilley, A. 'Financial centres as fields: Reflections on habitus and risk in the nineteenth and twentieth centuries' in this volume.
2. As practised by Matringe, N. 'Social capital versus commercial profits: The impact of networks on decision making in early modern banks' in this volume.

3. As researched by Pak, S. J. 'The House of Morgan: Private family bank in transition' in this volume.
4. See Wylegala, D. 'Top careers as a means of risk management in organisations' in this volume.
5. For example, the research project of Dr. Christian Marx (Trier) on the West European Chemical Industry. See also: BH Special Issue 'Rhenish Capitalism' (forthcoming).
6. See Sattler, F. 'Cooperative governance in banking: Consequences for decision-taking processes' in this volume.
7. To be named are Christian Marx, Tobias Gerstung and Arndt Neumann.
8. A first attempt will be Daniel Wylegala's PhD, forthcoming. See as mentioned above Wylegala, D. 'Top careers as a means of risk management in organisations' in this volume.

References

Ahrens, R. (2013). Bankenmacht im Aufsichtsrat? Der Bankier Jürgen Ponto und die Kontrolle deutscher Großunternehmen in den 1970er Jahren. In: R. Ahrens, B. Gehlen, & A. Reckendrees (Eds.), *Die „Deutschland AG". Historische Annäherungen an den Bundesdeutschen Kapitalismus* (pp. 195–220). Essen: Klartext.

Augustine, D. L. (1992). The banker in German Society. In: Y. Cassis (Ed.), *Finance and financiers in European history* (pp. 161–185). Cambridge: Cambridge University Press.

Berghoff, H. (2004a). *Moderne Unternehmensgeschichte. Eine themen- und theorieorientierte Einführung.* Paderborn: UTB.

Berghoff, H. (2004b). Wozu Unternehmensgeschichte? Erkenntnisinteressen, Forschungsansätze und Perspektiven des Faches. *Zeitschrift für Unternehmensgeschichte, 49*, 131–148.

Bonaldo, M. (forthcoming). *Resiliente Region Stuttgart? Anpassung und Entwicklung in einer Industrieregion nach dem Boom.*

Bourdieu, P. (1981). Kapital und Bildungskapital. Reproduktionsstrategien im sozialen Wandel. In: H. Köhler (Ed.), *Titel und Stelle. Über die Reproduktion sozialer Macht* (pp. 23–87). München: Europäische Verlagsanstalt. [English Translation: Bourdieu, P., Passeron, J.-C. (1977). Cultural capital and

Pedagogic Communication. In: Id., *Reproduction in education, society and culture* (pp. 71–106). London: Sage].
Bourdieu, P. (1988). *Homo Academicus*. Frankfurt: Suhrkamp. [English Translation: Id. (1988). *Homo Academicus*, trans: Collin, P. Cambridge: Polity Press].
Bourdieu, P. (1992). Ökonomisches Kapital – Kulturelles Kapital – Soziales Kapital. In: Id., *Die verborgenen Mechanismen der Macht* (pp. 49–79). Hamburg: VSA-Verlag. [English Translation: Id. (1986). Three forms of capital. In: J. G. Richardson (Ed.), *Handbook of theory and research for sociology of education* (pp. 241–258). New York: Greenwood Press].
Bourdieu, P. (1996). *Reflexive Anthropologie*. Frankfurt: Suhrkamp. [English Translation: Id., Wacquant, L. J. D. (1992). *Invitation to reflexive sociology*. Cambridge: Polity Press].
Bourdieu, P. (1997). Zur Genese der Begriffe Habitus und Feld. In: Id., M. Steinrücke (Ed.), *Der Tote packt den Lebenden* (pp. 59–78). Hamburg: VSA-Verlag. [English Translation: Bourdieu, P. (1985). The genesis of the concepts of habitus and field. *Sociocriticism, 2* (2), 11–24].
Bourdieu, P. (2004). *Der Staatsadel*. Konstanz: UVK-Verlag. [English Translation: Id. (1996). *State nobility. Elite schools in the field of power*. Cambridge: Polity Press].
Boyer, R., & Freyssenet, M. (2002). *The productive models. The conditions of profitability*. Basingstoke: Palgrave.
Boyer, R., & Saillard, Y. (2002). *Régulation theory. The state of the art*. London: Routledge.
Buchheim, C. (2006). Unternehmen in Deutschland und NS-Regime 1933–1945. Versuch einer Synthese. *Historische Zeitschrift, 282*, 351–390.
Cassis, Y. (1984). *Les banquiers de la City à l'époque Edouardienne (1890–1914)*. Gèneve: Librairie Droz.
Cassis, Y. (1987). *La City de Londres 1870–1914*. Paris: Belin.
Cassis, Y. (1994). *City Bankers, 1890–1914*. Cambridge: Cambridge University Press.
Crouch, C., & Streeck, W. (1997). *The political economy of modern capitalism. Mapping convergence and diversity*. London: Sage.
Erker, P. (1997). Aufbruch zu neuen Paradigmen. Unternehmensgeschichte zwischen sozialgeschichtlicher und betriebswirtschaftlicher Erweiterung. *Archiv für Sozialgeschichte, 37*, 321–365.
Erker, P. (2002). „A New Business History"? Neuere Ansätze und Entwicklungen in der Unternehmensgeschichte. *Archiv für Sozialgeschichte, 42*, 557–604.

Erker, P. (2006). „Externalisierungsmaschine“ oder „Lizenznehmer der Gesellschaft“? Trends, Themen und Theorien in der jüngsten Unternehmensgeschichtsschreibung. *Archiv für Sozialgeschichte, 46*, 605–658.

Feldman, G. D. (1999). *Unternehmensgeschichte des Dritten Reiches und Verantwortung der Historiker. Raubgold und Versicherungen, Arisierung und Zwangsarbeit*. Friedrich-Ebert-Stiftung: Bonn.

Feldman, G. D. (2001). *Die Allianz und die deutsche Versicherungswirtschaft 1933–1945*. München: H.C. Beck.

Freye, S. (2009). *Führungswechsel. Die Wirtschaftselite und das Ende der Deutschland AG*. Frankfurt: Campus.

Freyssenet, M. (2009). *The second automobile revolution. Trajectories of the world carmakers in the 21st century*. Basingstoke: Palgrave.

Freyssenet, M., Mair, A., Shimizu, K., & Volpato, G. (1998). *One best way? Trajectories and industrial models of the world's automobile producers*. Oxford: Oxford University Press.

Gerstung, T. (forthcoming). *Glasgow's Miles better*.

Grabher, G. (1993). *The Embedded firm. On the socioeconomics of industrial networks*. London: Routledge.

Hall, P. H., & Lamont, M. (2013). *Social resilience in the neoliberal era*. Cambridge: Cambridge University Press.

Hancké, B. (1999). Revisiting the French model: Coordination and restructuring in French industry in the 1980s. *Discussion Papers Wissenschaftszentrum Berlin für Sozialforschung, Berlin*. http://www.ssoar.info/ssoar/bitstream/handle/document/12907/ssoar-1999-hancke-revisiting_the_french_model.pdf?sequence=1 (Accessed 18 Oct 2016).

Hartmann, M. (2007). *Eliten und Macht in Europa. Ein internationaler Vergleich*. Frankfurt: Campus.

Henke, K.-D. (2006). *Die Dresdner Bank im Dritten Reich*. München: Oldenbourg.

Hesse, J.-O., Kleinschmidt, C., & Lauschke, K. (2002). *Kulturalismus, Neue Institutionenökonomik oder Theorienvielfalt. Eine Zwischenbilanz der Unternehmensgeschichte*. Essen: Klartext.

Jansen, D. (2003, 2nd ed.). *Einführung in die Netzwerkanalyse. Grundlagen, Methoden, Forschungsbeispiele*. Opladen: Leske+Budrich.

Kocka, J. (2002). *Sozialgeschichte in Deutschland seit 1945. Aufstieg – Krise – Perspektiven*. Gesprächskreis Geschichte 47. Bonn: Friedrich-Ebert-Stiftung.

Krenn, K. (2012). *Alle Macht den Banken? Zur Struktur personaler Netzwerke deutscher Unternehmen am Beginn des 20. Jahrhunderts*. Wiesbaden: Verlag für Sozialwissenschaften.

Marx, C. (2013). *Paul Reusch und die Gutehoffnungshütte. Leitung eines deutschen Großunternehmens*. Göttingen: Wallstein.

Neumann, A. (2008). *Kleine geile Firmen. Alternativprojekte zwischen Revolte und Management*. Hamburg: Edition Nautilus.

Neumann, A. (forthcoming). *Unternehmen Hamburg. Eine Geschichte der neoliberalen Stadt*.

Pierenkemper, T. (1999a). Was kann eine moderne Unternehmensgeschichtsschreibung leisten? Und was sollte sie tunlichst vermeiden. *Zeitschrift für Unternehmensgeschichte, 44*, 15–31.

Pierenkemper, T. (1999b). Business History in Deutschland. Zur Ortsbestimmung einer Disziplin. In: A. Teichova et al. (Eds.), *Business History. Wissenschaftliche Entwicklungstrends und Studien aus Zentraleuropa* (pp. 33–53). Wien: Manz.

Pierenkemper, T. (2000). Sechs Thesen zum gegenwärtigen Stand der deutschen Unternehmensgeschichtsschreibung. *Zeitschrift für Unternehmensgeschichte, 45*, 158–166.

Plumpe, W. (2003). Die Unwahrscheinlichkeit des Jubiläums – oder: warum Unternehmen nur historisch erklärt werden können. *Jahrbuch für Wirtschaftsgeschichte, 44*, 143–156.

Plumpe, W. (2014). Gerufene Geister: Die Überdehnung des Staates und die Abhängigkeit von den Finanzmärkten. *Journal of Modern European History, 12* (1), 44–52.

Pohl, M. (1999). Zwischen Weihrauch und Wissenschaft? Zum Standort der modernen Unternehmensgeschichte. Eine Replik auf Toni Pierenkemper. *Zeitschrift für Unternehmensgeschichte, 44*, 150–163.

Priemel, K. C. (2014). Littératur engagée: Gekaufte Zeit und das historische Gedächtnis. *Journal of Modern European History, 12* (1), 30–36.

Rachel, H., & Wallich, P. (1934-1938). *Berliner Großkaufleute und Kapitalisten* (Vol. 3). Berlin: Gsellius.

Raphael, L. (2003). *Geschichtswissenschaft im Zeitalter der Extreme. Theorien, Methoden, Tendenzen von 1900 bis zur Gegenwart*. München: H. C. Beck.

Reitmayer, M. (1999). *Bankiers im Kaiserreich. Sozialprofil und Habitus der deutschen Hochfinanz*. Göttingen: Vandenhoeck & Rupprecht.

Reitmayer, M. (forthcoming). *The concept of social fields and the productive models*. BH.

Reitmayer, M., & Marx, C. (2010). Netzwerkansätze in der Geschichtswissenschaft. In: C. Stegbauer & R. Häußling (Eds.), *Handbuch Netzwerkforschung (Vol. 4)* (pp. 869–880). Wiesbaden: Verlag für Sozialwissenschaften.

Reitmayer, M., & Rosenberger, R. (2008). *Unternehmen am Ende des "Goldenen Zeitalters". Die 1970er Jahre in unternehmens- und wirtschaftshistorischer Perspektive*. Klartext: Essen.

Rischbieter, L. (2014). Die Schönheit vergangener Zeiten und die dunkle Macht des Marktes. *Journal of Modern European History, 12* (1), 37–43.

Rosenberger, R. (2008). *Experten für Humankapital. Die Entdeckung des Personalmanagements in der Bundesrepublik Deutschland.* München: Oldenbourg.

Schnee, H. (1953-1967). *Die Hoffinanz und der moderne Staat. Geschichte und System der Hoffaktoren an deutschen Fürstenhöfen im Zeitalter des Absolutismus* (6 Vol.). Berlin: Duncker & Humblot.

Schröter, H. G. (2000). Die Institutionalisierung der Unternehmensgeschichte im deutschen Sprachraum. *Zeitschrift für Unternehmensgeschichte, 45*, 30–48.

Schwarz, W. (1958). A Jewish Banker in the nineteenth century. *Leo Baeck Institute Yearbook, 3*, 300–310.

Scott, J. (1982). *The Upper classes. Property and privilege in Britain.* London: Macmillan.

Scott, J. (1991). *Who rules Britain?* Cambridge: Polity Press.

Streeck, W. (2014a). *Buying time. The delayed crisis of democratic capitalism.* London: Verso.

Streeck, W. (2014b). Aus der Krise nach „Europa"? Vergangenheit und Zukunft in Geschichte und politischer Ökonomie. *Journal of Modern European History, 12* (3), 299–316.

Tanner, J. (2014). Die nationale Restdemokratie als politisches Leitfossil. *Journal of Modern European History, 12* (1), 71–79.

Tooze, A. J. (2014). Who is afraid of Inflation? The Long-shadow of the 1970s. *Journal of Modern European History, 12* (1), 53–60.

Wallich, P. (1978). *Lehr- und Wanderjahre eines Bankiers*. Frankfurt: Knapp.

Wellhöner, V. (1989). *Großbanken und Großindustrie im Kaiserreich*. Göttingen: Vandenhoeck & Rupprecht.

Windolf, P. (2005). *Finanzmarktkapitalismus. Analysen zum Wandel von Produktionsregimen*. Wiesbaden: Verlag für Sozialwissenschaften.

Windolf, P. (2006). Unternehmensverflechtung im organisierten Kapitalismus. Deutschland und USA im Vergleich 1896-1938. *Zeitschrift für Unternehmensgeschichte, 51*, 191–222.

Wingert, L. (2014). Von Krisen und Grenzen: Staatsvolk und Marktvolk im entgrenzten Kapitalismus. *Journal of Modern European History, 12* (1), 61–70.

Wixforth, H., & Ziegler, D. (1994). The niche in the universal banking system: the role and significance of private bankers within German industry, 1900–1933. *Financial History Review, 1*, 5–25.
Wixforth, H., & Ziegler, D. (1997). Deutsche Privatbanken und Privatbankiers im 20. Jahrhundert. *Geschichte und Gesellschaft, 23*, 205–235.

Index

Note: Page numbers with "n" denote notes

K. Schönhärl (ed.), *Decision Taking, Confidence and Risk Management in Banks from Early Modernity to the 20th Century*, DOI 10.1007/978-3-319-42076-9

D

The manufacturer's authorised representative in the EU is Springer Nature Customer Service Centre GmbH, Europaplatz 3, 69115 Heidelberg, Germany. If you have any concerns regarding our products, please contact ProductSafety@springernature.com

Printed and bound by CPI Group (UK) Ltd, Croydon, CR0 4YY
22/09/2026
02221067-0012